Also in the Variorum Collected Studies Series:

WENDY DAVIES
Welsh History in the Early Middle Ages
Texts and Societies

PAUL MEYVAERT
The Art of Words: Bede and Theodulf

ANNE HUDSON
Studies in the Transmission of Wyclif's Writings

JANET L. NELSON
Courts, Elites, and Gendered Power in the Early Middle Ages
Charlemagne and Others

ANNE J. DUGGAN
Thomas Becket: Friends, Networks, Texts and Cult

PAULINE STAFFORD
Gender, Family and the Legitimation of Power
England from the Ninth to Early Twelfth Century

MICHAEL JONES
Between France and England
Politics, Power and Society in Late Medieval Brittany

MARJORIE CHIBNALL
Piety, Power and History in Medieval England and Normandy

H.S. OFFLER (Ed. A.I. Doyle and A.J. Piper)
North of the Tees
Studies in Medieval British History

PATRICK SIMS-WILLIAMS
Britain and Early Christian Europe
Studies in Early Medieval History and Culture

CHARLES W. JONES (Ed. Wesley Stevens)
Bede, the Schools and the Computus

DAVID N. DUMVILLE
Histories and Pseudo-Histories of the Insular Middle Ages

VARIORUM COLLECTED STUDIES SERIES

Brittany in the Early Middle Ages

Wendy Davies

Brittany in the Early Middle Ages

Texts and Societies

This edition © 2009 by Wendy Davies

Wendy Davies has asserted her moral right under the Copyright, Designs and Patents Act, 1988, to be identified as the author of this work.

Published in the Variorum Collected Studies Series by

Ashgate Publishing Limited
Wey Court East
Union Road
Farnham, Surrey
GU9 7PT
England

Ashgate Publishing Company
Suite 420
101 Cherry Street
Burlington, VT 05401–4405
USA

Ashgate website: http://www.ashgate.com

ISBN 978–0–7546–5970–9

British Library Cataloguing in Publication Data
Davies, Wendy, 1942–
   Brittany in the early Middle Ages : texts and societies.
   – (Variorum collected studies series ; 924)
   1. Brittany (France) – History – To 1500 – Sources.
   2. Cartularies.
   I. Title II. Series
   944.1'014–dc22

ISBN 978–0–7546–5970–9

Library of Congress Cataloging-in-Publication Data
Brittany in the early Middle Ages : texts and societies / by Wendy Davies.
   p. cm. – (Variorum collected studies series)
   Includes bibliographical references and index.
   ISBN 978–0–7546–5970–9 (hardcover : alk. paper)
   1. Brittany (France) – Social conditions. 2. Power (Social sciences) – France – Brittany – History. 3. Brittany (France) – History – To 1500 – Sources.
   4. Brittany (France) – Politics and government – Sources. 5. Civilization, Medieval.
   I. Davies, Wendy, 1942–
   DC611.B856B76 2009
   944'.1013–dc22

                           2009030149

VARIORUM COLLECTED STUDIES SERIES CS924

Printed and bound in Great Britain by
TJ International Ltd, Padstow, Cornwall

CONTENTS

Introduction   ix

Acknowledgements   xvi

BRETON CHARTERS

I   The composition of the Redon cartulary   69–90
Francia. Forschungen zur westeuropäischen Geschichte 17/1, Mittelalter, ed. Deutschen Historischen Institut Paris. Sigmaringen: Jan Thorbecke Verlag, 1990

II   Forgery in the *Cartulaire de Redon*   265–274
Fälschungen im Mittelalter. Internationaler Kongreß der MGH München, 16–19 September 1986, ed. Monumenta Germaniae Historica, Schriften 33 (6 parts). Hannover: Verlag Hahnsche Buchhandlung, 1988, pt 4

III   Les chartes du cartulaire de Landévennec   85–95
Landévennec et le monachisme breton dans le haut moyen âge, ed. Marc Simon (Actes du Colloque d'avril 1985). Landévennec: Association Landévennec 485–1985, 1986

EAST BRETON SOCIETY

IV   On the distribution of political power in Brittany in the mid-ninth century   98–114
Charles the Bald: Court and Kingdom (revised edition), eds M.T. Gibson and J.L. Nelson. London: Variorum, 1990

V   Priests and rural communities in East Brittany in the ninth century   177–197
Études Celtiques 20. Paris, 1983

VI   Disputes, their conduct and their settlement in the village communities of eastern Brittany in the ninth century   289–312
History and Anthropology 1, pt 2. Chur, 1985

VII	People and places in dispute in ninth-century Brittany *The Settlement of Disputes in Early Medieval Europe*, eds W. Davies and P. Fouracre. Cambridge: Cambridge University Press, 1986	65–84
VIII	Suretyship in the *Cartulaire du Redon* *Lawyers and Laymen*, eds T.M. Charles-Edwards, M.E. Owen and D.B. Walters. Cardiff: University of Wales Press, 1986	72–91
IX	Intra-family transactions in south-eastern Brittany: the dossier from Redon *Mélanges de l'école française de Rome 111.* Rome, 1999, pt. 2	881–894
X	*Wynebwerth* et *enepuuert*: l'entretien des épouses dans la Bretagne du IXe siècle *Dots et douaires dans le haut moyen âge*, eds F. Bougard, L. Feller, and R. Le Jan. (Collection de l'école française de Rome 295). Rome, 2002	407–428
XI	A note on *ville* names and settlement development in the Morbihan *Mondes de l'Ouest et villes du monde. Mélanges en l'honneur d'André Chédeville*, eds C. Laurent, B. Merdrignac, and D. Pichot. Rennes: Presses universitaires de Rennes, 1998	139–147
XII	Field survey and the problem of surface scatters of building material: some east Breton evidence *La Bretagne et L'Europe Préhistoriques. Mémoires en Hommage à Pierre-Roland Giot, Revue archéologique de l'Ouest*, Supp. no. 2. Rennes: Presses universitaires de Rennes, 1990	321–332
XIII	Surface scatters of building stone: enhancing field survey work *Oxford Journal of Archaeology* 12.3. Oxford, 1993	337–353

BRITTANY IN THE WIDER WORLD

XIV	Ecclesiastical centres and secular society in the Brittonic world in the tenth and eleventh centuries *Govan and its Early Medieval Sculpture*, ed. A. Ritchie. Stroud: Alan Sutton Publishing, 1994	92–101

XV	'Protected space' in Britain and Ireland in the middle ages *Scotland in Dark Age Britain, ed. B.E. Crawford. St Andrews: Scottish Cultural Press, 1996*	1–19
XVI	Celtic kingships in the early middle ages *Kings and Kingship in Medieval Europe, ed. A. Duggan. London: King's College London Centre for Late Antique and Medieval Studies, 1993*	101–124
XVII	Alfred's contemporaries: Irish, Welsh, Scots and Breton *Alfred the Great, ed. T. Reuter. Aldershot: Ashgate, 2003*	323–337
XVIII	On servile status in the early Middle Ages *Serfdom and Slavery: Studies in Legal Bondage, ed. M.L. Bush. London: Longman, 1996*	225–246
XIX	Local participation and legal ritual in early medieval law courts *The Moral World of the Law, ed. P. Coss. Cambridge: Cambridge University Press, 2000*	48–61
Index		1–5

This volume contains xvi + 340 pages

PUBLISHER'S NOTE

The articles in this volume, as in all others in the Variorum Collected Studies Series, have not been given a new, continuous pagination. In order to avoid confusion, and to facilitate their use where these same studies have been referred to elsewhere, the original pagination has been maintained wherever possible.

Each article has been given a Roman number in order of appearance, as listed in the Contents. This number is repeated on each page and is quoted in the index entries.

INTRODUCTION

The papers in this collection include some technical analyses, though fewer than are printed in its sister volume *Welsh History in the Early Middle Ages* (Ashgate, 2009), and include some of the results of the long campaign of archaeological fieldwork that absorbed me through the 1980s and beyond; most of them, however, are investigations into social structure and they all derive from my second major set of research. By the time they were written I had already been in my second academic post, at UCL, for some years, after the initial very stimulating years in Birmingham. Most of the papers, then, derive from the 1980s and early 1990s but four are later reflections on material primarily studied in that period.

My second set of research focussed on the Redon charters, from eastern Brittany, work which I initially undertook in order to see if there were comparabilities between Breton and Welsh rural societies of the early middle ages. I quickly came to the view that there were some, but not many. At the same time I was involved, with Grenville Astill, in the field project, which focussed on the four communes which are most intensively covered by the Redon charters – Ruffiac, Tréal, Saint-Nicolas-du-Tertre and Carentoir. On my part this began as an attempt to understand the landscape of the charters, but it became much more: quite apart from years of fieldwalking and excavation, it took me into archives and into many other kinds of text, in particular texts which derived from the thirteenth to the twentieth centuries. So, despite the immensely detailed focus on a few hundred charters from the ninth century, there were always much wider perspectives in my mind. My Redon charter work was also my first venture into the world of electronic databases – in itself more reason to extend perspectives – and I remain deeply grateful to Chris Horsbrugh, then of UCL Computer Centre, for writing all the programmes with which I analysed the material; this was in the days before user-friendly packages, though I came to use those soon after, in analysis of the fieldwork data.

I was by no means the only person working on the Redon material and others published commentaries both on the texts of the charters and on their social and political significance. Hubert Guillotel stands out among these; in addition to his many papers, his contribution to the facsimile edition of the cartulary, published in 1998, is a fundamental analysis of the manuscript; it is essential reading, as are

Bernard Tanguy's comments on name-forms in the same volume.[1] Guillotel's arguments for the dates of the charters are also very important, and in some cases diverge from mine; he used the charters to illuminate politics throughout his work but much can be found in the survey he co-wrote with André Chédeville.[2] Noel-Yves Tonnerre also did important textual work, as well as social analysis, as he continues to do.[3] Bernard Merdrignac is another major Breton scholar, who has made many relevant contributions over the past twenty-five years.[4] And there are English scholars too who have made major contributions to Redon studies, like Julia Smith and Caroline Brett.[5] I benefited greatly from discussions with all of these people, and especially from their friendship over many years, as well as that of many others; and I recommend their work and approaches as an alternative to my own. Léon Fleuriot was even more generous: at an early stage in my own work he gave me copies of all his notes on name forms in De Courson's text of the Redon charters, as well as access to a microfilm of the manuscript; we argued long over many points but he was enormously helpful and an extremely good friend. Although he did not publish all the things he wanted to publish about these texts, there are some of his later thoughts in his revised edition of his *Dictionary of Old Breton*.[6]

Articles I–III here are textual criticism, on Landévennec as well as Redon charters, and should not be too difficult to read; they introduce many of the themes that I have continued to explore in collections from other regions. Article II is a minor piece, although it emanated from an extremely important conference, and although the general points about forgery are useful. Article I still seems to me to be important, both in respect of identifying local scribal practice and in its analysis of how a cartulary is put together; it is full of useful observations on charter writing, although analysis of the style and syntax of records of local origin could be taken much further as a contrast to those of monastic origin.

---

[1] *Cartulaire de l'abbaye Saint-Sauveur de Redon* (Rennes: Amis des Archives historiques du diocèse de Rennes, Dol et Saint-Malo, 1998), pp. 49–69.

[2] A. Chédeville and H. Guillotel, *La Bretagne des saints et des rois. Ve- Xe siècle* (Rennes, 1984).

[3] See his *Naissance de la Bretagne. Géographie historique et structures sociales de la Bretagne méridionale (Nantais et Vannetais) de la fin du VIIIe à la fin du XIIe siècle* (Angers, 1994); and more recently, for example, N.-Y. Tonnerre (ed.), *Chroniqueurs et historiens de la Bretagne du moyen âge au milieu du XXe siècle* (Rennes, 2001).

[4] Note, for example, his contribution to P.-R. Giot, Ph. Guigon, B. Merdrignac, *Les premiers bretons d'Armorique* (Rennes, 2003).

[5] J.M.H. Smith, *Province and Empire. Brittany and the Carolingians* (Cambridge, 1992). C. Brett (ed. and trans.), *The Monks of Redon. Gesta Sanctorum Rotonensium and Vita Conuuoionis* (Woodbridge, 1989).

[6] L. Fleuriot, *Dictionnaire du Vieux Breton*, in 2 parts: C. Evans and L. Fleuriot, *Part II. A Supplement to the 'Dictionnaire des Gloses en Vieux Breton'* (Toronto, 1985).

Note my words of warning on page 69, however: as ever, some problems are likely to remain insuperable. Article III came from an extremely memorable conference in the monastery of Landévennec – quite a small occasion but packed with local interest and overflowing with friendship. The Landévennec charters are a challenging group of texts and, despite a century and more of study, remain difficult to analyse. Mine was one attempt among several to apply some consistent principles of criticism (Guillotel took a different approach in the same volume); the paper remains an interesting attempt to deal with some intractable material and I continue to believe that there is usable material, largely overlooked, in that collection. It was my intention to publish a list classifying these Landévennec charters by type; this was omitted in the publication (though circulated with it) and it is now published here. As for revisions and emendations to the original publications in the light of the passage of nearly 25 years: Guillotel's arguments for the dates of the Redon charters, as indicated above, should be considered alongside my own (I 82–90); Caroline Brett's discussion of the hands of the manuscript is now available in her book, noted at note 5 above (I 71 n.9).

Articles IV–X are social analyses deriving from the Redon charters and are in some cases preliminary versions of material later developed in my book on early medieval Breton rural society;[7] other cases stand alone, and are merely summarized in the book. Article IV is a revised edition of a 1981 paper, the first piece of socio-political analysis I wrote from the Redon charters and for me a pioneering paper of discovery of people and places; the material was further developed in *Small Worlds* and is revisited, in a different way, in the paper I recently wrote for Jinty Nelson's Festschrift.[8] It has some historiographical interest, coming from such an early stage in my thinking, but it makes a cogent point about the nature and fragmentation of political power; the point is more widely applicable. Article V is a fundamental analysis of the roles of local priests; at the time of writing it was a completely new approach, conditioned by new kinds of question (although I was influenced by attending the Spoleto conference on rural parish formation[9]), and it has not been modified subsequently. It is summarized in the book but is best read in this version, particularly since it raises wider issues than the purely Breton. Articles VI, VII and VIII are again

---

[7] *Small Worlds. The Village Community in Early Medieval Brittany* (London and San Francisco, 1988).

[8] 'Franks and Bretons. The impact of political climate and historiographical tradition on writing their ninth-century history' in Paul Fouracre and David Ganz (eds), *Frankland: the Franks and the World of Early Medieval Europe* (Manchester, 2008), 304–21.

[9] *Cristianizzazione ed Organizzazione ecclesiastica delle Campagne nell'alto medioevo: Espansione e Resistenze*, Settimane di Studio del Centro Italiano di Studi sull'alto medioevo, 28 (1982).

fundamental analyses, of dispute settlement practice in this case, and are again best read in these versions. There is some overlap between VI and VII, although VI is about process and VII is about people. VIII – on suretyship – was again a new approach. My understanding was much enhanced by discussion of insular Celtic parallels, and by collaboration with Celticists, but it is important *not* to see these mechanisms as distinctively Celtic; there are, for example, very similar mechanisms to be found across northern Spain at a comparable period. There are similar messages in Article IX, with its warning not to expect 'Celtic' similarities (p. 885); this is a slighter piece, but makes a serious point about the way that family ownership worked in practice, as also about the constant process of fragmentation and reconstruction that characterizes much early medieval peasant proprietorship; it is also interesting on family strategies and on the alienability of property. Article X, like IX written in a phase of reflection subsequent to the main Redon work, is valuable because it offers a view of peasant practice in marriage arrangements, at a time when our evidence is usually firmly aristocratic; it is also useful on the power of women in property transactions.

As for revisions and emendations to the original publications of Articles IV–X: there has been much more work on the Breton interaction with Carolingians since I wrote and it is important to consider the work of Julia Smith and Noel-Yves Tonnerre, cited above, alongside mine, as well as that by J.-P. Brunterc'h (IV).[10] Bernard Tanguy's work on place-names has added some new dimensions to the analysis of priests and their responsibilities, while Gesine Jordan's very interesting book on pious donation does so too; and since we should think about potentially comparable societies as well, there has been much very good work on the church in late Anglo-Saxon England in recent years (V).[11] I would of course now add many more recent works on the Carolingians to my note in VI (308 n. 6), not least those of Dame Janet Nelson; and the publications on fieldwork mentioned there emerged regularly until 1997 (VI 308 n. 9);[12] the forthcoming work, named in VII 66 n. 4 and in VIII 88 n. 12, is the one ultimately named *Small Worlds*. I now know that requiring sureties to be available for goods

---

[10] J.-P. Brunterc'h, 'Le duché du Maine et la marche de Bretagne' in H. Atsma (ed.), *La Neustrie. Les pays au nord de la Loire de 650 à 850. Colloque historique international*, 2 vols. (Sigmaringen, 1989), i.29–127.

[11] For Tanguy, see above, p. viii and n. 1. G. Jordan, *'Nichts als Nahrung und Kleidung'. Laien und Kleriker als Wohngäste bei den Mönchen von St. Gallen und Redon (8. und 9. Jahrhundert)* (Berlin, 2007). For England, to cite the most obvious, J. Blair, *The Church in Anglo-Saxon Society* (Oxford, 2005) and F. Tinti (ed.), *Pastoral Care in Late Anglo-Saxon England* (Woodbridge, 2005).

[12] For example, J.L. Nelson, *Charles the Bald* (Harlow, 1992), but also many articles, such as those collected in *Rulers and Ruling Families in Early Medieval Europe* (Aldershot, 1999). For fieldwork publication, see below, p. xiii.

sold is not that unusual in the early middle ages and is not a distinctively northern European practice (VIII 85, 86); there are Spanish examples too.

Articles XI–XIII are a tiny proportion of the results of the archaeological field project carried out with Grenville Astill, a project which occupied almost twenty years from initial thoughts to final publication; in addition to the annual reports, that final publication was in two books: *The East Brittany Survey: Fieldwork and Field Data* (Aldershot, 1994) and *A Breton Landscape* (London, 1997), the latter also published in French as *Un Paysage breton* (Saint-Malo, 2000). The entire project was immensely stimulating – not just because of dealing with the *longue durée* of two thousand years of land-use change but for the sheer excitement of the modern archive work, the intimate concern with the land and the challenge of developing an appropriate methodology. Article XI is a small piece, though appropriate for the Festschrift for which it was written, because it brought together place-name evidence with that of changing land-use. It makes a negative point (on *ville* names as potential indicator of new settlements) but one that is important. Articles XII and XIII reflect fieldwork I did myself on stone scatters on the fields. I was very proud of it at the time, given its innovative and genuinely interdisciplinary character. XII is important as an introduction to new methods for assessing past land-use and land-use change; its implications are developed in *Breton Landscape*. XIII is a more mature piece, in which I had come to terms with all the methodological issues, and it includes much on changing farming practice of the late middle ages and modern period as well.

Articles XIV–XIX are discussion pieces which put Breton material into a wider, usually but not always Celtic, context; most were conference papers, in which I was making a point about including, and differentiating, Breton material. XIV ends with a good idea, but is quite slight, although it came from an inspiring conference at Govan, which gave appropriate attention to the extraordinary collection of sculpture there. XV came from another memorable conference (also in Scotland) and makes a substantial point about insular institutions which would be capable of much more extended exploration. XVI is a paper that students find useful. I remain committed to its point about differences in scale – a point that is easily, and often, ignored – and to the significant differences between Celtic areas; and I still passionately believe that 'some [kings] had very few functions at all' (123). Article XVII is the most recent piece in this collection, prepared for a conference organized by the late and much-missed Tim Reuter. It turned into a surprisingly interesting comparison and it is useful to bear in mind that contemporaries may well have seen Irish, Scots and Breton rulers as the equal of King Alfred. The conference which provoked Article XVIII was concerned with serfdom and slavery in many cultures at many periods and was not restricted to the middle ages; it is again a paper which students find useful; it gives Breton material a small place in a wider European context, whose interpretation continues to change.¹³ The last paper in this collection, Article XIX, also took its shape from a multi-period, multi-culture conference and also set the Breton evidence in a western European context, paying particular attention to English, French and Italian material. Since it was written, more examples of the study of judicial practice at local level have been published and these should now be taken into account too.¹⁴ As for revisions and emendations to Articles XIV–XIX, besides extending the bibliography: I would make much less of a public/private distinction in XVI and I would make less of a case for the size of Scotland at the point of comparison – and I would certainly say more about Alba and the large recent historiography, though see further on this at pp. 324 and 326 in the following paper.¹⁵ The excavations at Llanbedrgoch are now finished, though not yet fully published, although the relative Viking and native elements are still controversial (XVII 334). I would not nowadays talk about public notaries in ninth-century Spain, although there are people there who in effect performed notarial functions for local communities as well as for kings (XIX 52).

The papers I have written on Brittany are much more widely known than those I wrote on Wales and there is no need to make the point that Brittany needs consideration in the context of western European development. It is a particularly interesting area: it is more than a region of modern France now, with some very un-French features in its continuing heritage, just as it was much more than – indeed other than – a dimension of the Carolingian Empire in the early middle ages. It was neither typically Celtic nor Frankish, and that makes it very interesting indeed. To my surprise I have often been reminded of northern Spain, which has occupied me much in the last decade, while working on this collection. There are some very clear parallels in charter writing practice and in the transmission of peasant property, as there are also parallels and contrasts in judicial practice. I hope to explore some of this in the future, as I hope that

---

¹³ The continuing bibliography is enormous. Recent contributions of note include those by Alice Rio, 'Freedom and unfreedom in early medieval Francia: the evidence of the legal formularies', *Past and Present* 193 (2006), 7–40 and *eadem*, 'High and low: ties of dependence in the Frankish kingdoms', *Transactions of the Royal Historical Society* 18 (2008), 43–68.

¹⁴ For example, material in the central chapters of M. Innes, *State and Society in the Early Middle Ages. The Middle Rhine Valley, 400–1000* (Cambridge, 2000); in A.J. Kosto, *Making Agreements in Medieval Catalonia: Power, Order, and the Written Word, 1000–1200* (Cambridge, 2001); W.C. Brown and P. Górecki (eds), *Conflict in Medieval Europe* (Aldershot, 2003); J.A. Bowman, *Shifting Landmarks: Property, Proof, and Dispute in Catalonia around the Year 1000* (Ithaca, 2004).

¹⁵ Note in particular the work of Dauvit Broun, e.g. *The Irish Identity of the Kingdom of the Scots* (Woodbridge, 1999), but also many papers. I have reworked and extended some of the material in this paper in a forthcoming paper 'States and non-states in the Celtic world' in *Der frühmittelalterliche Staat - europäische Perspektiven*, eds W. Pohl and V. Wieser (Vienna, 2009).

someone may pursue the comparison between Brittany and Catalonia, each with its Carolingian overlay and very strong local culture.

WENDY DAVIES

Woolstone
19 June 2009

ACKNOWLEDGEMENTS

I am extremely grateful to the following publishers for their permission to reprint the papers in this volume: to Deutschen Historischen Institut Paris and Jan Thorbecke Verlag, Ostfildern (for Article I); to the Monumenta Germaniae Historica, Munich and Verlag Hahnsche Buchhandlung, Hannover (II); to l'Abbaye de Landévennec, Finistère, through the kind offices of Brother Marc Simon (III); to John Smedley and Ashgate Publishing Ltd, Farnham (IV and XVII); to CNRS Editions, Paris (V); to Taylor and Francis, Abingdon (http://www.informaworld.com) (VI); to Cambridge University Press (VII and XIX); to the University of Wales Press, Cardiff (VIII); to l'École française de Rome (IX and X); to Presses universitaires de Rennes (XI and XII); to Wiley-Blackwell, Oxford (XIII); to The History Press, Stroud (XIV); to Barbara Crawford, on behalf of Scottish Cultural Press, St. Andrews (XV); to King's College London (XVI); and to Pearson Education Ltd, Harlow (XVIII).

I remain very grateful to John Smedley, and colleagues at Ashgate, for their patience in dealing with this volume.

I

THE COMPOSITION OF THE REDON CARTULARY

The diplomatic of the earliest charter collection from Redon, in eastern Brittany, has provoked some summary discussion in recent theses, as also from its principal nineteenth-century commentators, although the dates of individual texts were certainly very fully considered by La Borderie[1]. It is curious that despite the importance of the material, despite a number of obvious corruptions and despite the two-hundred-year interval between the supposed origination of the charters and their copying into the existing eleventh-century cartulary, there has been no systematic analysis of formulation nor discussion of the way the cartulary was put together. This paper sets out to remedy this situation and much of it is therefore about the way people recorded transactions in the ninth century; it is inevitably also about the way a major and powerful monastic house used those records and generated its own. It is certainly possible – as well as interesting – to draw some broad conclusions about the materials from which the cartulary was constructed and the relationship between them, and this has no little significance for those who use the charters for historical or linguistic purposes[2].

There is no denying that there are problems in analysing this material, problems which are at present insuperable, and probably always will be. The different parts of the cartulary cannot be made to fall into a completely neat and tidy pattern and, although a broad overall structure is perceivable, anomalies persist which are difficult to explain. Further, it is impossible to disentangle some of the corruptions of

---

1 N.-Y. TONNERRE, Le diocèse de Vannes au IXe siècle d'après le Cartulaire de Redon, University of Paris X, Thèse de troisième cycle 1978 – on diplomatic of the Morbihan charters (cf. TONNERRE, Le cartulaire de Redon, in: Landévennec et le monachisme breton dans le haut moyen âge, ed. M. SIMON, Landévennec 1986, p. 115–21); J. M. H. SMITH, Carolingian Brittany, University of Oxford D. Phil. thesis 1985, p. 45–54 – on diplomatic of ninth-century charters; H. GUILLOTEL, Les Actes des ducs de Bretagne, 944–1148, University of Paris, Faculté de Droit, d'Économie et de Sciences Sociales, Thèse de doctorat en Droit 1973 – on some forgeries of eleventh-century material; also GUILLOTEL, Les cartulaires de l'abbaye de Redon, in: Mémoires de la Société d'histoire et d'archéologie de Bretagne 63 (1986) p. 36 and 46–7 – on forged ninth- and eleventh-century charters. Earlier considerations are Le Cartulaire de Redon, ed. A. DE COURSON, Paris 1863, p. cclix–cclxi; A. LE MOYNE DE LA BORDERIE, Histoire de Bretagne, Rennes-Paris 1896–1904 (6 vols.) vol. 2, p. 276–81; M. PLANIOL, Histoire des Institutions de la Bretagne, Mayenne 1981–4 (2nd edn, 5 vols.) vol. 2, p. 153–72. A. LE MOYNE DE LA BORDERIE, La Chronologie du Cartulaire de Redon, Rennes 1901.
I have used de Courson's numbering of the charters, cited as CR 1 etc., and CR A1 etc. for those of his Appendix; I quote from the manuscript throughout, however, and hence some deviation from de Courson's printed edition.
2 I really owe this undertaking to Mr. J. Sheringham of Machynlleth, who suggested to me about ten years ago that the Redon cartulary needed some systematic analysis and could not be treated as a text of uniform value. He was quite right.

Wendy Davies: 'The composition of the Redon cartulary'. First published in: Francia. Forschungen zur westeuropäischen Geschichte, Band 17/1: Mittelalter, hrsg. vom Deutschen Historischen Institut Paris, Sigmaringen: Jan thorbecke Verlag 1990, S. 69–90.

content; although solutions can often be suggested, some passages are near or total nonsense³. So also the problems of dating: many of the dates given in the texts are impossible, for errors of one or more minims, as also in computation of the appropriate phases of the moon, abound; one can often make sense of these irregularities by suggesting minor emendations to day of the week or day of the month, but the emendations do have to be made and the date intended cannot always be deduced⁴. However, despite these problems, some of the processes determining the makeup of the existing text can be glimpsed. What follows is a summary of their main aspects.

The principal extant cartulary of Redon is found in a manuscript compiled in the late eleventh century, consisting for the most part of copies of ninth-century charters⁵. These pertain to the monastery of Redon, founded in 832 by local clerics and gaining the patronage of the emperor Louis within two years of its foundation⁶. Although the monastery retained Frankish royal support and also won the support of the increasingly independent rulers of Brittany, many of the properties that accrued to it in the century after its foundation came from free peasant proprietors of the neighbourhood. Hence, most of the charters of the collection are private documents, concerning small properties and small-scale transactions.

The cartulary consists of 391 charters but there are nearly fifty folios missing from the manuscript; these folios probably contained some or all of the additional sixty-two ninth-century Redon charters known from early modern transcripts⁷. 288 of the charters of the cartulary are written in similar hands of the late eleventh century and

---

3 Corruptions range from scribal errors like *Conwoionem* for *coniugem* through the inconsistencies of the Lusanger/Derval transactions in CR 57 and CR 224–31 to the intentional corruptions of CR 143 or CR 199; see further DAVIES, Forgery in the Cartulaire de Redon, in: Fälschungen im Mittelalter. Internationaler Kongreß der MGH München 15–18 September 1986, Munich 1988 (6 vols) vol. 4, p. 265–274.

4 See the Appendix below for a list of suggested working dates. The errors arise because the year is indicated by the year of imperial rule, or by the floruit of one or more office holders, or by an AD date, or not at all; the day of the month is usually indicated by the Roman calendar, but also by church festivals, by the day of the month or not at all. The day of the week is often given; this can confirm the year, or even supply it in its absence though more usually can do no more than suggest a range of possible years. When the year is also computed by indiction and the day by the day of the lunar month, errors are more common than not.

5 Archbishopric of Rennes MS, no number; printed by de Courson as Cartulaire de Redon (abbreviated CR here). There were clearly other cartularies of Redon, some of which survive in small fragments; see GUILLOTEL, Cartulaires (see n. 1) p. 37–48.

6 CR 1, A 6, A 9; cf. 2, A 28, A 32, A 44. See DAVIES, Small Worlds. The Village Community in Early Medieval Brittany, London 1988, p. 26–8, 192–4, for foundation and rulers' patronage; also GUILLOTEL in A. CHÉDEVILLE and H. GUILLOTEL, La Bretagne des Saints et des Rois, Rennes 1984, p. 240–3; and J. M. H. SMITH, Culte impérial et politique frontalière dans la Vallée de la Vilaine, in: Landévennec et le monachisme breton dans le haut moyen âge, ed. M. SIMON (see n. 1).

7 All but seven of the additional charters are printed by de Courson in his Appendix to CR, using texts printed in Dom LOBINEAU's Histoire de Bretagne, Paris 1707, and transcribed in the Maurist collections in Paris, Bibliothèque Nationale MSS, Baluze 46, Baluze 376 and fr 22 330; the others (as also some more or less variant texts of the cartulary and additional material) may be found in H. MORICE, Mémoires pour servir de preuves à l'histoire ecclésiastique et civile de Bretagne, Paris 1742–6 (3 vols.) vol. 1, cols. 265, 271, 272, 295, 297, 308, and in the Abbé TRAVERS, Histoire de Nantes, Nantes 1860, vol. 1, p. 125. See further TONNERRE, Cartulaire (see n. 1) p. 117–18. There seems to be a twelfth-century note of another ninth-century text in Bordeaux MS 1, fol. 259v.

283 of these relate transactions of the ninth or early tenth centuries. A further 103 charters were added to the first cartulary by different and varying hands during the later eleventh and first half of the twelfth century; most of these additional charters detail transactions of the eleventh century, as do the odd five of the original 288, although a third belong to the first half of the twelfth century and two (possibly three) to the tenth[8]. The act of making the cartulary therefore seems to belong to the late eleventh century: since the latest charter of the original collection is dated to 1066–81, it is likely that the compilation was made near this time[9]. Collection then seems to have continued for the next half century or so. The process of acquiring, ordering and recording documentation was therefore an especial concern of the years between c. 1075 and 1150, although much of the material initially collected was of ninth-century reference[10]. It is, indeed, the density of private ninth-century transactions that is the distinctive quality of this collection and gives it its remarkable value[11]. (In fact, three quarters of these ninth-century texts, with the additional 62 from transcripts, relate to the two generations spanning the years 830–880, while most of the rest relate to the years before the foundation of Redon; very few are of tenth-century date). The following comments are concerned with the initial compilation of the cartulary and hence deal essentially with ninth-century charters.

Distinctions in diplomatic practice

Although several recent writers have commented on the use of Frankish formulary collections, particularly the formularies of seventh-century Neustria, by what they presume to be Redon scribes, there are in fact six types of diplomatic practice distinguishable in the ninth-century charters; three of these are only occasionally represented[12]. The types are:
(1) Neustrian formulary-derived diplomatic, using first-person records; two models overwhelmingly predominate: those recording (a) grants beginning *Mundi termino*

---

8 CR 305, 357, ?329; there are very few tenth-century charters in the earlier part of the cartulary: CR ?270, 274–281, ?282, 283; all date from before July 924.
9 CR 286; cf. GUILLOTEL, Cartulaires (see n. 1) p. 34–5, who argues that the last scribe of the early cartulary was working in the 1070s, contemporary with the energetic Abbot Aumod. See Caroline BRETT's discussion of hands of the CR MS, comparing them in the first instance with late eleventh-century hands from Mont St Michel, Texts from early mediaeval Redon: their value for the history of Brittany, University of Cambridge Ph. D. thesis 1986; publication forthcoming. For a full description of the manuscript, see GUILLOTEL, Cartulaires (see n. 1) p. 28–36; cf. TONNERRE, Cartulaire (see n. 1) p. 115–16 (who argues alternatively that the first eight folios were written in the early eleventh and others in mid-eleventh century).
10 The other cartularies are also witness to the same interest; see for example the short, fragmentary mid-twelfth-century Paris, BN MS, nouv. acq. lat. 2208.
11 LA BORDERIE made extensive use of the cartulary in vol. 2 of his Histoire de Bretagne, as have all subsequent writers on ninth-century Brittany, myself included. Its importance cannot be overemphasized.
12 Six types if we include the charters of de Courson's Appendix; type (6) does not occur in the cartulary itself. – For comment on the influence of Frankish-collected formularies, see for example PLANIOL (see n. 1) vol. 2, p. 153–5; TONNERRE, Diocèse (see n. 1) and Cartulaire (see n. 1) p. 119–20; SMITH (see n. 1) p. 48–9; DAVIES (see n. 6) p. 136–7.

I

adpropinquante and (b) sales beginning *Magnifico uiro*, although (c) other formulary-influenced models of sale and grant do occur. There are also:
(2) many third-person records of rural origin;
(3) many third-person records of Redon origin;
(4) a few third-person records of ›Celtic‹ type;
(5) a few records using what may be termed Breton ›courtly‹ diplomatic; and
(6) a few using Frankish imperial diplomatic. The charters of de Courson's Appendix and other additional material are often so heavily abbreviated that their type cannot be determined; this applies to 33 of the 62 but enough is recorded of the rest to suggest a classification.

To make the distinctions clear, there follow examples of each of these types, in full, without textual emendation:

1a *Mundi termino adpropinquante, ruinis crebrescentibus, iam certa signa manifestantur, idcirco ego, in Dei nomine, Ratvili, considerans grauitudinem peccatorum meorum, et reminiscens bonitatem Dei dicentis, Date elemosinam et omnia munda fiant uobis; si aliquid de rebus nostris locis sanctorum uel substantiae pauperum conferimus, hoc nobis, procul dubio, in aeternam beatitudinem retribuere confidimus; ego quidem, de tanta misericordia et pietate Domini confisus, per hanc epistolam donationis donatumque in perpetuum uolo esse ad illos monachos habitantes et exercentes regulam sancti Benedicti in monasterio quod uocatur Roton, ubi ego ipse locum petiui animam meam saluandi, quod ita et fecimus; donauimus eis Binnon totum, cum massis et manentibus, cum terris, siluis, pratis, pascuis, aquis, aquarumue decursibus, mobilibus et inmobilibus suis, et cum omnibus adpenditiis suis, cultis et incultis*[13]*, sicut a me hodie uidetur esse possessum, totum atque integrum, a die presenti trado atque transfundo ego in elemosina, sine censu, sine tributo ulli homini nisi solis monachis, ita ut quicquid exinde pro oportunitate monasterii facere uoluerint, liberam ac firmissimam in omnibus habeant potestatem; et si fuerit, aut ego, post hunc diem, aut unus de propinquis heredibus meis, uel quaelibet persona, qui contra hanc donationem aliquid repetere uel calumniam generare presumpserit, mille solidos multum conponat, et quod repetit non uindicet, et haec donatio, per omnia tempora, firma ac stabilis permaneat. Signum Ratvili, qui dedit et firmare rogauit; X Sulwal presbyter, X Iarnhaithoui, X Gurhoiarn, X Hebedan, X Arthveu, X Cumiau, X Maenvedet, X Maenwallon, X Haelwaloe, X Resmunuc, X Guethengar, X Nennan, X Arrtthel, X Minan presbyter, X Hoiarnmin, X Anguanuc, X Callon. Factum est hoc xii kal iulii, regnante domno Holodowico, xxi anno imperii eius* (CR 3, 20 June 834, re Bains).

There are forty-five of this type in the cartulary (16%) and a further fifteen in the abbreviated additional material.

Most of the ›Frankish‹ formulaic sales run as follows:

1b *Magnificis uiribus nomine Budworet, presbytero, uel germano suo, nomine Anauworeto, emptoribus, nos enim in Dei nomine, Cunmailus, et germanus meus Iudhaelus, constat nobis uendidisse et ita uendidimus rem proprietatis nostrae, hoc est, de terra modios vi de brace, nuncupantes Raniudwallon, et dimidium Rancomalton, sita in pago nuncupante Broweroch, in condita plebe Carantoerinse, in loco compoto Bachin, in uilla que uocatur Trebarail, finem habens de uno latere et fronte Rancampbudan et Ranriwocon, de altero uero latere et fronte Botwillan et Ranworhamoi, unde accepimus a uobis precium in quo nobis bene conplacuit, illis presentibus subtertenentur inserti, hoc sunt in totum solidos*

---

13 The specification of appurtenances varies from charter to charter.

xxxi habeatis, teneatis, faciatis exinde quicquid uolueritis, cum terris cultis et incultis, siluis, pratis, aquis, aquarumue decursibus, pascuis et omni supraposito suo, sicut a nobis, presenti tempore, uidetur esse possessum, ita tradidimus de iure nostro in uestra potestate et dominatione, in luh, in dicombito, in alode comparato, dicofrito, et sine ulla renda et sine ulla re ulli homini *sub caelo nisi Budworeto presbytero uel germano eius Anaworeto et cui uoluerint post se, ita ut ab hodierna die quicquid exinde facere uolueritis, iure proprietario, liberam ac firmissimam in omnibus habeatis potestatem ad faciendum*[14]; *et obligamus*[15] *uobis fideiussores uel dilisidos in securitate ipsius terrae his nominibus: Edelfrit, Rathoiarn et Cabud; et, quod fieri non credimus, si fuerit ulla quislibet persona aut nos ipsi aut ullus de heredibus meis, uel propinquis nostris uel quislibet persona qui contra hanc uenditionem istam aliqua calomnia uel repeticione generare presumpserit, illud quod repetit insuper et contra cui litem intulerit solidos lxii multa conponat; et haec uenditio firma et stabilis permaneat, manibus nostris firmauimus et bonis uiris adfirmare rogamus. X Cummail testis, Iudhail testis, Loiesworet testis* (and nineteen further names). *Factum est hoc, sub die xvi kalendas marc., vi feria, in loco uilla Arhael, die dominico* (CR 91, 14 February 822/28/33/39/50/56, in and re Carentoir).

There are twenty-six of this type in the cartulary (9%) and a further two in the additional material.

Other formulary-derived pieces had similar elements but were more varied and less regular:

1c   *Cum inter ementes atque uendentes fuerint tres diffinite pretio comparati quamuis plus ualeat reuocare, igitur ego, in Dei nomine, Gundowinus, cum concensu Odane coniugis meae, constat nos uendidisse et ita uendimus aliquem hominem nomine Agenhart et coniugem suam nomine Austroberta, hoc est, uendidimus uobis alodum nostrum qui est in pago namnetico, in condita Lubiaccinse, in uilla nuncupante Faito, in rem proprietatis meae, hoc est, tota possessionem nostram in Faito, et est circumcinctus de duobus lateribus et de uno fronte terra ipsius emptoris et de alio fronte uia publica, ita uobis uendidimus supradictum alodum, cum terris, siluis, uineis, mansis, scuris et omnibus adiacenciis suis, quantum hodierna die nostra uidetur esse possessio, unde accepimus a uobis pretium in quo nobis bene complacuit uel aptificum fuit, hoc est, solidos xl, tantum pretium in manibus nostris de manibus uestris accepimus, et cartam uenditionis eius una cum ipso alodo supradicto publiciter tradidimus ad possidendum uel ad faciendum quicquid exinde uolueritis. Si quis uero, post hunc diem, si fuerit, aut ullus de coheredibus uel propinquis nostris, seu quislibet emissa persona, qui contra hanc uenditionem uenire aut infrangere uel insultare presumpserit, cui litem intulerit solidos c multa conponat, et quod repetit non uindicet, sed haec uenditio firma et stabilis permaneat, cum stipulatione subnixa. Actum super ipsam terram, in anno vi regnante domno nostro Hlodowico imperatore, in mense aprilis, iiii die mensis. Signum Gundiwino, qui hanc uenditionem firmare rogauit; X Odane coniugis suae, X Sion* (and eleven further names). *Ego Landebertus scripsi* (CR 226, 4 April 819, in and re Lusanger).

There are seventeen of these in the cartulary (6%) and one in the additional material. Being much less standardized, they may have different introductions. Hence, for example,

     Licet unicuique de rebus suis propriis seu conductis uel conparadis per strumenta

---

14 The spaced roman passage is not a norm, although different elements of this string sometimes feature.
15 For *alligamus*.

74

> *cartarum, licentiam habeat ad faciendum quod uoluerit; igitur, idcirco ego*... (CR 33, 808, in Nantes, re Grandchamp).

Third-person ›local‹ records were much less regular than any of these formulary-derived pieces, in syntax, content and wording:

2   *Notum sit omnibus audientibus hominibus tam clericis quam laicis qui audierint, quod uendidit Wenerdon particulas terrae ad Sulcomminum presbyterum, id est sex argentiolas terrae Tonouloscan, cum monticulis et uallibus et pratis et pascuis et heredibus suis; et Sulcommin dedit pretium istius terrae ad Wenerdon, id est, duos equos et solidos d viii argenti, contra solidos xx, et unum solidum ad Morman, et unum solidum ad Catwalart, et unum solidum ad Hoiarn, et vi denarios ad Worgost, iii denarios ad Kerentin, et iii denarios ad Argantlowen, et iii denarios ad Hertiau, et x denarios aliis hominibus; et Wenerdon dedit istam terram pro isto pretio ad Sulcomin, sicut de trans mare super scapulas suas in sacco suo detulisset, et sicut insula in mare, sine fine, sine commutacione, sine iubeleo anno, sine exactore satrapaque, sine censu et sine tributo, sine opere alicui homini sub caelo nisi Sulcomino presbytero et cui uoluerit post se commendare, preter censum regis; et Wenerdom fideiussores dedit in ipsam terram ad Sulcomin; hi sunt fideiussores his nominibus: Morman, Catwalart, Gurgost, Erthiau. Factum est hoc ante aecclesiam Giliac, coram his testibus quorum haec sunt nomina: Sulcomin presbyter, Asoiucar testis* (and twenty-seven further names); *et haec uenditio fuit in tempore Maen episcopi, dominante Nominoe Brittaniae, in die dominico, v idus aprilis, luna xxv* (CR 136, 9 April 831/36/42, in and re Guillac).

There are forty of these in the cartulary (14%) and one more in the additional material.

Redon records also use the third person but are much more regular than those of local origin and are often very brief, with little local or particular detail; not all of the transactions were performed at Redon itself, though many were:

3   *Haec carta indicat atque conservat quod dedit Iarnhidin, filius Portitoe, terram quatuor modios de brace, id est Ran Weten, Sancto Saluatori et monachis rotonensibus, sitam in plebe Rufiac, tradens eam per manicam suam super altare Sancti Saluatoris in Rotono, in elemosina pro anima sua et pro regno Dei, sine censu, sine tributo ulli homini sub caelo, nisi supradicto Sancto Saluatori et supradictis, in monachia sempiterna, cum omnibus appendiciis suis et cum omnibus rebus supradictae terrae pertinentibus ita tradidit. Factum est hoc xv kal aprilis, in Rotono, die sabbato, regnante Karolo rege, dominante Salomone Brittanniam, Rethwalatro episcopo in Poutrocoet, coram Conwoion abbate et coram cunctis monachis qui ibi aderant: Iarnhitin, qui firmauit et firmare rogauit, testis* (and five further names) (CR 37, 18 March 859/64, in Redon re Ruffiac).

Redon records do not merely record grants; essentially the same format of record was used for other types of transaction. Hence,

> *Haec carta indicat atque conseruat quod pignorauit Duil ... salinam ... pro xx solidis karolicis usque ad caput vii annorum et si tunc redempta non fuerit maneat in monachia sempiterna Sancto Saluatori et monachis eius absque ulla redemptione usque in finem mundi; et dederunt ... fideiussores iiii in securitatem istius pignorationis*... (CR 86, 10 July 865, in and re Guérande).

There are sixty-four of these in the cartulary (23%) and three more in the additional material. There are also seventy-six records in the cartulary, of third-person structure, which have no formulaic features that indisputably associate them with Redon drafting; nor do they have distinctive features which strongly suggest a local origin. They could therefore be of monastic or of rural provenance. Since many of these benefit Redon, I suspect that the majority are in fact of Redon origin.

Third-person records of ›Celtic‹ type share diplomatic characteristics – both in form and formulas – with charters originating in Scotland, Ireland, Wales, western Britain and western Brittany in the early middle ages[16]:

4   *His igitur Dei munificentia peractis, Bili episcopus atque Dalitoc nuntius Matvedoi, v feria, luna xvii, eadem die dedicatio ecclesiae Sancti Saluatoris, uenerunt ad rotonense monasterium ut imolarent monachiam praedictam, id est partem tremissam Buiac ac dimedium plebis Guicbri, cum omnibus suis appendiciis, insulis, pratis, siluis, aquis aquarumue decursibus, Sancto Saluatori in rotonensi monasterio ac monachis Deo ibi seruientibus. Hoc factum est coram multis testibus dignis ac nobilibus: Bili, episcopus, qui dedit, testis; Dalitoc, testis; Benedic, testis* (and twenty-one further names). *Quicumque hoc firmauerit et custodierit a Deo caeli et ab omnibus sanctis benedictus sit; at quicumque mutauerit, anathematizatus sit* (CR 277, 28 October 913, re Guipry).

These records – of which there are only certainly five, though possibly six (2 %) – seem likely to originate from a religious centre farther west than Redon, since we know of others from Landévennec in Finistère, and we have traces of their distinctive formulas in Saints' Lives from Landévennec (or Saint-Pol) and from Saint-Malo[17]. Since four of the six have explicit connections with Vannes, they may reflect recording practice in that city in the late ninth and early tenth century[18].

Next Breton ›courtly‹ diplomatic: here again examples are few (two, possibly three, in the cartulary and two in the Appendix); they are associated with the later and grander Breton *principes* of the ninth century, are clearly influenced by Frankish imperial practice and are doubtless themselves an aspect of the prestige sought by Breton rulers, Salomon especially[19]. There follow the beginning and end of Salomon's record of his lavish gifts to the monastery that he founded at Plélan:

5   *In nomine sanctae et indiuiduae Trinitatis, Salomon, gratia Dei, totius Britanniae magneque partis Galliarum princeps, notum sit cunctis Britanniae tam episcopis quam sacerdotibus totoque clero necnon etiam comitibus ceterisque nobilissimis ducibus fortis-*

---

16 See DAVIES, Latin charter-tradition in western Britain, Brittany and Ireland, in: Ireland in Early Mediaeval Europe, ed. D. WHITELOCK, R. MCKITTERICK, D. DUMVILLE, Cambridge 1982, p. 258–80.
17 Ibid., p. 259, 264, 272–3. CR 275–9, ?280; I originally suggested that CR 249, 264 and 290 also conformed to Celtic charter type since they have religious sanctions (p. 259, n. 5); this is true, although the bulk of the formulation of 249 and 264 is less distinctive and looks of local Ruffiac/Molac origin. CR 275 lacks witness list and sanction, and CR 276 and 278 lack sanctions, but although not full ›Celtic‹ forms they nevertheless belong to this distinctive tradition. See also DAVIES, Les chartes du Cartulaire de Landévennec, in: Landévennec et le monachisme breton dans le haut moyen âge (see n. 1) p. 88–90, 92–4.
18 Alternatively, it is just possible that these reflect changing practice at Redon; there are certainly sanctions in some of the eleventh-century Redon charters, as de Courson pointed out, CR, p. cclx. However, on balance I think it more likely that they do not reflect Redon practice: the form is far from common in these later charters.
19 CR ?235, 240, 241, A31, A52. Salomon's charter for Prüm, of October 860, shows only some of these features; again influenced by Frankish imperial diplomatic, it also bears the marks of Prüm drafting; Urkundenbuch zur Geschichte der jetzt die Preussischen Regierungsbezirke Coblenz und Trier bildenden mittelrheinischen Territorien, ed. H. BEYER, L. ELTESTER, A. GOERZ, Coblenz 1860–74, vol. 1, no. 95.

simisque militibus omnibusque nostrae ditioni subditis, quomodo uenerabilis Ritcandus abbas...
(narrative of Ritcant's plea for a refuge from Viking attacks, the foundation of Saint-Maxent for the community of Redon, translation of the body of Saint Maxent to it, bestowal of many gifts on the new foundation, followed by confirmation of freedom of property rights)...
et quicquid nostro dominio ex abbacia Sancti Saluatoris recipiebatur ex illorum hominibus, tam colonis quam seruis siue ingenuis, super ipsorum terram commanentibus, tam de pratis et siluis et aquis necnon et forastis, pro mercede in uita aeterna centuplici illis perdonaremus; quorum peticioni fauentes, cum consilio nostrorum nobilium, eis totum et ad integrum quantum mihi meisque hominibus ex illorum abbacia debebatur, tam ex pastu caballorum et canum quam de angariis et de omni debito indulsimus, pro regno Dei et pro redemptione animae meae et parentum meorum et filiorum et pro totius Britannici regni stabilitate; ita ex meo dominio illorum potestati trado atque tranfundo, ut quicquid exinde nostrae utilitati recipiebatur, totum in illorum utilitatibus ac stipendiis fratrum proficiat, quatinus ipsis monachis pro nostra populique christiani salute laetius ac deuotius Domini misericordiam exorare delectet; et ne quis, ex hac die, eos de hac re inquietare presumat nostris et futuris temporibus interdicimus. Statuimus etiam ac iubemus ut causa uel querela quae contra eos, tempore Conuoioni abbatis, de monachia uel de hominibus eorum seu contra homines eorum uentilata non fuit, numquam uentiletur, neque commeatur quislibet ab hominibus illorum negotia eorum siue terra, siue mari, siue quibuscumque fluminibus exercentibus, aliquem teloneum uel censum aut aliquid redibitionem recipere, sed omnia in utilitate supradictorum monachorum proficiant. Factum est hoc in pago nunccupato trans siluam, in plebe quae uocatur Laan, in monasterio supradicto quod uocatur monasterium Salomonis, xv kal. mai, i feria, luna i, indictione ii, anno ab incarnatione Domini nostri DCCCLXVIIII, Salomon totius Brittanniae princeps, qui hanc donationem dedit firmareque rogauit, testis; Ritcandus, abbas, qui accepit, testis; Riwallon et Guegon, filii supradicti Salomonis, testes; Ratwili, episcopus Aletis, testis (and thirty-nine further names) (CR 241, 17 April 869, in the monastery of Saint-Maxent, Plélan).

There are some similarities between this diplomatic and that recorded in the Chronicle of Nantes for the princeps Alan in the 880s; although there are no precise verbal parallels, it is similarly elaborate and wordy[20].

Examples of Frankish imperial diplomatic (6) are also very few and are not represented at all in the cartulary that survives. However, texts seem to have been available to early modern copyists and the three (of Louis the Pious and Charles the Bald) are preserved almost in full in de Courson's Appendix[21]. These follow ninth-century Frankish practice very closely and are not reproduced here[22].

---

20 See La Chronique de Nantes, ed. R. MERLET, Paris 1896, ch. 22, of c. 889, especially; cf. Alan Barbetorte's charter, also with Nantes connections, in Cartulaire de l'Abbaye de Landévennec, ed. A. DE LA BORDERIE, Rennes 1888, no. 25. See DAVIES (see n. 17) p. 92, n. 22. (However, the style is echoed in other tenth-century charters of northern France and of England; ibid., p. 91 and n. 19).
21 CR A6, A9, A28.
22 See Recueil des Actes de Charles II le Chauve, ed. G. TESSIER with A. GIRY, M. PROU, F. LOT, Paris 1943–55 (3 vols).

Redon practice

Type (1a) above, the common formulaic first-person grant beginning *Mundi termino adpropinquante*, was, I believe, the standard format used at Redon for recording grants to the monastery in the first couple of decades of its existence. This form is used almost exclusively for grants to Redon and only once for grants to anyone else[23]; the format is very, very regular; it is nearly always the form used when transactions were initially performed at Redon itself, rather than in the relevant locality[24]. We know, for example, that CR 69, of this type, was drafted by the Redon monk Fulcric in 860. It is notable that most grants by Breton rulers to Redon were recorded in this way – CR 2 and A13 of Nominoe, CR A32 and A34 of Erispoe and CR 52 of Salomon – though Salomon did also develop his own courtly diplomatic, as demonstrated above.

The preferred Redon form for recording grants changed in the 850s to the much simpler third-person record, (3); this was usually quite brief, nearly always introduced by *Haec carta indicat atque conseruat* and very often included the observation that the grant had been made *in monachia sempiterna* – into the monastery's everlasting proprietorship; hence, explicitly again, in 860 the monk Liberius was named as the scribe of CR 213, of this format. The records are usually so brief and the monastic interest so overwhelming that it is difficult to imagine them the product of any other source. These Redon third-person records were made from 851 and became the norm for Redon recording from c. 860[25]; the older *Mundi termino* type of record continued in regular use until the mid-850s (854, on the evidence of the additional material in de Courson's Appendix). However, there was a tendency for ›special‹ grants – that is, those made by aristocrats – to continue to be recorded in the longer *Mundi termino* form even after that date[26]. In this the difference between CR 20 and CR 35 is instructive: both of these charters record grants made to the monastery on the same day, 21 September 852, at Redon; they have many witnesses in common and presumably record different parts of the same ceremony. However, CR 20, which deals with a grant of some land in (?) Molac by the local machtiern Alfret, is recorded in the short form, (3), while CR 35, which details a grant of several properties from the aristocrat Pascwethen – count and subsequently Breton ruler – is recorded in the more elaborate *Mundi termino* form (1a). The basic change in Redon practice from elaborate to brief records can easily be explained by the increasing volume of business in the 850s, and 860s especially; there were many more transactions, particularly small-scale ones. Nevertheless, the long and elaborate form seems to have been retained for grand people: that high status required appropriate language is not surprising and is in itself a useful comment on the growing pretensions of the Breton aristocracy.

---

23 In CR 143; but this is a very corrupt record, with considerable Redon contamination; see DAVIES (see n. 3).
24 Although transactions so performed were often subsequently repeated in the appropriate localities.
25 CR 116 and 165 have this form and are apparently earlier (816–35 and post–832, perhaps 840s); however, CR 116 seems to be largely a Redon ›fake‹ and CR 165 has several irregular elements; neither can be early texts as they stand.
26 Cf. Alan I's grant of May 878, CR 238.

78

Haec carta indicat atque conseruat, though not invariable, is the usual introduction to the Redon short form. It was still in use in the first half of the eleventh century, although other types of notification increasingly replaced it. Given this eleventh-century use, I would not wish to discount the possibility that the *haec carta* formula was added during the copying of the cartulary; it is in any case clear that it was sometimes added to local records when they were copied[27]. However, I think it unlikely that it was a late addition and certainly do not think that *in monachia sempiterna* was an eleventh-century addition – it is too integral to the syntax of the texts. Indeed, nothing suggests that these third-person records were in essence made at any time other than in the ninth century: they have too much circumstantial detail in their witness lists and locations to be later concoctions. In any case their format changed a little over time, as might be expected of a format in use over a long period: those of the later ninth century, especially those drafted for grants to or occasions at the refuge house of Saint-Maxent, are less distinctive and less formulaic[28]. So, too, the practice of dating from the Incarnation developed from 866 – just as dating by the imperial/regnal years of Frankish rulers dropped out of use from that time[29].

Local practice

The records of Redon drafting account for a high proportion of the ninth-century material in the cartulary – at least 39%, and up to 26% more if those without clear Redon elements be included. However, whatever the origin of the latter (and most are likely to be Redon documents), there remains a substantial proportion of records of ›local‹ origin; these records were drafted outside the monastery, usually in the village centres or machtiern's residences where the transactions were performed, and they were often drafted for the participants by local clerics[30]. Although constituting a smaller proportion of the cartulary, this material is of considerable importance. Much of it came into the Redon collection because existing documents – the title deeds of the properties in question – were handed over with property when it was given or sold to Redon. However, it is sometimes the case that records of alienation to Redon were themselves prepared in the villages, especially for locally transacted sales. Once in Redon these records of local origin were sometimes contaminated by the Redon scribes, who made minor endorsements shortly after they acquired the

---

27 CR 135 (813), 151 (820), the corrupted 166 (801–13), 212 (814–21), 267 (pre–834). It also appears in a number of other records with significant corrupt elements: CR 88, 145, 177.
28 Cf. CR 236 (which begins *Mundi termino* but does not follow with type 1a), 237.
29 There are two earlier records with an A.D. date, CR 199 and A16 (835 and 842), but the former is incorrect and contaminated with Redon additions and the latter is only known from the abbreviated Appendix version and does not necessarily represent an early text. The ›courtly‹ charters also have A.D. dates, as does one of the formulaic sales, CR 244; all of these are likewise later than 866.
30 The machtiern was a local transaction president, an aristocrat with a special position in village communities; see DAVIES (see n. 6) p. 138–42. For performance of transactions in the villages (the centres of the *plebes*), for record-making at the *lis* (the machtiern's residence) and for local scribes, ibid., p. 134–8, and also DAVIES, People and places in dispute in ninth-century Brittany, in: The settlement of disputes in early medieval Europe, ed. W. DAVIES and P. FOURACRE, Cambridge 1986.

Composition of the Redon cartulary

properties and deeds, usually to secure the property against claims by relations of the donor or vendor[31]. However, the local origin remains evident.

Occasionally there survive two variant records of the same occasion, and this suggests that sometimes each party had its own scribe, be they both local or one local and one monastic. CR 250 and 252, for example, record the same Molac sale of c. 830; CR 250, though corrupt, must be a version that came to the purchasers since it later became the basis of a record originating from them; CR 252 may then have been the vendors' record[32]. CR 56 and 110 are also different versions of the same dispute in Carentoir in 866: CR 56 indicates that Abbot Conwoion sought the return of a property previously given to Redon; CR 110 does not make this point explicitly, but adds other information and specifies a rent to be paid in future[33]. CR 6 and 123 – though very similar – have quite different modes of dating, the one using imperial years of Louis and the other the years of his son Lothar[34].

The format of these local records is both first-person, formulary-derived and also third-person, unrelated to formularies (or not related to those formularies now known). Formulary-derived records were used especially for sales, particularly the type (1b) above, beginning *Magnifico uiro;* this seems to have been in use in Ruffiac/Carentoir and environs in the very early ninth century, well before the foundation of Redon – used for example by the scribes Tuthowen and Mailon. Thereafter it was used extensively by Haeldetwid in the 830s and 840s, initially in the Ruffiac/Carentoir area but extending to the Redon *seigneurie* with Haeldetwid's increasing involvement in Redon affairs; the type was certainly in use during the period 814–47, and possibly 800–857 if we take outside limits of charters which are not precisely datable[35]. Other first-person formulas were used in Bourg-des-Comptes, Grandchamp, Lusanger and especially places east of the river Vilaine, at least between 808 and 871; occasionally these types were used for recording grants as well as sales[36]. In fact, seven different scribes are named, who all used essentially the same diplomatic, and presumably the same (surely antiquated) formulary. Simple third-person records were also used to record a few sales, as also most grants and pledges, and include those records made by Lathoiarn and Condeloc at the early dates of 801–13, 820 and 814–21; sales were recorded in this simple way both in areas not using the formulary-derived types – Batz, Guillac, Peillac and so on – and in Ruffiac and neighbourhood from the 850s onward[37]. Though most pledges were recorded by Redon, some were

31 See DAVIES (see n. 3); CR 58, 143, 199 etc.
32 See DAVIES (see n. 6) p. 18, n. 24.
33 There is yet another record of the return of this property to Redon, a few years later, in 869, printed in MORICE (see n. 7) vol. 1, col. 308.
34 See also CR 34/133, 54/149, 66/158, 71/A41, 128/219, 178/179. Not all of these are necessarily records of different origin: some contain additional elements and may simply be the result of more accurate copying; see further below, p. 81–82. (Other doublets have orthographic differences but not differences of content, and again need not necessarily be records of different ultimate provenance.)
35 Tuthowen and Mailon: CR 168, 250; Haeldetwid: CR 64, 111, 112, 121, 146, 148, 153 etc. For the Redon *seigneurie* (Bains, Renac, Brain, Langon and later Massérac), see DAVIES (see n. 6) p. 188–99 especially.
36 CR 109, for example; sales: CR 209, 210, 211, 226, 227, 228 etc.
37 The latter of course reflects the change in Redon practice itself; the two may not be unconnected: the very large number of small grants from Ruffiac to Redon suggests personal connections between the monastery and the village almost 25 km away – perhaps reflected in the career of the scribe

drafted locally, usually in the first half of the ninth century, and often in areas using the *Magnifico uiro* format for sales, that is places with the antiquated diplomatic tradition[38]. In other words, some villages seem to have had a long-standing record-making tradition, for essentially local reasons. However, it is interesting to note that the prolific Haeldetwid used local elements in pledges and not the full formulaic diplomatic; as also did two other named scribes – Lathoiarn and Agnus – for Carentoir, Ruffiac and Molac[39]. Dispute records must for the most part have been made locally, even when they concerned Redon. As might be expected, they have very few formulaic elements and sometimes have some considerable narrative[40]. As for the ›Celtic‹ records, they are really another – though more distinctive – type of local practice[41].

The structure of the cartulary

The above distinctions in diplomatic practice are clear enough to allow us to make some deductions about the organisation of the early cartulary (that is, up to and including CR 288). The first third – that is records up to and including CR 102 – consists very largely of Redon records, although those between CR 31 and 43 are of mixed types and mixed origins. Within this block, charters CR 1–17 are of the period 832–4; there follows a break in the manuscript with many folios missing; charters CR 18–30 (with one exception) then date from c. 857–60; CR 31–43 are of mixed dates; and CR 44–102 are mostly of the 860s. It looks as if this section of a hundred or so charters represents records produced and kept at Redon in the first generation after its foundation, now organized in a rough chronological order; charters from the period 835–56 presumably lay in the missing folios, just as charters from this period preponderate in the additional material now in de Courson's Appendix.

The second section of the early cartulary, that is CR 103–220, includes charters of very mixed dates, in very mixed order, of miscellaneous origins. They are often organized in sets, however, sets relating to one place or property; in this the Ruffiac set, CR 138 to 161, is the most striking, but there are others too, relating to Guer, Bains, Médréac and so on. It looks as if this section represents material miscellaneously acquired by Redon, at various dates, ordered haphazardly.

The last section of the early cartulary, CR 221–288, principally involves material from the late 860s and later, from the abbacy of Ritcant onwards, largely ordered in

---

Haeldetwid. Abbot Conwoion was of Comblessac origin, 15 km north east of Ruffiac, and it is not unreasonable to suppose that some of his co-founders may have been of Ruffiac origin; Gesta Sanctorum Rotonensium, I. ii, in: L. D'ACHÉRY, Acta Sanctorum ordinis sancti Benedicti, ed. J. MABILLON, Paris 1668–1701 (9 vols) vol. 4, pt 2, p. 194. Lathoiarn and Condeloc: CR 166, 151, 212; later Ruffiac sales: CR 172, 173. Lathoiarn's early third-person sale relates to Carentoir and is an exception to general practice in that area. Other third-person local sales: CR 136, ?264; and grant: CR 267.

38 Local pledges: CR 34/133 (Haeldetwid), 135, 182, the corrupted 199, 200, 251, 265; the local CR 104 is later (857–70) and the local 193 (856) may have been drafted by Haeldetwid for Redon.
39 CR 34/133, 193; 135, 251.
40 CR 106, 107, 108, for example; for full discussion see DAVIES (see n. 30).
41 For full discussion of characteristics see DAVIES (see n. 16).

chronological fashion; hence, CR 221–5 Ritcant, CR 232–63 largely 870s, CR 266 and 268 onwards post July 878. There are interpolated, however, small sets of charters of earlier date, which nearly always comprise earlier deeds relating to one of the Ritcant and later properties. This is most striking in the case of the Lusanger material: CR 225 about Lusanger, of 16 September 868, is followed by CR 226–31 about Lusanger, of 816–33; so also CR 257 about Pleucadeuc, of 10 February 872, is preceded by CR 255–6 about Pleucadeuc, of 820–66. It looks as if this third of the cartulary represents charters added as acquired after the 860s, in broad chronological order of acquisition.

Thereafter, in the cartulary that we have now, there is a major dislocation between charters 283 and 284; CR 283 records an agreement made in Poitou on 20 June 924, that is after the translation of relics and resettlement of the community in Poitou following severe Viking disruption. CR 284–88 record transactions that took place in the third quarter of the eleventh century. They suggest that, although the community returned to Redon, the original compilers of the cartulary were faced with a jumble of post-924 records which they began transcribing in accordance with no obvious plan – except perhaps a preoccupation with the most recent records.

The nature of these three sections of that early cartulary and their relationship to each other suggest that the basic organization of the Redon archive took place under Abbot Ritcant (867–71): hence, Redon records of the abbacy of Conwoion (d. 868) were placed first[42]; then other records in possession of the monastery were added in a somewhat haphazard fashion; thereafter the collection was augmented as new documents were acquired. We can envisage Ritcant, or his men, collecting together all the Redon documents, arranging them in rough chronological order – with some deviations – and putting them in one box; then gathering everything else and putting them in another box; and then starting a new box with Ritcant's own documents; new deeds would then be thrown in that box as acquired. There is no need to suppose that this archival activity involved a massive act of copying and recopying: it may simply have been a process of organizing in bundles and endorsing where necessary[43]. Quite apart from the organization of the respective sections of the cartulary, it makes sense to suppose this began under Ritcant; although his abbacy was short he was extremely active in securing confirmation of previous grants to the monastery and in getting tenants to renew their tenancies, with new commitments to himself. On one occasion he brought several tenants some distance to Bains church to renew tenancies in one major ceremony[44]. There is therefore good evidence that this was a period of energetic property management.

It is interesting to note that one member of most doublets lies between CR 1 and 102 and the other between CR 103 and 220, hence CR 12 and 156, 34 and 133, 54 and 149, and so on. This means that duplication can usually be explained by the different principles of organization of the cartulary: the first of the pair occurs in the initial

---

42 CR 36 – in the mixed part of the first section – is a text of February and March 869, while the doubtful CR 89/90 purport to derive from about 870; these are the latest texts in the CR 1–102 section and must suggest that that section took shape in or after 869.
43 The rather late orthographic forms of CR 1–17 could suggest that this material was re-organized in the 870s or later. These folios occupy a separate quire and are written in a separate hand.
44 CR 134, 208; see DAVIES (see n. 6) p. 90–1, 129, 133, 190–1.

Redon collection, and represents Redon's early record; the second occurs in the miscellanea – it sometimes represents the other party's record and at others Redon's organization by place rather than by time. There are only five pairs which cannot be explained like this: of these CR 82 is actually a retrospective summary, made c. 863, of the whole group CR 38–40; CR 128/219, CR 178/179 and CR 250/252 are different versions of single transactions and not strictly doublets – 178/179 and 250/252 are therefore recorded with their respective sets by place – Guer and Molac[45].

All this is of no little significance for assessing and using the cartulary itself; and for stressing the major influence of the monastery of Redon on local behaviour, in this as in so many other aspects of life[46]. But it is also important in its indication of recording practice in rural localities of eastern Brittany in the ninth century at periods before as well as after the foundation of Redon: it is a major witness to local practices in the villages as also to the continuing use of formularies, some two centuries after their collection in the form we now have them, and some three centuries after some of the formulas in them were devised. The material is witness, therefore, to a type of lay literacy: these were record-using societies even if most of their members did not read or write themselves[47].

APPENDIX

List of dates and types of Redon cartulary charters

KEY:
CR no. = no. of edition and Appendix of de Courson (see n. 1)
1a   = *Mundi termino* grant
1b   = *Magnifico uiro* sale
1c   = Other formulaic
2   = Local diplomatic
3   = Redon diplomatic
4   = ›Celtic‹ charter form
5   = Breton ›courtly‹ diplomatic
6   = Imperial diplomatic
n.d. = no date given
?   = unknown or uncertain
/   = either/or (i.e. 854/58 means either 854 or 858)
–   = within the period (i.e. 854–58 means between January 854 and December 858)
Morice, Abbé Travers and Bordeaux Bible: see n. 7

---

45 See above, p. 79, for CR 250/252. I cannot determine why CR 128/219 and CR 77/100 are in their present positions. 128 relates to 129 and 219 may have been thought to relate to 218 or 220; 77/100 could be seen chronologically to fit both after 76 and after 99 – but possible explanations are endless.
46 See DAVIES (see n. 6) especially p. 211–13.
47 Cf. R. McKITTERICK, The Carolingians and the written word, Cambridge 1989.

Composition of the Redon cartulary

CR No.	Type		Date[48]
1	2/3	1)	Thursday, pre June 832
		2)	Wednesday, June 832
2	1a		Thursday 18 June 834
3	1a		Saturday 20 June 834
4	1a		Wednesday 17 June 834
5	1a		Thursday 15 May 833
6	1a		Wednesday 10 December 833
7	1a		Sunday 9 February 833
8	1a		Sunday 26 October 833
9	1a		29 January 833–28 Jan. 834
10	1a		Sunday 28 December 833
11	1a		Tuesday 27 January 834
12	1a		Sunday 18 January 834
13	2/3		? Saturday 28 November 834
14	1a		n.d. (c. 834)
15	1a		n.d. (? c. 834)
16	1a		Tuesday 14 October 833
17	1a		Sunday 25 January 834
18	3		Wednesday 25 January 859
19	3		Tuesday 7 February 859
20	3		Wednesday 21 September 852
21	2/3		Tuesday 14 September 868
22	3		Saturday 15 December 854
23	3		Wednesday 31 May or Friday 9 June 859
24	3		Thursday 11 May 859
25	3		Sunday 18 June 859
26	3		Thursday 8 July 857
27	3		28 October 832–67
28	3		Monday 25 July 858
29	2/3		832–68
30	3		Saturday 2 March 860
31	3		832–68
32	2/3		Saturday 31 May 861/67
		or	Saturday 12 June 863
33	1c		October, ? 808
34	2		Friday 13 July 826
35	1a		Wednesday 21 September 852
36	3	1)	Friday 18 February 869
		2)	Sunday 6 March 869
37	3		Saturday 18 March 859/64
38	2/3		Friday 18 February 836/41/47/58/64
39	2/3		Sunday 20 February 847/58
40	2/3		20 April 858–67

[48] In this list I have noted strict alternatives, on the basis of dates supplied in the charter texts. In fact, where we have alternative possible dates one date is often much more likely than others. – LA BORDERIE's work remains fundamental (see n. 1), although it is sometimes unclear why he prefers one date or period to others. – Where more than one date per charter is given in this list (1, 2, etc. as in CR1) it reflects the fact that more than one transaction is recorded.

I

84

41	1a		Wednesday 12 August 845/51
42	1c		Sunday, October 846/49
43	1c		March 833
44	3		Sunday, 860–68
45	2		Sunday, pre 866
46	2		Tuesday 20 February 832/37/43/54/60/65/71
47	2/3		Wednesday 21 Feb. 843/48/54/65/71/76/82/93/99
48	2/3		10 December 833–January 868
49	2/3		Saturday 13 July 866
50	1a		Sunday 15 September 860/66
51	3		Saturday 18 January 839/50/56/61/67
52	1a		Monday 12 August 866
53	1b		Wednesday 31 March 846
54	3		Wednesday 17 or Thursday 18 May 864
55	2/3		Wednesday 17 or Thursday 18 May 864
56	2/3		Wednesday 19 or Friday 21 June 866
57	1a		Saturday 29 July 864
58	1b		Tuesday 30 April 849
59	1a		Monday 18 February 849
60	2/3		Tuesday 23 May 842/53/59/64/70
61	2/3		Saturday 5 August 836/42
62	2/3		Wednesday 9 January 866
63	2/3		Wednesday 11 August 863
64	1b		Tuesday 1 March 847
65	2/3	1)	Tuesday 30 April 866
		2)	Sunday 11 August 866
66	3		Sunday 22 December 866
67	2/3		Sunday 22 December 866
68	3		Wednesday 30 July 867
69	1a		Tuesday 2 January 860
70	3		851–55
71	2/3		Monday 20 November 836/42/53/59/64
72	3		Monday, November 857–69
73	3		Tuesday 22 August 859
74	3		15 July 832–67
75	1a		14 and 16 February, post 831
76	3		Sunday 26 April 862
77	3		Sunday 8 June 861/67/72
78	3		Saturday 6 March 863
79	3		Monday 15 March 863
80	2/3		Wednesday 17 March 863
81	2/3		832–68
82	3		858–67
83	3		Monday 24 March 833/39/44/50/61/67
84	2/3		Saturday 4 October 861
85	2/3		Wednesday 17 June 862
86	3		Tuesday 10 July 865
87	2/3		Monday 18 August 861/67/72
88	2/3		832–50
89	–		c. 871

Composition of the Redon cartulary

90	–		871/72
91	1b		Friday 14 February 822/28/33/39/50/56
92	3		Wednesday 2 April 861/67
93	3		Wednesday 18 September 855/60/66
94	3		post 862/66
95	3		Tuesday, September 861
96	2/3		Monday 24 February 867
97	1a		Thursday 9 February 842/48
98	2/3		Wednesday 30 January 866
99	1a		Wednesday 23 October and Sunday 10 November 832/38/49/55/60/66
100	3		Sunday 8 June 861/67/72
101	1c		n.d.
102	1a		Monday 10 November 850/61/67
103	2/3		Thursday 10 June 868
104	2/3		Sunday, 857–70
105	2/3		c. 857–58
106	2		c. 841–51
107	2		Saturday 8 March 844/50
108	2		Friday, 841–51
109	2		Tuesday 29 November 869
110	2/3		Wednesday 19 or Friday 21 June 866
111	1b		Friday 1 June 843/48
112	1b	1)	Tuesday 6 May 844
		2)	Saturday 10 May 844
113	1a		Monday 6 May 849
114	3		Wednesday 8 January 861/67
115	2/3		Sunday, February 848/49
116	3		Sunday, July 816–35
117	2/3		Tuesday 19 June 843/48
118	2/3		832–68
119	2/3		n.d.
120	?		July 851–September 855
121	1b		Monday 12 April 846
122	2/3		c. 840–50
123	1a		Wednesday 10 December 833
124	2		837–51
125	1c		Sunday, August 850
126	3		Friday 1 April 858
127	2		Friday 29 January 852
128	1a		Friday 1 May 834
129	2		pre 1 May 834
130	3		Friday 1 May 834
131	2		Monday 1 April 821/27/32
132	3		Wednesday, 832–67
133	2		Friday 13 July 826
134	2/3		5 January 868–January 871
135	2		Friday 30 December 813
136	2		Sunday 9 April 831/36/42
137	3		28 October 842–67

138	1b		Tuesday 2 March 835/40/46/57
139	2		Monday 17 June 860/66
140	3		Sunday, 860–68
141	1b		Monday 30 January 842/48
142	3	1)	Saturday 19 July 867
		2)	Wednesday 13 August 867
143	1a		851–57
144	2		Wednesday October, post 866
145	3		Thursday 10 July 867
			Sunday 13 July 867
146	1b		Sunday 3 February 821
147	2		821–39
148	1b		Sunday 19 January 839
149	3		Wednesday 17 or Thursday 18 May 864
150	3		Wednesday 13 August 867
151	2		Friday 6 April 820
152	1c		Friday, 29 January 829–28 January 830
153	1b		pre 867
154	2/3	1)	Friday 11 July 867
		2)	Wednesday 13 August 867
155	1b		Sunday 16 January 830
156	1a		Sunday 18 January 834
157	2		Sunday, pre 866
158	3		Sunday 22 December 866
159	3	1)	Saturday 27 December 867
		2)	Monday 2 February 868
		or	Friday 2 February 871
160	1b		Tuesday 9 March 846
161	1a		March 846–January 868
162	2/3		Friday 7 December 854
163	3		Monday 12 August 860
164	1b		29 January 819–28 January 820
165	2/3		post 832
166	2		April 801–13
167	1b		n.d.
168	1b		25 December 800–28 January 814
169	3		Wednesday 21 August 866
170	3		Wednesday 21 August 866
171	1b		Friday 26 March 840
172	2		Thursday 23 April 856
173	2		Thursday 23 January 867
174	3	1)	Friday 18 February 869
		2)	Sunday 6 March 869
175	2/3		Wednesday 13 April 841/47/52/58
176	1a		14 November 832–50
177	2/3		Saturday, December 837
178	1a		Saturday, October 832–39
179	2/3		Saturday, December 837
180	2/3		841–51
181	1b		c. 833

182	2		Sunday 4 May 833
183	1a		833–68
184	2		n.d.
185	2/3		15 January 858–67
186	2	1)	Sunday 3 August 839/44/50
		2)	Friday 5 August 841/47/52/58
187	2/3		Tuesday 22 January 844
188	1a		838–48
189	2		pre 848
190	2		Saturday 24 April & Sunday 2 May 840/46/57/63
191	2		Wednesday 29 September 801
192	2		19 December 832–24 January 838
193	2		Saturday 18 January 856
194	1a		Wednesday 4 February 840
195	2/3		Friday, 841 (pre 25 June)
196	1b		Friday 1 July 824/30
197	1a		Saturday 18 January 833/39
198	1b		Tuesday c. 840–50
199	2		Sunday 25 April 835
200	2		5 December 831–39
201	3	1)	Monday 3 November 878
		2)	Sunday 8 March 879
202	2/3		Thursday 24 February 858
203	2/3		Sunday 11 October 834/45/51/56/62
204	3		Thursday 11 May 859
205	2		December 833–January 868
206	2/3		Sunday 30 January 836/41/47/52/58/64
207	3		Monday 8 April 866
208	2/3		868–71
209	1c		March 841/48/51
210	1c		January 837/38
211	1c		January 837/38
212	2		Saturday, 814–21
213	3		Tuesday 12 November 860
214	1a		20 June 842–19 June 843
215	2/3		848–68
216	2/3		Friday 1 August 833/39/44/50/61/67
217	1c		15 June 841–67
218	2/3		832–68
219	1a		Friday 1 May 834
220	1b		Saturday 7 April 843/48
221	3		Saturday 7 August 868
222	2/3		Friday 27 January 870
223	3		Friday 18 June 868
224	2/3		3 February 867–70
225	2/3		Thursday 16 September 868
226	1c		Monday 4 April 819
227	1c		Monday 26 May 816
228	1c		October 819
229	1c		March 830

230	1c		April 831
231	1c		June 833
232	2/3		pre 870
233	2/3		Friday 25 August 870
234	3		Sunday 5 February 870
235	? 5		Thursday 12 June 878
236	3	1)	Wednesday 29 June 875
		2)	Friday 12 January 876
		3)	Wednesday 14 May 878
237	3		Tuesday 24 April 876
238	1a		Saturday 3 May 878
239	3		Thursday 1 August 888
240	5		Sunday 29 August 868
241	5		Sunday 17 April 869
242	2/3		Tuesday 24 May 869
243	3	1)	874
		2)	Monday 1 August 875
244	1c		Wednesday 2 May 871
245	3	1)	Wednesday 27 December 870
		2)	Sunday 28 January 871
246	2/3		Sunday 28 January 871
247	2/3		Monday 9 July 871
248	2/3		Wednesday 21 November 871
249	2		Sunday 5 October 850
250	1b		Friday 29 June 820
		or	Wednesday 29 June 830[49]
251	2		Monday 29 July 849
252	1b		Thursday 6 June 827
253	2/3		Sunday 12 November 870
254	2/3		Sunday 2 November 872
255	1b		Tuesday 3 July 820/26
256	1b		Friday 25 October 860/66
257	3		Sunday 10 February 872
258	1a		Tuesday 22 May 865/71
259	2/3		28 June or 29 May 871–77
260	3		Sunday 7 January 876
261	2/3		June 874–77
262	1a		Sunday 19 June 875
263	2/3		Sunday 20 July 878
264	2		840–48
265	2		Saturday and Friday, 840–48
266	2/3		? Wednesday 15 January 895[50]
267	2		pre 834
268	2/3		Saturday 2 August 895
269	1a	1)	Sunday 28 December 878
		2)	Sunday 25 January 879
270	2		Tuesday 21 January 917

49 Corrupt; this charter records the same transaction as CR 252.
50 This is strictly correct, but hidden errors might mean that it should rightly be dated earlier in the reign of Alan, i.e. from 878.

271	2/3		Tuesday 2 May 892
272	2/3		Thursday 14 September 892
273	?		? Friday 8 November 888
274	2		Monday 15 March 913
275	4		Friday 22 January or 18 June 913
276	4	1)	Friday 22 January or 18 June 913
		2)	Monday 25 October 913
277	4		Thursday 28 October 913
278	4		30 November 907–24
279	4		Sunday 27 November 908
280	3/4		? 914–24
281	1a/3		Tuesday 1 May 904
282	3		pre 922
283	–[51]		Sunday 20 June 924
A1	?		Sunday 17 April 819/30
A2	?		Monday 11 November 832
A3	?		Friday 18 July 833/39/44/50/61/67
A4	1a		Wednesday 8 October 833
A5	1a		Sunday 25 January 834
A6	6		Friday 27 November 834
A7	?		28 January 834–27 January 835
A8	1a		28 January 834–27 January 835
A9	6		Wednesday 30 August 836
A10	?		Tuesday 16 April 838
A11	?		Wednesday 2 July 844
A12	?		23 May 834–39
A13	1a		Thursday 26 January 842
A14	3		24 March, post 832
A15	?		25 June 841–24 June 842
A16	1b		Monday 19 June 842
A17	1b		Monday 13 November 842
A18	?		December 844
A19	?		December 844
A20	?		832–68
A21	?		Wednesday 24 or Thursday 25 March 846
A22	?		Wednesday 24 March 846
A23	3		Thursday 10 June 846
A24	?		Thursday 1 July 846
A25	?		Sunday 849
A26	?		6 January 841–49
A27	?		Wednesday 14 May 850
A28	6		Sunday 3 August 850
A29	?		16 March pre 857
A30	?		Maundy Thursday 851–57
A31	5		19 May 851–57
A32	1a		10 March 851–55
A33	?		Sunday 1 May 852
A34	1a		Tuesday 23 August 852

[51] A piece of narrative, not a charter text.

I

35	1c		Monday 12 September 852
A36	1a		Tuesday 3 May 852
A37	1a		Wednesday 22 August 854
A38	?		Sunday 11 November 837/43/48/54/65/71/76/82
A39	?		Saturday 15 December 854
A40	2		Thursday 1 March 854
A41	?		10 August, post 832
A42	1a		854, post 20 June
A43	1a		Sunday 11 August 855
A44	1a		10 March 851–55
A45	1a		pre March 854
A46	?		848–68
A47	?		Sunday 832–68
A48	?		Monday 10 June 860/66
A49	?		Sunday, May 826
A50	?		Sunday 11 November 837/43/48/54/65/71/76/82
A51	2/3		Friday 8 November 888
A52	? 5		Friday 8 November 888
A53	2/3		Thursday 14 September 892
A54	?		Sunday 28 August 903
A55	?		Tuesday 2 May 892
Morice, I. 265, first text			
	1a		Thursday 11 November 835
Morice, I. 271, fourth text			
	1a		Thursday 24 January 838
Morice, I. 272, fifth text			
	1a		Wednesday 9 March 841
		or	Thursday 9 March 842
Morice, I. 295, third text			
	?		Sunday 15 October 853
Morice, I. 297, third text			
	3		832–68
Morice, I. 308, second text			
	2/3	1)	Sunday 13 March 869
		2)	Sunday 4 December 869
Abbé Travers, I. 125			
	?		January 834–June 843
Bordeaux Bible			
	?		? 871–78

II
Forgery in the Cartulaire de Redon

The Redon Cartulary is a manuscript compiled in the late eleventh century, largely consisting of copies of ninth-century charters pertaining to the monastery of Redon in south-eastern Brittany, some 40 km south west of Rennes[1]. This monastery was founded in 832 by local clerics, supported by a grant from Ratvili, a minor aristocrat from the neighbourhood[2]. Within two years of its foundation, the monastic community had secured the patronage of the emperor Louis and of his missus for Brittany, Nominoe, and by the early 850s imperial support was sufficient to have created the basis for a major territorial seigneurie surrounding Redon[3]. The monastery continued to attract the support of Breton rulers, the successors of Nominoe (who were increasingly independent principes), and it became one of the most rich and powerful monastic communities of north-western France, remaining so until the French Revolution. Although Viking raids created some disturbance in the ninth and tenth centuries, in the long term the monastery seems to have retained control

---

1) Archives of the Archbishopric of Rennes; published as Cartulaire de Redon, ed. A. DE COURSON (1863), hereafter abbreviated as CR, with charters cited by number and those of its Appendix cited as A 1, etc. The readings below are those of the manuscript where they diverge from de Courson's edition. 288 of the charters (five of which belong to the third quarter of the eleventh century) are written in hands of the late eleventh century. A further 103 charters were added by different hands during the first half of the twelfth century; most of these additional charters date from the eleventh century (all parts of it) although a third belong to the first half of the twelfth century and two (? three) to the tenth (CR 305, 357, ?329).

2) CR 1; cf. CR A2.

3) CR A6, A9, A28; cf. Gesta Sanctorum Rotonensium I 2, 9–12, ed. J. MABILLON, Acta Sanctorum ordinis sancti Benedicti, 9 vols. (1668–1701) vol. 4 pt 2 p. 193–4, 200–3 (Caroline Brett of the University of Cambridge has prepared a new edition of this text, of which publication is forthcoming). For discussion of imperial support see A. CHÉDEVILLE and H. GUILLOTEL, La Bretagne des Saints et des Rois, V^e-Xe siècle (1984) p. 240–6, 275–9; J. M. H. SMITH, Culte impérial et politique frontalière dans la Vallée de la Vilaine, in: Landévennec et le monachisme breton dans le haut moyen age, ed. M. SIMON (1986); and W. DAVIES, Small Worlds. The Village Community in Early Medieval Brittany (1988) p. 193, n. 23. For the seigneurie see my Small Worlds, ch. 8.

Originally published in: Monumenta Germaniae Historica, Eds, Fälschungen im Mittelalter (Schriften der MGH vol. 33, in 6 parts). © Verlag Hahnsche Buchhandlung, Hannover (Germany) 1988, part 4, pp. 265–274.

of most of its ninth-century properties and can be seen to have been working them in the fifteenth and sixteenth centuries[4].

The cartulary includes 284 ninth- and early tenth-century charters; there are several folios missing from the manuscript and these probably contained some or all of the further sixty-two ninth-century charters known from early modern transcripts; three-quarters of these 346 charters arise from the two generations spanning the years 830–880[5]. Although only surviving in copies, this material is of considerable importance: most of the charters are private documents, concerned with small properties owned by independent peasant proprietors; most of the properties lie within 35 km of Redon[6]; the collection of charters includes records made previous to the foundation of the monastery and others not directly concerning it, that is records of the sales, pledges and gifts affecting properties before they were alienated to Redon (for properties were clearly transferred together with any extant relevant documents – their bundle of title deeds). We therefore have in this collection relatively dense coverage of a small region for two generations, with records concerning more than the monastery's interests. Since the records are overwhelmingly concerned with small-scale peasant interests, the density enables investigation of peasant social structure at an unusually early period – and thereby their especial value[7].

All this material is well known and for the last century and more has been plundered by Celticists in search – in particular – for evidence of Celtic institutions. Its considerable detail has also been used, though to a lesser extent, by

---

4) See DAVIES, Small Worlds, p. 190, n. 13 and p. 212–13; J. M. H. SMITH, Carolingian Brittany (University of Oxford D. Phil. thesis 1985) p. 312–17.

5) All but seven of these additional charters are printed by DE COURSON in his Appendix to CR, using texts printed in Dom LOBINEAU's Histoire de Bretagne (1707) and transcribed in the collection in Paris, Bibliothèque Nationale, MS Baluze 46; the others may be found in H. MORICE, Mémoires pour servir de preuves à l'Histoire Ecclésiastique et Civile de Bretagne, 3 vols. (1742–6) vol. 1 cols. 265, 271, 272, 295, 297, 308 and in the Abbé TRAVERS, Histoire de Nantes (1860) vol. 1, p. 125.

6) See DAVIES, Small Worlds (as note 3) fig. 31, for a distribution map. Redon owned some properties in every parish in a 30 × 55 km block of territory in its neighbourhood, although some of its lands were as much as 70 km away.

7) The even larger – and in some senses comparable – collection of eighth-century charters from St Gall has much less detail; the many eighth- to tenth-century charters from Italy and northern Spain, though rich in detail, are often less concerned with peasant proprietors and deal with more scattered properties – they do not therefore provide such dense coverage of the localities they touch.

Forgery in the Cartulaire de Redon

those with predominantly Carolingian interests, seeking to assign eastern Brittany its place in the Carolingian world. Both types of search are justifiable, although the texts have been used somewhat indiscriminately: apart from a very suspect papal letter, the ninth-century material has essentially been treated as genuine, largely without attempt at critical assessment – despite the fact that we only know of it from eleventh-century or much later copies[8].

Moreover, there are some obvious corruptions in the charter texts: in addition to widespread inconsistencies in dating clauses, charters 250 and 252 give conflicting versions of the same Molac transaction[9]; charters 57 and 224–231 give conflicting versions of Lusanger/Derval transactions[10]; the scribe of charters 231 and 276 added later endorsements to his main charter texts; and there are a number of texts with nonsensical passages, of minor significance – testamentary crosses in a list of place-names, *conwoionem* for *coniugem,* and so on[11].

Of course, many of these corruptions arise from errors in transmission, and have nothing to do with forgery. However, in some cases I think that we can demonstrate some intentional alteration of existing documents in the interest of the monastery and to this extent the collection does include 'forgeries'. It is possible to detect these alterations because of the circumstance that the peasant society was itself a record-using society and also because their diplomatic practices can be distinguished from others. Irrespective of the activities of the monastery, this ninth-century peasant society of south-eastern Brittany used records, both before and after its foundation. Conveyance by sale normally seems to have been recorded in writing, as the pre-832 records make clear, with cartae handed over at or after transactions[12]; cartae were also cited both in

---

8) CR 90. La Borderie, however, made a very detailed study of the many dating problems of the collection: A. DE LA BORDERIE, La Chronologie du Cartulaire de Redon (1901), reprinted from Annales de Bretagne 5 (1889–90) p. 535–630, 12 (1896–7) p. 473–522, 13 (1897–8) p. 11–42, 263–79, 430–58, 590–611; and H. Guillotel makes further comments on dates in the course of his discussion of ninth-century Breton history in CHÉDEVILLE and GUILLOTEL, La Bretagne des Saints et des Rois (as note 3) p. 307–8, 310, 313, for example. His thesis includes a very thorough treatment of some eleventh-century forgeries in the cartulary: H. GUILLOTEL, Les actes des ducs de Bretagne, c. 952–1148 (University of Paris, Faculté de droit, Thèse 1973).

9) See DAVIES, Small Worlds (as note 3) p. 18, n. 24.

10) See DAVIES, Small Worlds, p. 65, n. 10.

11) CR 5, 29, 33, 136, 182.

12) CR 220, 225, for example; cf. 283, *unum molendinum cum cartula.* See DAVIES, Small Worlds (as note 3) pp. 134–8.

court cases and in informal meetings for dispute settlement – both formal and informal machinery was important to local settlement procedures and both types of machinery might use documents in arriving at a solution to problems[13]; once settlement had been reached, it might be sealed with a public reading of the document recording the agreement[14]. We know of several local scribes who drew up the records for the participants, and these were usually local (non-monastic) priests of the relevant communities[15].

Different diplomatic practices are distinguishable within the ninth-century charter texts, five of which are clearly and consistently apparent.

I. The local scribes tended to draw heavily upon models closely related to those of the seventh- and eighth-century Frankish formularies, especially those of Tours and Angers, favouring formulas like *Magnifico viro emptori ego enim venditor constat me tibi vendidisse et ita vendidi rem proprietatis meae... unde accepi a te pretium in quo mihi bene complacuit, illis presentibus qui subtertenentur inserti... habeas, teneas, possideas, facias exinde quicquid volueris, ita ut ab hodierna die quicquid exinde facere volueris, iure proprietario, liberam et firmissimam in omnibus habeas potestatem ad faciendum*[16].

II. However, some of them used a much simpler, less sophisticated, rather 'home-made' style of writing, like that of a series of records from Augan and others from nearby Guer: *Notum sit omnibus venturis populis qualiter veniens Alunoc ad monachos... ut moderare posset retributum illius terrae, quod et fecerunt, id est, tres modios de frumento, in die kl octobris, consenserunt, et propriis voluntatibus, per singulos annos, reddere Sancto Salvatori...*[17].

---

13) CR 139, 144, for example; see further DAVIES, People and Places in Dispute in ninth-century Brittany, in: The Settlement of Disputes in Early Medieval Europe, ed. W. DAVIES and P. FOURACRE (1986) p. 75–6. Although charter evidence could be very useful, it was not necessarily decisive and oral evidence might prevail over it; see further below, p. 272.

14) CR 139, for example.

15) It is possible that more than one record was made of some occasions; the variant versions of the transaction recorded in CR 250 and 252 may be a case in point; cf. also CR 6 and 123. For scribes see DAVIES, People and Places in Dispute (as note 13) p. 68–70.

16) CR 148; cf. Formulae Turonenses, nos. 5, 8 and Formulae Andecavenses, nos. 4, 25, in: MGH Formulae Merowingici et Karolini Aevi, ed. K. ZEUMER (1886) p. 138, 140, 6, 12. See further DAVIES, Small Worlds (as note 3) p. 136 and n. 11. Cf. P. GASNAULT, Les Actes privés de l'Abbaye de Saint-Martin de Tours du VIIIe au XIIe siècle, BECh 112 (1954) p. 24–66.

17) CR 48; cf. 127, 175; 177, 179; 135.

III. By contrast, the few records emanating from the bishopric of Vannes, further west, are quite distinctive, using formulas more reminiscent of the 'Celtic' Latin charter-writing tradition (which favoured words like *immolare* and *grafiare* and sometimes included religious sanctions): *Bili episcopus atque Dalitoc... venerunt ad rotonense monasterium ut imolarent monachiam praedictam, id est, partem tremissam Buiac... Sancto Salvatori. Hoc factum est coram multis testibus dignis ac nobilibus* (24 names follow)... *Quicumque hoc firmaverit et custodierit a Deo caeli et ab omnibus sanctis benedictus sit; at quicumque mutaverit, anathematizatus sit*[18].

IV. The diplomatic of the *principes*, the Breton rulers, especially that of Salomon, is different again and is influenced by charters emanating from the Frankish imperial court, although it includes the occasional local institutional particularity: hence *quicquid exinde nostrae utilitati recipiebatur, totum in illorum utilitatibus ac stipendiis fratrum proficiat... Et ne quis, ex hac die, eos de hac re inquietare presumat nostris et futuris temporibus interdicimus. Statuimus etiam ac iubemus ut causa vel querela quae contra eos... de monachia vel de hominibus illorum seu contra homines eorum ventilata non fuit, numquam ventiletur. Neque commeatur quislibet ab hominibus illorum negotia eorum sive terra, sive mari, sive quibuscumque fluminibus exercentibus, aliquem teloneum vel censum aut aliquid redibitionem recipere, sed omnia in utilitate supradictorum monachorum proficiant* but *tam ex pastu caballorum et canum quam de angariis et de omni debito indulsimus*[19].

V. Finally, the diplomatic of Redon itself can also be distinguished: charters drafted at the monastery, without pretence of being drafted elsewhere, lack the elaborate proprietary formulas of the Frankish formularies and depend on less specific words, with an explicitly monastic colouring: *in monachia sempiterna* is frequent and rights are rarely specified in detail; hence, *Haec carta indicat atque conservat quod dedit Hirdhoiarn, filius Haelin, Ran que vocatur Bothgellet... Sancto Salvatori... pro anima sua et pro regno Dei, inconvulsa et in monachia sempiterna, totum et ad integrum, cum omnibus appendiciis suis, Sancto Salvatori et supradictis monachis. Factum est hoc in monasterio Roton, VI kalendas ian., VII feria, coram Ritcanto abbate et ceteri loci illius monachis. Posuerunt*

---

18) CR 277; cf. 275–6, 278–9. For this Celtic tradition, see W. DAVIES, The Latin charter-tradition in western Britain, Brittany and Ireland, in: Ireland in Early Mediaeval Europe, ed. D. WHITELOCK, R. MCKITTERICK, D. DUMVILLE (1982) p. 258–80.

19) CR 241.

supradictus Hirdhoiarn...istam donationem per manicam super altare Sancti Salvatoris[20].

By analysing the diplomatic in accordance with this five-fold classification, together with observation of inconsistencies and irregularities in content, some manipulation of original charter texts can be perceived. There follow four examples to illustrate this. A charter of the 850s, recording a grant to the local Ruffiac priest Maenwethen by a Ruffiac peasant Wordoital – a document that went to Redon with the property when the priest later donated it to the monastery – was altered to suggest that the priest was a Redon monk at the time of the gift to him (as he later became) and that the grant was made with free powers of alienation (CR 143): *trado atque transfundo tibi Menweten monacus, id est, do tibi III modios de brace de terra, hoc est de Ran Mewin, pro anima mea et pro anima patris mei Cathoiarn, in dicombito et in monachia sempiterna, cum suo herede nomine Iarngrinn et filios eius Gleudain et Wetencain et filiabus et quod ex eis procreatum fuerit, habeas, teneas, possideas, exinde quicquid volueris liberam et firmissimam in omnibus habeas potestatem, iure proprietario, ad faciendum, cum terris cultis et incultis, pratis, pascuis, aquis, et cum omni supraposito suo, sicut a me, presenti tempore, videtur esse possessum...ego Haeldetwid, abbas, scripsi; et propter hoc cantavit Maenweten, presbyter, inter missas et psalteria CC, pro anima Wordoital*[21].

This was done despite the fact that – as we know from another text – there was a court case subsequent to the initial grant; as a result of this court case the original donor, Wordoital, secured a payment of four *solidi* from the priest in order that he might be persuaded to agree that there would henceforth be free powers of alienation[22]. The alteration to CR 143, using the local diplomatic, made it appear that the priest had always had the power to alienate this property, and therefore to give it to Redon; it therefore added to the security of Redon's 'ownership' against family and other claims.

A charter of 867, recording a precarial grant to Redon from a Ruffiac peasant is very garbled: there are errors in the spelling of names; one place-name has been made into two property units (*inter duas villas que nuncupantur Loin et Cnoch* for *Loincetcnoch* – Conoch's wood (cet), modern Quoiqueneuc); there

---

20) CR 159; cf. 183; A4.
21) There are orthographic inconsistencies in this, as in other, charters.
22) CR 144; cf. 99.

are three vague references to a *censum* alienated, although normally – if meaningful – renders are specified in terms of the goods that were actually due; and one witness, Eusorgit, is explicitly said to have attended a related transaction, which happened forty-six years earlier (CR 145)[23]. I do not believe that this is or that it represents a genuine text: it lacks a coherent core and the charter looks as if it was devised by monks of Redon to give the monastery rights in perpetuity to a land unit in northern Ruffiac, and devised from some brief earlier record of the grant of income from land in that area for a short term[24].

A charter of c. 835, recording a pledge of a land unit in Bains from one Bains peasant to another (the relatively wealthy Arthviu) has, for a pledge transaction, an unusually full – and overemphasized – statement of the totality of ownership of the pledgee in the event of non-redemption of the land: *maneat inconvulsa... in alode in dicombito, in luth, iure proprio, sine censu, sine tributo ulli homini nisi sub caelo nisi ad Arthwiu et cui voluerit post se* (sic) (CR 199)[25]. Though not uncommon in records of grants, this is not the normal diplomatic of pledge transactions. Moreover, in this case the pledge was not redeemed and the land did pass completely to Arthviu, who subsequently sold it to his wife. Since she passed it on to Redon (in the 840s or 850s), it seems likely that the monastery has expanded the earlier document in order to protect itself from any claims by the original pledgor's family[26].

A charter of 849, ostensibly written by the Ruffiac/Carentoir scribe Haeldetwid, recording a sale in Brain from two peasants to the priest

---

23) Though this is not impossible it is somewhat unlikely that one man in his maturity would witness occasions separated by 46 years: it is very difficult to find any individual witnessing over more than twenty or thirty years in this collection. Eusorgit may indeed have witnessed two transactions but the sentence suggesting it (*erat testis qualiter vendidit Catweten ad Roiantken, sororem suam*) does not make sense in the context of its own document; I suspect that this list (or part of it) has been borrowed from some other document.

24) The collection includes many charters from Ruffiac.

25) Pledges were transactions in which property rights were handed over, for a limited term, for payment; at the end of the term the period could be extended but ultimately both property and payment were due to return to their original owners. When the payment was n o t returned, the property did not revert and the transaction effectively constituted a sale on rather light terms.

26) CR 186. Cf. 183, a record of a supposed grant from Arthviu to Redon; this charter seems to have been produced by Redon to explain and/or justify the monastery's ownership – the gift may have been made but this charter does not, as was presumably intended, record the occasion of the transaction.

Driwallon, has interpolated passages, cites the most unusual number of twelve guarantors for the sale and reads very chaotically: *unde accepimus a te precium in quo nobis bene complacuit, illis presentibus qui subter tenentur incerti, cum uno colone nomine Haelhoiarno, et semine eius, habeas, teneas, possideas, facias et inde quicquid volueris, iure proprietario, liberam et firmissimam in omnibus habeas potestatem ad faciendum, hoc est, precium solidos XVI et denarios VI* (sic) (CR 58).

I suspect that this record has a small credible core but has been expanded from another charter of Haeldetwid and two Brain witness lists: the list of guarantors includes a very unlikely *Abraham et ipsius coloni* and Haeldetwid is not otherwise known in this area until the late 840s. Again, Driwallon's properties ultimately went to Redon, and again it looks as if the monastery made emendations in order to cover itself against family claims; there were hereditary interests in the priestships and priestly properties tended to be the preserve of particular local families in the villages surrounding Redon[27].

The process exemplified above is that of the alteration of existing texts – often entirely credible and serviceable ones – to serve the interests of the monastery. It is not a process of outright forgery but one of tampering and emendation. Almost all identifiable cases are changes that would give Redon additional protection from claims made by families with some earlier connection with the properties. The claims of the extended family could be a real problem in the ninth century: although there were some permanent divisions of family land, breaking a tradition of shared ownership and endowing some individuals with permanent, privately owned portions, those divisions could be questioned by first cousins or siblings. The capacity of individuals to alienate though undoubtedly acknowledged with reference to acquired and sometimes to inherited land – could also be questioned in some circumstances[28]. Accordingly, we know of many disputes within families in this area in the ninth century[29]. The context of the Redon emendations is therefore particularly germane to local proprietorship and its ninth-century problems.

---

27) Cf. CR 166, in which a witness list has been added to the record of a sale to the priest Driiunet by five brothers from Carentoir. Driiunet's properties eventually came to Redon. For the power of priestly families, see W. DAVIES, Priests and rural communities in east Brittany in the ninth century, Études Celtiques 20 (1983) p. 177–97.

28) For a lengthy treatment of this issue, see DAVIES, Small Worlds (as note 3) ch. 3.

29) CR 147, 162, 192, 246, for example; for disputes, see further W. DAVIES, Disputes, their conduct and their settlement in the village communities of eastern Brittany in the ninth century, History and Anthropology 1, 2 (1985) p. 289–312.

Partly for this reason of appropriate socio-economic context, I think that many of these intentional corruptions were perpetrated in the ninth century. One might also suggest this for reasons of the arrangement of the collection: it would be hard to explain the placing of charter 143 beside the partly contradictory charter 144 if the alterations to 143 were only made at the time of copying them both in the eleventh century. It is easier to suppose that the two were copied consecutively by a non-too-thoughtful scribe. There is also relevant orthographic evidence: despite minor inconsistencies, the collection as a whole exhibits clear and consistent orthographic differences between material of the ninth and that of the tenth and eleventh centuries. But the name forms of additional and emended passages tend to follow ninth-century rather than later practice, suggesting that emendations happened earlier rather than later: hence, charter 145 uses *Catlowen, Domwalart, Tudwal*, where we might have expected *Catloguen, Domgualart, Tudgual*[30]. And the very fact that there a r e variations between ninth- and eleventh-century orthography suggests that the eleventh-century copyist tended to copy what he had in front of him, and not update it. All this, then, points to the ninth century as the period of many emendations. Indeed, at least one ninth-century charter is witness to the fact that contemporaries acknowledged the possibility that false documents could be used in doubtful cases or as the basis of claims to property: round about 840, a peasant called Wrbudic accused the abbot of Redon of wrongfully being in possession of a weir in the river Vilaine, in the stretch between Avessac on the one bank and Bains on the other, and he rested his accusation on the fact that the abbot's charter was false[31]. The matter was only finally settled by the verbal testimony of local people.

This 'forgery' in the Redon Cartulary, then, was largely a contemporary activity – contemporary, that is, with acquisition of the properties; it was essentially an early activity, rather than some backward-looking justification devised centuries after the purported transactions took place[32]. It was one of the ways in which the monastery sought to secure ownership in a world in which the rules of ownership were themselves changing and acquisitions (especially

---

30) Cf. K. JACKSON, Language and History in Early Britain (1953) p. 68–9.
31) CR 195.
32) Cf., similarly, ecclesiastical forgery in tenth-century Anglo-Saxon England, as Patrick Wormald has pointed out: P. WORMALD, Charters, law and the settlement of disputes in Anglo-Saxon England, in: The Settlement of Disputes (as note 13) p. 161.

gifts) were liable to be challenged. The 'forgery', then, had a real and immediate social purpose and should be studied in that light.

I should like to end by adding my voice to points that have already been made in this conference – we cannot make them often enough. Since the primary evidential value of any single text must have reference to attitudes, and since the production of a 'forgery' is not in itself any comment on the historicity of the transaction there recorded, we can often learn as much from a 'forged' text as we can from the formal record of an uncorroborated conveyance without verifiable marks of authentication[33]. Such tampering as we can identify does not in itself invalidate the texts, for the worth of a text does not only lie in its face value: the nature of alterations, emendations, additions, tells us something useful about the aims, intentions and desires of the person who made those alterations. A forger very rarely works from nothing, and there are usually at least two levels of information derivable from a forged text – from the changes he made as also from the original text with which he worked. As charter scholars, it must obviously be our primary aim to identify altered passages; but this is not in order to debar those texts from further use and scrutiny, rather to determine more easily the intentions of the writer(s). The forged text potentially is of equal historical significance to the substance of any 'original' text; whether or not it actually has such significance depends on the questions asked of it[34].

---

33) Of course, strictly, it is quite impossible to establish that a text that only exists in a copy has been forged: we could only establish forgery if we could establish intention to defraud.

34) My debt to Léon Fleuriot is enormous; he has always been generous with advice and comment and has allowed me to see his own notes on the manuscript of the cartulary. I also have a debt to the Bucknell charter group: our many lengthy discussions of charter problems of the early middle ages (see The Settlement of Disputes [as note 13]) have immeasurably extended my understanding of the way charters were written and have contributed not a little to my ideas about forgery.

III

LES CHARTES DU CARTULAIRE DE LANDÉVENNEC

Le document dénommé Cartulaire de Landévennec se présente de telle façon qu'il fait penser à des enregistrements de donations faites au monastère de saint Guénolé antérieurement au XIe siècle; trois seulement de ces enregistrements comportent une date (le fragmentaire n° 23 b — Xe siècle; le n° 24 — 954; le n° 39 — 955). Le texte commence par une longue série de donations faites ou confirmées par le légendaire roi Gradlon (nn° 2-23, 26); on pense généralement que ces notices impliquaient intentionnellement une date très haute dans le Moyen Age. En grande partie à cause de ces enregistrements concernant Gradlon, le cartulaire a été longtemps considéré comme presque entièrement incroyable — une série de «faux pitoyables» (1) — impropre par suite à tout usage historique. L'étude la plus systématique qui ait été publiée est celle de Latouche qui, en 1911, soutint que le corpus tout entier en était une sorte de polyptique, échafaudé au milieu du XIe siècle en prenant pour modèles deux chartes authentiques du milieu du Xe siècle (les nn° 25 et 40). Bien que le principal objet de son étude ait été de prouver que la plupart des textes du cartulaire n'avaient pas une origine antérieure, il déclarait, de façon quelque peu illogique, pouvoir accepter l'historicité de huit des actes qui y sont transcrits, et se servait en outre de son analyse pour rédiger une étude précieuse des origines des comtes de Cornouaille. Ainsi son travail n'a pas été totalement négatif, et il demeure fondamental pour toute appréciation de ce matériel; à tout le moins sa démonstration de la validité des nn° 25 et 40 est d'une importance extrême, et, de façon plus générale, son travail sur la chronologie des personnes citées est très utile (2).

Les problèmes que rencontre quiconque s'occupe de ce matériel sont considérables: il est parfois en contradiction interne avec lui-même, il se peut que ses leçons textuelles soient corrom-

---

(1) F. LOT, *Mélanges d'histoire bretonne* (Paris, 1907), p. 189, n. 4.
(2) R. LATOUCHE, *Mélanges d'histoire de Cornouaille, Ve-XIe siècle* (Paris, 1911), p. 47-90; cf. A. CHEDEVILLE et H. GUILLOTEL, *La Bretagne des saints et des rois, Ve-Xe siècle* (Rennes, 1984), p. 133; LOT, *Mélanges*, p. 189 n'était pas prêt à tenir pour authentiques les nn° 25 et 40.

pues, et ses usages orthographiques varient apparemment au petit bonheur. La place éminente faite au *Roi Gradlon*, dont rien d'autre n'atteste l'existence, éveille des soupçons, de même que la forme des notices: leur structure et leur style ne sont guère conformes aux usages continentaux du haut Moyen Age, de sorte qu'on ne peut leur appliquer les critères courants en diplomatique; et il n'y a pas d'originaux auxquels comparer les pièces du Cartulaire. De plus, avec seulement quarante-neuf pièces, la collection est trop réduite pour permettre une analyse diplomatique statistiquement significative; et trop peu des personnes qui y sont mentionnées sont attestées par ailleurs; il est donc presque impossible de trouver des éléments de confirmation. Étant donné qu'il y a trop d'inconnues et trop de variables, il y a des difficultés qui ne peuvent être résolues et il restera inévitablement beaucoup de problèmes. Il vaut pourtant la peine de les explorer et de reconsidérer la position de Latouche. C'est dès lors mon intention de le faire dans cette communication, de prendre la collection en son entier et d'examiner jusqu'à quel point son matériel peut légitimement être qualifié de «chartes» (3).

J'emploie le terme «charte» au sens où l'entendent habituellement les érudits de la fin du XXe siècle pour l'appliquer aux rapports de transfert ou de confirmation de droits de propriété ou de privilèges (4). La plupart des chartes européennes utilisent pour ce faire un formulaire standardisé, un formulaire qui comporte presque toujours une disposition (décrivant la nature du transfert et les personnes qu'il concerne), une liste des témoins présents ou des subscriptions, une clause de datation et une sanction pénale; souvent aussi il comporte des mots introducteurs d'invocation, de notification et/ou d'adresse, ainsi qu'une clause de bornage; des expressions standardisées (*formulae*) sont communément employées dans chaque section, elles varient naturellement avec les époques et les lieux (5). En dépit de leur formulaire conventionnel, la plupart de ces rapports sont, littéralement, des *rapports*; ils ne confèrent pas par eux-mêmes la propriété mais rapportent plutôt les circonstances dans lesquelles le droit de propriété a été transféré ou confirmé; il s'ensuit que la légitimité de la propriété ne repose pas sur la possession de ce document, encore que le témoignage des chartes puisse être précieux au cas où le droit de propriété serait mis en contestation (6). Le fait que beaucoup de chartes du haut Moyen Age furent dressées par leurs bénéficiaires n'en limitent donc pas nécessairement la valeur, car ces rapports pouvaient servir à identifier les personnes susceptibles d'être appelées à fournir un témoignage oral décisif. Il est important d'être au clair dès le départ sur la nature de la charte du haut Moyen Age, du moment que les évaluations faites dans le passé du matériel de Landévennec ont souvent été grevées d'un défaut d'appréciation — ou du moins de définition — de ce point.

Le Cartulaire de Landévennec comprend une collection de chartes et autres éléments se rapportant à des droits de propriété qui suit les *Vitae* de Guénolé et Idunet dans le Ms 16 de la Bibliothèque Municipale de Quimper. La plupart de ces pièces sont d'une seule main, mais pas de la même main que les *Vitae*, et ont été transcrites dans la seconde moitié du XIe siècle, probablement peu après 1047 (7). Un petit nombre de pièces a été ajouté par la suite, par des mains du XIIe et

---

(3) Les contraintes de temps et de distance m'ont empêchée de réexaminer le manuscrit, que j'avais brièvement examiné il y a dix ans; il eût été préférable de le faire.

(4) Voir H. FICHTENAU, *Das Urkundenwesen in Osterreich* (Vienne, 1971), p. 73-87 ; et ma propre étude «The Latin charter-tradition in western Britain, Brittany and Ireland in the early mediaeval period», dans *Ireland in Early Mediaeval Europe*, éd. D. Whitelock, R. McKitterick et D. Dumville (Cambridge, 1982), p. 266-269, spéc. n. 29.

(5) Voir tout manuel courant de diplomatique; par exemple, A. GIRY, *Manuel de Diplomatique* (2 vol., Paris, 1925) ou H. BRESSLAU, *Handbuch der Urkundenlehre für Deutschland und Italien* (3e éd., 3 vol, Berlin, 1958-60).

(6) L'utilisation d'un témoignage écrit en cas de conflit est discutée en détail dans l'ouvrage à paraître de mes collègues des Bucknell charter weekends: *The Settlement of Disputes in Early Medieval Europe*, éd. W. Davies et P. Fouracre (Cambridge, 1986).

(7) Daté du dernier abbé qui apparaît de la même main dans la liste des abbés qui précède les chartes, i.e. CL, n° 1 ; cet abbé était Elisuc, 1047-55.

du XIIIᵉ siècles. La collection principale est numérotée de 1 à 49 par ses éditeurs, et les additions continuent jusqu'au n° 55 ; une série de notes marginales par des mains du XIIᵉ et du XIIIᵉ siècles (la plupart du temps au sujet de rentes) a été numérotée de 56 à 66 par La Borderie (8).

Pour commencer, quelques observations sur la collection dans son ensemble : en premier lieu, les quarante-neuf documents qui constituent le soi-disant Cartulaire sont de caractères très variés. Vingt-et-un d'entre eux ne peuvent être par aucun effort d'imagination appelés « chartes » : ils ne consistent qu'en simples mots, listes ou récits. Même ceux qui se rapprochent de la forme d'une charte ne sont pas conformes à un unique modèle : il existe au moins trois types différents de documents et ils sont diversement répartis à travers la collection et non groupés par types. Les listes mêmes sont traitées de façons variées ; quelquefois les éléments dont elles sont constituées reçoivent des titres séparés (comme au nnᵒ 4-8, 33-35b), et quelquefois ils restent groupés (comme aux nnᵒ 11 ou 14). C'est donc que le matériel transcrit à la fin du XIᵉ siècle était très divers dans sa forme. Dès lors il est intrinsèquement improbable au plus haut point — étant donné les nombreux types de documents et leur distribution dans la collection — qu'ils aient été simplement inventés à la fin du XIᵉ siècle.

En second lieu, on peut observer que la collection est organisée selon une base géographique. Les nnᵒ 2-4 et 6-11 se réfèrent à des propriétés qui se trouvaient près de Landévennec dans la presqu'île de Crozon (5 peut être considéré comme une anomalie — l'île de Sein, proche du littoral) ; 12-18 étaient également proches les unes des autres, sur le territoire de Trégourez, Briec, Gouézec ; 19 et 21 se trouvent essentiellement sur la côte sud, près de Concarneau et Pont-Aven (bien que 20 puisse être Lanzent en Plonévez-Porzay, et donc une anomalie) ; 22-24 se concentrent dans la Cornouaille centrale et forment avec 21 une suite géographique ; 25 concerne la lointaine embouchure de la Loire ; de nouveau 26-41 constituent une séquence géographique, depuis l'île de Tibidy, à travers Daoulas, Irvillac, Pleyben, Brasparts, Huelgoat jusqu'à Lanrivoaré et Beuzit-Saint-Conogan (exception faite de l'anormal 40, situé dans le Morbihan) ; ils suivent une route que l'on aurait pu parcourir (voir fig. p. 89). Le dernier groupe, 42-49, qui représente des donations faites par ou en lien avec la famille comtale de Cornouaille, est plus dispersée (9). Il y a certainement des anomalies dans cet arrangement géographique, en partie parce que certains documents comportent toute une série de propriétés et en partie parce que certaines identifications sont incertaines ; mais essentiellement le matériel a été mis en ordre — « en grandes zones géographiques » (10) — en référence à la localisation des propriétés de Landévennec. A l'exception du n° 25, la plupart des propriétés dans les articles qui vont jusqu'au n° 39 auraient pu effectivement être visitées dans l'ordre indiqué. Que les documents de chaque zone géographique soient de types divers, cela suppose de nouveau qu'ils aient eu une existence propre avant la rédaction du Cartulaire ; des documents, représentant une gamme de types divers, ont été classés dans leur ordre actuel.

En troisième lieu, la forme des documents. Comme on l'a noté ci-dessus, plusieurs de ces pièces du Cartulaire ne sont pas des chartes (11). Des quarante-neuf, le n° 1 est une liste d'abbés.

---

(8) *Cartulaire de Landévennec*, éd. R.F.L. Le Men et E. Ernault, *Mélanges Historiques*, vol. 5 (Paris, 1886), p. 533-600 ; *Cartulaire de l'Abbaye de Landévennec*, éd. A. de la Borderie (Rennes, 1888), qui contient les deux *Vitae* aussi bien que les chartes (désormais noté CL).

(9) Je suis très reconnaissante à M. B. Tanguy et au Frère Marc pour leurs avis concernant l'identification récente de toponymes dans le Cartulaire ; voir en outre B. TANGUY, ci-dessous, p. 141 ss, et aussi Marc SIMON, *L'Abbaye de Landévennec de saint Guénolé à nos jours* (Rennes 1985),p. 184-190.

(10) Marc SIMON, *L'Abbaye de Landévennec*, p. 184-5, d'une façon différente souligne également ce point ; B. TANGUY (« cette distribution présente une logique interne ») le fait aussi, ci-dessous, p. 149 sq.

(11) J'ai proposé cela dans un précédent commentaire publié par moi, mais une étude ultérieure montre que *cette* liste de chartes était incomplète n'était pas la prendre en compte (« Latin charter tradition », dans *Ireland in Early Medieval Europe*, éd. Whitelock, McKitterick, Dumville, p. 259, n.4). Aujourd'hui je regarderais les nnᵒ 2, 12, 13, 15, 16, 39, 41 et le fragment 49 comme des chartes, et ne compterais pas comme tels les nnᵒ 27 et 28 ; voir l'appendice ci-dessous pour une liste complète.

III

Les nn^{os} 4-8 et 31-35 sont des éléments d'une liste de propriétés, avec addition de quelques formules; ils sont si brefs (parfois uniquement le nom d'une propriété) qu'ils ne présentent aucun rapport de transfert ou de confirmation ni ne nomment aucune des personnes concernées : ainsi, «*De Eadem* [*Pleiben*]. Sepultura Pritienti, patris Mormani, Caer Tanett » (N° 32); ou bien, «*De Cvmmanna*. Caer Niuguinen, Caer Thnou » (N° 35); les titres ont été ajoutés par un copiste. Certains documents sont plus longs, mais de nouveau constituent à peine des chartes (les nn° 11, 19, 26, 29, 30, 38) : plutôt qu'une seule propriété, ils énumèrent une longue liste de propriétés; ils comportent un petit nombre de formules mais donnent très peu de détails concernant l'action ou les personnes. Le n° 37 est plus long et possède quelques formules, mais il lui manque le format standardisé essentiel courant; c'est en réalité un court récit, mais non une charte. D'entre les quarante-neuf pièces originales trente seulement pourraient raisonnablement être considérées comme chartes, mais toutes ne le sont pas en fait (12). Ces trente se rapprochent plus ou moins de la forme d'une charte, comportent plus ou moins de formules, et enregistrent le transfert de propriétés en la possession de Landévennec (S. Guénolé). (Voir l'appendice.)

Plusieurs des trente documents qui se rapprochent de la forme de charte, bien qu'ils s'écartent quelque peu des conventions continentales, sont néanmoins étroitement conformes à ce que j'ai ailleurs défini comme forme de la charte «celtique» standardisée (13). Ils sont écrits à la troisième personne et aux temps du passé, et comportent de façon caractéristique notification, disposition, liste de témoins et sanction. Des chartes «celtiques » ont survécu de tout un éventail de lieux, en Irlande, Écosse, Pays de Galles, Cornouailles et Ouest de l'Angleterre, depuis le VIe jusqu'au XIe siècle. En voici un exemple représentatif, provenant du sud du pays de Galles :

Notification: Ostendit ista scriptjo quod

Disposition: dederunt Ris et luith Grethi Treb Gujdauc, i mal i ti duch cimarguith (i) ejt — hic est census eius, douceit torth ha maharuin in ir ham, ha douceit torth in ir gaem, ha huch ha douceit mannuclenn — deo et sancto Eliudo.

Liste de témoins: Deus testis, Saturnnguid testis, Nobis testis, Guurci testis, Cutulf testis; de laicis, Cinguernn testis, Collbiu testis, Cohorget testis, Ermin testis, Hourod testis.

Sanction: Quicunque custodierit benedictus erit, et qui franxerit maladictus erit a deo (14).

Plus de la moitié des documents du Cartulaire de Landévennec sont conformes à cette façon d'enregistrer le transfert des droits de propriété qui était courante durant le haut Moyen Age à l'extrême-Ouest de l'Europe. Il est donc tout-à-fait possible que ces enregistrements aient eu une origine antérieure à la moitié du XIe siècle.

De plus quelques-unes des chartes ont des sanctions religieuses — et non séculières —, usage tout-à-fait caractéristique de la pratique celtique (et insulaire). Certaines de ces sanctions sont très semblables aux sanctions que l'on a trouvées dans les chartes des IXe et Xe siècles provenant du sud

---

(12) Voir en outre ci-dessous.

(13) «Latin charter tradition», dans *Ireland in Early Med. Europe*, éd. Whitelock, McKitterick, Dumville; résumé dans «La charte celtique», *Bulletin de la Société Archéologique du Finistère*, t. CIX (1981), p. 195-207; les variations sont dues essentiellement à la nature plus archaïque de la pratique «celtique».

(14) *Marginale* de l'évangéliaire de Lichfield, ajouté au manuscrit à ou près de Llandeilo Fawr, au IXe siècle; texte imprimé dans *The Text of the Book of Llan Dâv*, éd. J.G. Evans et J. Rhys (Oxford, 1893), p. XLV. Voir aussi D. JENKINS et M. E. OWEN, «The Welsh Marginalia in the Lichfield Gospels, 1ere partie», *Cambridge Medieval Celtic Studies*, t. V (1983). p. 52-53.

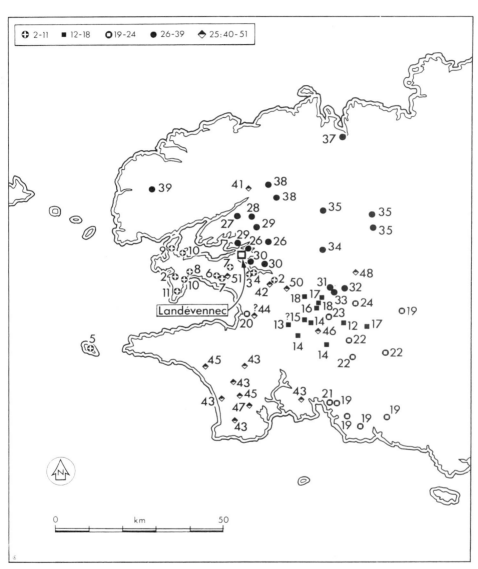

Les possessions de l'abbaye — Les numéros renvoient aux chartes.

du pays de Galles et de Cornouailles, et notamment celles qui sont dans les *marginalia* de l'Évangéliaire de Lichfield et de celui de Bodmin, encore que quelques-unes des formules caractéristiques apparaissent ailleurs en Bretagne. Ainsi, le n° 47 utilise les verbes caractéristiques *custodire, benedicere, frangere, maledicere*, comme dans l'exemple gallois ci-dessus: « Qui custodierit hoc donum a Deo caeli sit benedictus; qui vero frangere aut minuere voluerit a Deo caeli sit maledictus, nisi digna satisfactione emendaverit. Amen » (15). Dans ces chartes de Landévennec les mots choisis appartiennent donc souvent à un milieu culturel Breton-occidental, exactement comme le contexte dans lequel elles sont transcrites leur est commun avec l'ouest de la Grande-Bretagne et l'Irlande au haut Moyen Age — elles viennent après les *Vitae* des saints fondateurs, comme les chartes qui suivent la *Vita Cadoci*, une longue *Vita* du XIe siècle en provenance de Llancarfan au sud-est du pays de Galles, ou les « Additamenta » qui suivent la « Vie » du VIIe siècle de saint Patrick par Tírechán provenant d'Armagh dans l'Irlande du Nord (16). De nouveau ces parallèles notoires indiquent qu'il est totalement possible que ces enregistrements aient eu une origine antérieure au XIe siècle, et cela confirme l'observation faite plus haut que tout ce qui a été transcrit dans le Cartulaire vers 1050 l'a été à partir de textes existants (et peut-être archaïques).

Pour passer de la considération générale de la collection en son ensemble à une étude plus détaillée des textes particuliers: premièrement, bien que certains de ces textes ressemblent superficiellement à des chartes, et font usage de *formulae* caractéristiques, il leur manque quelques-unes des parties essentielles d'une charte, même de la charte « celtique »; plusieurs manquent de sanctions aussi bien que de listes de témoins, ce qui les rend impropres à servir d'instruments de vérification des transactions qui y sont rapportées. Ces textes (les nn° 3, 9, 10, 14, 17, 18, 23, 27, 28) ne peuvent être tenus pour des chartes dérivant d'enregistrements de transfert contemporains ou presque contemporains. L'utilisation des formules *sans* la forme appropriée doit, à la vérité, jeter un doute sur la présentation de leur contenu.

Ce qui reste à la fois ressemble à des chartes et peut raisonnablement être regardé comme tel. Il y a trois groupes diplomatiques distincts, que j'appelerai, par commodité, A, B et C. Le groupe A se définit par l'emploi des formules caractéristiques « commendare sancto... affirmo », et par le fait que tous relatent la recommandation d'un saint ou d'un clerc à saint Guénolé, et avec lui des propriétés dont il avait été doté. Ainsi:

> Eodem quoque tempore erat quidam vir sanctus Dei nomine Berduualt, qui et seipsum commendavit et omnia sua, id est, Lan Herprit et locum qui vocatur Lan Bertuualt, cum omnibus ei apendiciis sancto Uuingualoaeo... Ego Gradlonus... hoc affirmo in dicumbitione. (N° 15)

> Haec memoria retinet quod sanctus Riocus... omnen hereditatem sibi separatam ab omnibus parentibus spetialiter Deo et sancto Uuingualoaeo obtulit, in monachiam perpetuam. Idcirco seipsum commendavit sancto Uuingua-

---

(15) Cf. CL, n° 24: « Et qui bene conservaverit a Deo caeli benedictus sit. Et quicumque frangere vel minuere voluerit aut prohibere, anathema sit in die judicii coram deo et angelis ejus. Amen ». Cf. Dans l'évangéliaire de Bodmin: « Et quicumque fregerit hanc libertatem, anathema sit; et quicumque custodierit, benedictus sit » (n° 19, M. FÖRSTER. «Freilassungsurkunden des Bodmin-evangeliars », dans *A Grammatical Miscellany offered to Otto Jespersen,* éd. N. Bøgholm, A. Brusendorff et C. A Bodelsen (Londres et Copenhague, 1930), p. 77-99 et p. 87; et dans les quelques chartes du milieu du IXe ou du début du Xe siècle du Cartulaire de Redon qui montrent quelques traces de diplomatique celtique: « Quicumque hoc custodierit et firmaverit, a Deo caeli benedictus sit; at quicumque mutaverit, sit anathema » (*Cartulaire de Redon,* éd. A. de Courson (Paris 1863), n° 279).

(16) *Vitae Sanctorum Britanniae et Genealogiae,* éd. A. W. Wade-Evans (Cardiff, 1944), p. 124-136; *The Patrician Texts in the Book of Armagh,* éd. L. Bieler (Dublin, 1979), p. 166-178; voir en outre mon étude « Latin charter tradition » dans *Ireland in Early Med. Europe,* éd. Whitelock, McKitterick, Dumville, p. 258-9 et 269-274, et aussi mon « Property rights and property claims in Welsh «vitae » of the eleventh century », dans *Hagiographie, Cultures et Sociétés,* éd. E. Patlagean et P. Riché, Études Augustiniennes (Paris, 1981), p. 523-26.

loaeo cum omnibus suis, atque propriam hereditatem in aeternam possessionem. Ego Gradlonus gratia Dei rex affirmo (n° 21).

Les nn° 2 (malgré son long récit), 13, 15, 16, 20, 21, 22, 39 et 41 tombent dans cette catégorie ; le n° 12 offre des variantes des formules, mais tombe essentiellement dans le même groupe (17).

Le second groupe distinctif, groupe B, partage le même style et plusieurs des formules des nn° 25 et 40, les chartes «authentiques» du milieu du Xe siècle selon Latouche. Ce style est très boursouflé et plein de redites, il emploie d'interminables formules dans ses préambules et ses sanctions et aussi quelques citations bibliques. Par exemple :

> In nomine sanctae Trinitatis et unicae deitatis, divina concedente clementia, Alanus dux Britonum, videns sanctum corpus Uuingualoei exul a patria peregrinaturumque in aliena hostium crudelium perturbationis causa, et reminiscens Iohannis evangelistae verba «Quicunque viderit fratrem suum necessitatem habere» (n° 25).

On retrouve le même style d'écriture ailleurs dans le nord de la France au Xe siècle et, beaucoup plus fréquemment, dans les chartes anglaises de la même période (18). Les chartes de Landévennec du Groupe B, nn° 24, 36, 42, 43 et 44, aussi bien que 25 et 40, peuvent être, sans manipulation des textes, datées du Xe siècle (19). Dans ces conditions, je ne vois absolument pas de raison de supposer qu'elles sont des inventions du XIe siècle. Elles sont cohérentes, relatent des transferts de propriété qui sont en soi crédibles, et ont une forme de charte qui se tient (20). Latouche prétendait qu'elles décrivaient probablement des événements réels, mais que les textes avaient été forgés au XIe siècle en prenant 25 et 40 pour modèles. Il n'est nullement nécessaire de

---

(17) Voir en outre ci-dessous.

(18) Pour ce style herméneutique en général, voir M. LAPIDGE, «The hermeneutic style in tenth-century Anglo-Latin literature», dans *Anglo-Saxon England*, t. IV (1975), spéc. p. 73. Pour les chartes anglaises, voir W. de GRAY BIRCH, *Cartularium Saxonicum* (4 vol., Londres, 1885-1899), nn° 620, 635, 663, 667, 692, 702, 703, par exemple. Bien que la langue des chartes anglaises soit beaucoup plus à l'extrême, Bullough a avancé que les noms sont peu nombreux et caractéristique pourraient se trouver en Bretagne, grâce aux contacts anglo-bretons de la fin du IXe et du début du Xe siècle : D. A. BULLOUGH, «The educational tradition in England from Aelfred to Aelfric», dans *Settimane di Studio del centro italiano di studi sull'alto medioevo*, t. XIX. 2 (1972), p. 475-7.

(19) Pour résumer les points essentiels concernant la datation : le n° 25, comme l'a démontré Latouche, est de 944-52 (Alain Barbetorte est mort en 952, et Iuthouen est archevêque de Dol à partir de 944) ; le n° 40, qui a en commun avec le précédent six participants, est approximativement de la même période, au moins vers 940-960 (Hesdren est évêque de Nantes). La plupart des dates des chartes qui restent sont discutables, étant donné que les noms sont peu nombreux et que la forme s'en retrouve dans plusieurs générations successives (Alan, Budic). Les témoignages dont on dispose correspondent aux propositions suivantes : le n° 42 appartient avec le maximum de probabilité au milieu du Xe siècle, avec le Comte Budic tenu pour Budic II de Cornouaille, et l'évêque Salvator (témoin aussi au n° 25 ; voir R. LATOUCHE, *Mélanges*, p. 53, et A. CHEDEVILLE et H. GUILLOTEL, *La Bretagne des saints et des rois*, p. 381) ; les nn° 43 et 44 plus probablement appartiennent à la fin du Xe siècle, Dilès étant le prédécesseur du Budic III (début du XIe siècle). Le n° 36 présente les plus grandes difficultés : du point de vue chronologique son Comte Budic pourrait être Budic II ou Budic III ; du point de vue diplomatique il porte des traces du style ampoulé du Groupe B, mais seulement des traces ; sa place dans la collection suggérerait le milieu du Xe siècle plutôt que le début du XIe.

Il y a également de sérieux problèmes de datation pour le n° 24 : il porte une date de 954 après J.-C. et contient deux listes de témoins ; certains des témoins (toute la première liste, et le comte Helgaud et l'abbé Bénédic de la seconde) étaient morts une génération avant 954 ; de toutes façons, la diplomatique de ce texte a subi sans aucun doute l'influence du n° 25 et ne peut pas raisonnablement lui être supposée antérieure. Je propose de dire qu'il y a ici un simple enregistrement original d'une donation avec sa liste de témoins (la première), enregistrée entre 884 et 914, avant que la communauté de Landévennec ne quittât la Bretagne à la suite des ravages causés par les Vikings en 913 (Bénédic est abbé depuis 884 — cf. LOT, *Mélanges*, p. 84). La seconde partie du document suggère que cette donation fut confirmée à Montreuil, en présence du comte Helgaud, qui mourut en 926. Je ne vois pas comment cet enregistrement a pu être consigné *avant* le milieu du Xe siècle, et au moins cinq des moines de la seconde liste pourraient être des moines vivant à cette époque et témoins aux nn° 25, 40, 42. Il est *possible* que cette confirmation ait eu lieu avant 926, que l'on ait noté alors les témoins et que l'on ait plus tard incorporé leurs noms dans le rapport élaboré que nous avons ; de toutes manières, étant donné la façon caractéristique dont ce texte est écrit, il semble plus vraisemblable que les noms du comte et de l'abbé ont été ajoutés après leur mort à une liste de moines du milieu du Xe siècle. Par conséquent, bien qu'il y ait à ce document un noyau du début du Xe siècle, il semble bien qu'il ait été considérablement développé au milieu du siècle.

(20) CL, les n° 43 et 44 n'ont pas de liste de témoins.

III

compliquer ainsi les choses; il est parfaitement raisonnable de supposer que le n° 25 a effectivement inauguré une nouvelle manière diplomatique et que, à Landévennec, on fut influencé par ce style durant le Xe siècle (21). Ainsi:

> In nomine Dei summi et amore regis superni qui de Virgine dignatus nasci pro redemptione generis humani. Quidam vir indolis, moribus ornatus, stemate regalium ortus, nomine Hepuuou [Moysen], qui cuncta despiciens terrrena, modis omnibus cupiens adipisci caelestia (tradidit tref sancto)... pro [redemptione] anima[ae], ut ex rebus transitoriis, purgatis squaloribus facinorum, vera dispensatione supernae pietatis, regna mercaret gaudiflua soliditate perpetuitatis,sancti Uuingualoei precibus assiduis (n° 24) [40].

La charte n° 25 elle-même fut rédigée entre 944 et 952 pour Alain Barbetorte par Hesdren, primitivement évêque de Saint-Pol (Léon) et ensuite transféré à Nantes, et reflète sans doute le style d'écriture qui avait cours à Saint-Pol ou — ce qui est peut-être plus probable — à Nantes. Quelques-unes des chartes d'Alain le Grand de la fin du IXe et du début du Xe siècle font usage d'un langage très similaire (22). Bien que ce soit si étonnant, 25 fut donc rédigé selon une tradition diplomatique britannique-bretonne existante; la charte n° 243 du Liber Landavensis du sud du Pays de Galles, par exemple, est aussi du Xe siècle et partage le même style ampoulé (23).

Latouche prétendait également que le troisième groupe, Groupe C, dérivait de la même manière des « authentiques » 25 et 40. Or ces chartes, nn° 45, 46, 47, 48, et le fragmentaire 49, comme aussi les 50 et 51 ajoutés, sont de nouveau des chartes cohérentes, d'une forme convenable de charte (24). Certes, il y a quelques touches du style ampoulé du Groupe B dans le n° 46, mais il y en a vraiment très peu; le style de ce Groupe C est essentiellement différent — plus concis et plus simple —, et aux actions rapportées on peut attribuer des dates au début ou à la fin du XIe siècle (25). Il n'y a pas de raison d'y voir autre chose qu'une phase plus tardive de la diplomatique de Landévennec, ce que suggère aussi le fait que l'orthographe du n° 46 est plus tardive que celle des nn° 24 et 25, lisant « Blinliuguet » pour « Blenliuett », et « Catgua- » pour « Catuua- ». (Comme on pouvait s'y attendre, étant donné qu'elles ont été ajoutées et son indubitablement plus tardives, 50 et 51 sont encore plus divergentes d'avec le Groupe B). Ainsi:

> Haec cartula custodit quod Budic, nobilis comes, tradidit sancto Uuingualoeo de sua propria hereditate vicarium unum, Edern nomine, pro sui redemptione suorumque omnium utrorumque sexum, in sepulturam suam, totum omnino, sicut ipso vivente tenuerat. Sic affirmavit dicens: Quisquis hoc custodiendo servaverit Dominus custodiat eum ab omni malo; custodiat animam tuam Dominus. Amen.

---

(21) Ce style diplomatique a eu quelque influence sur l'écriture à Quimper au XIe siècle; on en trouve des traces dans la plus ancienne charte de Locmaria, aux Archives d'Ille-et-Vilaine, L'abbaye de Saint-Sulpice de Rennes, 1. 89, éditée par A. de la Borderie, «Chartes inédites de Locmaria de Quimper, 1022-1336», dans *Bull. de la Société Archéologique du Finistère*, t. XXIV (1897), p. 98-99. Cette grande et unique feuille de parchemin, écrite d'une main du milieu du XIe siècle, contient trois chartes de la première moitié du XIe siècle et des notes; voir en outre ci-dessous, n. 33.

(22) *La Chronique de Nantes*, éd. R. Merlet (Paris, 1896), cc. 25 et 22 spécialement, respectivement des environs de 900 et 889; *Cartulaire de Redon*, éd. A. de Courson, n° 235, charte de 878, qui consigne une occasion où l'évêque de Nantes était présent. (CL, le n° 25 traite de propriétés dans le voisinage de Nantes).

(23) *Book of Llan Dâv*, éd. J. G. Evans et J. Rhys, p. 243; pour la date (c. 980), voir mon étude *The Llandaff Charters* (Aberystwyth, 1979), p. 125 (Bien qu'aujourd'hui je douterais de l'influence anglo-saxonne sur l'écriture de ce texte).

(24) CL, le n° 45 n'a pas de liste de témoins; le n° 48 n'a pas de sanction.

(25) Pour une réflexion générale sur la datation, voir ci-dessus n° 19. De nouveau les témoignages ne sont pas concluants mais ils s'accordent avec les propositions suivantes: le n° 45 nomme le comte Budic, probablement Budic III de Cornouaille (1008-1031). Le n° 46 peut être daté en toute sécurité du début du XIe siècle par le comte Budic, Alain III (1008-40), Benoît évêque de Quimper (fils de Budic), et l'abbé Cadnou de Landévennec (jusqu'à 1031). Le n° 47 est daté par le même Benoît, Alain comte de Cornouaille (avant 1029 jusqu'en 1058) et Orscand évêque de Quimper (au moins à partir de 1029), du second quart du XIe siècle (probablement les années 1020); et le n°48 du second quart par le comte Alain et Alain III (1026-40); le n°49 n'a pas été achevé, et par suite est antérieur à 1058; les nn°50 et 51 sont de la fin du XIe début du XIIe siècle (les abbés Guillaume et Justin, 1085-1112).

III

Si quis vero temere frangere aut minuere voluerit, de libro viventium et cum justis non scribatur. Sit pars ejus cum Dathan et Abiron, quos terra deglutivit, nec non cum Juda et Pilato, qui Dominum crucifixerunt. Hujus donationis testes sunt plures : Alan dux Britanniae, qui obitui ejus affuit, testis ; Benedictus episcopus, filius istius Budic,testis ; Cadnou abba Sancti Uuingualoei,testis ; Euhuarn vicecomes, testis ; Saluten, testis ; Riuuelen, testis ; Blinliuguet, testis, Catguallon, testis ; Moruuethen, testis (n° 46).

Je pense donc que les chartes du Groupe B et du Groupe C sont des chartes du Xe et du XIe siècles. Les chartes du Groupe A sont un matériau d'un type différent. Dans l'ensemble leurs caractéristiques diplomatiques ne se distinguent pas suffisamment de celles des Groupes B et C pour suggérer une origine antérieure, avant le Xe siècle ; pas davantage, la plupart du temps, leurs caractéristiques orthographiques. Le n° 39, en tout cas, porte une date de 955 après J.-C., et certaines des chartes utilisent des formules qui furent en usage aux Xe et XIe siècles mais pas plus tard ; la plupart ont le très commun *in dicumbitione*, une expression (signifiant pleine autorité) caractéristique du matériel de Landévennec jusqu'au XIIe siècle et utilisée dans d'autres chartes bretonnes entre le IXe et le XIIe siècles (26). Il ne semble donc pas que les chartes de ce groupe aient une origine antérieure aux Xe ou XIe siècles, même si l'une ou l'autre peut avoir été reprise de textes plus anciens. Le n° 21, par exemple, a un nombre considérable de formules « celtiques » (y compris « obtulit in monachiam perpetuam », aussi bien qu'une sanction caractéristique), et serait en conformité avec des chartes « celtiques » écrites au IXe et Xe siècles. Bien que le récit qui l'ouvre paraisse tardif (et décousu), la fin du n° 20 peut être d'une charte et présente quelques traits orthographiques anciens (Uuinuual). Après tout, nous savons par la *Vita Pauli* de la fin du IXe siècle, écrite à Landévennec, qu'il existait des chartes et qu'elles étaient gardées avec soin en Bretagne occidentale avant le Xe siècle (27). Les chartes du Groupe A offrent un intérêt particulier en ce qu'elles enregistrent l'absorption par Landévennec de maisons religieuses existantes et de leurs dotations, en utilisant le modèle suivant : « Saint N... s'est donné lui-même, son monastère et ses terres à Guénolé ». Je ne vois pas de raison de douter que ce processus se soit réellement produit, c'est-à-dire que dans le voisinage il y ait eu de petites maisons qui s'affilièrent et se mirent dans la dépendance du monastère plus grand, et dont les terres furent administrées à partir de la maison-mère. La création de fédérations de monastères est la règle à travers le monde celtique dans la période qui va du VIIe au XIe siècle, et naturellement, elle ne fut pas moins caractéristique de l'Europe continentale au XIe siècle ; ainsi l'évêque Aed de Sletty en Irlande se recommanda lui-même et sa propriété à l'église d'Armagh à la fin du VIIe siècle (28). Elli donna son monastère, et une rente annuelle, au monastère de Llancarfan, au sud du Pays de Galles, au VIIIe (?) siècle ; l'église de Llandaff prit en charge toute la tradition — saint, archives et propriété — de l'église de saint Teilo (Llandeilo Fawr) au sud du pays de Galles au Xe ou au début du XIe siècle (29). Plus près de nous même, le monastère de Redon au cours du IXe siècle, absorbait de petits établissements en

---

(26) Voir M.P. PANIOL, *Histoire des Institutions de la Bretagne* (réimp. Mayenne, 5 vol.,1981-84), II, 169 f ; A. de LA BORDERIE, CL, p. 209-210 ; cf. *Cartulaire de Redon*, éd. A de COURSON. nn° 39, 40, 153, 200, 264, etc. ; A. de LA BORDERIE « Chartes inédites de Quimper », dans *Bull. de la Société Archéologique du Finistère*, t. XXIV (1897), p. 98-99. Le matériel de Landévennec utilise cette expression beaucoup moins fréquemment après le XIIe siècle ; voir les notes marginales éditées par La Borderie, CL, jusqu'au n° 57, mais pas au-delà.

(27) *Revue Celtique*, t. V (1881-83), p. 449-452.

(28) *The Patrician texts in the Book of Armagh*, éd. L. Bieler, p. 178.

(29) *Vita Cadoci*, ch. 63 ; *Vitae Sanctorum Britanniae et Genealogiae*, éd. A. W. Wade-Evans, p. 130-132 (« Ecce, ego construxi ecclesiam et domos in nomine Domini, et ipse cunctique successores mei familie Cadoci erimus obedientes,subiecti, atque beniuoli familie Cadoci ») ; mon étude *An Early Welsh Microcosm* (Londres, Royal Historical Society, 1978), p. 139-144.

Bretagne de l'est (30). Puisque la notion de recommandation dans ces divers contextes, comme à Landévennec, est si spécifique et caractéristique, impliquant l'acte d'engagement d'un homme envers un autre et une acceptation de dépendance, et par suite le transfert des propriétés, je suis prête à accepter les chartes du Groupe A comme l'enregistrement à Landévennec de son absorption de propriétés religieuses existantes. Le processus est en soit crédible, bien que la date de composition soit probablement tout-à-fait tardive.si le témoignage des n°° 12 et 21 est valable pour l'ensemble du groupe, alors l'absorption peut avoir eu lieu vers la fin du IXe siècle et l'enregistrement peut avoir été fait au Xe (31).

*
**

Reprenons donc ensemble les divers aspects géographiques, diplomatiques et chronologiques de cette analyse. Si nous considérons l'ensemble de la collection, les articles 2-23, les chartes « Gradlon », sont classés en référence à des zones géographiques et en grande partie indatables. Il y a un hiatus autour de 23b-25, mais les notices 24-41, et probablement aussi le fragmentaire 23b, sont, lorsqu'on peut les dater, une section du milieu du Xe siècle, classée dans un ordre géographique. De nouveau une rupture aux n°° 40-42, mais les notices 42-51 constituent une section du milieu du Xe à la fin du XIe siècle, rangée en ordre chronologique et ajoutée à la collection originale. (Le Cartulaire a été manifestement copié alors que la collection déjà s'accroissait ; ainsi les n°° 50 et 51 ont été purement ajoutés, en ordre inverse.) Mon opinion est que le travail principal de compilation et de rédaction a été fait au milieu du Xe siècle, une fois les moines revenus de leur exil à Montreuil. Les notices 23b-41 (qu'on puisse ou non leur faire confiance) sont des chartes et des listes composées au milieu du Xe siècle. Les notices 2-23 ont été construites au moment où l'on recueillait les pièces 23b-41, en vue d'apporter un témoignage antérieur au milieu du Xe siècle pour des droits de propriété sur des terres sans doute détenues en toute légitimité ; elles pourraient même représente des terres possédées avant le départ pour Montreuil. On les construisit à partir de tous les matériaux que l'on avait sous la main —listes, notes, Vitae (32) et même quelques chartes telles que les textes qui sont à la base des n°° 20 et 21. On les groupa par zones géographiques et on les plaça avant 23b-41. Je pense que ceci s'est fait du milieu à la fin du Xe siècle, plutôt qu'à une date plus tardive, pour deux raisons précises : le verbe *affirmo* est caractéristique de la série et il était visiblement courant au milieu du Xe siècle, comme le prouve le texte de confirmation joint au n° 25 : « Post obitum Alani, ego Tetbaldus, nutu Dei comes, hoc idem affirmo sicut supra dictum est... » De plus on *ne* le rencontre *pas* dans les chartes de la fin du Xe et du XIe siècles ni dans les additions de la fin du XIe et du XIIe siècles. Il ne rime à rien de supposer que c'est une invention du milieu du XIe siècle (33). Après quoi, selon que se présentaient les donations, les n°° 42-49 furent ajoutés à la collection, que l'on gardait probablement dans des coffres ou même dans un précédent cartulaire. Le tout fut retranscrit, dans cet ordre déjà fixé, au milieu du XIe siècle, et d'autres ensuite ajoutés.

---

(30) *Cartulaire de Redon*, éd. A. de Courson, n°° 247, App. 4, 97, App. 40 et App. 45, pour des absorptions dans les années 830, 840 et 850 (Sent Ducocca, Castel Uuuel, Sent Thovi).

(31) L'occurence de saint Rioc du n° 21 dans la *Vita Winwaloei*, II, 22 (A. de La Borderie, CL, p. 84-85) donne à penser que Landévennec avait le contrôle des propriétés associées au Xe siècle quand la *Vita* fut écrite (fin du IXe siècle) ; la localisation de *Tres* (sic) *Uuilermeaen* (Guelvain) dans la *vicaria* de Trégourez au n° 12 suppose qu'il a été écrit *avant* que n'existât la paroisse d'Edern, soit au XIe siècle, comme le souligne M. Tanguy, ci-dessous p. 145.

(32) Comparer la *Vita Winwaloei*, II, 22 et 23 (A. de La Borderie, CL, p. 84-87) avec les n°° 21 et 9.

(33) Malgré le point de vue respectable de M. Guillotel, ci-dessous p. 101, je trouve le milieu du Xe siècle plus vraisemblable, tout en reconnaissant qu'il n'y a pas pour le moment de preuve déterminante. Ni les formules qui se rencontrent dans les chartes de Locmaria de Quimper (ci-dessus, n. 21), ni la structure de ce document ne fournissent une preuve décisive pour sa datation : la première charte — que l'on peut dater des années 1020 — commence certainement par une version abrégée du préambule du Groupe B, mais le fait que celui-ci est utilisé au XIe siècle ne peut être une preuve qu'il ne l'était pas au Xe.

De plus, la version quimpéroise, puisqu'elle est abrégée, dérive probablement d'une autre. L'usage chronologiquement limité de *affirmo* me paraît être un argument plus fort. Je suis, naturellement, très reconnaissante à M. Guillotel de la discussion de ce point et de son obligeante correspondance.

Je suis donc portée à accepter toutes les *chartes* comme des textes de chartes produits au milieu du Xe siècle ou plus tard (i.e. 2, 12, 13, 15, 16, 20, 21, 22, 24, 25, 36, 39-49), le n° 24 étant le développement au milieu du Xe siècle d'une charte du début du siècle. Je pense aussi que les nn° 20 et 21 présentent un noyau de charte antérieur qui a été développé au milieu du Xe siècle (alors que plusieurs autres chartes — ainsi le n° 22 — pourraient avoir pour base des textes antérieurs mais non des chartes antérieures). L'opinion de Latouche selon laquelle les nn° 2-23 et 26-30 seraient uniquement fabriqués à partir de noms de lieux, avec des récits hagiographiques inventés au XIe siècle, est absolument insuffisante. En dehors même de l'analyse diplomatique, il est évident que derrière une bonne partie de tout ce registre il y a un matériau écrit de quelque espèce, étant donné que l'on y trouve sporadiquement des traits orthographiques anciens.

Naturellement, l'historicité des actes enregistrés dans les chartes est tout à fait une autre affaire. Même là où les textes sont parfaitement crédibles et paraissent d'authentiques enregistrements du Xe ou du XIe siècles, il ne s'ensuit nullement que les actes qu'ils enregistrent ont eu lieu. Sans une preuve qui vienne les corroborer on ne peut faire là-dessus aucun commentaire. De preuves il n'y en a dans la plupart des cas aucune, sinon le fait que Landévennec s'est trouvé plus tard en possession de plusieurs des propriétés dont parlent ces enregistrements.

En dépit de l'inévitable incertitude sur la valeur du contenu de ces enregistrements, un certain nombre de points méritent d'être soulignés. Même si le matériel en est difficile, il ne nous est pas permis d'ignorer le témoignage du Cartulaire de Landévennec. Il contient souvent d'utiles informations, et — compte tenu de la rareté du matériel médiéval ancien de la Bretagne occidentale — mérite une attention consciencieuse et détaillée. Le matériel des Xe et XIe siècles au moins est souvent extrêmement intéressant. Il nous fournit, par exemple, une information remarquable sur la pratique des héritages et la structure familiale, depuis les remarques explicites sur la pratique des familles nobles jusqu'aux implications de l'emploi du terme *transmarinus* — quoi qu'il en soit des origines réelles des gens décrits par ce terme, on l'invoquait probablement pour prévenir les réclamations de la famille (34). De même le grand nombre de cas où un achat est indiqué avant une donation avait probablement pour dessein de prévenir de telles réclamations, du moment que normalement un achat portait sur une terre aliénable. D'autres éléments de ce matériel ont une valeur potentielle : les paiements funéraires, comme les références à la dîme, pourraient rendre service dans les discussions sur l'implantation des structures paroissiales, à la fois en général et dans le problème particulier de l'origine des *plebes* en Bretagne (35). Et le contrôle de l'ensemble d'une *plebs* au moins au XIe siècle sinon avant, est d'un grand intérêt dans le contexte du développement de la *seigneurie*. C'est pourquoi ce matériel a son rôle à jouer dans la discussion des problèmes sociaux, religieux et économiques de l'histoire de l'Europe du haut Moyen-Age, et il serait peu perspicace de l'ignorer.

Les chartes des Groupes B et C sont des enregistrements presque contemporains de transferts des Xe et XIe siècles, et celles du Groupe A des enregistrements de transfert faits rétrospectivement à cette même époque à partir de documents antérieurs. Le reste des documents du Cartulaire de Landévennec est constitué de notices d'origines variées, qui *ne* sont *pas* des chartes ; il est donc impossible de les dater diplomatiquement, mais rien ne s'oppose à ce que quelques-unes aient eu une origine antérieure au Xe siècle — ici l'étude des noms est d'une importance cruciale en faisant faire un pas de plus aux problèmes d'analyse critique. L'opinion qui tient l'ensemble du Cartulaire pour une élaboration du XIe siècle me paraît donc intenable : sa nature est absolument plus complexe.

---

(34) Cl, nn° 13, 37.
(35) Ibid., nn° 13, 14, 28 ; 25, 38, 41 ; voir mes réflexions sur le problème de la *plebs* dans « Priests and rural communities in east Brittany in the ninth century », dans *Études Celtiques*, t. XX (1983), p. 177-180, 196-197.

III

Appendix: Le cartulaire de Landévennec

1	Liste d'Abbés	28	X
2	A	29	Liste
3	X	30	Liste
4	Elément d'une liste	31	Elément d'une liste
5	Elément d'une liste	32	Elément d'une liste
6	Elément d'une liste	33	Elément d'une liste
7	Elément d'une liste	34	Elément d'une liste
8	Elément d'une liste	35	Elément d'une liste
9	X	36	B
10	X	37	Narration
11	Liste	38	Liste
12	A	39	A
13	A	40	B
14	X	41	A
15	A	42	B
16	A	43	B
17	X	44	B
18	X	45	C
19	Liste	46	C
20	A	47	C
21	A	48	C
22	A	49	Fragment C
23	X		
24	B	50	C
25	B	51	C
26	Liste	52	X
27	X	53	C

Liste d'Abbés: 1
Eléments de listes: 4, 5, 6, 7, 8, 31, 32, 33, 34, 35
Listes: 11, 19, 26, 29, 30, 38
Narration: 37
Groupe A: 2, 12, 13, 15, 16, 20, 21, 22, 39, 41
Groupe B: 24, 25, 36, 40, 42, 43, 44
Groupe C: 45, 46, 47, 48 (49); (50, 51, 53)
Groupe X: 3, 9, 10, 14, 17, 18, 23, 27, 28

IV

ON THE DISTRIBUTION OF POLITICAL POWER IN BRITTANY IN THE MID-NINTH CENTURY

The political status of Brittany in the ninth century is problematic for us and was a problem, at the time, for Bretons as much as for Franks.[1] This circumstance arises in part because of migration from Britain into northwestern France - the Armorican peninsula - in the late Roman and very early medieval period, occasioning the name Brittany [*Britannia (Minor)*], and because of the consequent intrusion and maybe reinforcement of Celtic language and institutions, thereby distinguishing it from the rest of Francia. Everything points to a heavier concentration of British settlement in the western half of the peninsula, though, despite the strength of Frankish political interests in Rennes and Nantes, the medieval linguistic boundary seems to have run from the mouth of the Loire to the western base of the Cotentin peninsula (see Fig. 6.1). There is no doubt that the Franks constantly claimed to rule Brittany after the migration and that they had no small influence in the late sixth century, especially in east Brittany. Indeed, Rennes and Nantes, as *Frankish* strongholds, were attacked by the Bretons then and Gregory of Tours clearly considered the river Vilaine the Breton boundary. Similarly, early in the ninth century, the *Royal Frankish Annals* could record that Louis went *from* Vannes *into* Brittany. Relations in the intervening period, the seventh and eighth centuries, are quite obscure, as are relations between East and West Brittany, for there is almost no contemporary evidence; that obscurity must have itself affected relations in the ninth century.[2]

---

[1] A version of this paper was first read to members of the Medieval Society at the Institute of Historical Research, London, in February 1979. I am most grateful for the comments received on that occasion, as also, of course, for comments at the Charles the Bald conference. I owe a further debt of gratitude to Janet Nelson, Julia Smith and Chris Wickham for their very helpful criticisms of written drafts of the paper; and to M. Gildas Bernier for his advice on Breton names.

[2] For recent comment on the migration see Chadwick 1965, pp. 235-99; Fleuriot and Giot 1977, pp. 106-16; Fleuriot 1980; Chédeville and Guillotel 1984, pp. 21-49. There is some comment on the following centuries in Chadwick 1969, but the most detailed consideration, and one which refers the reader to most of the evidence, remains that in La Borderie 1896, vol. i. See also Planiol 1981-4 (this indispensable work was first published (1953, in part) some two generations after it was written [1891-4]); and Chédeville and Guillotel 1984. For linguistic and other boundaries see Flatrès 1977, p. 312; Tanguy 1980. See also *ARF*, s.a. 818.

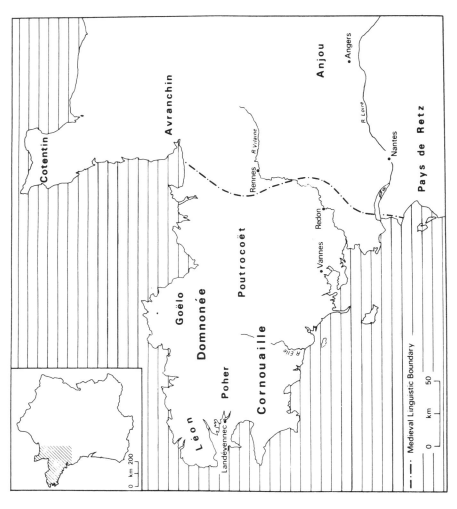

Figure 6.1: North-West France

We know of Frankish expeditions sent into Brittany by the Carolingian predecessors of Charles the Bald -Pippin, Charles the Great and Louis the Pious - in 753, 778, 786, 799, 811, 818, 824. All of these expeditions were made to state and to effect Carolingian control over the region; and Louis himself led the last two, penetrating as far as Landevennec far in the west of the peninsula. We know of the consequent appointment of the Breton Nominoë as Louis's *missus* and *dux* in Brittany in 831 and of Frankish bishops as far west as Quimper and S. Pol in the middle of the century. We know of some association of the aristocratic families of west Neustria with the Bretons already in 813-22, when the count of Vannes was Guy, brother of Lambert of Anjou, and subsequently in the 840s and 850s, and again in 878, when Gauzlin and Gauzbert got the fidelity of some (*pars*) of the Bretons. We know of further expeditions by Charles the Bald in 845 and 851, and of meetings and agreements between Charles and the Bretons Erispoë and Salomon. As a result of these meetings, Rennes, Nantes and the pays de Retz were given to Erispoë in 851; a 'third' of Brittany (the details were not specified) was ceded to Salomon in 852;[3] further lands were given to Salomon in Anjou as a benefice in 863 and in the Cotentin and Avranchin in 867; and joint Breton/Carolingian action was taken against the Vikings, in 868 and 873 (see Fig. 6.1).[4] Moreover, whatever the truth of the claims of the *Annals of St. Bertin* that Salomon was the *fidelis* of Charles and commended himself in 863, there is some evidence of the occurrence of Frankish terms and maybe institutions at least in eastern Brittany in the ninth century: commendation, *fideles* and *vassi* were occasionally to be found, as were the judicial instruments of *mallus* and *scabini*. Coins were minted in Rennes in the name of Charles.[5] Both the interest of the Franks in Brittany and their influence upon the country are therefore quite clearly demonstrable.

On the other hand, we know that Nominoë, Louis's *missus*, ravaged Anjou in the 840s, seized Rennes and Nantes in 849, working with Lambert of Anjou, and was regarded as a rebel, and that Erispoë continued this opposition. Charles suffered defeat at the hands of both of them.[6] Besides this, Breton bishops did not attend Frankish councils nor acknowledge the metropolitan authority of Tours. Consequently, both medieval and modern historians of Brittany have argued that Nominoë established an independent kingdom. The eleventh-century *Chronicle of*

---

3 *AB*, p. 64: 'Salomon Britto Karolo fidelis efficitur tertiaque Brittanniae parte donatur'. It is quite unclear to which part of Brittany this refers, though Smith 1985, p.138, argues for Rennes and Nantes; it is also unclear how this was intended to affect Erispoë's relations with Charles.
4 *AB*, pp. 63f, 96, 137, 151, 193-5. See La Borderie 1898, ii. 3-115, 264-72; Boussard 1968, pp. 15-21; Chédeville and Guillotel 1984, pp.249-352; Smith 1985; Davies 1988, pp.17-22 for the substance of this paragraph.
5 *Cartulaire de Redon*, ed. A. de Courson (Paris, 1863), no. cvii, cxcvi, lxi, cxcii for example. I am most grateful to Michael Metcalf for advice on the difficult area of the coinage.
6 See La Borderie 1898, ii. 49f., 70-2; Chédeville and Guillotel 1984, pp.259-87.

Nantes accordingly records that Nominoë was elevated to the kingship, while in the late nineteenth century La Borderie significantly headed his appropriate chapters 'La delivrance de la Bretagne (826-46)', 'Formation de la monarchie bretonne (846-51)', 'Le fils du libérateur (851-7)', 'Apogée de la monarchie bretonne (857-74)'.[7] Moreover, explicitly Celtic terms are as easy to find in eastern Brittany in the ninth century as are Frankish ones: *enepuuert* (morning gift), *loth* and *cofrit* -in the phrase *dicofrit* or *sine cofrito* -(charges on land), *machtiern* (local 'ruler'). All are obviously Celtic words but some also refer to distinctive institutions, which may have their parallels -like Welsh *mechdeyrn* and *wynebwerth* -in other Celtic countries.[8] Brittany therefore differs from many other areas of Frankish interest and control in that it provides plentiful evidence of distinctively non-Frankish institutions. It has a partly Celtic nature and supplies sufficient indication of separatist tendencies to suggest the possibility of a distinctive, non-Frankish identity.[9]

There is therefore a quite clear problem in considering the political status of Brittany in the ninth century. Both Franks and Bretons claimed overall political control; both Frankish and Breton socio-political institutions were evident. Historians of the Carolingian state are prone to see it as a Frankish appendage, but Bretons as an independent Celtic state. At its crudest, then, was Brittany Frankish or Breton? What was the relationship between Bretons and Franks? And, a point that is less obvious but as significant in any consideration of political status, what was the relationship between the Breton 'rulers' of Brittany and the Bretons? Was there any machinery of political control? What was the possibility of effecting the political will of the ruler at ground level? How, indeed, does rule at ground level compare, if at all, with other parts of the Carolingian world? This paper is about the nature and exercise of political power in Brittany in the ninth century. Much of it ranges over material that has often been discussed before, and I am aware that little that I have to say is totally new. However, this is a useful opportunity to state the problems and bring them before the attention of an English audience and to place Brittany in the Carolingian context as well as the Celtic; hopefully it will stimulate further and more sophisticated consideration.

We are fortunate in possessing unusually good sources for the history of east Brittany in the ninth century, a circumstance which distinguishes investigations of this period from those about the preceding or immediately subsequent centuries. Not only are there the expected incidental and other notices of Frankish annalists, those of the *Annals of St Bertin* being especially valuable, and a few letters of clerical interest, but there is also a useful corpus of saintly *Vitae* -of Paul, Guénolé, Tudwal, Machutes and the *Sanctorum Rotonensium* -and a very large

---

7   Merlet 1896, pp. 33-9; La Borderie 1898, ii. cc. ii-v, pp. 27-122.
8   See Fleuriot 1971, pp. 601-60, esp. pp. 650-2; *Cart. Redon*, no. ccxxxvi, xlix, cli, xxi, for example.
9   It is not, of course, alone in providing evidence of separatist tendencies; see Kienast 1968, pp. 4-9, for some discussion of this.

collection of charters from the monastery at Redon. Redon is south of Rennes, in east Brittany, and the monastic foundation was made in 832, with the support of Nominoë, who made grants to it by 834. Its eleventh-century cartulary contains 283 charters of the ninth and early tenth century and a further 108 of the tenth and eleventh centuries. 62 additional ninth-century charters are known from later transcripts.[10] Most of the ninth-century charters record grants and sales made within 50 years of foundation, but a few detail transactions which had taken place in the generation before 832. They refer to lands scattered all over the southeastern third of Brittany, with the greatest concentration occurring just west of a line between Redon and Rennes, though a few are more widely scattered. The charters are exceptionally rich in personal and topographic, institutional and circumstantial detail. Hence, this concentration of material from a short space of time, together with the close connections of the foundation with the 'rulers' of Brittany, permits some detailed investigation of mid-ninth century Brittany to be undertaken.

We may begin by asking what can be said of the 'rulers' of Brittany, the Bretons of the ninth century whose political powers had some associated aura of independence. The principal rulers, as I shall refer to them, were five, covering three generations.

Nominoë, the first, emerged as imperial *missus* in 831 but was rebelling at least from 843, if not earlier. On his sudden death in 851, he was followed by his son Erispoë. Erispoë was killed in 857 by his own cousin, Salomon, who was himself killed in 874 as the result of a conspiracy by the *primores* of Brittany led by Pascwethen, his son-in-law, and by Guorhwant, son-in-law of Erispoë. These two were jointly dominant until they were succeeded three years later by Pascwethen's brother, Alan, and Guorhwant's son, Iudicaël. Thereafter, Alan's descendants became dukes of Brittany.[11]

All available evidence would suggest that this series of prominent men had responsibility for the whole of Brittany, Pascwethen and Guorhwant sharing it. Hence, Nominoë was originally and initially designated *missus (imperatoris) in Brittannia*, was described by the *Gesta Sanctorum Rotonensium* as ruling almost all Brittany at the time of foundation of Redon, and as *princeps Britanniae* subsequently.[12] The titles used to describe these men by those who drafted the Redon charters often emphasise the wide span of their power: *totius Brittanniae, dominante Brittanniam usque Medanum flumen, gubernante totam Brittanniam,*

---

[10] The manuscript is at present in the care of the archbishop of Rennes; it was published in a somewhat unreliable edition, whose accuracy is very inconsistent, in the nineteenth century (*Cart. Redon*). La Borderie 1890, pp. 535-630, indicated some corrections, and the charters pertaining to the diocese of Vannes have recently been re-edited, but not published, by Tonnerre 1978, vol. ii.

[11] La Borderie 1898, ii. 43-51, 59-65, 70-5, 82f., 114-16, 318-24, 405-18; Chédeville and Guillotel 1984, pp.298-321, 354-74.

[12] See, for example, *Cart. Redon*, no. clxxvii and clxxix, both of the year 837; 'Gesta Sanctorum Rotonensium' in Mabillon 1738 pp. 203, 210, 216, 220. Caroline Brett has prepared a new edition of the *Gesta* (Brett 1986), publication forthcoming.

totum dominium Brittanniae, and even *totius Britanniae magneque partis Galliarum*, used of Salomon in 869.[13] Further, the comments of Frankish annalists suggest that the principal rulers negotiated for the whole region, as, for example, on the occasion in 863 when Salomon agreed to the payment of tribute from Brittany and caused all the *primores* of Brittany to swear to Charles.[14] Similarly, Salomon appears to have had defensive responsibility for the entire area: in 871 the *principes* of Brittany refused to let him make a pilgrimage to Rome because they feared a Norse attack in his absence.[15] Clearly he was expected to protect them all. Given the consistency of the evidence on this point it would be unreasonable to doubt that the rulers theoretically had responsibility for all of Brittany, though it is worth remembering that we have very little material from west Brittany and it is by no means inconceivable that the prominent men had little effective power in those parts.

The charters provide an additional perspective on the position of the ruler in the particular case of Salomon, for they contain indications that he (or his recording source) considered his authority royal, with the greater or lesser connotations of status that that term brings. From 868 he was called *rex*, rather than the miscellaneous descriptive terms and circumlocutions applied to him and his predecessors before that date - *dux, comes, N gubernante/dominante/possidente*.[16] Indeed, increasingly since 858, transactions had been dated by reference to the principate of Salomon rather than to the year of the Frankish king's rule: *...anno principatus Salomonis in Brittannia* rather than *regnante domno... anno imperii ejus*. This also happened during the last year of Erispoë's life, 857.[17] The change of practice in dating and in titles is very marked under Salomon, and contrasts strongly with the *com(m)es in tota Brittannia* which Nominoë was still using in 850. So, there is little in contemporary evidence to support the notion of the elevation of Nominoë to the kingship,[18] as maintained by the *Chronicle of*

---

[13] *Cart. Redon*, no. ccxxv, cv, clxxviii, lxxii, ccxli.
[14] *AB*, p. 96.
[15] *Cart. Redon*, no. ccxlvii.
[16] *Cart. Redon*, no. xxi, ccxxv, ccxliii, ccxlvii, cclvii. However see *dux* in the suspect letter to the pope 871; *Cart. Redon*, no. lxxxix.
[17] *Cart. Redon*, no. xxvi, xix, xxiii, xxiv, xxv, etc. Cf. the comments of Lot 1907, pp. 33-5.
[18] Regino of Prüm, who died in 915, and who referred to Nominoë as king is commonly held to have used some lost annals of Prüm which were exceptionally well informed about Brittany. This may have been so, but if so it is clear that Regino had insufficient information about the mid-ninth century since his annals up to the 870s are very badly collated: he has an annal for 818 s.a. 836, 833 s.a. 837, 851 s.a. 862 and 863, 857 s.a. 866; at 874 the collation is correct and here he has a long entry which does seem to depend on local Breton knowledge: Regino s.a., pp. 107ff. (See also Werner 1959, pp. 106-16, on the range of Regino's sources.) Regino's references to Nominoë as king are therefore of doubtful value.

Nantes.[19] On the other hand, Salomon clearly appears to have been considered king of Brittany in the late sixties and seventies by a number of different sources, a circumstance which may have something to do with a change in his relations with Charles the Bald: the Viking pressure on western Francia is very marked in the 860s; Robert had not been powerful enough against Salomon, who was assisting the Vikings, in 862, though he had killed more than 200 Breton *primores* who were raiding in that year; and more Bretons allied with the Vikings in 865.[20] It is more than possible that Salomon was at least as powerful as Charles and his officers in west Francia in this period and that the peace negotiations and grants to Salomon of 867 represent a treaty which Charles was forced to seek.[21] Salomon is not recorded as paying tribute on this occasion. The change in the terms of reference to Salomon may well therefore reflect a real change in political status and strength. However, the very fact that some sources call Erispoë *rex* would indicate that we are dealing with a changing trend rather than with sudden changes: there was no moment of creation of a kingship, as the *Chronicle of Nantes* would have us think, but Breton (and other) thoughts turned more and more to a view of the Breton ruler as king.[22]

However we assess the relationship of the principal rulers with the Carolingians, and especially the opposition of Salomon, the above range of developments represents changes for Brittany in the emergence of a series of men with at least a notional responsibility for the whole of it. La Borderie must surely have been right in seeing the ninth century as a period in which a Breton monarchy did emerge, even if he anticipated the development somewhat. Pre-Carolingian Brittany appears to have been politically very fragmented, according to the evidence of Gregory of Tours and the (largely ninth-century) corpus of *Vitae*.[23] Rulers termed *duces* and *comites* made their appearances, but always in limited geographical contexts: Riwal, one of the better evidenced, is called *dux* of merely part of Domnonia (northern Brittany) in the *Life* of Guénolé. Only one of these

---

[19] Merlet 1896, p. 39. The combined evidence of the charters in this respect is more credible than the retrospective eleventh-century report. (Cf. Planiol 1953, ii. 37f.) Moreover, the elevation of Nominoë is not reported in the 'Gesta Sanctorum Rotonensium', a source much in favour of him (Mabillon 1738, pp. 202-31), and the so-called 'Annals of Redon' refer to Nominoë as *subregulus* but to Salomon (and Erispoë) as *rex* (Migne, *PL*, 202, col. 1323 - this latter text is extremely brief and represents an abstract made for Robert of Torigny, abbot of Mont S. Michel in the mid- to late twelfth century. It presumably drew upon earlier records but we cannot know if they were contemporary or not). The *Chronicle of Nantes* also includes a letter of confirmation of ecclesiastical privilege which refers to Erispoë as *rex*; Merlet 1896, pp.44-8; cf. Planiol 1953, ii.39.

[20] *AB*, pp. 89f., 117-24.

[21] See above, p. 100.

[22] Cf. Planiol 1953, ii. 43f., who argues that the Franks too must have seen Brittany as a kingdom (but this did not prevent them expecting tribute).

[23] The exception to the ninth-century date of the Lives is in the Life of Samson, which still appears more likely to have been written in the seventh century, *pace* Poulin 1977; see now Wood, 1988. The Life is not, however, distinctive in its political terminology.

rulers, Iudicaël, contemporary of Dagobert, acquired the title *rex* from a contemporary source, and even he was so termed by the distant Fredegar. His connections were in fact confined to Domnonia.[24] Hints of movement towards political unification only come with the Carolingian onslaught. Before Louis selected Nominoë, resistance seems to have been focused about a certain Morvan, who is called king (*rex*) by the contemporary Ermold and by the Astronomer and 'a tyrant who elevated himself to the kingship' by the later *Life* of Conwoion.[25] It is difficult to assess what was happening, but the concentration of references suggests the beginnings of some movement of wider import at that time. The *Royal Frankish Annals* note that Morvan asserted a claim to royal power, against the usual custom of the Bretons -a clear indication of change.[26] And Ermold may have commented that Morvan did not deserve to be called *rex* because he had no powers of government, but this too is notice of the fact of development.[27]

From Morvan, then, there seems to have been a new element in the political structure of Brittany: the notion of a single political -not merely social - identity and with it a prospect of the role of single ruler to be filled.

In the case of Salomon, at least, there is good indication that he used institutions in support of his authority, for he seems to have utilised some machinery of government within Brittany. We hear of counts with territorially-defined countships during the ninth century: *comes provintiae Brouueroch, commes* (sic) *Poucaer*, and of other countships without territorial designation - though never more than five at any one time.[28] Rennes and Nantes seem to have been kept in the hands of the principal rulers; the remaining counties were often hereditarily transmitted.[29] Every count of whom we have knowledge appeared with Salomon on the major occasions 'of state' in 868 and 869 when he confirmed privileges and made gifts to Redon.[30] This suggests some capacity to compel attendance and the possibility, therefore, of the dependence of the counts on the principal ruler, and their potential use as his functionaries. Pascwethen, as count of Broweroc, was certainly used as envoy (*vicarius*) by Salomon in the mission to

---

[24] See La Borderie 1896, i.350-488; Planiol 1953, i.254-64; Chédeville and Guillotel 1984, pp.67-8.

[25] La Borderie 1898, ii.7-26; Faral 1932, line 1308; Astron, MGH, SS II, p. 623.

[26] *ARF*, s.a. 818, p. 148: 'Nam postquam Mormanus, qui in ea praeter solitum Brittonibus morem regiam sibi vindicaverat potestatem, ab exercitu imperatoris occisus est...'. Cf., however, the assertion of the cartulary of Landevennec (an eleventh-century cartulary containing edited earlier material) that Gradlon had been king in the time of Charles the Great; La Borderie 1888, p. 152, though Davies 1985a, pp.94-5, suggests that this text is of no earlier than mid-tenth-century date.

[27] Faral 1932, line 1309. For all this see now Chédeville and Guillotel 1984, pp.211-12, 219-20.

[28] *Cart. Redon*, no. xxi, ccxlvii, cclviii, cvii.

[29] See Planiol 1953, i. 254-75, ii.65-8; La Borderie 1898, ii. 137-41, Davies 1988, pp.166, 172-3, 203. We do not know the relationship of these counties with pre-ninth-century units.

[30] *Cart. Redon*, no. ccxl, ccxli.

Charles in 867.³¹ Salomon's ability to raise tribute from Brittany, for payment to Charles in 864, may further suggest the existence of some administrative machinery.³² It was levied, so say the *Annals of St. Bertin*, s.a. 863, 'according to ancient custom'. The possibility of the existence of some fiscal machinery is also indicated by Salomon's order for donation and construction from his 'public rights', *ex nostro publico* in 869.³³ Further, both Nominoë and Salomon used *missi* for making grants and presiding over cases, in their own names.³⁴ And Salomon and Pascwethen, at least, seem to have had some powers of jurisdiction over the more powerful Bretons. Complaints went to the ruler, who presided and on three occasions resolved the cases - whereas judgement itself was more usually, in less politically sensitive cases, a matter for locals.³⁵ All of the above considerations, though sketchy, suggest the exercise of some powers over the whole community by the principal ruler and the existence of some machinery by which his will might be effected.

Rulers and counts were not, however, the only element in the political structure, for there was also the machtiern (sometimes *tiarn* or even *tirannus*), a person distinguished by his own proper term of reference, of whom there is plentiful evidence in the Redon cartulary. Machtiern is a Breton word which includes the element *tiern*, from common Celtic *tegernos/tigernos* 'ruler', and hence modern Welsh *teyrn* 'ruler, monarch' and the occurrence of the element in personal names such as Vortigern and Tegernomalus.³⁶ The word occurs in Welsh and Cornish - W. *mechteyrn*, C. *mychtern* - where it usually has the meaning of 'great ruler, overlord'; in Cornish it is used of Pharoah, of David, and of Christ.³⁷ There is evidence, then, of rulers other than the principal ruler in Brittany in the ninth century. What may be said about them?

The machtiern was of extremely localised significance. There is much that associates him with what was apparently the primary unit of social organisation in east Brittany at that period, the *plebs*, a word which survives in modern Breton

---

31   *AB*, p. 137.
32   *AB*, p. 113; cf. s.a. 863, p. 96. (See also Ermold, Faral 1932, line 1376: Morvan refused to pay tribute.) See further Davies 1988, pp.205-6.
33   *Cart. Redon*, no. ccxli.
34   *Cart. Redon*, no. cvi, cxi, lxxxvii, cxxxix, ccxxv, for example. See further Davies 1988, pp.203-5.
35   *Cart. Redon*, no. xxi, ccxlvii, cclxi; cclxvii, cxcii, clxxx, etc. Cf. also La Borderie 1898, ii. 136, on Salomon giving judgement. See further Davies 1986a.
36   See Fleuriot 1971, pp. 622f.; Planiol 1953, ii. 95-102; Jackson 1953, pp. 446f.
37   The meaning of the initial element in this word is disputed: *mach* means 'surety' but it has been suggested that there may have been a lost adjective, cognate with Irish *mass*, meaning 'fine', and hence the usage 'great ruler' in insular contexts. In Brittany, as we shall see, it makes much more sense to understand *mach* as 'surety'. Whatever the discussion about the meaning of the separate elements in the word *machtiern* there is no disagreement that the term signifies 'ruler', both in its root meaning and its use in other Brittonic contexts at a comparable period. Williams 1939-41, pp. 39f.; see also Williams 1972, p.26. For an exhaustive treatment of the occurrence of the word, see now Sheringham 1981.

place-names as *plou*.[38] Plebs, basically, means 'group of people'; by the ninth century it quite clearly had a territorial connotation too: the land inhabited by the group. Men identified themselves with reference to their *plebs*; transactions took place and property lay in this or that *plebs;* it is not uncommon to find that transactions had to be notified to the men of the *plebs*, or enquiries were addressed to them. The word has much the same connotation as a modern civil parish. (Medieval *plebes* usually became modern 'communes', the smallest units of civil administration in France, and were the ecclesiastical parishes of the time before 1789.) Now, it is most unusual to find more than one machtiern officiating in a *plebs* in any one period, though he might personally have held properties in several *plebes* and though it is not unusual to find one person holding the machtiernship of a few *plebes*, which were not necessarily those in which he had properties; hence, Portitoe had properties in Pleucadeuc but appeared as machtiern in Pleucadeuc, Ruffiac, Molac, and Carentoir, and the machtiern Trihoiarn may have sold property in Guillac though Riwalt was machtiern there.[39] Moreover, the terms of reference sometimes explicitly associate the machtiernship with the *plebs*; *machtiern in plebe Ruffiac* or *plebe Carentoerense, machtiern in illa plebe*, and even *princeps plebis*.[40] (Reference to Iarnhitin as machtiern, *tyrannus* and *princeps* in one single charter seems to establish the identity of machtiern and *princeps*.) In Pleucadeuc, therefore, we find Guorvili as machtiern, followed by Portitoe, followed by Bili; in Ruffiac, Portitoe, followed by Guorvili, him by Catloiant, him by Iarnhitin and him by Hinualadr. The only exceptions lie in the dual machtiernship of the two brothers Portitoe and Guorvili, who are explicitly designated 'duo machtiern in plebe Catoc', so marking the peculiarity. The role or office of machtiern therefore appears to have been defined in relation to the unit of civil association, the *plebs,* and the implication is that each *plebs* had its machtiern.

His own properties were not widely scattered, as were those of the counts and principal rulers; the extent of the area in which he might perform functions as machtiern was very limited - 25 miles in diameter at the most. Hence Count Bran and Count Pascwethen appeared in places as scattered as Cléguérec, Retiers and Guérande, places more than 75 miles apart.[41] Indeed, Pascwethen appears so frequently that we can determine changes in the pattern of his appearances: at first, c. 850-60, he occurs as witness in a very limited area - Molac, Redon, Plélan; subsequently, and just before he was termed count, we find him in Fougeray, in Retiers, in Cléguérec.[42] The machtiern Iarnhitin, son of Portitoe, on the other hand, appeared from Molac to Ruffiac (about 13 miles apart) and had properties in

---

[38] *plebem* < *plou*; cf. modern Welsh *plwyf*, 'parish'. Most *plebes* had a corresponding church. There is much discussion of the possible Breton ecclesiastical origin of these civil units; see Largillière 1925. Compare, however, Flatrès 1956, pp. 11f., for suggestions of the pre-Breton origin of the *plou* of Brittany. For *plebes* in the ninth century see further Davies 1983.

[39] *Cart. Redon,* no. cxvi; and see below, n. 46.

[40] *Cart. Redon,* no. ix, xvi, cxxxi, cclv; clxxviii, cclxvii.

[41] *Cart. Redon,* no. ccxlvii, xxi, xxx, lii

[42] For example, *Cart. Redon,* no. ccxlix, xx and then xxi, ccxlvii, ccxv, ccxlii, etc.

Ruffiac;⁴³ Machtiern Deurhoiarn appeared as machtiern in Augan, and perhaps Ploërmel, as witness in Caro, Plélan and Carentoir, and had properties in Augan, Campénéac and Plélan.⁴⁴ (Augan to Plelan is about 12 miles; Augan to Carentoir about 11 miles.) His father Riwalt appeared as machtiern in Augan, Ploërmel, Campénéac and Guillac, as witness in Augan, and made donations from Campénéac and Augan.⁴⁵ The greatest span of appearances are those of Portitoe from Molac to Guer, less than 20 miles, and of Guorvili his brother from Pleucadeuc to Guer.⁴⁶ (See Fig. 6.2) Though the occurrence of two machtiern brothers is unusual, the family interest is not; there are several machtiern families and the position was clearly often hereditary. Hence Iarnwocon, 858-78, son of Deurhoiarn, machtiern c.840-68, son of Riwalt, machtiern 816-35;⁴⁷ machtiern Iarnhitin, 821-39, and his two sons Portitoe, machtiern 821-34, and Guorvili, machtiern 821-40, Portitoe's son Iarnhitin, machtiern 843-72, and Guorvili's son Catloiant, machtiern 840-50;⁴⁸ Ratfred, machtiern 842, and his son Bili, machtiern 848.⁴⁹ The sum of the above considerations indicates clearly enough that the machtiern was some sort of small-scale hereditary ruler.

The charters are sometimes explicit about the attributes and functions of these rulers. The machtiern might expect the loyalty of the men of the *plebs*⁵⁰ and might have powers over vacant properties in the *plebs*.⁵¹ It is implied that the machtiern might receive payment of dues in some cases: in 868 Altfrid was accused of holding monastic income as if it were *sub censu*.⁵² The very complaint indicates, of course, that exemptions were possible, if not common; many grants were made *sine censu*, after all, like the sale made by a layman to his sister in 821.⁵³ In the 830s a grant was made in order to pay what was due to the *princeps*. This material suggests, therefore, that payments were sometimes due to the machtiern, although there is more reason to suppose these were payments arising from his seigneurial powers than from his machtiernly status.⁵⁴

---

43   *Cart.Redon*, no. cxlv, cxliii, ccxx, cxxxix, cclvii, ccli, cl, lv, xxxvii. Cf.Planiol 1953, ii. 84-92, 114-20, for details of all machtierns cited in the cartulary and Davies 1988, pp. 175-83.
44   *Cart. Redon,* no. xxiv, clxxv; lxxix, cvii, cxxii, ccxxxvi.
45   *Cart. Redon,* no. cxvi, cxciv; v, cc; cvii, cxxiii, vi, cxxii, ccxxvi.
46   *Cart. Redon,* no. ix, xi, xiii, xii, xiv, xvi, cxxxi, cxlvii, clv, clvi, clxx, cxcvi, cclii, cclv; cxii, cxxxi, cxlvii, cxlviii, clv, clvi, clxvi, clxi, clxxviii, cclv, viii, xii, xvi, xxxiv, xlix, cxxxiii. See Davies 1988, pp.176 and 178 for individual maps.
47   *Cart. Redon,* no. clxxv, ccxxv, ccxli, ccxxxvi, lxxix; cvii, cxxii, ccxl; cxvi, cxxviii, ccxix. The dates given here are the extreme range of the dates of each individual's appearance.
48   *Cart. Redon,* no. cxlvi, cclxvii, cxlvii; xvi, ix, xii, xiii etc; xii, xvi, clv etc; cxxxix, cxliii, cxlv etc.
49   *Cart. Redon,* no. Axvii; cvx.
50   *Cart. Redon,* no. xcvi; cf. Planiol 1953, ii. 100.
51   *Cart. Redon,* no. clxxxv; cf. Tonnerre 1978, pp. 176f.
52   *Cart. Redon,* no. xxi.
53   *Cart. Redon,* no. cxlvi.
54   *Cart. Redon,* no. clxxviii; cf. clxxix and vi, and the discussion of La Borderie 1905, ii. 157. For full discussion of this complex issue see Davies 1988, pp. 139-42.

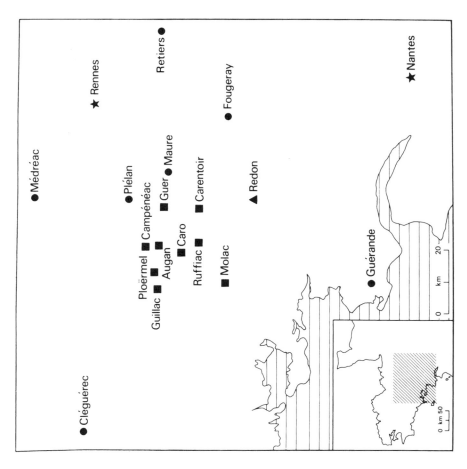

Figure 6.2: Redon and its Neighbourhood

The clearest functions exercised by machtierns were, however, those relating to transactions. They presided at transactions of sale and loan, donation and confirmation of donation, though transactions could also take place without reference to them; hence, from the early ninth century we find reference to this or that happening *ante machtiern* and sometimes *verbo machtiern*.[55] Occasionally they appear to have played some part in securing transactions: Ratuil accordingly received 6 pence in 843 after a sale (as did Nominoë's *missus* and the *fideiussores* -the machtiern was not the only guarantor).[56] They also presided over the resolution of disputes: when a layman had a grievance against Redon in 854 he took his plaint to the machtiern, who ordered an investigation. Several machtierns were present at a hearing about disputed property rights between an abbot and a layman, under the presidency of one of their number.[57] *But,* they were not the only presidents and were not the judges. Disputes between ordinary laymen were sometimes heard by the principal ruler's officers (*missi* or *comites*), with judgement being given by *scabini* in the earlier period.[58] (After Nominoë, there are no references to *scabini* and few to the *mallus*, and the implication is that the Carolingian terminology dropped out of use, though this did not prevent the continuation of meetings or the use of respected local men in judicial cases.) Planiol makes the sensible observation that the machinery of justice clearly existed at two different levels, that of the 'prince' for quasi-political affairs - to whose jurisdiction the machtiern himself was subject - and that of the machtiern for local affairs.[59] Complaints might be made to the machtiern at a *lis*, a word meaning 'court' or 'residence' in Modern Welsh (*llys*) and associated with rulers in Old Welsh poetry. The *lis* was clearly a residence, with private rooms: Riwalt had a *domus*, Lisuison, and Salomon lay ill at Lispenfau.[60] Sometimes records and facilities for writing were specified: one transaction was done at Augan but recorded at Liscoet.[61] Normally only one *lis* was found in each *plebs* and only one machtiern was associated with each *lis* though the principal ruler or his agent might be found in company there with him.[62] The *lis* might well have appurtenant property, like Lisbroniuin and *hoc quod adjacet ei, ex plebe Kempeniac,* 844/50;[63]

---

55   *Cart. Redon,* no. cxii, cxv, clxxii, clxxx; clxviii. Transactions were performed in different locations: on the land itself, in or in front of a church, at a *lis* or *aula* (court), occasionally in someone's house (*domus*). The place where the transaction was performed was not necessarily in the same *plebs* as the land which changed hands, though there was a tendency for this to happen where the machtiern presided; this perhaps suggests that the machtiern, if presiding, travelled to the relevant local centre.
56   *Cart. Redon,* no. cxi.
57   *Cart. Redon,* no. clxii, cf. no. cclxxi; clxxx.
58   *Cart. Redon,* no. ccxlvii, xxi, cxcii, cclxi, xxix, ccxlii.
59   Planiol 1953, ii.97-9. See further Davies 1985b and Davies 1986a.
60   *Cart. Redon,* no. cxxii, cxciv, lxxxv.
61   *Cart. Redon,* no. v.
62   *Cart. Redon,* no. xxix, clxxvi.
63   *Cart. Redon,* no. cvii.

but for that reason alone, though there was usually only one per *plebs*, it is clear that the whole *plebs* was not considered appurtenant to the *lis*. One machtiern might have several, however, and the *lis* was alienable: Riwalt had Lisbroniuin and Lisuison, and gave the former to Nominoë.[64] It was therefore quite clearly a private residence, but one which might often have associations with public duties, the place from which the machtiern acted; there may have been distinctions between those treated merely as properties, in which the term *lis* was merely residual, like the half *randremes* of Liswern given to Nominoë in the 840s, and those where the machtiern still acted out his public function.

The machtiern therefore seems to have been a local ruler with civil functions, who might expect some payment for his services. There is nothing which suggests he had a military *function* -whereas there are suggestions that the counts did have such a function[65] - although, of course, the anecdotes of the tyrannous machtierns suggest that they had some military capacity. Maybe there were machtierns amongst the 200 raiders killed by Robert in 862 or amongst the fighting forces attached to counts.[66] Whichever way this problem is answered, it is clear that the function of the machtiern as such was civil.

Was he a public official or a person of independent authority? This question has vexed scholars for generations and it is quite clear that present evidence is not adequate to supply a conclusive answer.[67] The chief problem turns on the *plebs* of Bains and on Redon itself. The statements of the *Gesta Sanctorum Rotonensium* that Nominoë, as Louis's *missus*, handed over a quarter of the *plebs* of Bains to the foundation at Redon, property itself granted by the machtiern Ratvili, and that Louis himself subsequently gave Bains and another *plebs*, Langon, to Redon indicate that the emperor was in a position to alienate *plebes*; and suggest that Nominoë, as *missus* had been assigned a quarter as income.[68] If this was so, and there is no reason to disbelieve the *Gesta*, then either Louis did so as emperor because he had ultimate powers of control over all *plebes*, or he happened to have come into personal possession of them.[69] This therefore clearly raises the possibility that power over the *plebs* was an aspect of the 'puissance publique', the apparatus of the Carolingian state.[70] Some indication of the political status of the machtiern is supplied by three separate statements of his relationship with the *plebs*: *(princeps) qui possidebat plebem, qui Bain haberet in potestatem, princeps qui dominaretur in Bain*; moreover, in 872 Aourken was *tirannissa* and legate in

---

[64] *Cart. Redon*, no. cvii cxxii lxxviii, cviii, clxxxviii.
[65] See La Borderie 1898, ii.140f; Davies 1988, pp. 170-1, 182-3.
[66] *AB*, p. 90.
[67] See La Borderie 1898, ii. 158-61; Planiol 1953, ii. 110f., 127f: Fleuriot 1971, p. 652.
[68] Mabillon 1738, pp. 210f.
[69] Louis had made grants of lands near Morvan's place (near the river Ellé) to an abbot (Faral 1932, lines 1344/5). We do know, therefore, that Louis had properties, or power over properties, in Brittany.
[70] Planiol 1953, ii. 83, for full discussion of all this see Davies 1988, pp.192-3 and notes.

Pleucadeuc *sub potestate Salomonis*.[71] Now these are proprietary terms and suggest an essentially proprietary relationship with the *plebs*. Hence, both *plebs* and *lis* were alienable: the *plebs* of Bains and *plebs* of Langon were given to Redon; Riwalt gave Lisbroniuin to Nominoë and Salomon gave Lis Iarnwocon away.[72] The case of the lady who, in default of heirs, willed *Seminiaca plebs* to Salomon provides an alternative case of a proprietary relationship with the *plebs*.[73] Presumably these cases do not imply the possession of all properties in the *plebs*, but rather the possession of some specified rights and dues; hence, in the 840s tolls taken at Balrit were due to the man who had the *plebs* of Bains *in potestatem*, and in the 860s the two properties of Bron-Winoc were reserved, in default of heirs, for him who *dominaretur* in Bains.[74] Of course, the use of proprietary terms need not make the relationship between *plebs* and *princeps* a purely private one;[75] after all, the rulers of Brittany were mentioned in similar terms: *N possidente, dominante Brittanniam*. That use merely stresses the prevalence of proprietary attitudes to political power. The genuinely proprietary element, as manifest in the alienability of *plebs* and *lis* and possibility of accumulation of numbers of them, does mean, however, that if the machtiern was in reality exercising a public office for which he was responsible to some higher level of government -be it count or Breton ruler or king -then already by the 840s, within a generation of Louis's conquest, there was much that was private in his exercise of the office. In this Brittany was scarcely distinguished from the west Frankish kingdom as a whole.

If the above is true, then the crux of the problem does not lie in determining the source of the machtiern's power as we perceive it in the mid-ninth century. By anybody's assessment there was much that was private about machtiernly power at that period. Hence, Planiol writes of the 'hérédité de fait' of the prince's agents being transformed into 'hérédité de droit', as a means of explaining ninth-century developments.[76] The crux of the problem is twofold. The real crux lies in origins: were the earliest machtierns agents of some higher authority or virtually independent local rulers? The ninth-century writers of saintly *Vitae* conceptualised the original *princeps plebis* as leader and founder of the community: Fracanus established the *plebs* which subsequently took his name, Ploufragan.[77] They saw the origins as independent. This does not mean they were, but it does at least emphasise the contemporary view of them. The secondary crux is this: if there was

---

[71] *Cart. Redon*, no. clxii, cvi, clxxxv, cclvil.
[72] *Cart. Redon*, no. i, cvii, lxxviii.
[73] *Cart. Redon*, no. cix: I see no reason to argue, as some have done, that this must really have been a royal grant.
[74] *Cart. Redon*, no. cvi, clxxxv.
[75] I cannot help wondering, despite the cases in which the *princeps* and machtiern of a *plebs* were the same person, if this was always so.
[76] Planiol 1953, ii. 123.
[77] *Vita Sancti Winwaloei* in La Borderie 1888, pp. 9f: '(Fracanus) fundum quendam repperiens non parvum, sed quasi unius plebis modulum.... inundatione cujusdam fluvii qui proprie Sanguis dicitur locupletem'.

some private aspect of the machtiern's power, it clearly was not solely exercised for the private benefit of his family. A sense of public responsibility is perfectly clear in the deliberations and procedures that follow complaint. To that extent at least machtiernly power is public. But did the machtiern of the mid-ninth century have a responsibility *ex officio* to anyone other than the community of the *plebs*?

Some consideration of other Celtic areas offers possibly useful suggestions. The existence of special peace-keeping officers in medieval southern Scotland and Northumbria (*mair* and *iudex*),[78] as also in Wales and western parts of England (serjeant of the peace),[79] officers whose functions are commonly considered to be of Celtic origin, strengthens the case for the pre-Carolingian origins of the functions performed by the machtiern. In the North the *mair* is notable for receiving dues for the performance of local policing functions, while the *iudex* is even more comparable to the machtiern in the prominent part he played in the attestation of lay transactions and hence in *traditio* itself, and in the occasional rulings he gave in court. The serjeant of the peace is notable not merely for his policing functions but for his role in forcing suspects to find sureties for their due appearance in court. Though all the material which relates to the function of these officials is of late origin, normally twelfth-century or later, and though there are clear differences between these and machtierns, nevertheless the occurrence of a local official much concerned in transactions and another much concerned with sureties must raise the possibility that the machtiern is an earlier, Breton example of the local peace-keeper and that the several cases represent differing manifestations of some early Brittonic peace-keeping institution.[80] The sixth- to eighth-century law code sometimes known as *Canones Wallici* may possibly supply evidence of the operation of such institutions in Brittany at an earlier stage, when it refers to the *iudex* who presided over cases.[81]

If the existence of comparative institutions in other Celtic areas may point in the direction of the independent origins of machtiernly power, there are further ninth-century considerations which point in the direction of the retention of a measure at least of independence and of a lack of responsibility *ex officio* to any higher authority. Though there is evidence of vassalage in Brittany at this period, there is absolutely no evidence of the vassalage of machtierns to the counts, the officers who might be expected to have been their natural immediate superiors.

---

[78] Dickinson 1977, pp. 52-5; Barrow 1973, pp. 67-74.
[79] Stewart-Brown 1936, esp. pp. 87-98.
[80] I am most grateful to Patrick Wormald for initially suggesting this line of enquiry. It seems to me that, in fact, the offices of *mair* and serjeant of the peace are not close parallels of that of machtiern, particularly with respect to the contexts in which sureties were acquired, but the existence of peace-keeping officers in Brittonic contexts remains extremely interesting in the light of the machtiern's functions.
[81] 'Canones Wallici' (A), 30 in Bieler 1963, p. 142; for the date and provenance of this collection see Dumville 1984 and Davies 1986b; see also Fleuriot 1971, pp. 601-18. See also the comments of Professor Fleuriot, citing Professor Jenkins, on the machtiern as 'private' law officer.

Where the principal ruler of Brittany communicates with machtierns he does so directly. Moreover, the principal rulers moved about with their own retinues, which were not composed of machtierns: Nominoë visited Redon with his *optimates*; Salomon's son Wigon had his own *fideles*.[82] Further, Salomon, apparently, could not compel the attendance of all machtierns at his principal meetings, even those who resided near the place of meeting. In 868, at Maure, therefore, Deurhoiarn was there but neither Iarnhitin of Ruffiac nor Altfrid of Medréac nearby were; the same was true at Plélan in 869.[83] Such considerations suggest that the principal rulers had no power to compel the performance of machtiernly functions by the machtierns, though they might establish personal relationships with them. Portitoe and Guorvili were therefore vassals (*vassi dominici*); and Salomon could call on the *tirannissa*, wife of Iarnhitin, machtiern of Ruffiac, to act as his representative in Pleucadeuc.[84] I would suggest therefore that the machtiern structure was utilised by the mid-ninth century rulers of Brittany, Breton or Carolingian, in order to reach the localities, but that it did not depend upon these rulers.

The distribution of political power in Brittany in the ninth century therefore has an unusual air, because of the existence of local rulers. It is unlike the distribution of powers in Wales and Scotland and Ireland. Was it so unusual in Francia? There seem to have been local regulators of social relationships and transactions, with proprietary rights over the units of regulation, and with a power to demand and receive tax. They had an economic and social power which permitted arbitrary exploitation: some machtierns were literally *tiranni* as one charter wryly noted - 'Alfritum tyrannum et vere tyrannum'.[85] Their power was transmitted hereditarily, and they were not *ex officio* answerable to any superior authority, though they might have contracted a personal relationship with such a powerful man.

If this was so, then the capacity of the principal rulers of Brittany -Nominoë, Erispoë, Salomon especially - to govern, the capacity to command and to relate to the men of the *plebs* was limited by their capacity to establish individual relationships with the machtierns. Government existed on two levels, and there was no clearly established machinery of contact between those levels. Hence, the relationship of the Carolingian rulers with the Breton was conditioned by the two separate factors of their fluctuating relationship with the principal rulers on the one hand and on the other of those rulers' relationship with the machtierns. Despite the interest and activity of the early Carolingian kings in Brittany, therefore, the capacity of Charles to intervene in and affect Breton affairs was limited not merely by the military power of the principal ruler but by the local powers of local rulers.

---

82 Mabillon 1738, p. 210; *AB*, s.a. 873, p. 193.
83 *Cart. Redon*, no. ccxl, ccxli. If the machtiern is to be identified with the *iudex publicus* of Salomon's charter for Prüm of 860, then the fact that he is distinguished from the royal servants (*ministri*) would emphasize the same point; Beyer 1860, p. 99.
84 *Cart. Redon*, no. cclvii.
85 *Cart. Redon*, no. ccxlvii.

BIBLIOGRAPHY CHAPTER IV

Primary sources

AB *Annales de Saint-Bertin*, ed. F. Grat, J. Vielliard and S. Clemencet, with introduction and notes by L. Levillain (Paris 1964).
ARF *Annales Regni Francorum*, ed. F. Kurze, MGH *Scriptores Rerum Germanicarum* (1895).
Astron. *Anonymi Vita Hludovici Pii*, ed. G. Pertz, MGH *Scriptores in folio* II (1829).
Beyer H. ed., 1860. *Urkundenbuch zur geschichte der mittelrheinischen Territorien* (Koblenz).
Bieler, L. ed., 1963. *The Irish Penitentials* (Dublin).
Cart. Redon *Le Cartulaire de l'abbaye de Redon*, ed. A. de Courson (Paris 1863).
Faral, E. ed., 1932. Ermold Le Noir, *Poème sur Louis le Pieux et épitres au roi Pépin* (Paris).
Gesta Sanctorum Rotonensium *The Monks of Redon. Gesta Sanctorum Rotonensium and Vita Conuuoionis*, ed. and trans. C. Brett (Woodbridge 1989).
Mabillon, J. ed., 1738. *Acta Sanctorum Ordinis S. Benedicti*, saec. iv, pt. 2 (Venice).
Merlet, R. ed., 1896. *La Chronique de Nantes* (Paris).
PL J.-P. Migne ed., *Patrologia Latina*.
Regino Regino of Prüm, *Chronicon*, ed. F. Kurze, MGH *Scriptores Rerum Germanicarum* (1890).
Vita Sancti Winwaloei in: La Borderie, A. (Le Moyne) de ed., 1888. *Cartulaire de l'Abbaye de Landévennec* (Rennes).

Secondary sources

Barrow, G.W.S., 1973. *The Kingdom of the Scots* (London).
Brett, C., 1986. 'Texts from early medieval Redon: their value for the history of Brittany', University of Cambridge Ph.D. thesis.

Boussard, J., 1968. 'Les destinées de la Neustrie du ixe au xie siècle, *Cahiers de civilisation médiévale* 11, pp. 15–28.
Chadwick, N.K., 1965. 'The colonisation of Brittany from Celtic Britain', *Proc. Brit. Academy* 51, pp. 235–99.
Chadwick, N.K., 1969. *Early Brittany* (Cardiff).
Chédeville, A. and Guillotel, H., 1984. *La Bretagne des saints et des rois. V–X siècle* (Rennes).
Davies, W., 1983. 'Priests and rural communities in east Brittany in the ninth century', *Études Celtiques* 20, pp. 177–97.
Davies, W., 1985a. 'Les chartes du *Cartulaire de Landévennec*' in *Landévennec et le monachisme breton dans le haut Moyen Age. Actes du Colloque du XV centenaire de l'abbaye de Landévennec*, ed. M. Simon (Landévennec), pp. 85–95.
Davies, W., 1985b. 'Disputes, their conduct and their settlement in the village communities of eastern Brittany in the ninth century', *History and Anthropology* 1, pt. 2, pp. 289–312.
Davies, W., 1986a. 'People and places in dispute in ninth-century Brittany' in *The Settlement of Disputes in early medieval Europe*, ed. W. Davies and P. Fouracre (Cambridge), pp. 65–84.
Davies, W., 1986b. 'Suretyship in the *Cartulaire de Redon*' in *Lawyers and Laymen*, ed. T.M. Charles-Edwards, M.E. Owen, D.B. Walters (Cardiff), pp. 72–91.
Davies, W., 1988. *Small Worlds. The Village Community in Early Medieval Brittany* (London).
Dickinson, W.C., 1977. *Scotland from the earliest times to 1603*, 3rd edn, ed. A.A.M. Duncan (Oxford).
Dumville, D.N., 1984. 'On the dating of the early Breton lawcodes', *Études Celtiques* 21, pp. 207–21.
Flatrès, P., 1956. 'Les divisions territoriales de Basse-Bretagne comparées à celles des contrées celtiques d'outre-mer', *Annales de Bretagne* 63, pp. 3–17.
Flatrès, P., 1977. 'Historical geography of western France' in *Themes in the historical geography of France*, ed. H. Clout (London), pp. 301–42.
Fleuriot, L., 1971. 'Un fragment en Latin de très anciennes lois bretonnes armoricaines du vie siècle', *Annales de Bretagne* 78, pp. 601–60.
Fleuriot, L., 1980. *Les origines de la Bretagne* (Paris).
Fleuriot, L. and Giot, P.-R., 1977. 'Early Brittany', *Antiquity* 51, pp. 106–16.
Jackson, K.H., 1953. *Language and History in Early Britain* (Edinburgh).
Kienast, W., 1968. 'Die französischen Stämme bei der Königswahl', *Historische Zeitschrift* 206, pp. 1–21.

La Borderie, A. (Le Moyne) de, 1889–90. 'La chronologie du cartulaire de Redon', *Annales de Bretagne* 5, pp. 535–630 (also 12 (1896–7), 13 (1897–8)).

La Borderie, A. (Le Moyne) de, 1896, 1898. *Histoire de Bretagne*, vols. I and II (Rennes).

Largillière, R., 1925. *Les saints et l'organisation chrétienne primitive dans l'Armorique bretonne* (Rennes).

Lot, F., 1907. *Mélanges d'histoire bretonne* (Paris).

Planiol, M., 1953. *Histoire des institutions de la Bretagne*, 5 vols. (Mayenne); 2nd edn 1981–4.

Poulin, J.-C., 1977. 'La première vie de S. Samson de Dol', *Francia* 5, pp. 1–26.

Sheringham, J.G.T., 1981. 'Les machtierns', *Mémoires de la société d'histoire et d'archéologie de Bretagne* 58, pp. 61–72.

Smith, J.M.H., 1985. 'Carolingian Brittany', University of Oxford D. Phil. thesis.

Stewart-Brown, R., 1936. *Serjeants of the Peace in Medieval England and Wales* (Manchester).

Tanguy, B., 1980. 'La limite linguistique dans la péninsule armoricaine à l'époque de l'émigration bretonne (IV–V siècle) d'après les données toponymiques', *Annales de Bretagne* 87, pp. 429–62.

Werner, K.F., 1959. 'Zur Arbeitsweise des Regino von Prüm', *Die Welt als Geschichte* 19, pp. 96–116.

Williams, I., 1939–41. 'Mechdeyrn', *Bulletin of the Board of Celtic Studies* 10, pp. 39–41.

Williams, I., 1972. *Armes Prydein*, trans. R. Bromwich (Dublin).

Wood, I., 1988. 'Forgery in Merovingian hagiography' in *Fälschungen im Mittelalter, MGH Schriften* 33, 6 vols. (Hanover), vol. 5, pp. 369–84.

V

PRIESTS AND RURAL COMMUNITIES IN EAST BRITTANY IN THE NINTH CENTURY

The formation of the territorial units of Brittany is a process which has vexed scholars for more than a century and has occasioned a considerable body of discussion, especially with reference to place-names incorporating the vernacular element *plou* and units called *plebes* in Latin; the problem is a wide-ranging one and both bears on and is dependent upon the problems of migration to the continent from Britain and the nature of early Breton religious institutions. The Breton word *ploue* is an extremely common element in settlement names—Ploufragan, Pleugriffet, Ploermel, Plélan, Plessé, Pluméliau, and so on—and is an early borrowing from Latin *plēb-*, in fact borrowed early enough to produce on Old Breton form at least by the ninth century and certainly in use as a name-forming element at that date.[1] Now although the root meaning of Latin *plebs* refers to 'the common people' the term was widely used in Europe in the early middle ages to refer to *Christian* people, a group of believers or 'flock', especially under the care of a bishop or priest, and hence the primary unit of pastoral care ('parish', in later terms, both people and territory).[2] The evidence for which meaning from the wide semantic range of *plebs/plebes* was associated with the borrowing of *ploue* is inconclusive, and it has sometimes been suggested that the use of *plebs* in Brittany must itself have been distinctive. In the light of this problem, the following considerations deserve some attention: since the loanword from *plebs* also occurs in Welsh and Cornish (W. *plwyf*, OC *plui*, MidC *plu*) it is likely to have been borrowed in the Brittonic period, before the separation of Primitive Breton, Primitive Welsh and Primitive

---

1. OB *pluiu, plueu, ploeu* (where final *u* is for [v] in all three examples), *ploi-, ploe-* (also *blobion* for *ploibion*); MidB *ploe, ploue, plu-, ple-, plo-*, etc.; K. H. Jackson, *A Historical Phonology of Breton* (Dublin, 1967), p. 221; L. Fleuriot, *Dictionnaire des Gloses en Vieux Breton* (Paris, 1964), p. 165; idem, *Le Vieux Breton. Éléments d'une Grammaire* (Paris, 1964), pp. 118, 163.
2. Du Cange, *Glossarium mediae et infimae Latinitatis* (7 vols., Paris, 1840-50), V, s.v. *plebes*; A. Blaise, *Dictionnaire latin-français des auteurs chrétiens* (Turnhout, 1954), p. 629; P. Imbart de la Tour, *Les Paroisses Rurales du IVe au XIe siècle* (Paris, 1900), p. 99, n. 2; P. Aebischer, 'La diffusion de *plebs* 'paroisse' dans l'espace et dans le temps', *Revue de linguistique romane*, XXVIII (1964), 143-65; A. Castagnetti, *L'organizzazione del Territorio rurale nel medioevo* (Turin, 1979), pp. 9-30.

Cornish (even though Breton parochial institutions developed differently from insular Celtic ones); it is therefore likely to have been borrowed with reference to its fourth-, fifth- and early sixth-century range of meaning —'people' or 'Christian people'—rather than with reference to the later 'parish' and the territory it occupied. In Brittany it is clear that by the ninth century *plebs* was used to denote a civil, social unit, with clearly defined characteristics, and the territory that that unit occupied; use of *plebs* therefore does seem to have been distinctive, as were the characteristic Breton methods of localising places and units of property.³ Breton *ploi-*, *pluiu-* were quite clearly used as the equivalent of *plebs* in the ninth century, and the plebeian sense of the word is apparently evidenced in *eru blobion*, which glosses *proletarios*. In insular religious sources 'household' is a common connotation of *plebs*: Irish *induile tegdais i. plebs* glosses *domus* and we find 'in domu alicujus plebei divitis' in Adomnán's *Life of Columba* and 'uocauit ad se familiam suam hoc est plebem suae patriae' in the twelfth-century 'Vita Teliaui'; sometimes, however, it carries the meaning (non-territorial) 'unit of pastoral care' and its connotation can vary within a single text. Breton *ploue* retained a strong sense of 'lay community' in the later middle ages—'rural district, countryside, village'—and, as Oliver Padel has pointed out, can hardly have been in use for 'parish' by the fifteenth century since the French word for 'parish' was borrowed into Breton then.⁴

The problem, therefore, is not merely a difficult problem of semantic range and linguistic meaning: it has social, political and ecclesiastical implications and becomes a complex problem of origins. When and in what circumstances were the *plebs* units formed? Were they a result of British migration into Brittany, or of subsequent developments, or even some reflection of pre-migration structures? Moreover, were they secular or ecclesiastical in origin? And if they were of ecclesiastical origin, how is it that *ecclesiastical* associations determined the shape of *secular* units in the ninth century and later and left such a marked influence on Breton topo-

---

3. See further below, p. 196 and nn. 12, 61. Cf. the *plebs Fracani* in the ninth-century 'Vita Winwaloei'; Fracanus migrated to Brittany with some companions, finding land just big enough for the group to settle; the name survives in Ploufragan (*Cartulaire de l'Abbaye de Landevenec*, ed. A. Le Moyne de la Borderie (Rennes, 1888), pp. 9f).

4. L. Fleuriot, *Dictionnaire*, p. 165; *Thesaurus Palaeohibernicus*, ed. W. Stokes and J. Strachan (2 vols., Cambridge, 1901-3), I.707; *Adomnan's Life of Columba*, ed. A. O. and M. O. Anderson (London, 1961), II.17 (p. 362); *The Text of the Book of Llan Dâv*, ed. J. G. Evans with J. Rhys (Oxford, 1893), p. 113; 'Synodus I S. Patricii', c. 3 and 'Paenitentiale quod dicitur Bigotianum', II.11 (*The Irish Penitentials*, ed. L. Bieler (Dublin, 1963), pp. 54, 224). E. Ernault, *Dictionnaire étymologique du breton moyen* (Nantes, 1887), p. 354; R. Hémon, *Dictionnaire Breton-Français* (3rd. ed., Brest, 1964), s.v. *ploue*; O. J. Padel, 'Cornish *plu*, "parish"', *Cornish Studies*, II (1974), 76, who also cites the Welsh meaning 'people' for *plwyf* in the late medieval poetry of Dafydd ap Gwilym.

nymy? Because of the paucity of fifth- to eighth-century evidence about the date of *coining* place-names (and precise meaning at the time of coining) explanations have been many. They have ranged from those favoured in the late nineteenth century, when La Borderie, among others, argued that the *ploue* was originally a group of settled migrants with their territory ('la tribu bretonne émigrée'), laymen with their own secular and religious leaders, to those of the 1920s in the classic toponymic work of Largillière, who argued that the *ploue* was essentially a rural parish, functioning as a 'petite république autonome', the grouping of parishioners being an indirect effect of evangelisation by priests in the disorder of Brittany after the migration (fifth and sixth centuries). More recently M. Flatrès has suggested that, although the *ploue* was an ecclesiastical parish, whose prominence in Brittany is due to the ninth-century ecclesiastical reorganization, earlier Gallo-Roman territorial units may well have provided the framework of some of them. Most recently M. Bernier has argued that the development of free, secular communities during civil dislocation in post-migration Brittany allowed priests to exercise exceptional powers and intentionally mould the communities into parishes, creating a parochial structure which was to all intents and purposes independent of bishops; hence *ploue* was a baptismal parish of secular origin—an institution peculiar to Brittany—and *plebs* had a specialised meaning by the ninth century.[5]

As may be observed, the power of priests is frequently called upon to explain the formative stages of *plebs* and/or *ploue* and, on the surface at least, the terminology itself appears to suggest that an ecclesiastical basis underlies secular units of association and organization and that powerful clerics had some hand in it. Now there is a useful corpus of material on the role and function of priests in rural communities in the ninth century. Although this obviously postdates the formative stages of social and ecclesiastical structures in Brittany, it allows us to view the power of Breton

---

5. A. Le Moyne de la Borderie, *Histoire de Bretagne* (6 vols., Rennes, 1896-1914), I. 281f, II. 142-4; R. Largillière, *Les Saints et l'Organisation chrétienne primitive dans l'Armorique bretonne* (Rennes, 1925), pp. 197-219—see especially pp. 197, 212, 214; P. Flatrès, 'Les divisions territoriales de Basse-Bretagne comparées à celles des contrées celtiques d'outre-mer', *Annales de Bretagne*, LXIII (1956), 3-17; idem, 'Historical geography of western France', in *Themes in the Historical Geography of France*, ed. H. Clout (London, 1977), pp. 321-3; G. Bernier, *Les Chrétientés Bretonnes Continentales depuis les origines jusqu'au IXe siècle* (Rennes, 1982), pp. 51f, 88, 92. (M. Bernier diverges from Largillière in several particulars.) The strongest argument for the early emergence of *territories* dependent on churches (as in Italy) is the substitution of *provincia* for *bassilica* in parallel clauses in one text of the compilation known as 'Excerpta de libris Romanorum et Francorum', of fifth- to eighth-century date: *The Irish Penitentials*, ed. L. Bieler, pp. 152, 140 (where the text is misleadingly called 'Canones Wallici'); see L. Fleuriot, 'Un fragment en Latin de très anciennes lois bretonnes armoricaines du vi[e] siècle', *Annales de Bretagne*, LXXVIII (1971), 655.

clerics from a different, and useful, perspective. The material is contained in the well-known corpus of charters in the *Cartulaire de Redon*, a source which—though central to discussions of *plebes*—has scarcely been touched for its evidence on priests.[6] It is therefore the purpose of this paper to investigate the function of the priests of the Cartulary in relation to their local communities and demonstrate that their role was an important one.

The Redon Cartulary is very well known to modern scholars and needs little introduction. It has been in print since 1863, in an edition which is inconsistently inaccurate, and has been much cited and quoted. The collection exists because of the foundation of the monastery of Redon in 832, and because for forty or so years after its foundation this monastery was the recipient of many small grants of property in south-east Brittany. Since, however, many lands came to Redon together with extant documents about previous transactions the corpus includes material from at least three decades previous to 832. The cartulary is an eleventh-century manuscript containing nearly three hundred charters from the years between 800 and 925; a further 60 or so were not included in the collection but are known from early modern transcripts of Redon material. About three quarters of this total relate to the years 830-80. This number is unparalleled for a small district in northern Europe, at such a date, as is the fact that virtually all are records of the acts of private individuals rather than of kings, in what was clearly a record-using peasant society. The charters detail grants, sales, mortgages and leases of property, and records of disputes about property and property rights; they normally name donors, beneficiaries and witnesses who attended the transactions, and any one else who might have had an interest in them. The properties whose history is so documented lie from Cléguerec to Guérande, although the greatest concentration straddles the boundary between the *départements* of Morbihan and Ille-et-Vilaine and is especially notable for the communes of Ruffiac, Carentoir and Bains-sur-Oust. The localisable detail about the units of ownership and of tenure and about the people associated with them is considerable. The material is exceptionally rich, therefore, not only because of its quantity but also because of its character and the density of its coverage of one region for a limited period during the ninth century.

It is quite clear from the Cartulary that a unit of civil association known as the *plebs* existed in east Brittany in the ninth century—*plebs Catoc/Cadoc* (the modern commune and village [bourg] of Pleucadeuc), *plebs Rufiac* (Ruffiac), *plebs Motoriac* (Médréac), and so on[7]—and that it was the primary

---

6. *Cartulaire de l'Abbaye de Redon*, ed. A. de Courson (Paris, 1863)—hereafter cited as *Cart. Redon*.
7. *Cart. Redon* XIII, LXII, CXC, etc.; cf. A. Meynier, 'La commune rurale française', *Annales de Géographie*, LIV (1945), 161-79, and F. Lot, *L'état des paroisses et des feux*

unit of social organization. Hence, men were seen as belonging to this or that *plebs* and as members of the *plebs (plebenses)* they had some sort of corporate existence, to which individuals were obliged to account; transactions, therefore, were announced to the men of the *plebs*, as in the oft-cited example of King Salomon's (female) envoy who was commissioned to declare his Pleucadeuc transactions to the men of that society.[8] (The identity of the groups continues to be evidenced in later centuries.) Local offices were performed with reference to the unit of the *plebs*: most commonly we find machtierns of this or that *plebs* (a man who presided at transactions and over dispute proceedings and had some fiscal and vacant property powers), but there might also be a *mair* and sometimes a priest.[9] The equivalence of *plebs* and *ploue* is perfectly clear in the case of the *plebs Caloc*, which was alternatively *Ploicaduc*, gave the name 'Pleucadeuc' to the modern bourg and commune, and had *plebenses* called *pluiucatochenses*. It is also clear, from this as from other sources, that by the ninth century the word *plebs* had a territorial as well as a social connotation in Brittany for parcels of land were frequently located by reference to their appropriate *plebs*—the parcel called Ranmaeltiern, for example, was sited in the *plebs Carentoerensis* in the area known as *compot Roenhoiarn*.[10] The term *plebicula* is also used, of *Plaz* (Brain) for example, but although it always seems to imply a social/ territorial unit of smaller than average size no more precise implication is made.[11] In many cases the *plebs* had an associated church, which also bore the name of the *plebs*—*ecclesia Carentoerensis*, *ecclesia Rufiac*, and so on— and the implication of much of the material is that the association was not fortuitous: the church was in some sense focal to the life of the community.

---

de 1328 (Paris, 1929) for the relationship between modern communes and earlier parishes in Brittany.

8. *Cart. Redon* CCLVII.

9. La Borderie, *Hist. de Bretagne*, III. 134f. *Cart. Redon*, IX, XVI, CXXXI, CCLV; CCLXVII; CCLXVIII. For machtierns see Wendy Davies, 'On the distribution of political power in Brittany in the mid-ninth century', in *Charles the Bald: Court and Kingdom*, ed. M. Gibson and J. Nelson with D. Ganz (BAR International Series 101, 1981), pp. 93-8 and references there cited; J. G. T. Sheringham, 'Les machtierns', *Mémoires de la Société d'Histoire et d'Archéologie de Bretagne*, LVIII (1981), 61-72. For priests see further below, pp. 187f.

10. *Cart. Redon* CXXXIV; cf. 'uillam in plebe', 'mansionem in plebe', *Vie de Saint-Malo*, ed. G. Le Duc (S. Malo, 1979), I.84, II.9, pp. 214, 237; 'Gesta Sanctorum Rotonensium', I.2, 4, 8, 11, etc., *Acta Sanctorum Ordinis Sancti Benedicti*, ed. J. Mabillon, IV part 2 (Paris, 1680), pp. 194, 196, 199, 201; *Cartulaire de l'Abbaye de Landevenec*, ed. A. de la Borderie, pp. 147, 149.

11. Du Cange, *Glossarium*, gives the meaning 'ecclesiola' for this term, but since he cites Breton (including Redon) examples and since the precise signification is not clear from the contexts, I am not sure that he was correct. I am grateful to Richard Sharpe for pointing out that the (rare) occurrence of the term in insular contexts refers to small groups of people rather than to territories or churches.

So, although other locations were also used, it was common for transactions to be performed in or before the church of the *plebs*, and for disputes about property rights to be heard there.[12]

Although priests held tenancies and benefices,[13] served some proprietary churches, and were sometimes chaplains to aristocrats, it is by contrast clear that much presbyterial land was allodial. Many of the priests who feature in the transactions recorded by these charters, either as participants or witnesses, had their own property and clearly this was sometimes family land. Many therefore either had full personal control over their lands or shared full control with parents, children, siblings or cousins. The property interests of priestly families are best demonstrated by those transactions which occurred soon after or even before the foundation of Redon in 832. Hence, the next year, a meadow in Carentoir was given to Redon by the priest Condeloc, whose father Groecon had previously bought the land, acquiring it with full allodial power, at some time during the first two decades of the ninth century.[14] In the same year or the next another priest, Uuorcomin, gave away land in Pipriac, and its tied serf with it, and the record of this grant includes a sanction against contravention of the arrangement by the priest's family *(parentes)*, a penalty of a hundred *solidi* to be incurred in that event.[15] Later in that decade we hear of the priest Agon in dispute with his brothers over the distribution of family land in Langon: he had given them some money, but they appear to have held on to the land; he wanted, therefore, to get the money back and opt for equal shares in the property.[16] Now in later decades the allodial powers of priests continue to be evidenced, but their grants often have a new character. Sometime between 842 and 867 a priest gave his allod in Guillac to the

---

12. See Wendy Davies, 'Disputes, their conduct and their settlement in the village communities of eastern Brittany in the ninth century', *Anthropology and History*, I (1983), forthcoming.
   In other areas where *plebes* were commonly found in early medieval Europe, such as Italy, the usage was distinctive by this period: *plebs* still had a range of meanings but by the ninth century it was most frequently used to denote: *a)* baptismal churches and *b)* the territory dependent upon a baptismal church; cf. such frequent usages as 'territorium de plebe Sanctae Mariae' and 'territorium plebis Sanctae Mariae'; P. Aebischer, 'Diffusion', *Rev. linguistique romane*, XXVIII (1964), 150, 154, and A. Castagnetti, *L'organizzazione*, pp. 16-18, 26f. Although, as I shall argue below, the church was probably an invariable element in the ninth-century Breton *plebs*, one cannot ignore the differences between ninth-century Breton and Italian patterns: this is marked at least in the differing modes of expressing location and in the clear evidence of civil, not merely Christian lay, association in Brittany.

13. *Cart. Redon*, CLVIII, CXXXVII, XLIV, CXLIX, for example.
14. *Ibid.*, XVI, CLXVIII.
15. *Ibid.*, CCXIX, CXXVIII.
16. *Ibid.*, CXCII.

monastery at Redon, but he gave it on condition that he might continue to hold it himself, for payment of rent to Redon, until he became a monk, if he should so wish, provided he was considered worthy at the time of his request.[17] This priest seems to have been investing for his future. A variation on this type of grant is provided by a transaction recorded for 864: here, a priest's grant of land in Ruffiac was made on condition that he and his brother continued to hold it for rent, and that it revert to Redon only on his brother's death.[18] These latter cases are classic examples, of course, of a process evidenced elsewhere in northern Frankia at the same period, that of the commendation of allodial land to great ecclesiastical landowners by small men, on condition that they retained the lands as tenants; it is the substitution of limited (precarial) property rights for full control.[19] These examples are sufficient to demonstrate that priests might have their own personal and/or family lands, both at the time of the establishment of Redon and afterwards. Their properties not only consisted of lands, for, as is scarcely surprising in ninth-century Europe, they owned and alienated rights over rents, rights over people and rights over churches and monasteries too, just as laymen did: in 808 a priest sold the church of St Mary and St Peter at Grandchamp (Loire)—apparently to a layman—for the very large sum of 200 *solidi*, and in the 840s another priest gave his monastery in Avessac to Redon, a sanction against the intervention of his co-heirs being recorded along with the record of the gift.[20]

The property interests of priests were more various than the simple transmission of their inherited rights. Some were involved in the purchase of new properties and some took properties as security for loans: there were two estates in Carentoir purchased for thirty *solidi* in c. 810, parcels of land for payments in kind in Molac in 830, another estate in Ruffiac for twenty-four *solidi* in 830, later a parcel of land in Pleucadeuc for forty *solidi* in 860 or 866, and the many purchases in Renac and Sixt by the priest Dreuuallon in the years 842-4. We often find priests accumulating property.[21] The phenomenon is particularly notable in the period up to the mid-840s, after which accumulation tends to be characteristically the province of the monks of Redon. Accumulation also came by way of loans. These are the so-called 'pledges' of property for a limited term in return for cash payments; at the end of the term the pledger would pay back the money and, thus

---

17. *Ibid.*, CXXXVII.
18. *Ibid.*, CXLIX, LIV.
19. Cf. M. Bloch, *Feudal Society*, trans. L. Manyon (London, 1965), pp. 245f (= *La Société Féodale* (Paris, 1939), I. 375f).
20. *Cart. Redon*, XXXIII, XCVII; cf. the well-known grant by Anouuareth to the monastery of Glanfeuil of Anast, with its church of St. Peter and dependent chapels: M. Planiol, 'La donation d'Anouuareth', *Annales de Bretagne*, IX (1893), 233f.
21. *Cart. Redon*, CCLII, CLXVI; CLV; CCLVI; App. XI, XVI, XVII.

V

184

redeeming it, recover the property. Hence, in 826, a man called Merthinhoiarn pledged his *ran* in Carentoir for twenty-six *solidi* and some grain, for seven years, to the cleric Riuualatr; under the terms of the original agreement, this arrangement was extendable for two further sets of seven years, i.e. a total of twenty-one years. If the money had not been returned after twenty-one years then the land would remain with the cleric for ever.[22] Occasionally we hear that the money was repaid to the priest and the land returned, as happened when Argantlon recovered her brother's pledge from the priest Driuinet some time before 827.[23] Much more commonly, however, there is no record of redemption and the land stayed with the priest, to be used or given away. Although it is possible that the initiative for the transactions lay with the clergy in some of these cases and that they wanted additional properties and rents and were prepared to pay for them, more often it was the laity's need for cash—perhaps to meet some fiscal demand— which stimulated the process; the lands were given literally as a pledge for the return of the cash.[24] In these cases local priests were effectively operating as moneylenders. These transactions again seem to indicate that priests had liquid capital; laymen sometimes performed the same function (and priests did sell sometimes[25]) but the proportion of priests remains notable.

These were not the only worldly roles played by priests in Brittany at this period. It was priests who were employed as the envoys and representatives of the greater landowners, and this may well imply that priests were characteristically literate and articulate: they could be trusted to make a case in the event of dispute and to perform the necessary formalities when property was transferred to or from their lords. Hence, it is usual to find priests used as the representatives of the abbot and monks of Redon, sometimes in pairs,[26] but they also occur as representatives of smaller monasteries, such as Ballon,[27] and of secular lords. Accordingly, the lady Roiantdreh sent her priest to announce a transaction she had occasioned in Médréac to the people of that *plebs*, while the machtiern Jarnhitin used his chaplain, the priest Doithanau, to mediate between himself and a suitor.[28] It is more than possible that priests sometimes presided at local meetings in place of the appropriate machtiern: one sale in Ruffiac was transacted on the

---

22. *Ibid.*, XXXIV, CXXXIII, CXXXIV.
23. *Ibid.*, CXXXI.
24. Cf. *Cart. Redon*, CCXXXIV, where the initiative is explicitly attributed to the pledger.
25. Cf. *Cart. Redon*, XXXIII, XXXVIII.
26. *Ibid.*, CCLXI, LII, CII, CXXVII, etc.
27. *Ibid.*, CVI; the priests are here termed *sacerdotes* and not the more usual *presbyteri*; it is not clear if some distinction is intended by the use of the two terms.
28. *Cart. Redon*, CXC; CCLXVII; cf. LXXIX.

land in question in front of witnesses, with the presence of the priest separately noted, as also the machtiern's word; the point is not made explicitly but seems to be implied. The same may be implied by dispute proceedings heard in or before a church—as happened at Bains, Carentoir, Ruffiac—when no machtiern or *missus* was present.[29] Apart from this, priests performed scribal duties for members of the local community as well as for themselves and for any institutions with which they might be associated. In the exceptionally full series of records for the *plebes* of Ruffiac and Carentoir we find that the cleric Haeldetuuid recorded transactions of gift, sale and pledge, in which he had no personal or institutional interest, in the 820s and 830s, usually at Lisnouuid though sometimes in Ruffiac church, and that he moved to Bains/Renac in the 840s. Before him Lathoiarn performed similar services for Carentoir.[30] They appear to have acted as notaries. In their other (non-religious) public functions priests behaved in some ways like the lay elders of the community: occasionally, as at Bains in 841-51, priests were named among the local *seniores*, making the point explicit: 'seniores ex Bain, Jarnhatoe, Uurhoiarn, Roenuuallon, Suluual presbyter, Uuetencar...'.[31] More strikingly, however, priests do *not* normally feature among the elders, nor among those *idonei testes* (law-worthy witnesses) called on to give impartial evidence in court cases. However, they did play some of the social roles of leading worthies and acted as sureties in other people's transactions of sale and pledge: in such transactions it was usual for vendor or pledger to name several local men as a guarantee to the purchaser/pledgee that the terms of the contract would be met (usually two, three or four, exceptionally one or twelve). So, in 850 the priest Arblaut was named as one of nine sureties in a sale by two laymen to a machtiern of land in Molac, while some time between 846 and 868 the priest Achebui was named as one of four sureties in the course of settlement of a dispute between a man from Peillac and the monastery of Redon, and in 826 the priest Buduuoret was one of three sureties for the pledge of land from a layman to a priest. (Their functions as sureties were to guard against financial loss, resign any interest of their own, and sometimes distrain.)[32] However, only just over 10% of sureties in all transactions were priests, and this suggests that their performance of this function was relatively rare. They seem to have stood outside it. In addition to this, as might be expected, priests constantly acted as simple witnesses to

---

29. *Ibid.*, CXLI; XXXII, LVI, CXLIV, CCLXXIV. Machtierns and *missi* also sometimes presided in church.
30. *Ibid.*, CLV, CXLVIII, CCLXIV, CCLV, CCXX, etc.; CLXVI.
31. *Ibid.*, CVI; cf. below, n. 45.
32. *Ibid.*, CCXLIX, CXVIII, XXXIV; see Wendy Davies, 'Suretyship in the *Cartulaire de Redon*' in *Mach ac Ynad. Law and its Enforcement in the Middle Ages*, ed. T. M. Charles Edwards, D. Walters, M. E. Owen, University of Wales Press, forthcoming.

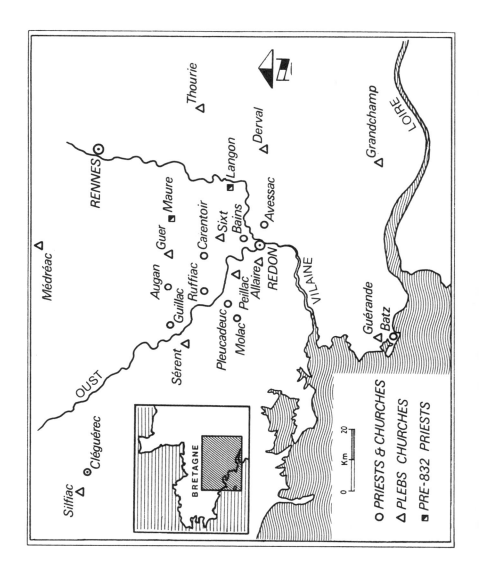

transactions of gift, sale, and pledge and to the settlement of disputes, as did laymen of the *plebs*, and were usually noted high on the list of witnesses, with an implication thereby of superior status.

The most striking aspect of the occurrence of priests at transactions, however, is not their role as witnesses nor their status in witness lists but the fact that their occurrences have different patterns. Of the named ninth-century priests who appear with any regularity there are two quite distinct patterns of occurrence. The first has a wide geographical reference: priests who witnessed transactions relating to widely scattered properties, whether the transaction was performed on the land itself, or by the local church of the *plebs*, or at the monastery of Redon. The second pattern is of much more limited scope: priests who only witnessed transactions relating to a very small area—often confined to a single *plebs*—the performance of the acts of transfer almost invariably taking place within the *plebs* of the land granted (or at least confirmed there subsequent to the transfer). In the first category, for example, one may note Comalton, who witnessed grants of property between 859-68, relating to Locmariaquer, Plélan and Ruffiac, being present at least in Plélan and Ruffiac (26 km apart);[33] Hinconan, who witnessed grants between 854-69 relating to properties in Guérande, Renac, Bains and Ambon/Plaz (the latter performed in Avessac and the rest in those localities—Guérande and Renac are 56 km apart);[34] Liberius, who witnessed between 848-76 in relation to Peillac, Guérande, Caro, Locmariaquer, Rhuys, Avessac, Bains, Carentoir, Ruffiac and Derval, personally appearing in at least Peillac, Guérande and Bains, and Redon many times;[35] Tribodu, who witnessed between 858-65 in relation to Ruffiac, Locmariaquer, Rhuys, Pluherlin and Guérande, appearing at least in Redon, Pluherlin and Guérande (Pluherlin is 20 km west of Redon and Guérande 44 km south; in the order cited the places are—respectively—24 km, 64 km, 56 km, 20 km and 44 km from Redon).[36] In the case of the three latter priests the properties range from the mouth of the River Loire 100 km north west to the edge of the inland forests of Plélan, ranging over south-east Brittany. In the second category (of which there are slightly more examples than the first), we find by contrast that Adaluuin appeared in Ruffiac only, although he was often cited as a witness between 858 and 870;[37] Buduuoret appeared predominantly in Carentoir, and

---

33. *Cart. Redon*, LXIX, CIII, CXIV, CCXXIII; indication of distance here as elsewhere is as the crow flies, and not by modern road.
34. *Ibid.*, XXII, XCV, CIV, LXXXII, CLXIII, CCXLII.
35. *Ibid.*, XXV, XXVII, LXIX, LXXVI, LXXXIV, LXXXVII, XCV, XCVIII, CXXXIV, CLXI, CLXXXVIII, CCXIII, CCXXI, CCXXIV, CCLXI, etc.
36. *Ibid.*, XLIV, LXIX, LXXIII, LXXVI, XCIII.
37. *Ibid.*, XLIV, CXXXIX, CXL, CXLII, CXLIV, CXLV, CLIV.

188

purchased there with his brother, but once in neighbouring Ruffiac;[38] Maelcar at Augan only in the 860s;[39] Maencomin at Avessac only in the 840s and 850s;[40] and so on. Further, many of the priests with consistent associations with one *plebs* also clearly had allodial property in those *plebes*; hence Comaltcar, Conatam and Rihouuen had lands in Ruffiac;[41] Buduuoret, Driuinet, Condeloc and his father Groecon in Carentoir;[42] Oremus in the Isle de Batz and Guérande;[43] and Sulcommin in Guillac.[44] By contrast, priests without consistent associations apparently did not have property interests in the localities.

I would suggest that the reason for the difference in patterns of appearance is that the priests of the first category—those whose witnessing activities relate to a wide scatter of properties—belonged to the community of the major monastery at Redon while those of the second category were resident in their respective *plebes*. The first were the representatives of the community who travelled out to pursue Redon's interests; indeed, the representative role of such priests is sometimes (though by no means always) specified and some of them are described as priest and monk. The priests of the second category appear to have been continuously resident in one *plebs*, and often to have had property interests therein; they must therefore to some extent have performed priestly functions for the community of the *plebs*—appropriately the priests of Guillac and of Sixt are referred to as priests of their respective *plebes*.[45] The same conclusion is suggested by another approach to the witnessing patterns: if the distribution of appearances of all the priests who appear in a given *plebs* be considered—and this will include priests who appear infrequently as well as those who do so regularly—then it is clear that most of them have an extremely limited territorial range. Of the twenty-three priests, therefore, who witnessed transactions relating to Carentoir, two thirds appeared only in Carentoir; Anauuoret was once also in Augan, 16 km away; Buduuoret and Driuinet were each once in neighbouring Ruffiac, 10 km away; while Maenuueten appeared predominantly in Ruffiac but came over once from the 'home *plebs*'. Only the scribe Haeldetuuid appeared equally frequently in Ruffiac and Carentoir.[46] Of the ten priests who appeared in relation to Pleucadeuc,

38. *Ibid.*, XCI, CXII, CXIII, CXLVIII, CCXXXII; cf. LVI.
39. *Ibid.*, XLV, LXVIII, CLVII.
40. *Ibid.*, LXI, CXVII, CLXII, CXCV, CCVI.
41. *Ibid.*, CXLIX, LIV, CL, CLX; CXIV; CLV, XII.
42. *Ibid.*, LVI, XCI; CLXVI, CXXXI, App. XXI; XVI; CLXVIII.
43. *Ibid.*, LXXXIV, XCVIII, App. XLII.
44. *Ibid.*, CXXXVII.
45. *Ibid.*, CCLXVIII; App. XVII.
46. *Ibid.*, LVI, LXVIII (Anauuoret); for Buduuoret see above n. 38; XVI, XCI, CXII, CXXII, CXXXI, CLXVI, CXCVI, App. XXI (Driuinet); LXIV, XLIV, XLV, LXV, CXXXVIII, CXL, CXLI, CXLIV, CXLVIII, CLVII, CLX, etc. (Maenuueten); for Haeldetuuid see n. 30.

eight appeared in that *plebs* only but Rihouuen and Comaltcar appeared more frequently in Ruffiac (10 km away).⁴⁷ (This pattern does *not* apply to priests of Langon, Renac and Bains, all places nearer Redon, for these interchanged frequently.)

Now, it may be imagined that even though each individual in this second category of priests had consistent, long-term associations with a single *plebs*, nevertheless he was there because he had been sent out from the dominant monastery of Redon to serve the local community; that is, that although life-style was different, he was effectively a member of the Redon community too. However, the family interest in many of their properties must make this situation very unlikely, as indeed does the length of their local associations. But there are also several positive indications that this was not so. Firstly, and obviously, there are plenty of references to local priests in the years before 832 and the foundation of Redon: three priests witnessed a settlement at Langon in 802;⁴⁸ some time before 824 another three priests witnessed a settlement in Pleucadeuc, one of them acting as a mediator to achieve the settlement in his machtiern's dispute with a layman;⁴⁹ four priests witnessed a sale at Carentoir in 826 and in the same year, at the same place, three witnessed a pledge undertaken by a fourth;⁵⁰ in 830 a priest and his brother purchased land in Molac, a transaction witnessed by two other priests;⁵¹ and so on. Further, four priests of Bains were named as such and distinguished from the representatives of Redon, who included priests, who heard a case in Bains in the course of a dispute during 892; and the priest Suluual was named in the 840s as one of the elders of Bains responsible for hearing, assessing and resolving a dispute to which Redon was party.⁵² Moreover, several of those priests who made grants to Redon—either in totality or reserving a life tenancy for themselves—did so with the request that by virtue of their grants they be permitted to join the Redon community;⁵³ in such cases it is clearly extremely unlikely that they were already members of the community. Indeed these cases suggest the converse: an already existing structure of village priests with local interests was gradually influenced and changed by the establishment of Redon. Hence, village priests retired to Redon for their last days; proprietary churches were given to Redon; outposts of Redon were established in some localities—like the *locus receptionis* in Anast (Maure) by 871; and by

---

47. *Ibid.*, CCLVI, CCLXVII, CCLV, XIII, CCV.
48. *Ibid.*, CXCI.
49. *Ibid.*, CCLXVII.
50. *Ibid.*, CCLV, XXXIV.
51. *Ibid.*, CCLII.
52. *Ibid.*, CCLXXI, CVI; cf. CIV.
53. *Ibid.*, CXXXVII, XVI, CCI, App. XXIII.

the eleventh century Redon clearly had acquired possession of many village church tithes.⁵⁴

If there was a rural priesthood that did not owe its establishment to the pastoral and proprietary interests of Redon, it should not be imagined that these priests were evenly distributed among the rural communities on the basis of one per 'parish' or one per church. The indications of the charters are that some if not all *plebes* had groups of priests. Indeed, in areas where there is full documentation, there are usually two, three or four priests with the same contemporary, consistent local associations. In the case of the twenty-three priests named in association with Carentoir, the maximum number of priests with consistent contemporary associations is four: Condeloc, Driuinet, Taetal and Uuiuhoiarn in the periods 827-33 and the latter three also in the period 838-46.⁵⁵ Indeed, the maximum number of priests named at one time is never more than four, and more usually three.⁵⁶ Very occasionally the same sort of case for local associations can be made for deacons and minor clergy, although it cannot be ignored that deacons are much more frequently associated with Redon or with the ruler's court.⁵⁷ Now even allowing that our evidence is incomplete, it is clear that a high proportion of rural communities that *are* evidenced had attached priests. In the extant charters the number of *plebes* with consistently associated priests is nine: Augan, Avessac, Bains, Carentoir, Guillac, Molac, Pleucadeuc, Ruffiac and the 'island' of Batz; in addition there is slight though clear evidence of local priests at Langon and Maure before 832.⁵⁸ Church buildings are mentioned for all of these places. Reference to churches at other *plebes*—Allaire, Derval, Guer, Guérande, Grandchamp, Médréac, Peillac, Sérent, Silfiac, Sixt, Thourie and (?) *Vilaria* (Nantes) must suggest the provision of still more groups of priests for it is unlikely that the structures had no permanent responsible officers in attendance. Some of these may have been proprietary, as Grandchamp undoubtedly, and Médréac possibly, was.⁵⁹ In fact only six of the twenty-two *plebes* mentioned in the

---

54. See above, p. 183; Comaltcar, Haeldetuuid and Maenuueten also seem to have followed this retirement pattern. For tithes, cf. CCCXXII (Sérent 1041), CCCXLIV (Marzac, 1080), CCCLVIII (1086-91).

55. *Ibid.*, XVI, XXXIV, CXXXIII, CCXII; for Driuinet see above n. 46; XVI, CXIII, CXXXI, CCXXXII, CCLXIV; VIII, XXXIV, CXI, CXII, CXIII, CXXXIII, CLXXII.

56. Of course, we cannot assume that *all* priests named in the Carentoir charters belonged to that *plebs* since the number of appearances of some individuals is too small to permit comment on the pattern of their associations, although the absence of other associations must make it likely that they were local; see above, p. 188.

57. Hence, most clearly, deacons Catuualart at Sérent (CCLXIII), Gustus at Grandchamp (CCX, XLIII), Iunmonoc at Ruffiac (CXLII, CLIV, CCXXI, CCXLVIII).

58. *Cart. Redon*, CXCI, CXXIX.

59. *Ibid.*, CCXXXV, LVII, CLXXVI, XCV, CXC, CCXIII, CCLXIII, CCXLVII, XLVI, XLI, LXXV, XXXIII, XLII. (Largillière, *Les Saints*, pp. 200f., argued that virtually all *ploue* had churches and all early parishes had *ploue* names.)

core area that is well provided with charters do *not* have consistently associated priests and/or churches named—i.e. 73% do. Since the focal villages of these *plebes* are usually no more than eleven km apart, and sometimes only six, the provision of priests for village communities is therefore —for the ninth century—surprisingly dense.[60] The evidence suggests that each *plebs* in ninth-century south-east Brittany was served by its own small group of local priests and other clergy. The church of Allaire was, appropriately, explicitly termed *ecclesia plebis* in 878, a usage which also occurred in west Brittany in the late ninth century. Direct analogy with Italian practice would in any case suggest this, but clear differences in the use of the term *plebs* in Brittany mean that it is unacceptable merely to argue from analogy.[61]

There are two especially interesting aspects in all of this: the priests seem to have had a focal role within their villages; and the density of their occurrence must suggest the existence of at least a proto-parochial structure. With their own property interests in the *plebs*, they had a stake in the community, a stake also demonstrated by the fact that the office tended to be the preserve of certain families; priest father and priest son occur, as do priest brothers and priest cousins.[62] Family interest in the priestships is quite clear (and occasionally there are hints of a relationship between priestly and machtiernly or other powerful lay families). Omnis had a host of powerful lay relations and Haeluuocon was the son of the oft-appearing donor Argantlon.[63] Priests were literate and articulate, and had business skills; they performed essential business functions for their neighbours; they had money—resources to spare—and they loaned it. The priest's house *(domus presbyteri)* might serve as an alternative to the church or the machtiern's *lis* for the performance of business: transactions were sometimes performed there (and tonsuring might be carried out too).[64]

---

60. This point has frequently been made by earlier writers with reference to the fifth and sixth centuries and lies at the root of many of the arguments about the distinctiveness of Breton *plebs* and *ploue*; while the point is absolutely clear for the ninth century (and rarely made) it is not at all clear for earlier periods, for which contemporary evidence is lacking; the arguments rest on inference from place-names.
  61. *Cart. Redon*, CCXXXV; 'Vie de S. Paul', *Rev. Celt.*, V (1881-3), ch. 15; A. Castagnetti, *L'Organizzazione*, p. 21. The east Breton manner of localising units of property *(N in uilla N in plebe N)* is notably distinct from other practices in ninth-century Europe, north and south of the Alps; cf. above n. 12.
  62. Cf. *Cart. Redon*, LVI, CLV, XVI and CLXVIII, App. XXXVII, and the *clerici* Riscant and Budhoiarn at Carentoir (CXII).
  63. *Ibid.*, LXV: the priest Hinuualart's nephew appears to be the son of the machtiern Iarnhitin. The priest Omnis and family (uncle, cousin, brother, sister and priest nephew): CXXI, CLXXXI, CLXXXII, CLXXXIII, CLXXXVI, CXCIX, CXXXIV. Haeluuocon, priest, son of Argantlon: App. XXII; CLII, CLIV, CXXXI.
  64. *Ibid.*, CCLIV, LXXI, CLXXVIII, XLV, CLXXXI. Cf. *domus ecclesiae* in episcopal centres in sixth-century Gaul.

In many practical ways their presence and activities were central to the life of the community, even if a sense of distance distinguished them from the local lay elders. Presumably this was also so in spiritual matters although there is very little evidence about the performance of pastoral functions or of the crucial rites of baptism and burial; some ritual activity is at least evidenced in the singing of psalms and masses for the souls of the *plebenses*, and we do know something of the burial of rulers and aristocrats.[65] Of course, some of the machtierns, lay lords and large monasteries may well have had greater property interests than priests but the breadth of these interests meant that they were physically removed from village communities. Similarly in local politics, the most powerful person in the neighbourhood must have been the machtiern; but here again, the machtiern's political and professional interests were wider than the single *plebs* and extended, like his properties, to three or four of them. In that the priests were more consistently present in the *plebs* and had *plebs*-sized interests they were in *some* sense more powerful than these greater men and women.

In effect the local priests must have constituted a parochial framework, whether or not they actually performed all the functions that one would expect of a later parish priest. The essence of the framework must have been in existence in east Brittany before the foundation of Redon and cannot therefore be a consequence of the latter foundation. Moreover, it seems to have continued, irrespective of the establishment of Redon, although it is perfectly clear that the monastery had immense power in the neighbourhood, and began to influence the conduct of some 'parish' affairs from the middle of the ninth century. The existence of such a framework in ninth-century Brittany is extremely unlikely to be a product of the Carolingian conquest of the late eighth and early ninth centuries since the system was already hereditary by that period and lacks the characteristics of Carolingian regularisation: the parcellation of large parishes between existing churches of all types and the delimitation of ecclesiastical territories by bishops during the ninth century (frequently with reference to estates) often involved the foundation of more churches and resulted in the distribution of priests among them and the breakup of earlier communities of priests. The ninth-century archpriest might therefore supervise scattered priests in several parishes where his sixth-century counterpart supervised one community.[66] The Redon material shows no traces of this process.

---

65. *Cart. Redon*, App. XLIV; CXLIII, CLVII, CCXXXVII; cf. burial rights in CCXXXVI, CCLX, CCXLIII, CCXLI, XLIX, App. XV, and care for paupers in CCXXXIV. (Most of these burials are in Redon or Plélan, i.e. *not* in local *plebes*; cf. CCXCI in the eleventh century.)

66. See P. Imbart de la Tour, *Paroisses rurales*, pp. 96-105, 128f; G. Fournier, *Le Peuplement rural en Basse Auvergne durant le haut moyen âge* (Paris, 1962), pp. 401-47; J.-F. Lemarignier, 'Quelques remarques sur l'organisation ecclésiastique de la Gaule du

Indeed, in many ways the Breton communities are comparable to those of the rural churches established north of the Alps in the fifth and sixth centuries: these were usually staffed by a group of priests, often under an archpriest and often living communally, ultimately responsible to a city bishop, but administering baptism (after fetching the chrism from the bishop) and saying mass themselves; usually, however (unlike the Breton ones), a group served several village communities and therefore a wider territorial area, with minor churches and dependent chapels under its supervision. The Breton communities are also comparable to those of the rural churches of eighth- and ninth-century Italy, again served by groups of priests, living a communal life, coming from families with hereditary interests in the offices and in the properties associated with them; like the Merovingian rural communities they sometimes supervised minor churches, although in parts of north Italy *plebs* churches were no more than five to ten km apart.[67]

It is also interesting to observe that the ninth-century Breton parochial framework has a surprisingly close relationship with the later medieval and modern framework of Breton parishes in that the foci of the ninth-century *plebes* still tend to be parish (and commune) centres today; moreover, although the size of 'parish' territory has usually decreased since the ninth century, in some areas there has been little infilling with new parishes and in others many of the new creations are of recent date, in areas which seem to have been little populated in the ninth century: La Chapelle Gaceline, La Gacilly and Quelneuc were not detached from Carentoir until the mid-nineteenth century, and similarly Monteneuf and Porcaro from Guer.[68] This is unusual in comparison with parochial development in other parts of

---

VIIe à la fin du IXe siècle principalement au nord de la Loire', *Settimane di Studio del Centro Italiano di studi sull'alto medioevo*, XIII (Spoleto, 1966), pp. 451-86; M. Chaume, 'Le mode de constitution et de délimitation des paroisses rurales aux temps mérovingiens et carolingiens', *Revue Mabillon*, XXVII (1937), 61-73 and XXVIII (1938), 1-9; E. Griffe, 'A travers les paroisses rurales de la Gaule au VIe siècle', *Bulletin de Littérature Ecclésiastique*, LXXVI (1975), 3-26.

67. Cf. E. Griffe, 'Paroisses rurales', *Bull. Litt. Eccl.*, LXXVI (1975); C. Stancliffe, 'The Christianisation of the Touraine, 370-600', *Studies in Church History*, XVI, ed. D. Baker (Oxford, 1979), esp. pp. 50f; H. G. J. Beck, *The Pastoral Care of Souls in South-East France during the sixth century* (Rome, 1950), pp. 29-31, 79, 83; C. E. Boyd, *Tithes and Parishes in Medieval Italy* (New York, 1952), pp. 58f, 63, 67; A. Castagnetti, *L'Organizzazione*, p. 21.

M. Bernier has already pointed to the apparent absence of dependent minor churches in Brittany, *Chrétientés Bretonnes Continentales*, p. 92.

68. See J.-M. Le Mené, *Histoire archéologique, féodale et religieuse des paroisses du diocèse de Vannes* (2 vols., Vannes, 1891-4), I. 140, 302. Clare Stancliffe was of the opinion that everyone was within 10 km of a 'parish' church in the sixth-century Touraine, i.e. that populated areas were relatively well served with priests and churches, *Studies in Church History*, XVI (1979), p. 50.

194

Europe for parish centres were still being established in the tenth and eleventh centuries, parish boundaries were still being defined and the allocation of tithe payments was still being regularised at that period and even later; the concentration of baptism, burial and preaching rights for a given territory in the hands of a single, responsible parish priest, at his parish church, was a long slow process.[69] In most of Europe the territorial framework of pastoral care was fluid and unstable during the ninth- to eleventh-century period, although the process was largely completed by the fourteenth century. Moreover, in the ninth and tenth centuries pastoral functions were in practice increasingly exercised by monks rather than local, parish priests, despite the Carolingian legislation. At least in the relationship between ninth-century and later parish centres, and in their stability, the east Breton development appears precocious.

Now, whether or not the Breton system was fully parochial depends on the payment of tithe, allocation of baptism and burial rights, and the existence of an overseeing bishop: did the *plebenses* automatically pay tithe to the church of the *plebs* and necessarily seek baptism and burial from that church rather than any other? In fact, although the structure of village relationships might well suggest that this was so, direct contemporary evidence on these points is very limited and is inadequate for providing any firm answers.[70] We cannot perceive the bundle of rights exercised by the Breton priests nor the ability of the local group to monopolise them. It is by no means impossible, however, that local priests were receiving tithe from the *plebenses*; this might then explain the relatively easy availability of cash.[71] Similarly problematic is the question of the

---

69. These points were made very forcibly at the Ventottesima Settimana di Studi sull'alto medioevo, Spoleto, 1980; publication forthcoming. See especially the contributions of Hartmann, Settia, Lemarignier, Constable. Cf. J. Gaudemet, 'La paroisse au moyen âge', *Revue d'histoire de l'Église de France*, LIX (1973), 5-21.

70. It is usually assumed, however, that the *plebs* churches were baptismal; cf. M. Planiol, *Histoire des Institutions de la Bretagne* (2nd ed., 4 vols., Mayenne, 1981-2), I. 237f, who follows Du Cange, *Glossarium*. Since, however, Du Cange arrived at this meaning largely from Italian examples, and since the Italian usages themselves change, this cannot be sufficient to establish the Breton meaning without corroborative evidence. The so-called 'Bigotian Penitential' implies that the cleric of a *plebs* had responsibility for baptism; in that one manuscript of this Irish-influenced but unplaceable text appears to have been written by a Breton, this may be of relevance for some part of Brittany; *Irish Penitentials*, ed. L. Bieler, p. 224.

71. Voluntary payment of tithe was certainly encouraged throughout Europe for several centuries before this, and seems to have gone directly into the hands of rural priests in Italy by the late eighth century (C. Boyd, *Tithes and Parishes*, pp. 67f and A. Castagnetti, *L'Organizzazione*, pp. 26f); even in Ireland there seems to have been some movement towards the association of baptismal churches with churches to which tithe was paid round about 800 (J. G. O'Keeffe 'The Rule of Patrick', ch. 8, *Ériu*, I (1904). Carolingian legislation regularised payment of tithe into the hands of the bishop and made

priests' relationship with an overseeing bishop: did they acknowledge the ultimate jurisdiction of a diocesan bishop, even if contact was rare? It is usually assumed that they had no contact, or effectively none, and there is little indication of any episcopal presence at local transactions. However, occasionally bishops *were* present and the fact that transactions are usually dated with reference to an episcopate, even in the years before 832, might suggest that the bishops of Vannes, Nantes and Rennes retained some overseeing role in their respective 'dioceses'. Moreover, the owner of the church of Anast owed two *solidi* a year to the bishop in 843, one man from Guillac was called *custos ecclesiae* and there are deans at some transactions.[72] The *custos* was certainly dependent on someone, and it is difficult to see a place for the deans except as an indication of diocesan organisation.

All of this is not only in apparent contrast with the developing pattern of parochial provision in continental Europe but also with the pattern of insular institutions. There is at present very little to suggest the provision of non-monastic pastoral care in Celtic areas and the parochial arrangements that were eventually established have a very different relationship with settlement patterns.[73] In English areas some parts seem to have been as well supplied with small 'monasteries' as Wales and Ireland but others seem to have been characterised by rural 'collegiate' churches serving large areas, on the early continental model, with the trend towards the provision of one priest for each rural community beginning in the ninth century, although the main development did not take place until the tenth.[74] However, in the light of the Breton evidence the insular institutions do ask for revaluation: the Breton material raises the question of the nature of the small 'monasteries' of the west midlands, Wales and Ireland—perhaps they were churches served by small groups of priests, living a communal life,

---

it compulsory in the late eighth century in Frankia, but definition of tithe-paying areas took time and there was apparently much confusion and variety in practice during the ninth century; P. Viard, *Histoire de la dîme ecclésiastique principalement en France jusqu'au décret de Gratien* (Dijon, 1909) and R. McKitterick, *The Frankish Church and the Carolingian Reforms 789-895* (London, 1977), pp. 76-8.

72. *Cart. Redon*, XCVII, CXXXVI, CCXXII; M. Planiol, 'Donation d'Anouuareth', *Annales de Bretagne*, IX (1893), 234. *Decani*: Catuuotal, *Cart. Redon*, CXII; Jacob, *ibid.*, CCLXXV-VII; Madganoe, *ibid.*, CCXII; Cumdelo, *ibid.*, CLXXXVIII.

73. See the articles by Flatrès, cited n. 4 above, O. J. Padel, 'Cornish names of parish churches', *Cornish Studies*, IV/V (1976-7), 15-27, and Wendy Davies, *An Early Welsh Microcosm* (London, 1978), pp. 37-42, 63f; cf. the large number of small 'monasteries' in south-east Wales: Wendy Davies, *Wales in the Early Middle Ages* (Leicester, 1982), pp. 143-5.

74. See J. Godfrey, *The English Parish 600-1300* (London, 1969), pp. 32f, 44f. Cf., as in south-east Wales, the relatively large number of small 'monasteries' in the English west midlands: P. Wormald in *The Anglo-Saxons*, ed. J. Campbell (Oxford, 1982), pp. 123-7 and *idem* in M. Falkus and J. Gillingham, *Historical Atlas of Britain* (London, 1981), p. 35.

popularly known as 'monasteries'. Secondly, the material inevitably calls for comparison with the so-called 'clas' churches of pre-Conquest Wales, whose hereditary priestly communities are in many respects similar to those of the Breton churches[75].

The ninth-century evidence clearly indicates that east Brittany had relatively many rural churches, to which were attached groups of priests, often with hereditary interests in both office and property in their *plebes*; the churches were therefore in some sense 'collegiate' and were in many ways comparable to the rural churches of Merovingian Frankia and later Italy. The ninth-century evidence also clearly indicates that the Breton institutions were of pre-ninth-century (and therefore presumably pre-Carolingian) origin. This evidence also suggests that there were fewer proprietary churches than might be expected: certainly very few are mentioned, and there is an increase in seigneurial control in the later ninth century indicated by Redon's increasing influence in the churches of the surrounding *plebes*, with its absorption of some proprietary churches and developing bonds with local priests. Hence, the implication of the corpus of material is that the essence of the parochial structure of east Brittany was already in existence in the early ninth century; that it had its origins in the distant past; and that by comparison with other parts of the continent Brittany was curious in lacking indications of characteristic Carolingian developments and of the prevalence of estate churches and seigneurial control.

So, on the basis of this evidence, east Brittany appears to have been precocious in the stability of the ninth-century framework and therefore in its relationship with the ensuing parochial structure; conservative in its retention of what was essentially a sixth-century European pattern, perhaps unusually fully implemented; apparently distinctive in the comparative rarity of seigneurial churches as also in the strong sense of identity of its rural social units. Whether or not this is genuinely distinctive, the local power and role of village priests is perfectly clear in the ninth-century communities. As such, this adds some weight to the arguments for unusual priestly power in sixth-century Brittany, although that case must in the end rest on contemporary evidence. The issues, for the sixth century, ultimately hang on the level of episcopal control.[76] Equally, of course,

---

75. Cf. W. Davies, *Wales in the Early Middle Ages*, pp. 149-51; and C. Boyd, *Tithes and Parishes*, p. 63, on legislation about 'canons' living in 'monasteries'. The strong priestly element in early monastic communities has received too little attention, in Brittany as in Ireland; cf. 'Vie de S. Paul', ed. Ch. Cuissard, *Revue Celtique*, V (1881-3), cc. 7, 11.

76. The strongest argument for the unusual independence of Breton priests is the sixth-century letter from the bishops of Rennes, Tours and Angers complaining of the unsupervised and irregular ministry of two priests, who had women to assist them;

and just as significantly, both the ninth-century situation and that which may be implied for the sixth add some weight to the argument for the absence of *secular* political authorities. In many parts of Europe the pattern and terminology of territorial units is ultimately determined by the fiscal demands of ruling powers; the fact that this did not happen in Brittany lends considerable support to the suggestion that there was little attempt at state formation in the post-migration centuries. Further, the connotation of *plebs* in ninth-century Brittany is firmly secular although the secular units had associated churches and priests; this is interesting given the strong secular connotations of the vernacular term and given the difference in practice in localising property units between Brittany and other parts of Europe. This, together with the absence of developed state machinery and the comparative rarity of seigneurial powers, supports the suggestion that free, secular associations of people had determined the mould of the basic social structure and that these had already had a long history by the ninth century.[77]

A. de la Borderie, *Hist. de Bretagne*, II.526f. However, 'Excerpta de libris Romanorum et Francorum' does underline the requirement that clergy be subject to episcopal jurisdiction; *Irish Penitentials*, ed. L. Bieler, p. 144. (If we could localise these texts it might be more easy to resolve the inconsistencies at present apparent.)

77. This paper was originally written for a conference on Britain and Brittany held in Oxford in January 1981; I am most grateful to Trevor Rowley for asking me to prepare it and to the many people who expressed reactions to it at the time. I am also indebted to my friends the Rev. Wyn Evans, Oliver Padel and Ian Wood for their very helpful comments on written drafts and to Chris Wickham for some very valuable discussions about Italian material.

RÉSUMÉ. — *Étude du rôle et de l'importance des prêtres au IXe s. d'après les transactions conservées dans le Cartulaire de Redon. Les prêtres ont alors des propriétés personnelles, qui leur viennent de leur famille, peut-être comme leur propre charge. Ils accumulent parfois les possessions, grâce au prêt sur gages. Ils jouent un rôle important, comme lettrés. Comme témoins de transactions, certains prêtres ont un large champ d'action (ce sont des moines de Redon), d'autres interviennent dans un domaine restreint, dans le* ploue *où ils habitent, où ils ont des possessions (ce sont des prêtres attachés à une* plebs*). La grande densité de ces derniers permet de supposer qu'il existait dans chaque* plebs *une communauté de prêtres, souvent héréditaires, jouissant de larges pouvoirs. Comparée à d'autres pays d'Europe occidentale, la Bretagne a connu une organisation précoce du clergé rural et du service pastoral des campagnes.*

VI

Disputes, their conduct and their settlement in the village communities of eastern Brittany in the ninth century

> There were formal and informal means for the settlement of disputes within the village communities of ninth-century eastern Brittany, although both depended essentially on local knowledge of local history and on confidence in the good faith of those with the knowledge. Reference was not made to written law, nor sets of customs, nor principles; the answer to all problems was seen to lie in the past, and all problems were assumed to have an answer. Where the procedure was formal and the meeting presided over by some official, presidents do not appear to have determined the outcome; judgment was made and due settlement assessed by panels of 'suitable' local men. Peasant communities sometimes became involved in the disputes of high politics, through the property interests of more substantial landowners. In these cases the means of arriving at a judgment and the procedure of expressing it often differed: though local knowledge might be cited, cases were usually heard by the ruler, who then both judged and determined the due settlement. Sometimes this appears to have been done for obvious political purposes.

THE RECORDS THAT survive from Europe in the early middle ages include a rich and significant corpus of law codes, but relatively few accounts of cases. Where such accounts do survive in any numbers, as they do in Italy and Spain, the sporadic and incidental nature of their recording and collection produces considerable disparities in time and place, and this makes systematic analysis of practice exceptionally difficult. Medieval historians, therefore, are more accustomed to treat law as text than as process and to treat the prescriptive and quasi-descriptive clauses of the codes as sufficient indication of practice, discussion frequently concentrating on the descriptive potential of different types of text. Some areas, however, do produce records which allow insight into practice, and there exists a collection of charters from east Brittany which is not only unusually rich in detail of persons and place but also unusually large in quantity for a limited area and period. These charters include records of disputes, amongst a range of property transactions, and the size and character of the collection permits consideration of the occasions of dispute and the process of making them public, as well as the procedures adopted to bring about settlement and the range of persons who became involved. Since the problems are of small scale, since most of the protagonists are peasant farmers and since many of the disputes are conducted within the limits of a single village and its associated territory, we have an opportunity to consider aspects of life and relationships at village level in a period when most available documentation deals with the activities of emperors, kings and major clerics. This paper is consequently about village communities in ninth-century Brittany and the way that they handled their problems in public.[1]

Before engaging with these, two preliminary comments are essential to explain both the context and the limits of the investigation: these concern the available sources and the wider political context. To begin with the primary source material: in the year 832 AD a monastery was founded at Redon, at the confluence of the rivers Oust and Vilaine, 65 km south west of Rennes, the present capital of Brittany. Though the land for it was donated by a local magnate, the foundation was made with the patronage and involvement of the Frankish emperor Louis and his representative in and for Brittany, Nominoe. The monastery was the beneficiary of many small grants of property in eastern Brittany during the succeeding decades, and these properties came to Redon together with records of the gifts and other pertinent documentation. In the eleventh century many of the documents were compiled into a cartulary, and it is this, the *Cartulaire de Redon*, which is the principal source of our present knowledge.[2] (Though collection of the records occurred after a period of political dislocation partly occasioned by the Vikings, it is clear that the monastery retained control of many of the properties throughout the later medieval and early modern periods.[3]) A high proportion of the charters in the cartulary relates to the grants made to Redon in the decades shortly after its foundation; since those grants involved handing over extant documentation the cartulary includes material from at least a generation previous to 832 and records of other transactions too, i.e. the disputes, sales, loans, mortgages, leases and gifts which had touched the lands before they were absorbed by Redon. The range of business recorded is therefore far greater than might be expected from a monastic cartulary and the number of documents referring to small-scale transactions by private individuals is quite exceptional for northern Europe and unusual throughout Europe in the centuries previous to the record-making revolution of the twelfth century.

There are 283 charters in the cartulary from the years *c.* 800-925; a further 55 were not included in the collection but are known from early modern transcripts;[4] about three-quarters of this total refer to the years 830-880. The properties with which they deal lie within a polygon which stretches to 100 km at its furthest limits, but by far the greater proportion of them lies within a circle of 40 km diameter, whose base rests in the south at Redon itself. The charters not only record the actual transactions but also normally name all interested parties in and witnesses to them, and include considerable detail about units of property and tenure and the personnel associated with them. Now, it is clear that the proprietary interests of a major landlord rather than the endeavours of some would-be disinterested observer determined the circumstances of collection, that much crucial information must be lost and cannot be recovered, and that records of dispute settlement procedure will tend to focus on property disputes and not others; nevertheless, the density of information supplied by this corpus for a limited area for two generations in the ninth century is so extraordinary that it is worthy of very serious consideration. Though we must not forget the limitations imposed by the nature of the source material, it remains possible to comment in some depth on relationships at village level.[5]

Secondly, the wider world and politics: during the eighth century an unusually large state had been created by the Carolingian rulers of the Franks who, though often returning to a Lorraine base and its neighbourhood, were crowned as emperors in Rome on Christmas Day 800. The state included lands which comprise much of modern France, Germany, Italy, Switzerland, Austria and north-east Spain, but its integrity as a single political unit was always unstable and was not sustained for more than two generations. After the death of the Emperor Louis, in 840, a series of partitions produced successor states with increasingly separate political identities. West Frankia, comprising much of modern France, was ruled by Charles the Bald as king until 877, and as emperor also for his final two years. Throughout this time the extension of governmental activity was considerable and included innovation in administration and some standardisation of judicial procedure.[6]

The political status of Brittany throughout this period of change for western and central Europe was a fluctuating matter and was sometimes decidedly anomalous. From at least the sixth century the Franks had sought political control of it and had sometimes, at least partially, achieved this. But only under the Carolingians do we hear of any effective over-running of the whole peninsula: a series of expeditions in the late eighth and early ninth centuries ended with two that were led by the Emperor in person and occasioned the introduction of some Carolingian institutions in at least eastern Brittany. Moreover, a Breton, Nominoe, was appointed by the Emperor Louis round about 830 as his representative, with responsibility for all Brittany. After a decade Nominoe was in revolt against Charles the Bald, as successor to Louis in West Frankia; though relations between Bretons and Franks changed several times during the next forty years, it is clear that someone remained responsible for Brittany as a single unit and that this responsibility was transmitted hereditarily; at times this operated as independent kingship.[7] For the period during which there is the greatest charter cover, therefore, Brittany had a principal ruler (whom I shall refer to as the *princeps*[8]); this ruler was initially under Carolingian authority but after 840 was either unwillingly subject or in practice not subject at all. At times, therefore, and particularly in the period *c.* 865-74, Brittany was effectively an independent state.

The fundamental question of the relationship between government and localities is clearly complicated in this case by the comparatively recent introduction and probably imperfect application of Carolingian institutions to Brittany and also by the fluctuating political status of the area itself. Moreover, it is obvious that this was a period of major change for Brittany and for the eastern areas influenced by Redon: before the end of the century the monastery succeeded in establishing itself as a landlord of exceptional power and wide interests, quite probably on a scale not encountered in the locality before; and the Carolingian conquest clearly in some senses stimulated the unification of Brittany, for we have no indication of its existence as a single political unit before this period. The evidence of disputes, their publicising and their settlement is not necessarily typical, therefore, of other centuries in the middle ages or of other areas at the same time. Nevertheless, although the material is particular to a particular situation, the processes it records share many characteristics with those of other medieval societies.

VILLAGES

The area covered by the Redon charter material and worked from the ninth-century villages does not have a single geographical personality. Coastal parts, sometimes to an extent of 20-25 km inland, are low-lying and perforated by pools, lakes and water courses. Near the mouth of the Loire saltpans characterised the landscape and the economy in the ninth century as they do now. The river Vilaine runs south and west to the coast, and with its principal tributary the Oust, running south east, provides the major waterway of the area, which is cut by a pair of parallel ridges (the Landes de Lanvaux) running from east to west, six to seven km apart and 20 to 30 km back from the coast. Beyond this lies the area most intensively treated in the charters: an undulating landscape of mixed farming practices and many settlements stretches from the ridges of Lanvaux to the forests of central Brittany 25 km to the north (Forêts de Lanouée and Paimpont). This is a land that appears to have been worked, and well worked, from at least the Roman period until the present; arable farming seems always to have constituted a substantial part of the agrarian economy, with pastoral husbandry an important supplement. In the ninth century properties were small but packed together, their bounds much disputed, emphasising the intensity of the exploitation. There is little to suggest that the people of this area worked other than as farmers, though it is

VI

VILLAGE COMMUNITIES OF EASTERN BRITTANY

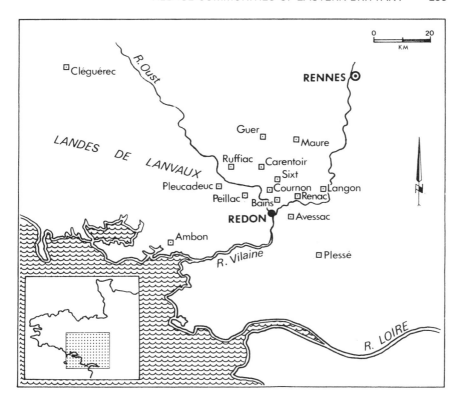

clear that in coastal and riverine parts some were engaged in the production of salt and in commercial activities. Redon itself must have functioned as a market centre and port.[9]

It is clear that agrarian society of this region in the ninth century organised itself in village-based units, known as *plebes* in Latin (and as some comparable-sounding word in the vernacular, since the Latin term was borrowed to give Breton *plou*, which still survives in modern place-names like Pleucadeuc, Pluherlin and Ploërmel). The basic meaning of *plebs* is simply 'the common people' but in the ninth century in this part of France it was used to refer to the primary unit of civil association between people, as also to the land inhabited by the group. Men referred to themselves, therefore, as belonging to this or that *plebs*; transactions might be formally notified to the men of the *plebs*; lands lay in this or that *plebs*; and often there is mention of the church of the *plebs* too. The territories were quite small — usually in the order of six to ten km in diameter — and frequently formed the basis of later ecclesiastical parishes and modern communes, though there has in many cases been some subsequent subdivision. In at least a social sense, and probably also in a spatial sense, the church was focal to the *plebs*: transactions might take place and disputes might be heard in it or before it; roads led to it and it was cited as a point of reference; mention of houses near it suggests some nucleation of settlement in its neighbourhood.[10] But however great the nucleation at the focus of the *plebs*, it is equally clear that there were other settlements within it: a scatter of hamlets is often implied and sometimes explicitly indicated, as are also the occasional seigneurial residence and small monastery.

Each *plebs* appears to have had its own regulator of public relationships, known as the machtiern. This man (and on one occasion a woman) presided over transactions of sale, loan and gift and sometimes stood as guarantor for such transactions. When members of the community had a grievance they might take it to the machtiern for resolution, who would thereupon order an investigation and who might himself preside over any formal hearing that ensued. In some cases there are suggestions that he had powers over vacant properties within the *plebs* and in others that he might expect both the loyalty and a proportion of the surplus of men of the *plebs*. There was undoubtedly a proprietary element in his exercise of these functions, although it would be misleading to present his activities as purely self-interested. In practice one machtiern often served for several *plebes*, and had relations who served for neighbouring communities, and he and his family often had personal properties in some of them; transmission of his 'office' was most frequently hereditary; indeed, no alternative means of succession are suggested in the material, and there are no indications of methods (if any) of appointment. He was therefore a local, powerful man whose personal and family interests might well stretch over several village communities: the greatest distance over which a single machtiern had interests is more than 30 km but half of that distance, spanning two or three *plebes*, is much more common.[11]

There were other men in the village community with specialized roles: occasionally we hear of a man called a *mair*, who was certainly used as a mediator in one case of dispute but whose function may have been primarily that of seigneurial agent and rent-collector.[12] The evidence is insufficient to comment more decisively on this case but that on the role of the Christian clergy is much clearer. Two, three or four priests seem to have served each church, being resident in the *plebs* and owning property in it. Some clearly had hereditary interests in their office and/or their property, and a few may have belonged to machtiernly families.[13] They played a major part in public business, not only as witnesses and guarantors but also — in effect — as moneylenders. Priests had sufficient liquid capital not merely to be more involved in purchasing property than others but also to make cash loans on the security of the loanee's property. The geographical range of a priest's interests, however, was much more limited than that of the machtiern for it was usually restricted to his own *plebs*. Some might travel to neighbouring villages to act as witnesses but that is as far as they went.[14]

Other named individuals are not distinguished by function and we can do no more than assume that the names which recur as the witnesses and guarantors of transactions were the respected and respectable, the leaders of these peasant farming communities. Most of those directly involved in property transactions seem to have been independent — though small — proprietors, for they are clearly distinguished from the servile dependents who were often alienated together with the lands they worked. Since the serfs (*manentes, coloni, mancipii, homines*) are hardly ever cited as witnesses to the transactions of which they formed a part (and apparently in no other cases) it would appear that it was the peasant proprietors that formed the body of witnesses. One aspect of their appearance is worthy of comment: of those names which occur repeatedly in the lists of witnesses, three-quarters only ever appear in transactions pertaining to one *plebs*; the remainder appear in neighbouring *plebes* but only rarely do people travel farther away — even to the increasingly dominant monastery of Redon, the beneficiary of so many transactions. This therefore seems to have been a society of highly localised interests and very limited mobility, with only the machtierns and their families habitually moving between village communities, at once a part of village society and beyond it. There existed an aristocracy — of a few counts and wealthy landowners[15] — which had wider interests, but their interests were so wide that they scarcely impinged as individuals on these communities, although we do know of one case in which the *princeps* himself (Salomon) used a machtiern to report to the *plebenses*. These are, then, peasant communities, with small-scale interests and very limited horizons.

DISPUTES AND THEIR SETTLEMENT

The ninth-century disputes of which we have evidence in this society number about forty, and nearly three-quarters of them date from the generation c. 840-70. They are very largely concerned with property rights and the commonest occasions of dispute are firstly — as might be expected — appropriation of land, stock or income from the monastery of Redon and, secondly, conflict over the allocation of property rights, especially between the members of a family. Hence, in the first category, we find the abbot of Redon accusing a priest of holding on to land which the priest's uncle had given to the monastery; accusing a peasant of stealing the monastery's pigs and cattle and beating up its men; accusing a machtiern of constructing a boundary bank on Redon's property; and so on (*CR* lvi, xxxii, ccxlvii). Almost as common are cases of the second category, in which, for example, two men claim that their cousin had no right to land that he had given to the abbot and that the gift was therefore invalid; or two brothers quarrel with another brother over a share-out of family property previously agreed; or a peasant maintains that he has sold rather less of his land than the purchaser subsequently uses; or another peasant maintains that land given to his local priest was not free to be bestowed on whomever the priest might think fit (*CR* clxii, cxcii, cxxxix, cxliv). Occasionally, however, there is evidence of other types of dispute which, although involving some property element, include non-proprietary aspects in the cause of offence. For instance, the abbot moved in one of the cases cited above not merely because of the theft of stock but also because of physical assault on his dependent serfs, and he moved again because of threats of burning in addition to theft (*CR* xxxii, cv). Very rarely there is notice of killing and of the action subsequently taken: grants were made to the abbot and to the *princeps* as a consequence of deaths — to the *princeps* as agreed compensation for killing his vassal and to the abbot for killing his serf (and in this latter case the amount was clearly more than the value of the property lost so that there is an element of penalty as well as of compensation); the abbot was also granted property as a consequence of an assault made on a priest (instead of the offender losing his right hand as initially judged; *CR* cvii, clxiii, ccii).[16] We cannot comment on the total range of disputes aired in these villages at this period, nor on the relative proportions of different types, but the evidence is sufficient to show that property disputes were not the sole source of conflict.

The procedure by which a grievance was made public — a necessary precondition to achieving a satisfactory settlement — is not always clear. In about a third of the recorded cases a direct request for intervention was made to political leaders — most frequently to the *princeps*, but also to machtierns, counts and even local village elders (*principes plebis*).[8] Occasionally, problems appear to have been aired for the first time in court: in these cases the charters state that the abbot came to a public court, before an appropriate official, and made his accusation, but we have no means of knowing if previous attempts at settlement had been made. In about half of the cases the first that we hear is that one man accused or questioned or made demands of another, in a context that clearly was not formal. Here we have a sense of a private grumble gradually being made known to more and more people, until the community at large knows that the two men are in dispute, before any formal action is taken. This process is explicit in one case that took place in Ruffiac in the 860s: a man called Uuordoital complained that the priest Maenuueten had improperly given away a parcel of land which he, Uuordoital, had previously given the priest for the use of himself and Ruffiac church. Hearing about this, Maenuueten started to gather his evidence — written documentation and witnesses of the gift — preparatory to raising a formal case. Seeing that Maenuueten was doing this, and not wishing to lose his friendship, Uuordoital sent him a message suggesting that if he were to pay a further four silver shillings Uuordoital would confirm the gift, together with free powers of alienation. Maenuueten did so and harmony was restored (*CR* cxliv). It is perfectly clear from this and from many other cases that formal proceedings were often not taken and that many disputes — though a matter of public knowledge and concern — were settled out of court (see below, p. 302).

When complaints were made to political leaders the action taken seems to have depended on the political level at which the complaint was made. When local leaders or machtierns were approached, the invariable outcome was an investigation and, if necessary, a ruling by local elders on the rights and wrongs of the case. When the *princeps* was approached he might do one of several things: he might refer the case to a local court; he might send representatives to the locality to collect information from local elders; he might demand that the accused appear at his own court to answer the accusation, first allowing him an opportunity to gather evidence (*CR* lxi, cv, cvi, cxci, ccxlvii, cclxi). His response appears to have been determined by the status of the persons accused: at the simplest level, peasant problems were referred back to their communities but machtiern offences were dealt with by the *princeps* himself. When the machtiern Ratfred and his brothers acquired eight shares of land in Bains and four and a half in Sixt by threatening Redon with burning, Salomon demanded that Ratfred appear in his court and explain why; on discovering that the explanation of monks and machtiern were inconsistent, he insisted that the disputed property be put into his own hands, and gave Ratfred ten days to assemble his case and present it at another of Salomon's courts (*CR* cv). When the abbot went to the *princeps* Nominoe and accused a peasant and his family of refusing to acknowledge the obligations of a parcel of land, Nominoe sent two representatives to hold a court in the locality. Six local men then testified as to the associations of the disputed parcel and a settlement was arranged (*CR* lxi). But when two priests from a minor monastery near Redon went to Nominoe to request the income from tolls taken at Balrit (presumably a subject of dispute in the locality), the *princeps* sent a representative to the neighbourhood to enquire of the elders of the *plebes* of Peillac, Bains, Renac and Sixt (which lay near the confluence of the rivers Oust and Vilaine) who had a right to these tolls (*CR* cvi).

Cases which were not resolved by the *princeps* or settled at an early stage were taken to court. Our information about the precise manner in which proceedings were conducted is very limited and there is no reason to suppose that the few cases of which there is detailed evidence are typical, given the variations between them. Here is one example:

... Couellic and Brithael, cousins of Lalocan, came to accuse the monks of Redon about their inheritance, which Lalocan had given the monks. Lalocan had given his inheritance, i.e. the villa called Trebhinoi in the *plebs* called Sei (Plessé), to St Saviour's and the monks of Redon. The cousins therefore came before Hoiarnscoit, who controlled that *plebs*, and asked him with many prayers to do justice to them over the case of Redon and Lalocan. They testified that the inheritance was more theirs than Lalocan's. Afterwards he summoned Lalocan with the monks, leading men and elders of that *plebs* and other *plebes*, whose names were: Maencomin the priest, Uuetenuuoion the priest, Catuuotal, Uuetenoc the priest, Catloiant, Rihouuen, Uuarnher ... [and six more names]. They all came with Lalocan before Hoiarnscoit in the villa called Sarant, and testified that he had more right than the cousins because in earlier times their family had divided the inheritance between them, and the villa in question had fallen to the share of Lalocan's ancestor. They [the cousins] were proved wrong, and after Lalocan had proved them wrong with his witnesses he again handed over his inheritance, as he had done before, to the monks who were in that court, Tribodus and Riuuere. ... This was done before these witnesses [13 names] on the seventh of the Ides of December, on Friday, in the fifteenth year of the reign of King Charles and the third year of Erispoe governing Brittany (after his father's death), Courantgen being bishop in Vannes and Conuuoion abbot in Redon (*CR* clxii).

Other cases diverge in several respects, but some general observations can usefully be made. A court might take place at a machtiern's residence (*lis*), in front of or inside a church, in a village or small town (*vicus*), or on the disputed land. A machtiern, or a group of machtierns, or a representative of the *princeps*, or some combination of these, presided. The recording of the names of judges and elders presumably indicates the presence of an official scribe or notary. It would appear that accuser and accused usually spoke for themselves and that investigation was made of the judges' suitability to judge before any judgment was made. Judgment was usually given and formally noted.

How was judgment made and by whom? It was occasionally made by the *princeps*, presiding in his own court; much more commonly it was made by a panel of local people, members of the village community who sat in a local court. For example, Abbot Conuuoion accused one Merchrit in a public hearing before several machtierns of forcefully holding on to property previously donated to Redon; no truth was found in Merchrit's statements, and he then "returned the land which he unjustly held, in accordance with the judgment of the *scabini* who were present, whose names were: Hitin, Framuual, Uuolechaec and Drihican" (*CR* clxxx). The judges were sometimes known by the distinctively Carolingian term *scabini* and at others by the more general *iudices* (judges) and *boni viri* (good men), and their number per case varied from three to fourteen. It is clear that their work involved responsibility for establishing the good faith of witnesses: in the 830s, twelve *franci* testified on oath in a property case, and the *scabini* then judged that these *franci* were worthy (*digni*) to testify and swear (*CR* cxxiv). Their testimony then determined the outcome of the case.[17] In a further case the *scabini* also had some part in vetting the good faith of oath-helpers: at Langon in 802 an accused man was required by six of them to establish his innocence by swearing by the saints to the truth of his position together with twelve others, who had to be 'suitable' (*CR* cxci). We do not know how the *scabini* were chosen although selection of them must have hinged on reputation, as did the suitability of those who might be called upon to give evidence.

Repeated reference to the notion of 'suitability' suggests that procedure depended very closely on the acceptance of a sufficient number of qualified men in the community to act as judges and witnesses and get the business done. For, both informally, when the *princeps* or an interested party sought local information, and formally, in court, it was the testimony of *nobiles* and *seniores* (leaders and elders) which was taken, a testimony that in all recorded cases was decisive (*CR* cvi, cxcv, cclxi; clxii, ccv). In a case about ownership between two laymen in the 890s heard in front of the church of Bains, the record actually specifies that, when all parties and their supporters had gathered together "suitable men (*idonei*) were chosen, proved in their conduct and character, who would not be seduced into giving false testimony by any bribe to do injustice, but who would know what was right and true" (*CR* cclxxi). These were duly selected and they then swore about the appurtenances of the disputed parcels of land, and this determined the outcome. There is no statement of essential qualifications beyond this, although the notion that witnesses should be 'suitable' is not uncommonly instanced in early medieval charters and canonical material, and some legal texts from other areas and other periods explicitly prohibited those convicted of certain offences from giving evidence.[18] However, though these Breton 'suitable' men might be clear of offence they certainly were not personally outside dispute: legal functionaries sometimes brought cases themselves. There are a few further indications in the charters of the status and character of those regarded as suitable: judges and suitable witnesses seem to have been propertied, since several occur on other occasions as donors and vendors, and as sureties for the sales, loans and settlements of other parties. There are no cases of serfs nor, apparently, of females performing these functions. The same men were called upon to act as witness and judge and surety over a period of several years: hence Tiarnan, who was *scabinus* at Langon *c.* 832-40, donor at Cournon *c.* 847 and surety used by Branoc in a sale at Renac *c.* 846 (*CR* cxxiv, cviii, liii); Catlouuen, who was *scabinus* at Langon in 802 and then oath-helper in the oath required by the *scabini* in the same case (*CR* cxci); Houuori, who was named as surety for a sale in Ruffiac in 821 and later appeared as *scabinus* in the court considering a dispute about that sale (*CR* cxlvi, cxlvii); Burg and Antrauual, who were among the *franci* who testified at Langon between 832 and 840 and were *scabini* in a different case at Langon between 834 and 838 (*CR* cxxiv, cxcii). All those who appeared more than once in this capacity did so with reference to small areas — either one *plebs* only or two/three in the case of Langon, Cournon and Renac.[19] Judges and witnesses, then, seem to have been free, male, village men with a property qualification, and there appears to have been a relatively small body of village notables available to perform such roles at any one time.

The actual means of finding judgment in the disputes where a settlement could not be reached without it was preponderantly by the use of these suitable local men, whether acting as *scabini* or special witnesses. A pronouncement of right or wrong was not the inevitable outcome: occasionally, as in the 802 case at Langon cited above, it was decided that the problem might be resolved if one of the protagonists could gather enough supporters of sufficient status prepared to swear to the truth of his claim. When a layman of Sixt was accused about property rights some fifty or sixty years later, the elders of the community required him to swear to the truth of his statement, with three others, on the holy altar (*CR* xlvi).[20] Judgment, however, is evidenced much more frequently than oath-helping, and it is clear that it was made in different ways at different political levels.

At village level community members and not any appropriate officer took responsibility for determining right, even if someone controlled the machinery through which this was done; machtierns did not judge and pass sentence even where they presided over the hearing of cases. How did these elders arrive at their judgments? Those formally required to make a decision, whether known as *scabini* or not, appear to have done so in three related ways: they heard and assessed 'evidence' produced by either party, the evidence consisting of documents about, sureties for, and witnesses of former transactions concerning the disputed property; alternatively the judges heard the (sometimes sworn) testimony of worthy local men on the nature of past practice, the understanding being that these were impartial witnesses. Or, thirdly, they themselves stated, from their own experience, who they believed to be the owner of the land or who had the greater rights. Their personal knowledge of local custom was therefore often sufficient for them to arrive at a decision, without the necessity of enrolling a panel with more detailed local knowledge. Hence, when the two men proceeded against the abbot of Redon on the grounds that their cousin had given him a parcel of land to which he had no right, the machtiern made enquiries of the local elders (*CR* clxii). Knowledge of previous events in the locality — effectively a knowledge of local family history — is therefore fundamental to the process of resolution, and there is no admission in this material of the possibility of other standards of right nor of the possibility of both claimants having equal rights. The answer to all problems was seen to lie in the past; and all problems were assumed to have an answer.

At a higher political level the process was different, although the methods used to arrive at judgments also sometimes had recourse to this local machinery. In cases of aggression by machtierns, heard by the *princeps* in his own court, it was customary for the *princeps* to preside, make a judgment and pass sentence himself. Here, the ruler had clearly established the power to exercise personal jurisdiction over the lesser aristocracy, who were therefore outside the customary judicial procedures. He arrived at his judgment by hearing statements, and sometimes evidence, from both sides, as in the Ratfred case cited above, and sometimes by making his own investigations in the locality, as in the case of the machtiern Greduuocon and the serfs of Bains (*CR* cclxi). The usual outcome was an order for the restitution of the disputed property, and in one case Salomon laid down a penalty of 5000 *solidi* in the event of contravention of the judgment — an enormous sum (*CR* ccxlvii; cf. xxi, cv, cclviii). The tyrannous Alfrit, accused by two successive abbots of constructing a boundary across Redon's property in Cléguérec and appropriating a small monastery there for himself, confessed that he had no right to do this when questioned by Salomon. The ruler then went to the disputed lands and personally walked the boundaries, proclaiming his sanction against further contravention.

Machinery for the enforcement of judgments was as minimal as political considerations might lead one to expect. In most cases there is reference to none, but there is one practice — the use of sureties — which indicates some institutionalisation of machinery, while the actions of rulers indicate that they might take personal responsibility in political cases. There is also a hint in a fragmentary charter that machtierns would investigate mortgage transactions in which the terms of redemption had not been met (*CR* cclxv). More usually, however, sureties were named at the time of making the arrangement, whose duty was to see to the implementation of the terms. In transactions where there are no suggestions of dispute, this appears to have been normal practice where money changed hands, but sureties were also very frequently named when property was handed over as a result of dispute settlement at village level. (Machtierns were *not* required to produce sureties.) Hence, where a tenant's payments had lapsed, sureties might be named for the future payment of render; if the terms of settlement of disputed ownership were that A owned but B became his tenant, sureties might again be given for the payment of render; in ownership cases resolved by one party resigning all interest, sureties might be named as a guarantee of withdrawal of claim, sometimes to the extent that neither the loser nor his offspring would ever bring a further case (cf. *CR* lxi, lxxxviii, cxviii).[21] It is clear that in practice most of these sureties agreed to cover the loser's financial obligations, guaranteeing the victor that he would not lose income. In other cases, it would appear that the sureties were members of the loser's family; effectively they were agreeing to a resignation of their interest too. One case is very clear on the multiple functions of sureties, though, in the nature of the case, it is unlikely that this was anything other than exceptional: the cleric who assaulted a priest and avoided losing his right hand by making a grant in compensation to Redon named three sureties as security for the grant and then those three with a further three as security that he would do no wrong to Redon's men and property in future. The charter then goes on to specify the action they were to take in the event of the latter: if they thought he was about to do anything they were to try and prevent it and warn the abbot; and if he did anything, they were to give his worth to the abbot and pursue him to death. These sureties had both a financial and a physical obligation, and apparently an obligation to engage in a feud against the malefactor (*CR* ccii). Such varieties of suretyship appear to have been the principal method of enforcing the terms of judgments; they again depend on local contacts and the mutual interdependence of the network of local relationships.

In informal cases the procedure for arriving at a settlement was obviously different, although there were many similar elements. It was usually effected by a meeting of the parties, or occasionally their representatives, and a solution being found; sureties might then be given by one party and promises of future good behaviour made. The solution itself varied: money might change hands, or the agreed owner might lease the disputed property to the loser, or the opinion of some respected local person might be sought and boundaries consequently reestablished with the disputed plot divided. Only rarely is the means of arriving at this solution detailed, but it is interesting to note that when the abbot was accused of wrongly holding land in Augan, he sent three of his most experienced monks to the locality to enquire of the respected men of the *plebs* the truth of the matter. Since the outcome was the lease of a second property by the abbey to the accuser, we may suppose that the abbot took note of the local wisdom in determining his future course of action (*CR* cxxvii). When another man accused the abbot about a dam on the River Vilaine near Avessac, the men of Bains and Avessac collected on the river bank which formed their common boundary and maintained that the man was telling lies — whereupon he confessed (*CR* cxcv). Alternatively, there are two occasions on which mediators were used: round about 820 a man asked the machtiern in Pleucadeuc to give him his father's hermitage: the machtiern used the local *mair* and his own chaplain as mediators before conceding the grant. Fifty years later, the abbot of Redon sent three mediators to question another man about his right to properties near the coast; on the advice of the mediators he paid the man 60 *solidi* and then made him a tenant (*CR* cclxvii, ccxlii).

In some senses a distinction between local gatherings such as the Avessac case and local 'courts' is a false one, for they were all public assemblies in which the business of the community was conducted. Nevertheless, from the terminology used, it appears that contemporaries did see a distinction and did regard some public occasions as having a special status. The Carolingian terms *mallus* and *placitum* ('court' and 'session') are used for most of the formal occasions and expressions like *cum lege, in lege, secundum legem et veritatem et rationem* and *in ratione* are used to distinguish their proceedings from those of the more or less amicably produced settlements out of court.[22] We can only guess at the visible difference between the two types of occasion, for courts might take place at locations also used by the less formally described gatherings and local men, of law-worthy status, often played a part in determining the outcome of both. Some distinction there may have been, however, in the status of the presiding chairman, for in most of the court cases machtierns or representatives of the *princeps* sat in the chair. It would not be unreasonable to

VILLAGE COMMUNITIES OF EASTERN BRITTANY

argue — from the proportion of such cases — that this must always have been so. Another distinction may lie in the fact that judgment was almost always given and formally noted. The overwhelming impression is that procedure was more formal in the court cases, even if the crucial role of local knowledge in achieving a settlement was effectively the same as in the informal local gatherings. Presumably someone chaired the informal gatherings — or did he? We have *no* indications of this. The further implication, of course, is that formal proceedings were at times an aspect of state apparatus — sometimes explicitly an aspect of Carolingian regularisation and at others of Breton politicisation — whereas the informal gatherings were not.[23]

POLITICS

Any attempt to assess the way that political influence worked at village level is hindered by the nature of the available sources. It is nevertheless possible to make some suggestions, on the basis of the frequency of citation of certain names in association with their known property interests. Although there is less information about dispute settlement at a high political level, the operation of political influence in these cases is easier to assess. There is no evidence in this material of the intervention in disputes of the highest level of ruler, the Carolingian emperor or king, but, as we have seen, there are clear indications of the role of the Breton ruler, whether acting as the agent of the Carolingians or independently. Firstly, it is evident, although nowhere explicitly formulated, that the ruler acted as a court of appeal for those with grievances which could not be settled at county or village level. These were nearly always disputes involving machtierns, though not invariably so; the other cases were raised by the abbot and it is plausible if not probable that these disputes involved major landowners, aristocracy rather than peasantry (*CR* lxi, ccxlii). Secondly, it is clear that although the ruler allowed the accused an opportunity to speak and produce evidence in his own support — witness the ten days which Salomon allowed the machtiern Ratfred to prepare his defence; and although he often went to some pains to collect local opinion on problems — as Nominoe did when he sent his envoy to gather opinion from the elders of four *plebes* in the case of the tolls of Balrit — nevertheless in making the judgment he adopted a procedure which diverged from local practice. Since he himself presided, judged and passed sentence, he used political power in an obvious manner in order to control the aristocracy.

No similar practice is apparent at the lower political level of the machtiern. He might receive a complaint, he might preside over the proceedings which sought to resolve the problem, but he neither judged nor prescribed the necessary compensatory action or penalty. If machtierns used the political power which they undoubtedly exercised over small groups of villages then they must have done so indirectly in cases of dispute. Nor could they be used by the ruler as an automatic channel for his own influence in the localities, since they represented entrenched local families of long standing, and much about them was independent.[24] The person of the president, therefore, was only significant in formally conducted cases at the highest level, since presidents do not appear to have determined the outcome at the lower levels.

Within the village community, there are a few indications of the distribution of power. In nearly half of all cases the initiative in making a dispute public was taken by ordinary laymen, whose range of recorded property interests suggests that they were peasants rather than significant landowners — they only appear in one *plebs*, with small parcels of land. Sometimes their grievance was against the abbot of Redon, sometimes against other laymen. Though there is a slight tendency for the number of cases against Redon to decrease from *c.* 860, when the monastery was presumably making its power felt, it would appear that members of the peasant community in the ninth century were not inhibited from claiming against the abbot: two brothers were able to go to their machtiern and complain that their cousin had no power to grant their land to the monastery, and Uurbudic was able to challenge the abbot over control of his inheritance (*CR* clxii, cxcv). Further, though the abbot did frequently win such cases, and those raised by himself, there are occasions when he did not. Though the language of the records is nearly always such as to suggest that the monastery was the victor (why else would the record be preserved?), the content of some of them suggests otherwise: when the abbot accused a man of appropriating land near the coast at Plaz, in 869, it is curious to find that he ended up by giving the man a not inconsiderable sum of 60 *solidi* for the property *and* installing him as a tenant (*CR* ccxlii).[25] Of cases where the abbot was not involved, a high proportion were intra-family problems and it is not possible to comment on the relative power and status of the contenders. Of the remainder, it is worth noting that one layman succeeded in forcing his local priest to hand over an additional sum of money for a past sale; another seems to have successfully proceeded against his local machtiern, who — using mediators — ceded the man's father's hermitage to him; and another brought a successful case over ownership, but nevertheless made the loser a small payment of three *solidi*, 'for peace' (*CR* cxliv, cclxvii, cclxxi). The reasons for these successes remain hidden if they are other than the immediate explanation — the drive to maintain harmony in a small community whose members were in the last resort dependent on each other.

The close network of inter-relationships (and even of functions) in these communities is explicitly stated when we find that members of the panel of judges, *scabini* et al., also acted on the side of one of the contenders.[26] So, when the six *scabini* at Langon in 802 judged that Anau should clear himself of a charge of appropriation with an oath and twelve oath-helpers, three of them served as his oath-helpers; and when six local elders testified *c.* 840 that Puz belonged to the Urblon inheritance, two (or three) of them then stood as sureties for the payment of render from the property; and when four *scabini* judged that Merchrit had no claim on the properties of Rethuuobri in Guer, at about the same time, two of them then stood as sureties that Merchrit would make no further claim (*CR* cxci, lxi, clxxx). The same intertwining of interests is evident in other contexts: when an agreement to pay rent by four men in Peillac was renewed in 867, sureties were given for its future payment, and three of these were three of the men liable: of the four men — a), b), c), d) — a) gave b) and d); b) gave a), d) and another (x); c) gave x and two others (y and z); and d) gave z) (*CR* xcvi). Obligations and responsibilities must have been extremely difficult to separate, and it does not necessarily follow that a man who performed two functions acted with wickedness, partiality or cynical self-interest. In the end it is impossible for us to perceive the reasons for local alignments — sometimes family members provided support but this too did not necessarily happen for as often brothers or cousins or children were in conflict.

The only interest whose operation can clearly be identified is that of the abbey of Redon itself, though it is evident that the abbey's interest was not totally predominant. Independence of Redon *was* possible, for Uurbudic who testified on behalf of Redon near Avessac between 836 and 842 also brought a case (unsuccessfully) against Redon *c.* 840 (*CR* lxi, cxcv). Laymen who brought cases against Redon did not always lose, though notably those who won tended to have more than one unit of property, i.e. they were more than minimally propertied. The effect of Redon's victories was usually to institute a new rent-paying relationship; the absence of reference to subsequent problems over these properties — there are no cases at village level where questions were re-opened — suggests that the rent was thereafter paid and the dispute ended, but one cannot argue too strongly from negative evidence. At the higher political level Redon had sometimes repeatedly complained to the *princeps*, or successive *principes*, about machtierns' depredations: such repetition must imply Redon's initial failure and imply further that when Redon did fail, it continued until an effective judgment was made in its favour. Persistence brought victory.

In non-Redon cases any attempt at assessment of interest is confused by the fact that information about them is preserved because the disputed property and associated documentation subsequently (and independently) was transferred to Redon. All we can say is that apparently the resolution of these cases was interest free and apparently groups of local men attempted to produce amicable settlements by re-allocating realisable resources, or if that failed, they genuinely attempted to establish truth by calling upon evidence (normally oral — documents were only cited in a quarter of cases[27]) and local knowledge. Charter xcii suggests that the judgment in cclxxi was correct for although it was not cited in the latter case it substantiates the main burden of the argument which won the decision.

DISCUSSION

The Redon charter material has a unique character and permits exceptional insight into the dealings of a group of co-terminous village communities in ninth-century Europe. It is notable that disputes were settled both informally and formally — by village gatherings outside court and in court, and also by recourse to the ruler. The latter has an element of both the formal and the informal, procedure being less standardised and political interest being much more overtly expressed. Many cases were settled out of court, informally, a compromise being reached and most interested parties conceding a little. Judgment, if necessary, was made by the ruler, when he was involved in the case by either party, and more usually by local people. At village level, formal and informal, the means of arriving at a decision and at a settlement depended essentially on local knowledge and on good faith about the character of those who possessed it; this also entered into some of the ruler's judgments, although he wielded political weight in accordance with the status of the accused. In political cases procedure therefore diverged from the norm. In that judges and testifiers had to be of suitable reputation, and in that village interests were clearly immensely entangled, we must suppose that particular influences operated within village communities; but we cannot perceive *how* they operated. A knowledge of local history emerges as the most consistent means by which problems were solved, and reference to neither local nor 'national' principle plays much part in the process. There is only one case which could even remotely be construed as involving principle — whether a son inherit his father's hermitage, cultivated from the waste (*CR* cclxvii) — and this principle is inevitably tied to property, and was in fact resolved by mediators mediating between the conflicting property interests. It can scarcely be overlooked that a corpus of material which is so rich in reference to disputes and the process of their settlement is strikingly lacking in reference to law and lawyers. Though contemporaries might refer to going to court as going 'to law', professional lawyers do not appear to have been involved in the solution of these cases — at any level, from *princeps* to village — and principles of law are never stated or mentioned. On the other hand broad principles — on the level of killing requiring compensation and marriage requiring negotiated payments between the families involved — must have been acknowledged.[28] The impression given is that rules for the regulation of social relations were not *perceived* as being common to areas beyond the single *plebs* and not committed to writing. This may be an impression moulded by some peculiar bias of the records but it is notable that no collection of written legislation survives from early medieval Brittany. Only the 63 (67) clauses of the 'Excerpta de libris Romanorum et Francorum' remain and these clauses were almost certainly compiled (at some point between the fifth and eighth centuries) from a range of written sources of varying cultural provenance.[29] Now it may be that the absence of reference to law and lawyers is entirely occasioned by the nature of the source material and that in reality both were significant. My view is that this was not so, for it would be extraordinary in a corpus so rich in detail if no incidental reference to them survived. We must therefore consider the possibility that these communities operated without professional lawyers and written law. The lack of law books contrasts with the large corpus of early medieval law tracts from Ireland and rather later law-books from medieval Wales and the lack of lawyers with the number of high status, highly trained, highly professional lawyers which characterize the insular societies.[30] This may partly be explained by the recent emergence of Brittany as a single state and by the absence of any other notable political units previous to the ninth century — it is exceptionally rare to find reference to a king, even of part of the peninsula, and such references tend to come in foreign sources.[31] Brittany, for all its common background with western Europe and Britain, was politicised late; until hit by the Carolingian onslaught it may really have been a land of small, independent, inward-looking, self-sufficient communities, communities that were more self-contained, with narrower horizons than their Irish and Welsh counterparts.[32] The combination of the absence of state responsibility for the law *and* the introverted nature of village communities perhaps explains the contrast.

The problems and procedures of these communities will sound familiar to anyone who is accustomed to the village records of medieval Europe. What is curious in this case is that procedures make so little reference to principle, either as formal lawcodes or collections of customs. Perhaps surprisingly, a simple, non-professional approach to resolving the property disputes of small-scale peasant communities appears to have worked. We have no evidence of cases for which it proved inadequate, and we must presume that it was workable because communities were small and discrete — people had little contact with other *plebenses* and therefore little chance to encounter principles that were contrary. It means that there was apparently no problem in applying fixed rules to real cases; in mediating between the centre and a range of localities; in manipulating the rules to allow for a variety of legitimate interpretations. Where Carolingian institutions are evidenced there is little to suggest that these had occasioned any real change in local procedure.[33] The contrast with Wales and Ireland can hardly be explained by the mere fact of limited politicisation in Brittany, for both insular areas were politically undeveloped. The contrast therefore presumably implies some difference in the inter-relationship between state, village and aristocracy. Size, economic and social self-sufficiency, internal cohesion, communications, must all be critical variables; hence, not only does this ninth-century material permit insight into dispute settlement procedures within rural communities but it also suggests insights into political processes in a period of fundamental change. Moreover, the contrast between village and aristocratic machinery for settling disputes emphasises the distinction between non-political and political cases. The combination of contrasts ultimately serves to throw light upon the very creation of political power at a formative stage. In much of Europe the manipulation of judicial institutions by all levels of the aristocracy was fundamental to the exercise of political power throughout the central middle ages and the opportunity to perceive the early stages of that development is therefore of considerable interest and importance.

Notes

1. I am indebted, for much helpful discussion on the particular subject of this paper and on dispute settlement in medieval Europe in general, to the friends and colleagues who meet regularly at my house in Bucknell to study early medieval charters; our own collection of papers, *Dispute settlement in early Medieval Europe*, ed. W. Davies and P. Fouracre, will shortly be sent to press. I am also especially grateful to Tom Davis, Jinty Nelson, Morfydd Owen and Chris Wickham for their detailed comments on drafts of this paper.
2. *CR*, with references to charters as numbered in the edition; the manuscript is at present under the care of the archbishop of Rennes. The published edition is an extremely and inconsistently inaccurate transcript. The charters of the diocese of Vannes have been helpfully re-edited by M. Tonnerre (Tonnerre 1978) but this is not easily available.
3. Cf. Jausions 1864; de Corson 1880-6:II.164-218; Morice 1742-6: III.961.
4. These are printed in an Appendix to *CR*: 353-402.
5. There are other relevant sources from the area but they are too varied and discursive to permit systematic analysis. They have, nevertheless, to be taken into account. They are principally 'De Gestis Sanctorum Rotonensium'; *Annales de Saint-Bertin*, other sets of Frankish annals and the series of letters about the Breton church (principally *MGH Epistolarum* VI: 619-22, 639-40, 646-9), inasmuch as they involve the rulers who were patrons and protectors of Redon, include material that is generally but not specifically relevant.
6. This is a very superficial survey of a long series of well-documented developments. There is a vast modern literature on the Carolingians; there are brief surveys of many of the issues in Fichtenau 1957, Halphen 1947, and more recently James 1982. More detailed consideration can be found in Braunfels 1965-8, Lot and Halphen 1909. Guillotel 1975-6 and Werner 1980:210 are especially pertinent to the issues discussed here. Modern discussion concentrates on Charlemagne and it is therefore difficult to acquire a balanced overview of events after 814.
7. The best modern discussion of these developments, though it is extremely questionable in its interpretation, remains La Borderie 1898; Durtelle de Saint-Sauveur 1935 is more easily accessible. I have considered the political status of Brittany briefly in Davies 1981.
8. He is most consistently termed *princeps* in this material, but also *dux* and *rex* (especially in the 860s and 870s). The Latin terminology of political authority is clearly not precise, however; *princeps* (*plebis*) is also used of machtierns and village leaders, while *comes* is used of counts with wide territorial responsibilities — counties — but also sometimes of machtierns and village leaders. Both the words *princeps* and *comes* therefore seem to have been used to signify political leadership at a number of levels.
9. Dr. Grenville Astill and I are conducting a survey of landscape and land use over the past two thousand years; publication of the results will be in progress over the next five years,

especially in *Archéologie en Bretagne*. For ninth-century land use, I am preparing a book on the villages of east Brittany, which will deal with it. Flatrès (1971) has argued for distinctively Frankish and Breton patterns of land use in the Loire and Oust/Vilaine regions respectively.
10. I have briefly discussed this in Davies 1981:93; for fuller discussion see La Borderie 1898: 142-4 and Planiol 1981:II. 60f. *Ecclesiae plebis* were not exclusive to France; see Castagnetti 1979: 16-30 on the ecclesiastical nature of the *plebs* in eighth- and ninth-century Italy.
11. See Davies 1981: 93-9; La Borderie 1898: 142-64; Planiol 1981: II. 63-96; Sheringham 1981.
12. See Planiol 1981: ll.149-52; *CR* cclxvii, ccli, xlii, cxi, cxvi, App. xvii. Cf. Welsh *maer*, collector of dues, agent of a king; *Armes Prydein*, ll.18, 21, etc.; there is a useful discussion of the occurrence of the Welsh term in Jones 1972:373-80. Cf. also the Carolingian *maior*, steward of an estate; 'Capitulare de Villis', cc. 10, 26, 60 etc. and Ganshof 1968:38; cf. the several *maiores* cited in mid-ninth-century contexts, Ganshof 1975:s.v. *maior*.
13. If Hinuualart the Ruffiac priest of *CR* lxii (866) is Hinuualart the Ruffiac donor of *CR* lxv (866), he was related to the Ruffiac machtiern Iarnhitin.
14. See Davies 1983.
15. Brittany was divided into seven or eight distinct counties at least at times during the ninth century, including the two, most Frankish influenced, eastern counties of Rennes and Nantes. The Breton *princeps* tended to keep the latter under his own personal control; the counts of the remainder appear to have been directly answerable to the *princeps*, although transmission of the countship was often hereditary. See Davies 1981:92; Planiol 1981.II:48f.; La Borderie 1898:137-41. The occasional occurrence in the Redon cartulary of persons with property interests spanning several *plebes*, who had agents to carry out their business, suggests in addition the existence of a landowning aristocracy; cf. *CR* cix.
16. In the last case it is not clear if the grant was made to the abbot as priest's lord or to the abbot as the person with powers of (private or delegated) jurisdiction over offences committed in the neighbourhood.
17. The term *franci* may signify Frankish rather than Breton people, but this seems unlikely in view of the fact that most of them have Breton names; it more probably refers to their status as law-worthy freemen, whatever their cultural associations; cf. Ganshof 1968:76; Werner 1980:213.
18. For charters see Davies 1982:277-8. The pre-ninth-century Breton legal compilation known as 'Excerpta de libris Romanorum et Francorum' suggests remedies for those not qualified to testify on their own behalf, cc. A4, 28, 43 etc. (Bieler 1963); see further below n.29 and Fleuriot 1971:626f. Legislation from seventh-century Spain banned murderers, thieves, perjurors and other evil-doers from giving testimony (*Leges Visigothorum* II.iv.l) and late ninth-century charters from northern Spain continued to refer to the requirement; cf. a Cuxa charter of 874 where the judge directed witnesses *absque ullo crimine* to be produced (Marca 1688:796-7). Charlemagne also proclaimed measures providing for the examination of witnesses before testimony was given and prohibition of any found dishonest or without local knowledge, e.g. 'Capitulare missorum' of Thionville, 805, c.11 (*MGH Legum* II.i:124).
19. All formal cases of which we have evidence were heard at different locations in the ninth century. Since there was no overlap in personnel between Ruffiac, Guer, Maure (Anast) and Renac within the same decade, nor Ruffiac, and Sixt in another decade, it appears that a different panel operated for each *plebs*. (These places are within 15-17 km of each other.) Though the locations for meetings vary, the same individuals appeared in formal capacity in Langon and Renac (and they owned property in Cournon and Ambon — the latter some distance away). This area, which is close to Redon, appears to have had a panel acting for several *plebes*; it is notable that these are the *plebes* given to Redon by the Emperor Louis and it therefore seems possible that these men operated with reference to the seigneurial jurisdiction of Redon. See further Davies in Davies and Fouracre 1986.
20. Oath-helping was one of the standard modes of proof in early medieval European court procedures. In most circumstances the oath-helpers were gathered by the accused and swore to his good reputation, reliability and honesty, and not to any particular points of

fact. See 'Formulae Salicae Lindenbrogianae' (*c.* 800) c.21, 'Capitulare legi Ribuariae additum' (803) c.4, 'Capitulare Karoli Magni de latronibus' (804) c.3, Ganshof 1968:86-7; for oath-helping in non-European contexts see Gellner 1969:104-25. These Breton cases appear to be variants of the usual practice since the records state that the oath-helpers were required to swear to fact rather than reputation; they therefore functioned more like partial sworn witnesses.

21. Fleuriot 1971:650-1; I have discussed the question of suretyship in a forthcoming paper (Davies 1985).
22. *CR* lxi, cxxiv, cxxix, cxxxix, clxxx, cxcii, cclxxi; xxix, cxlvii, cv, cxxiv, lxi.
23. This is only certain when the *missus principis* appeared; machtierns were used by the ruler at times but it is not clear that they were his appointees; in my view they were persons of independent authority and the procedures they regulated were of local, non-state, pre-ninth-century origin. See Fleuriot 1971:622-3; Davies 1981.
24. The position of the machtiern is controversial; see above n.23. Salomon appears to have been especially successful in establishing contact with, and control over, machtierns; witness his success in disciplining them, cited frequently in this paper. The presence of the ruler's representative *and* machtierns in the chair in some cases may provide us with an opportunity to see the visible coalescence of two systems — the Frankish, under the count or his envoy, and the Breton, under the machtiern.
25. Cf. *CR* xlvii, ? lxi, cxxvii. All suggest victory against the abbot.
26. See above, p. 299.
27. The question of forged documents is only of limited significance since the value of documentation was itself limited; not only were documents cited in a small proportion of cases but when they *were* cited oral evidence was also taken. It is in fact possible that the record of the grant in *CR* cxlviii was emended by Redon, in its own interest.
28. See *CR* cvii, clxiii for compensation for killing and ccxxxvi for *enepuuert*, 'morning gift'.
29. Published in two versions in Bieler 1963:136-59 — where it is misleadingly headed 'Canones Wallici'; it has been plausibly but inconclusively argued by Professor Fleuriot that it belongs to the sixth century (Fleuriot 1971); Thomas Charles-Edwards argued very persuasively at a conference in Oxford in January 1981 that it was a handy digest of answers for common problems, compiled from extant sources.
30. For Irish law see Binchy 1978 and his many papers on particular aspects, of which Binchy 1943 remains a good introduction to the nature of early Irish law. The Welsh texts in Owen 1841 are gradually being replaced by modern editions: Wiliam 1960, Williams and Powell 1942, and Wade-Evans 1909; there is useful introductory material on the nature of Welsh law in *WHR* 1963, Owen 1976, and Jenkins 1981.
31. *Chronicle of Fredegar* c.78.
32. The southern Welsh law books instance the use of non-professional judges, however, and I have argued for the importance of 'self-regulating communities', without professionals and without state machinery, in eighth- and ninth-century south-east Wales (Davies 1978a, 1978b).
33. Cf. the comments of Nelson 1977:64-5, but n.b. those of Werner 1980:224 on the requirement that Carolingian *comites* and *missi* should know the law when administering their regions.

Abbreviations

CR   *Cartulaire de Redon*, ed. A. de Courson, Paris, 1863.
MGH   *Monumenta Germaniae Historica*
WHR   *Welsh History Review*, special volume.

Bibliography

Annales de Saint-Bertin, ed. F. Grat, J. Vielliard and S. Clémencet (1964) Paris: Klincksieck.
Armes Prydein, ed. I. Williams, trans. R. Bromwich (1972) Dublin: Institute for Advanced Studies.
Bieler, L., ed. (1963) *The Irish Penitentials*, pp. 136-59, Dublin: Institute for Advanced Studies.
Binchy, D.A. (1943) "The linguistic and historical value of the Irish law tracts" *Proceedings of the British Academy* 29:195-227.
Binchy, D.A., ed. (1978) *Corpus Iuris Hibernici*, six vols., Dublin: Institute for Advanced Studies.
Braunfels, W., ed. (1965-8) *Karl der Grosse. Lebenswerk und Nachleben*, five vols., Düsseldorf: Schwann.
'Capitulare de Villis' see *MGH Legum* Sectio II, pp. 82-91.
'Capitulare Karoli Magni de latronibus' see *MGH Legum* Sectio II, pp. 180-1.
'Capitulare legi Ribuariae additum' see *MGH Legum* Sectio II, pp. 117-18.
Castagnetti, A. (1979) *L'Organizzazione del Territorio Rurale nel Medioevo*, Turin: Giappichelli.
Charles-Edwards, T.M., a.o., eds. (1985) *Mach ac Ynad. Law and its enforcement in the Middle Ages*, Cardiff: University of Wales.
Chronicle of Fredegar (1960) *The Fourth book of the Chronicle of Fredegar*, ed. and trans. J.M. Wallace-Hadrill, London: Nelson.
Davies, W. (1978a) *An Early Welsh Microcosm*, London: Royal Historical Society.
Davies, W. (1978b) "Land and Power in early medieval Wales" *Past and Present* 81:3-23.
Davies, W. (1981) "On the distribution of political power in Brittany in the mid-ninth century" in *Charles the Bald: Court and Kingdom*, ed. M. Gibson and J. Nelson, British Archaeological Reports, International Series, CI, pp. 87-107.
Davies, W. (1982) "The Latin charter-tradition in western Britain, Brittany and Ireland" in *Ireland in Early Mediaeval Europe*, ed. D. Whitelock, R. McKitterick, D. Dumville, Cambridge: University Press, pp. 258-80.
Davies, W. (1983) "The role of the priest in the local community in east Brittany in the ninth century" *Études Celtiques* 20:177-96.
Davies, W. (1985) "Suretyship in the *Cartulaire de Redon*" in T.M. Charles-Edwards, D. Walters, M.E. Owen, eds., 1985.
Davies, W., and Fouracre, P., eds (1986), *Dispute Settlement in Early Mediaeval Europe*, Cambridge: University Press.
de Corson, G. (1880-6) *Pouillé Historique de l'archevêché de Rennes*, six vols., Paris: Fougeray.
'De Gestis Sanctorum Rotonensium' (1738) in L. d'Achery, *Acta Sanctorum Ordinis S. Benedicti*, ed. J. Mabillon, saec. IV pt. 2, pp. 202-31, Venice: Colet and Bottinelli.
Durtelle de Saint-Sauveur, E. (1935) *Histoire de Bretagne des origines à nos jours*, two vols., Rennes: Plihon.
Fichtenau, H. (1957) *The Carolingian Empire* (trans. P. Munz from *Das Karolingische Imperium*, Zürich, 1949), Oxford: Clarendon Press.
Flatrès, P. (1971) "Les anciennes structures rurales de Bretagne d'après le Cartulaire de Redon" *Études Rurales* 41: 87-93.
Fleuriot, L. (1971) "Un fragment en Latin de très anciennes lois bretonnes armoricaines du vi[e] siècle" *Annales de Bretagne* 78:601-60.
'Formulae Salicae Lindenbrogianae' see *MGH Legum* Sectio V, pp. 265-84.
Ganshof, F.-L. (1968) *Frankish Institutions under Charlemagne*, trans. B. and M. Lyon, Providence: Brown University Press.
Ganshof, F.-L. (1975) *Le Polyptyque de l'Abbaye de Saint-Bertin (844-859)* Paris: Klincksieck.
Gellner, E. (1969) *Saints of the Atlas*, London: Weidenfeld.
Guillotel, H. (1975-6) "L'action de Charles le Chauve vis-à-vis de la Bretagne de 843 à 851" *Mémoires de la Société d' Histoire et d'Archéologie de Bretagne* 53:5-32.
Halphen, L. (1947) *Charlemagne et l'Empire Carolingien*, Paris: Michel.
James, E. (1982) *The Origins of France*, London: Macmillan.
Jausions, Abbé (1864) *Histoire de la Ville et de l'Abbaye de Redon*, Redon: Thourel.
Jenkins, D. (1981) "The medieval Welsh idea of law" *Legal History Review*, 49:323-48.
Jones, G.R.J. (1972) "Post-Roman Wales" in *The Agrarian History of England and Wales* I pt. 2,

ed. H.P.R. Finberg, Cambridge: University Press, pp. 281-382.
La Borderie, A. Le Moyne de (1898) *Histoire de Bretagne* II, Rennes: Plihon and Hervé.
Leges Visigothorum, ed. K. Zeumer (*MGH Legum* Sectio I.1), Hanover, 1902.
Lot, F. and Halphen, L. (1909) *Le Règne de Charles le Chauve*, Paris: Champion.
Marca, P. de (1688) *Marca Hispanica sive Limes Hispanicus*, Paris: F. Muguet.
MGH Epistolarum VI, *Epistolae Karolini Aevi* IV, ed. E. Dümmler, E. Perels *et al.*, Berlin, 1925.
MGH Legum Sectio I, see *Leges Visigothorum*.
MGH Legum Sectio II, *Capitularia Regum Francorum* I, ed. A. Boretius, Hanover, 1883.
MGH Legum Sectio V, *Formulae Merowingici et Karolini Aevi*, ed. K. Zeumer, Hanover, 1886.
Morice, H. (1742-6) *Mémoires pour servir de preuves à l'histoire ecclésiastique et civile de Bretagne*, three vols., Paris: C. Osmont.
Nelson, J. (1977) "On the limits of the Carolingian renaissance" *Studies in Church History*, XIV, ed. D. Baker, pp. 51-69.
Owen, A., ed. (1841) *Ancient Laws and Institutes of Wales*, London: Record Commission.
Owen, M.E. (1976) "Functional Prose" in *A Guide to Welsh Literature*, I, ed. A.O.H. Jarman and G.R. Hughes, Swansea: Christopher Davies, pp. 248-76.
Planiol, M. (1981) *Histoire des Institutions de la Bretagne*, three vols., Mayenne: Association pour la publication du manuscrit de M. Planiol.
Sheringham, J.G.T. (1981) "Les machtierns" *Mémoires de la Société d'Histoire et d'Archéologie de Bretagne* 58:61-72.
Tonnerre, N-Y. (1978) "Le diocèse de Vannes au IXe siècle d'après le cartulaire de Redon", Thèse de troisième cycle, University of Paris X.
Wade-Evans, A.W. (1909) *Welsh Medieval Law*, Oxford: Clarendon Press.
Werner, K.F. (1980) "*Missus-Marchio-Comes*" in *Francia*, Beiheft IX (Histoire Comparée de l'Administration IV-XVIII siècles), Munich, pp. 191-239.
Wiliam, A.R., ed. (1960), *Lbyfr Iorwerth*, Cardiff: University of Wales.
Williams, S.J. and Powell, J.E., eds. (1942) *Cyfreithiau Hywel Dda yn ôl Llyfr Blegywryd*, Cardiff: University of Wales.

VII

People and places in dispute in ninth-century Brittany

The records of dispute and dispute settlement from northern Europe, although few by comparison with those of the South, include an unusually large set of useful material in the collection of charters relating to the monastery of Redon in eastern Brittany. Redon, on the River Vilaine, 65 km south-west of Rennes, was founded in 832 and soon gained the patronage of the Carolingian emperor Louis and of his representative in Brittany, Nominoe. It received many small grants of property in its neighbourhood in the decades following the foundation, and records of the grants, along with other documents, were copied in the eleventh century into the *Cartulaire de Redon*[1].

This cartulary contains 283 charters of the ninth and early tenth centuries; and a further sixty-two charters, which may not have been included in the medieval cartulary, are known from early modern transcripts[2]. Three-quarters of these charters relate to the forty years following the monastery's foundation and constitute – for the ninth century – an unusually large number of documents to deal with a small region[3]. The lands with which the charters are concerned lie between Rennes, Nantes and Vannes, but most of the properties fall within 40 km of Redon itself (fig. 2). Many of the grants were of small areas (in the order of

---

[1] I have discussed several aspects of the dispute material in 'Disputes, their conduct and their settlement', *Hist. and Anth.*, 1, pt 2 (1985) and 'Suretyship in the *Cartulaire de Redon*' in T. Charles-Edwards, M. E. Owen, D. Walters (eds.), *Lawyers and Laymen*. In this present paper I summarize those discussions and only deal in detail with other aspects. The material in the latter part of the paper depends on analysis of the results of programs run on my Redon database, filed on the mainframe computers at University College London. I am indebted to the British Academy for financial support in setting up the database and to the staff of UCL Computer Centre, and in particular to Chris Horsburgh, for considerable assistance in creating the database and for writing the appropriate programs. I am also grateful to Rosamond McKitterick for her comments on a draft of this paper.
[2] *Cartulaire de Redon*, ed. A. de Courson (hereafter *CR*, with charters cited by number); most of the additional charters are printed by de Courson in an Appendix to *CR* and the rest can be found in H. Morice, *Mémoires pour servir de preuves*, vol. 1, cols. 265, 271f, 272, 295, 297, 308; the transcripts from which they were printed can sometimes be identified but many are difficult to locate.
[3] The density of coverage only seems to be paralleled by east Frankish collections such as those of St Gallen; *Urkundenbuch der Abtei Sanct Gallen*, ed. H. Wartmann, vols. 1 and 2. See further Nelson above, pp. 45–6, for comment on other Frankish material of the same period.

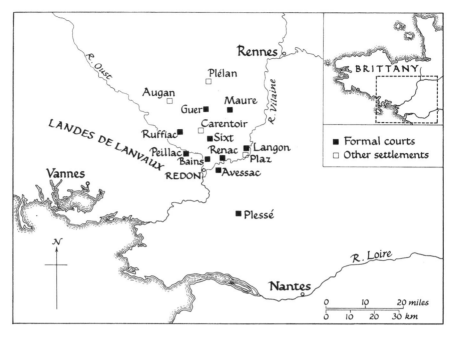

2 Formal and informal courts in the *pays de Redon*

10–25 hectares), and the donors, vendors and plaintiffs of the records were peasant farmers: most of the individuals mentioned worked the land themselves and confined their business to their own village communities[4]. The collection, then, is largely a collection of private, rather than government, acts and is particularly valuable in allowing insight into the workings and relationships of peasant communities[5]. It is also valuable in the range of its material: since many properties passed to Redon together with extant documentation about them, the collection includes records from at least one generation previous to 832 and records of transactions to which Redon was not party, both before 832 and after[6]. It therefore preserves far more than a dossier of grants to the monastery.

The area which is most frequently the subject of the charters was well worked in the early middle ages, largely for arable production, and had many settlements. Agrarian society was organized in village-based units, known as *plebes* in Latin

[4] For detailed discussion see my forthcoming book, *Villages, Villagers*.
[5] See below, pp. 78–82, for discussion of the means and social status of the men of these records.
[6] This is not unknown in other charter collections of the same period, although the proportion in *CR* is notable; cf. *Cartulaire de Beaulieu*, ed. M. Deloche, which includes six charters previous to Beaulieu's foundation date of 855; the material in the several Cluny collections includes several score of records from the generation before the foundation, that is, from the 870s onwards, *Recueil des chartes de l'abbaye de Cluny*, ed. A. Bruel, vol. 1. See also above, p. 54.

Dispute in ninth-century Brittany

and as some similar-sounding term in the vernacular (hence Medieval Breton *plou*, a loanword from Latin *plebem*). Men referred to themselves as members of this or that *plebs* and transactions might be formally notified to the men of the *plebs*, although by the ninth century the term was used to refer to the land inhabited by the group as well as to the group itself. The territories of the *plebes* were quite small, ranging from 3 to 10 km across (but were often about 5 km): on the accompanying figure, Ruffiac and Carentoir are neighbouring *plebes*, as are Langon and Renac, Augan and Guer (fig. 2)[7]. Each *plebs* appears to have had its own officer for public business, called a machtiern. This man presided over transactions involving the transfer of property rights, which were performed in public; he might also be approached to find a solution for village problems, and accordingly might order an investigation or preside over any consequent hearing[8]. He was usually the most powerful character in the locality and in practice might serve several *plebes* and have relations who served neighbouring communities. Characteristically he lived at a distinctive type of settlement, away from the nucleated focus of the *plebs*, known as the *lis*.

Although the material in the Redon cartulary is exceptionally useful as evidence of social process at village level, it also allows some glimpses into a wider world. There was an aristocracy, of counts and major landowners, although there were few large-scale property interests in these particular *plebes* until the extension of those of Redon itself. There was also a Breton ruler (the *princeps*), at least from *c.* 830, when the emperor Louis appointed the Breton Nominoe as his representative for government, following a series of Carolingian expeditions across the country. Thereafter, the whole of modern Brittany, and sometimes some of the lands to the east of it, seems to have been ruled as a single polity, although rule was sometimes shared by two leaders. The relationship of these rulers with the Carolingians was unstable, for Nominoe rebelled in the early 840s; afterwards some of the rulers – notably Salomon (*princeps* 857–73) in the 860s and early 870s – were effectively independent[9]. Since the *princeps* favoured Redon with their patronage and especial protection, their presence was sometimes felt in the village communities considered here.

There are forty-nine ninth-century texts in the Redon collection which record dispute settlement processes, although six make only indirect reference to

---

[7] For further discussion of the *plebs* see my 'Priests and rural communities', *Études Celtiques*, 20 (1983), 177–80.
[8] See further below, pp. 72–3; for machtierns see also my 'On the distribution of political power' in M. Gibson, J. Nelson, D. Ganz (eds.), *Charles the Bald*, and M. Planiol, *Histoire des Institutions*, vol. 2, pp. 63–96.
[9] The relevant sources for the political history of this period are cited by A. Le Moyne de La Borderie, *Histoire de Bretagne*, vol. 2, pp. 3–122; interpretations differ nowadays. For more recent consideration see A. Chédeville and H. Guillotel, *La Bretagne des saints et des rois, V^e–Xe siècle*, pp. 201–332.

them[10]. These average five per decade between 832 and c. 880 but there are at least eleven from the 860s and a further eight, which cannot be dated more precisely than to the abbacy of Conuuoion (832–68), are probably also from the 860s. There are also four from the generation before the foundation of Redon and four that occurred after c. 880. The records do not conform to a standard pattern: some briefly indicate the essential details of a judgement; others have a narrative of the events leading up to a case, or of a settlement, or of proceedings in court, the latter sometimes including what look like verbatim reports; others are too cryptic to make much sense. Despite the variety of recording practice, it seems to have been usual to record court proceedings. Although there is only occasional mention of a notary, many of the Ruffiac and Carentoir records – of transactions as well as of disputes – conclude with a statement of the writer's identity and make it clear that the task of making a written record *was* someone's responsibility. Haeldetuuid, for example, cleric then abbot, recorded at least eighteen transactions of sale and pledge in Ruffiac and Carentoir (and also one in Pleucadeuc) between 821 and c. 850, and he was preceded as recorder by the cleric Latmoet[11].

Twenty-three individuals are named as scribes in the complete corpus of ninth-century records and this has some bearing on the recording of disputes[12]. Of the twenty-three scribes, three seem to have been working for Redon, since they either were termed monks or produced records for a wide range of locations in which Redon had interests[13]. The rest of the scribes are notable for their limited range: there were some at major centres like Angers and Nantes but the others only appeared in one of the *plebes* of, for example, Laillé, Grandchamp or Derval in the more Frankish East or at Médréac, Augan or Peillac in the more Breton West (see fig. 3). Records were made at seven of these places, and at another unidentified place, *before* 832 (by nine of the scribes) and therefore *cannot*

[10] Princely courts: *CR* 21, 29, 105, 107, 108, 215, 216, 242, 247, possibly 258, 274, A40, A53. Formal, local courts: 46, 47, 61, 96, 106, 124, 129, 139, 147, 162, 180, 191, 192, 271, A3, A20. Informal, local meetings: 32, 56, 88, 103, 118, 127, 144, 163, 184, 185, 190, 195, 202, 205, possibly 236, 237, 246, 261, possibly 265, 267. R. Hübner, 'Gerichtsurkunden', *ZRG, Germ. Abt.*, 12 (1891), omitted the twenty records of settlement in which no judgement was given.

[11] Haeldetuuid is named as scribe in *CR* 34, 53, 58, 64, 111, 112, 121, 131, 133, 143, 146, 148, 152, 153, 155, 160, 171, 193, 196, 198, 220, 255, 264, A11. Transactions of pledge were those in which a loan of cash was raised using landed property as security; see my 'Suretyship'.

[12] The scribes are Agnus, Benignus, Bernarius, Condeloc, Conuuoion, Cumdelu, Daramnus, Frodebert, Fulcric, Gallianus, Gundobald, Hilric, Landebert, Lathoiarn, Letaldus, Liberius, Mailon, Otbert, Ratuuethen, Siguinus, Tethion, Tuthouuen. The usual way of referring to a scribe is 'N scripsit'. Notaries are named in *CR* A6, A28, apparently attached to the Carolingian court.

[13] Fulcric (*CR* 69, 234); Liberius (213, 260); Conuuoion (128, 177, 179, A1, A4). In the case of Haeldetuuid it might be argued that he ended his life working for Redon: although his association with Ruffiac and Carentoir was consistent for about twenty-five years, from the middle of the 840s he also made records for the Bains and Renac area; *CR* 53, 121, A11 (although 58, dated to 838, seems to refer to Brain; if so, it is anomalous). We do know of several local priests who retired to Redon in old age, so the pattern is quite credible.

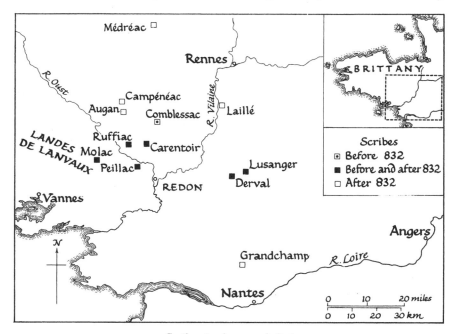

3 Scribes in the *pays de Redon*

have been made using services provided by Redon. Hence, scribal facilities were available at an early date in at least Molac, Ruffiac and Carentoir (both served by one scribe), Comblessac, Peillac, Derval and Lusanger. Not surprisingly, at least four of the early scribes – like Haeldetuuid and Latmoet – were in orders, termed priest or cleric: acting as scribe for local business may have been a normal part of the priests' duties in the *plebs*, although the records were sometimes made at the machtiern's residence, the *lis*, which occasionally seems to have functioned as an office for the performance of local business[14]. Now, more than half of the records that name scribes deal with sales, and these records have a consistency in form and *formulae* which is notably absent from the dispute records. In effect there seems to have been provision of secretarial services for the transfer of property rights in these villages, perhaps the consequence of a need to record sales correctly[15]. So, there were skilled people in the villages, who could write

[14] *CR* 34, 112, 152, 255; cf. R. McKitterick, *The Carolingians and the written word*, ch. 4.
[15] A concern that the correct legal procedure should be followed in cases of sale is indicated at least by the unprovenanced 'Excerpta de libris Romanorum et Francorum', cl. A18–20, in *The Irish Penitentials*, ed. L. Bieler, p. 140; see further my 'Suretyship', pp. 85–6. (This text may be Breton but if not it is likely to derive from Anjou or Maine; it may be of sixth-, seventh- or eighth-century date.) See L. Fleuriot, 'Un fragment en Latin de très anciennes lois bretonnes', *Ann. de Bret.*, 78 (1971) and D. Dumville, 'On the dating of the early Breton lawcodes', *Ét. Celt.*, 21 (1984).

according to a 'proper' form when necessary. They were therefore available to record dispute settlements, both before and after the foundation of Redon, although a standard format was apparently not considered necessary for this type of record.

One element is common, however, to records of every type in the Redon collection, including those which are explicitly about dispute settlement: the witnesses of public proceedings are listed very fully. This was presumably a major reason for *making* the records, for in the event of subsequent dispute, or of the revival of an old one, the witnesses could be located and questioned about the transaction[16]. In some of our recorded ninth-century disputes former witnesses were traced in this way, as in the case of Uuetenoc cited below: his rights to a property he had purchased were questioned but were confirmed on the production of witnesses and other evidence (*CR* 139). In another case of the 860s, when the donor of a property cast doubts on the quality of the donee's ownership, the latter, a priest called Maenuueten, gathered together the witnesses of the transaction in which he had received the grant; this was sufficient to provoke a compromise and prevent a court case (*CR* 144).

The occasions of dispute which are recorded in this collection largely concern property rights, as might be expected, given that the copy was made by a major landlord with substantial interests in many of the properties. Appropriation of land or income from the monastery of Redon is the commonest cause of dispute. Accusations were made by the abbot (or occasionally by his deputies) against men who continued to work and profit from properties given to Redon by their kinsmen; against others who encroached on the monastery's land, often when it was sharing a boundary with their own; against tenants who had defaulted on the payment of rent; and occasionally against men who went to monastic property, stole stock and attacked the farmers who lived there. These account for about half of the cases. Nearly as common, however, are records of disputes within lay families, especially disputes about the allocation of property rights between members of the family and about powers to alienate individual shares. Hence, brothers quarrelled with brothers, and cousins with cousins. In addition to these types of case there are records of lay quarrels in which there seems to have been neither strong family nor monastic interest; and, rarely, there are accounts of the procedures that followed assault and killing[17].

The means of arriving at a settlement in these disputes varied in accordance

---

[16] See my 'Latin charter tradition' in D. Whitelock, R. McKitterick, D. Dumville (eds.), *Ireland in Early Mediaeval Europe*, pp. 275f, for the importance of witnesses to registration of property transfer in late Roman Europe.

[17] See my 'Disputes' for full discussion of the subject of this paragraph and for what follows in the succeeding few pages. Cf. 'Gesta Sanctorum Rotonensium', I. viii, in L. d'Achéry, *Acta Sanctorum ord. s. Benedicti*, ed. J. Mabillon, for a comparable ninth-century Redon case recorded in a Saints' Life: Abbot Conuuoion offered Risuueten 20 *solidi* to withdraw a claim on hereditary lands.

Dispute in ninth-century Brittany

with the status of the parties. In normal circumstances, when a dispute arose, requests to solve the problem might be made to political leaders – notably to the *princeps* but also to machtierns, counts and, very occasionally, village elders. But there were also other methods of initiating settlement proceedings: sometimes a grievance appears to have had its first airing in court, recorded in such terms as 'N came to court and there accused NN'; at other times demands were made privately of the offender by the injured party, with the knowledge of friends and neighbours. In fact, it seems highly likely that the latter procedure was normal: presumably most cases first recorded in court had already been through some such process.

In practice, many disputes seem to have been settled before they reached litigation, and settled locally, without recourse to political leaders. For example, the following case, which took place on 29 January 852, in Augan, was not taken to court since the abbot of Redon, who was here the subject of an accusation by a layman, sent some monks to test local feeling on the matter as a preliminary to reaching an agreement.

Notice of the way that Fomus came to accuse the monks of the Holy Saviour of Redon about the Arbiuan Inheritance (*hereditas*[18]), for he said that it was his. Abbot Conuuoion consulted with the brothers about this and they advised him to send three of the most learned brothers to the land to meet the respected men who lived in the *plebs* and ask them whether the complaint were true or not. Leumelus, priest and monk, Uuinkalunus, priest and monk, and Rituuere, monk, went off to the land, on Wednesday the feast of St John. The gave him (Fomus) a third of the Dignum Inheritance; and he gave them sureties (*fideiussores* and *dilisidos*), Iarnhobrit and Dumuuoret, so that he would not complain further over the Dignum Inheritance nor the Arbiuan Inheritance, nor [would] his son, nor his son's son, for ever as long as the world lasted. He promised to give them, from the third part [i.e. from Dignum], a half measure of wheat and 18 pence every year. This was done in the *plebs* of Augan, at Coluuoretan, before many respected men. Their names are Reinbert (priest), Haelhoiarn (priest), Catuueten, Cenetlor (priest), Arthanael, Uuoletec, Rethuualt, Alunoc (cleric), Iarnican, Uuorbili, Maenuuallon, Pascuuoret, Seferia. It was done ... in the twelfth year of the reign of King Charles, with Erispoe [*princeps*] governing Brittany (*CR* 127). (App. XI)

Since Fomus was given tenancy of a third of a property which was not the subject of recorded dispute, and since he appears to have remained in control of the disputed property, although as tenant, it looks as if the abbot and his advisers did a deal; by this Fomus kept the use, but not the ownership, of the Arbiuan Inheritance but his acquiescence and silence were bought by allowing him use of a further property, a third of the Dignum Inheritance. Full reconstruction of the episode is impossible, since there is no further documentation. Even in this out-of-court settlement witnesses were noted – local Augan priests and peasants – implying some local informal meeting. Fomus himself was clearly a well-off

---

[18] *Hereditas* refers to land, and to family rather than acquired land; in practice I think the *hereditas* was often managed as a unit.

peasant and appeared in Augan as ordinary witness; in 867 he pledged another property in Augan for 24 *solidi* (*CR* 68).

The drive to settle amicably was a forceful one and even in formal court proceedings a compromise solution was often reached[19]. It was in most people's interest to establish and preserve harmony, especially in relationships within the *plebs*. It is only at a higher – supra-*plebs* – social level that there are suggestions of resistance to compromise: the abbot was often persistent in his attempts to preserve and extend Redon's rights, especially against local machtierns, and could make repeated visits to the *princeps* to do so; at the other end of the social scale, peasant farmers sometimes refused to accept the extension into their communities of seigneurial interests from outside.

What happened when there was no immediate settlement? When a request for intervention was made to the *princeps*, he referred the case to a local court, or he sent representatives to the locality to gather information, or he commanded the accused to appear at his own court and answer the accusation. It was usually peasant problems that were referred back to their local community machinery (*CR* 106, 261), while the *princeps* showed an interest himself in cases involving machtierns and major landlords. Aristocrats might well be given time to gather evidence, as in the case quoted below, and local knowledge might be used to arrive at a solution. In the end, however, it was the *princeps* himself who made the judgement and ordered what consequences should ensue. This was very different from the procedure followed in local courts[20].

The following record is representative of the aristocratic process. In it the abbot of Redon complained to Salomon about a machtiern called Ratfred and his attacks on monastic property in Bains and Sixt. It was heard soon after 857.

Notice that Salomon, *princeps* of Brittany, asked Ratfred why he had broken his protection of Abbot Conuuoion and the monks of the Holy Saviour during the disturbances that followed the death of Erispoe. Ratfred and his brothers had gone to the monastery of Redon, saying that they were heirs of Bains and that, unless the abbot and his monks returned their inheritance, they would burn the entire abbey and loot it. Then the abbot and monks, unwilling but driven by necessity, gave them what they sought, that is, eight parcels of land (*partes*) in Bains and four and a half in Sixt. Even this was not enough for they required the monks to give them four sureties for the gift; forced by this, the monks did so, lest the whole *plebs* be burned. Afterwards Salomon acquired control of the whole of Brittany and heard about it, and he was very annoyed. He ordered Ratfred to come to him and asked him why he held monastic property by force and tyranny. He replied that he did not hold anything by force, for Abbot Conuuoion and his monks had given the

---

[19] *CR* 47, 96, for example. Compare the comments of S. Weinberger, 'Cours judiciaires, justice et résponsabilité sociale', *Rev. Hist.*, 267 (1982), 282–6, on compromise in Provençal courts of the tenth and eleventh centuries (although he is somewhat quick to link this with a decline in 'state' power).

[20] Most of the aristocratic cases involve machtierns, although the case of Pricient appears to have been about a wealthy man, with large and wide-spread property interests, who held no office (*CR* 242).

Dispute in ninth-century Brittany 73

property freely, willingly and peacefully. Salomon, angered, then asked Conuuoion and the monks why they had given the religious property (*monachia sempiterna*[21]) of the Holy Saviour to tyrants (*tirannis*[22]) . . . [The abbot objected but] Salomon took over the disputed property and said to Ratfred, 'Now I have in my hands what you held of the property of Redon. Now lay your charge and show that it is your inheritance, according to law, truth and right, and I will show that "proof" to the monks and return it to you.' Ratfred replied that he could not produce proof because he did not have any law-worthy local men (*pagenses*) there. So Salomon said, 'I give you ten days to gather your proof and your witnesses in the court of Penard.' Then Ratfred confessed that he had neither witnesses nor proof to show that he had an inheritance in Bains. Then Salomon said, 'If you cannot prove that it is your inheritance, promise and give security, for yourself and all your family, that neither you nor your family will seek an inheritance in Bains.' [He did so.] Then Salomon returned the property to Abbot Conuuoion and the Holy Saviour in eternal alms, for his own soul and that of Nominoe his fosterfather. It was done in the court of Colroit, before many noble men, whose names are Salomon, Bran, Boduan [and thirteen further names] (*CR* 105). (App. XII)

This was a very explicitly aristocratic occasion, the witnesses at Salomon's court including several counts, with Salomon using his power as ruler to control the machtiern and allocate (perhaps re-allocate) the property. Ratfred was presumably the man called Ratfred who was machtiern of Sixt, who appeared often in the *plebes* near Redon as ordinary witness and who acted as surety in the very special case of the arrangement following an assault made by one Anau. He was frequently at Salomon's court in the 860s and 870s. He is probably to be identified with Ratfred brother of Ratuili (*CR* 221) and this would make him the brother of the machtiern of Bains. His interest in these properties is therefore understandable and he might have regarded them as his by right. In the above record Ratfred did not merely seize the property but he asked for, and received, sureties from the abbot; this was unusual procedure for a grant, although it was common in transactions of pledge, sale and exchange, and it suggests that Ratfred may have been more concerned to observe the proper forms of behaviour than the record at first indicates. The outcome is common for cases of this type – restoration of the disputed property to the 'rightful' owner and provision of guarantees; very occasionally, however, the *princeps* went further by making a personal visit to the area in question or by imposing a monetary sanction.

The outcome of requests to *local* leaders was invariably an investigation and usually a court case, although disputes in the *plebes* were sometimes settled outside local courts, at informal assemblies, as in the Fomus case above. Disputes were settled on all days of the week and in all months of the year but there are no records of formal hearings on Sundays nor in January, March, April, October and November; most, in fact, were heard early in the week. Dispute hearings took

---

[21] Literally 'eternal monastic property'; the phrase is common in the Redon material and has echoes in the Celtic charter tradition; see my 'Latin charter tradition', pp. 276f.
[22] And also 'to machtierns' (sometimes Latinized as *tiarnus, tirannus*); a double-entendre is probably intentional – a play on the word is explicit in *CR* 247.

place at more than half of all known ninth-century *plebes* in this area and formal local proceedings were held in at least ten different *plebes* in the region near Redon. Informal settlements occurred in the same *plebes* and in other *plebes* too (see fig. 2). This is so high a proportion that it suggests that every *plebs* had its own meetings, meetings which might easily be constituted as courts. Most of the witnesses, as well as the major participants, were local to the *plebs*. In some cases, however, a couple of *plebes* may have been grouped together: it looks as if Caro business was done in Guer and Pleucadeuc business was done in Ruffiac. Within the *plebs*, courts might be held at a range of locations – in church, or on the land in question, or even at a machtiern's *lis*; and we know of at least three different court locations used in the single *plebs* of Langon[23].

There are some standard elements of procedure in local courts. Most parties seem to have spoken for themselves for advocates are only mentioned for two aristocratic cases[24]. Presidents are named for a high proportion of court cases although their status and 'office' varied. They acted singly and also in groups; they were usually drawn from local machtierns or from representatives of the *princeps* (*missi principis*) and sometimes from a combination of the two. However, one elder of the local community seems to have been used in Avessac in 836 or 842 (*CR* 61). In one very early case (*c.* 801) the presidents were *missi comitis*, presumably representatives of the Carolingian count; and in another, very late, case (892) the abbot of Redon was president, presumably as *seigneur* of the *plebs* of Bains, where the case was heard. Very occasionally the *princeps* himself appeared in the *plebs* and presided[25]. Local panels of judges, sometimes referred to by the characteristic Carolingian term *scabini* but at others by more general terms like *boni viri*, are also mentioned in at least half of the recorded court cases. It is implied that their presence was standard in formal procedure, although the number of them certainly varied between three and twelve (and on one occasion it may have been fourteen).

In local courts right could be established in a number of different ways. Most commonly 'evidence' was produced, although even this was done by various means; duel and ordeal did not feature. When they had heard an accusation, the judges sometimes asked local men, often on oath, to provide information about the past history of the disputed property and associated persons; the charters include at least one record which appears to be a statement taken from a sworn witness[26]. The witnesses who provided this information were clearly supposed to be impartial: effectively the judges were conducting a small-scale local inquest. The judges might also direct that the case be resolved by the use of oath-helpers, although this is not frequently recorded. In a case at Langon in 801,

---

[23] Cf. F. Estey, 'The *scabini* and the local courts', *Speculum*, 26 (1951), 120.
[24] *CR* 107, 108. Both appeared at *Lisrannac* (one of Nominoe's centres) in the 840s and both cases involved settlement of problems of direct interest to Nominoe himself.
[25] *CR* 191, 271, 47.   [26] *CR* 205; cf. 185.

Dispute in ninth-century Brittany

Anau, accused of wrongly holding that *vicus* (village), had to establish his right by swearing to the truth of his position together with twelve 'suitable' men (*CR* 191); in another case, in Sixt, round about 850, the accused had to swear on an altar to the right of his possession, together with three others (*CR* 46).

At other times the judges heard evidence produced by one or both parties; this might take the form of documents detailing, witnesses to or guarantors of past transactions, or some combination of these. The following record from Ruffiac demonstrates the significance that 'evidence' could have; it took place on 17 June, in 860.

Notice of the way in which a man called Uuobrian accused another called Uuetenoc about an allod which Uuobrian had sold him a long time before. Uuobrian said that he had not sold him as much land as he was working. Thereupon, Uuetenoc raised a court case, gathering his supporters; these were called Fomus, Iacu, Rethuualart, Drehuuobri. When his charter had been read and his witnesses and sureties (*dilisidis*) had testified, it was revealed that all that he worked had been purchased from Uuobrian. Then Uuobrian, vanquished as much by the charter as by the witnesses and guarantors, confessed. This was done in Ruffiac church, on the fifteenth of the kalends of July, Monday, before Machtiern Iarnhitin and Hinuualart[27] and Litoc, the representative of *Princeps* Salomon, and before many noble men[28], whose names are Uuorcomet, Nominoe, Miot, Omnis, Tuduual, Hoiarn, Abbot Sulmin, Abbot Iuna, Comaltcar (priest), Adaluuin, and Eusorchit (cleric); Eusorchit then read the charter in public, to the effect that all had been sold to Uuetenoc just as he had said from his own charter (*CR* 139). (App. XIII)

This is a very ordinary local occasion of dispute settlement, and Uuobrian and his family were normal, active peasants. Uuobrian certainly made frequent appearances as an ordinary witness in Ruffiac and his brother, at least, was a donor of lands to Redon (*CR* 248). The witnesses on this occasion were peasants drawn from the *plebs* and not far beyond, the abbots being local abbots of minor monasteries. Within five years the victor, Uuetenoc, had given the property to Redon (*CR* 44), which presumably explains the preservation of the record. In fact, the record of the original sale (*CR* 138) reveals that Fomus and his colleagues had been sureties, in Ruffiac church, in 846. The oral evidence of the original sureties was crucial to the resolution of this case, although it is interesting that the settlement stresses the importance of the documentary record.

Documents could be important in providing proof but they were not automatically regarded as decisive: round about 840 a man called Uurbudic accused the abbot of Redon of being in wrongful possession of a weir on the River Vilaine and he made a point of the fact that the charter held by the abbot was false. His efforts to deny the force of documentary proof failed, but the matter was only finally settled by the verbal testimony (and local knowledge) of the men of

---

[27] A machtiern Hinuualart is noted in *CR* 248 and 265; this may be the same man, but he is not called machtiern in this record.

[28] 'Noble' here means 'men of standing, of proven worth', not 'aristocratic'; cf. K. Nehlsen-von Stryk, *Die boni homines des frühen Mittelalters*, pp. 251f.

Avessac and Bains on either side of the river (*CR* 195). In fact, documents were not always used when they existed: *CR* 92, recording a grant from Bains by a son of Uesilloc, substantiates the argument in the later case detailed in *CR* 271, recording the unsuccessful attempt of three sons of Uesilloc to claim that they were *not* heirs to that villa; it was not apparently cited in the hearing.

Since settlements were sometimes made in court, and one party sometimes conceded the case or confessed to dishonesty, a formal judgement was not an inevitable part of all proceedings. When it did happen, it was made by the local panel of judges, either with reference to the 'evidence' that had been brought forward or to the local knowledge of the *scabini* themselves. It was never made in these records with reference to stated legal nor customary principles, whether oral or written, and notably it was never made with reference to anything described as *lex*[29]. The only factor determining the judgement seems to have been knowledge of past events, transactions and relationships in the locality.

Out of court the informal procedure for settling disputes was very similar, with public assemblies in which trusted local men gave evidence on past transactions and relationships, although there were neither presidents nor judges at these occasions. The material which led to settlement was very much the same as in formal court cases and sometimes mediators – named as such – were used. The meetings were held in the same type of place as formal courts, although within or in front of churches were favoured meeting points, and sometimes the same terminology as that used for formal cases was used to describe the proceedings, presumably because they were recorded by the same individuals. Charter 144 is very like the Uuetenoc case of *CR* 139, quoted above, in its detail of production of witnesses and charters, but there was no formal court case, merely a publicly announced dispute, followed in turn by argument, pressure and settlement: the donor, Uuordoital, succeeded in extracting a payment from the donee, Maenuueten, in order that the latter might have the power to alienate the property as he wished: 'seeing that Maenuueten was gathering together his witnesses, guarantors and charter, and not wishing to lose his former friendship, Uuordoital sent to Maenuueten suggesting that he should give him 4 *solidi*, and he would then confirm the grant; Maenuueten did so'.

Since a high proportion of the cases detailed in this material are about rival claims to property rights, there is not much information about 'criminal' areas such as sentencing and punishment. It is therefore not at all clear if there is any evidence of 'criminal' jurisdiction and of the way it operated; indeed, it is not at all clear if such notions are appropriate to judicial practice in this society. As far as we can see, law *enforcement* was normally achieved by the use of sureties. When agreement on a disputed issue was reached, either by a judgement or by a settlement, it was common for sureties to be named, who had to be acceptable to

---

[29] However, going to court might be described as going *in lege*. This is in stark contrast with practice in ninth- and tenth-century northern Spain; see Collins below, pp. 85–6.

Dispute in ninth-century Brittany 77

both parties. These would either effectively guarantee that the victor would not suffer any financial loss – by paying themselves or by distraining on the guilty man's property – or they would effectively resign any personal claims on the property assigned to the victor. Members of the family of the loser might therefore be named as guarantors, but other, unrelated, supporters might line up behind him. Acting as surety was part of a local, small-scale pattern of alliance-making that is largely hidden from the records. Very occasionally the function of some sureties is specified in detail: in the case of a cleric, Anau, who had assaulted one of Redon's priests, a grant was made to Redon in compensation for the attack and three sureties were named for the property; another three were then named, to act with the first group, to restrain Anau from any future assaults. If they heard that he was likely to do further damage, they were to stop him and warn the abbot; if they failed to stop him, they were then to pursue him to death and give his worth to the abbot (*CR* 202). Here the sureties had a policing and punishing, as well as a distraining, function and punishment was administered by using the purely private machinery for guaranteeing obligations[30].

Apart from the sureties, evidence of enforcement and of punishment machinery is limited. In a case involving the machtiern Alfret and Redon, the *princeps* Salomon imposed a sanction of 5,000 *solidi* to be paid in the event of a contravention of the judgement (*CR* 247). This was exceptional, and a sum far larger than the stated value of any property. A sanction of double the value of the stated price was usually attached to records of sale, but there are no indications of *who* administered it nor of the destination of the sum. Anau himself, in the sureties cases quoted above, was at first condemned to lose his right hand for his assault but it is not absolutely clear if Redon sentenced him, exercising either public or seigneurial jurisdiction, or if someone else did. In the few recorded cases of killing and their consequences, compensatory land grants were made to the associates of the injured party: Nominoe was given land for the death of his injured vassal (*CR* 107); land and a serf were given to Redon in compensation for the killing of one of Redon's own serfs (*CR* 163); another serf was given to Redon in compensation for a range of depredations (including theft of cattle) (*CR* 32). All of these seem to have been arranged between the interested parties and were not the subject of judgements. The grants made to Nominoe as a substitute for

---

[30] See further my 'Suretyship'. Cf. the Irish *Cáin Adamnáin*, ed. K. Meyer, ch. 33, where the punishment for killing a woman was maiming (right hand and left foot) followed by death; after this the kindred were to pay compensation, rather than the appointed sureties, as here, where private agreement not family obligation is the enforcing machinery. The statement of a monk travelling in the late ninth century that Breton 'law' required anyone who had seen an injury done to take action against the injuror is puzzling; it would be difficult to work in practice. Perhaps the monk confused the onlooker with an agreed third party (that is, a surety); 'Itinerarium Bernardi', ch. 23, *Descriptiones terrae sanctae*, ed. T. Tobler. I owe this reference to Julia Smith, to whom I am very grateful.

payment of render are described as being done *pro fraude*; this could merely have been compensation for default in payment of the render but the transaction may conceal something more complex (*CR* 108)[31]. It is therefore clear that a notion of punishment and/or penalty was attached to certain sorts of offence, as well as compensation to the injured bodies; it is also clear that sometimes the penalty was administered by private machinery; it is *not* clear if the 'state' had responsibility for any stage of the process (or benefited financially) other than in the particular circumstance of the Breton ruler's dealings with the aristocracy. That might have been as much a matter of crude power politics between the individuals concerned as of evidence of 'state' responsibility.

In a princely court it was the *princeps* himself who presided, judged and sentenced. 'State' interest in the village processes was minimal either from the highest (Carolingian) level or from that of the Breton *princeps* whether dependent or independent. Formal and informal occasions often had no representative of government noted – neither *missi principis* nor *missi comitis* – although the Langon case, of the very early date of 801, did show comital intervention (*CR* 191)[32]. Otherwise, representatives of 'state' only appeared when *principes* intervened personally at a local level on receipt of complaints or appeals. Even in these cases decisions tended to be thrown back to the local community of farmers who were permanent residents.

Who were the people of the *plebes* called on to act as judges and impartial witnesses? The *suitability* of individuals to give testimony – their legal competence or law-worthy status – was essential to the provision of effective evidence, and the judges are sometimes recorded investigating or pronouncing upon it; everyone's evidence was not equally admissible. What constituted 'suitability' was not usually specified in these texts, although an Avessac record of 892 comes very close to a definition: good behaviour, good character, an unbribable nature and a love and knowledge of justice, right and truth were essential requirements. People with local knowledge and free from conviction or suspicion of offence were presumably in mind here[33]. We can also observe that law-worthy people were male and not servile. But, given the unusual detail of this material, we can go further and investigate the circumstances and range of interests of many individual impartial witnesses, and of judges too.

The terms used to refer to the judges are several: *scabini, boni viri, principes* and *iudices*[34]. No regional or temporal distinctions in the usage are apparent. The

---

[31] Conceivably the inquiry at Langon involving the other Anau was some sort of criminal case, since it was conducted by representatives of the count (*CR* 191). The travelling monk (see n. 30 above) reported that Bretons imposed a death penalty for theft of goods worth more than 4 pence.

[32] Although machtierns were sometimes *used* by *principes* they were not appointees of state; see further my 'Distribution of political power', pp. 96–8.

[33] *CR* 271. Cf. Estey, '*Scabini*', 122, and see further my 'Disputes', 298f.

[34] Cf. La Borderie, *Histoire de Bretagne*, vol. 2, pp. 136, 150f, 161f; see also Estey, '*Scabini*', 121–4, for

Dispute in ninth-century Brittany

twenty-five judges that are investigable (that is, those who appear on several occasions) were more often than not demonstrably propertied; they were donors, vendors and purchasers in other transactions, and sureties for the participants in yet more[35]. Their property interests were not vast but their own property did not always lie in the *plebes* in which they served as judges, sometimes lying in the immediately neighbouring *plebes*. So, for example, Framuual served as judge in Guer, was a donor of property in Caro and was surety for property in Guer – he owned property in Caro and performed services for the community and for individuals in the next *plebs*, Guer; Iarndetuuid was judge in Ruffiac, purchaser of property in nearby Pleucadeuc and often surety for property in Ruffiac; and Tiarnán acted as judge in Langon, was the donor of an unlocated property, and was surety for properties in Bains and Brain (Plaz) (see fig. 4a)[36]. They were not normally office holders; although Huuori was *mair* of Pleucadeuc and Riduuant was a priest, these cases are unusual: since priests normally featured prominently in all village business, their absence from the panels of judges is notable[37].

Although they did not usually serve as judge in more than one *plebs*, people from the panel of judges were often ordinary witnesses to ordinary transactions of sale or grant in several neighbouring *plebes*. Now, the total range of places where some might appear extended to Carentoir and Guer, or to Ruffiac and Carentoir, or to Ruffiac, Guer and Augan; however (after 832) others consistently and frequently appeared in all four *plebes* near Redon – Renac, Langon, Bains and Brain (in fact a *plebicula*), or this combination with the addition of one of the neighbouring *plebes* of Avessac or Peillac. The range of locations of the properties in relation to which they witnessed tends to be the same as the range of places where they appeared in person; it is again strikingly consistent in the *plebes* near Redon, with the addition of Avessac, often, or of nearby Massérac or Alarac (see fig. 4b). Further, unusually, many of these men also served as judges in *several* of the *plebes* in the block: Bains men served in Renac and Langon, and so on. Behaviour therefore markedly differed in this Redon zone from behaviour in the surrounding *plebes*. In the outer areas, a judge might serve in one *plebs* and appear in two or three, and one man's range was unlikely to be the same as another's; in the *plebes* near Redon, judges operated *throughout* the area and might additionally appear in one *plebs* outside it; so, for community and judicial purposes, this zone was treated as a single *plebs*.

comparably mixed terminology in other parts of Francia; and Nehlsen-von Stryk, *Boni Homines*, for an exhaustive survey.

[35] Sureties must have been propertied. For full discussion of the suretyship issue see my 'Suretyship', pp. 81–3.
[36] Tiarnán: *CR* 53, 58, 71, 124, 181; Framuual: *CR* 8, 25, 152, 177, 178, 179, 180, 194; Iarndetuuid: *CR* 130, 147, 148, 153, 174, 196, 255.
[37] Huuori: *CR* 12, 146, 147, 151, 155, 156, 196, 205, 267; Riduuant: 192. It is not clear what distinctive functions the *mair* performed; whether the term is a Breton borrowing from Latin *maior* or is the same vernacular word as Welsh *maer*, someone's deputy is implied – perhaps the machtiern's.

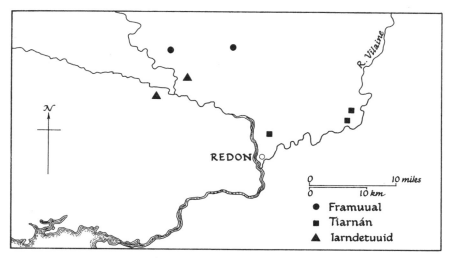

4a Some judges in the *pays de Redon*

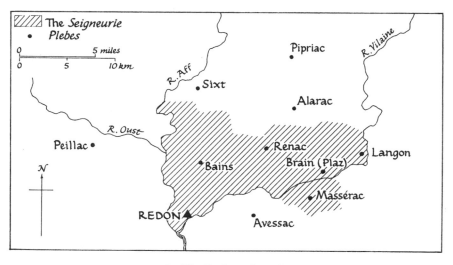

4b The Redon *seigneurie*

The texts refer to the impartial witnesses as *franci, nobiles viri, idonei viri, idonei testes, seniores* (especially), *seniores et nobiles* and *seniores et optimates*. The circumstances of the investigable impartial witnesses (fifty-six in number) were a little different from those of the judges; as might perhaps be expected their geographical range was more limited. In fact twenty-eight of them are explicitly associated with – respectively – the *plebes* of Renac, Sixt, Peillac or Bains, by being termed *senior* (elder of) Bains, *senior* Renac and so on; presumably this indicated residence in those *plebes*. They constitute only a small proportion of all the people who – in a decade – featured as ordinary witnesses to transactions in their *plebes*; this suggests that impartial witnesses tended to be chosen from a *limited* sector of the free, male, propertied population, although we can only guess at but we do not know the nature of the limitation[38]. Within their *plebes* it was not uncommon for men who were impartial witnesses to hold specific office: two held the office of *mair* and several were priests. A few were demonstrably propertied persons, but their property interests were usually in the *plebs* in which they appeared as impartial witness and their property dealings are not so evident as those of the judges[39]. A few of the impartial witnesses also served as judges but most had no other public rôle than ordinary witness of transactions. Hence, Arthuuiu, elder of Bains, was judge in Langon, impartial witness in Bains, had property in Bains, stood surety in Brain and was a frequent ordinary witness in these places. Catlouuen, elder of Renac, was impartial witness in Bains, and surety in Renac and Brain; but Uuetenuuoion was impartial witness in Avessac and had property there; both were also ordinary witnesses. The range of places at which they appeared was more limited than that of the judges but the distinctive quality of the zone near Redon is again clear. Many appeared within its limits only (Bains, Renac, Langon, Brain); several, including men who were explicitly termed *seniores* of Bains and Renac, appeared in the zone together with one neighbouring *plebs* (especially Avessac, but also Pipriac, Peillac and Sixt). By contrast, the Sixt *seniores* tended to appear in Sixt only, apart from the occasion when Nominoe called them to Bains; an Avessac group appeared in Avessac, or Avessac and Allaire, or Avessac and the Redon zone; a single man appeared in Ruffiac and Pleucadeuc[40]. The properties that were the subject of their evidence were comparably located except that men of Bains tended to witness to a wider range than the others. (This presumably reflects the fact that general Redon business was often performed in the church of Bains, using local Bains witnesses, even if the donation concerned a distant property.)

The distinctiveness of the behaviour of men from the Redon zone and the consistency of the group is very interesting. The four *plebes* of Renac, Bains, Langon and Brain were those 'given' to Redon by Carolingian rulers soon after

---

[38] Where meaningful statistics are possible the proportion of impartial witnesses to ordinary witnesses is in the order of a fifth or less. Of the nine *seniores* of Bains (*CR* 106, AD 841–51), four witnessed a lay sale pertaining to Bains in 846 (*CR* 121), as did two from Renac and one from Sixt; the remaining seventeen witnesses who were not actors in the transaction did not feature in special rôles in other cases in the locality.

[39] There is one exception to this pattern: Cadalun gave evidence in Avessac and had properties in two or three *plebes* to the south in St Étienne de Montluc (*CR* 59, 97, 162, 195).

[40] *CR* 62, 106, 161.

its foundation. These 'gifts' gave Redon proprietary rights over a whole territory without affecting the ownership of individuals within the *plebes*; in practice this probably meant rights to certain dues (including tolls), rights over vacant properties and some rights of jurisdiction; effectively it also created an area of immunity from state intervention, as the monks were well aware and sometimes stated[41]. Other *plebes* were later given to Redon too but, with the exception of Massérac, which lay beside the original four, the others were scattered. The existence of the block of four (later five) around Redon gave a territorial coherence to the monastery's political powers in the neighbourhood; and the grants clearly marked the inauguration of the *seigneurie* of Redon. It is very striking that the territorial range of the judges and the impartial witnesses of this area coincides with the *seigneurie*, underlining the juridical significance of the territory, and marking it off from the ordinary *plebes*.

The dispute material in the Redon cartulary is of considerable interest in the context of ninth-century political and social development in Europe. It clearly indicates that there was local machinery in eastern Brittany at village level for the settlement of disputes, as well as for the recording of transactions and keeping of records. This machinery was in existence and well established at least a generation before the foundation of Redon and clearly cannot be a consequence of the establishment of the monastery itself. Dispute procedure differed fundamentally at this peasant level from procedure at aristocratic level for, in the latter case, the *princeps* himself carried out a range of functions that were performed by several different bodies in local courts; most strikingly, he both presided and judged, rôles which were always separate in the local courts, where judgement was never made by machtierns or other officials. Each village and its surrounding territory, the *plebs*, held its own meetings for dispute settlement, and a high proportion had courts; business relating to one *plebs* was normally heard in the *plebs*, with people of the immediate locality in attendance. 'State' interest in the proceedings was either minimal or non-existent; hence, many 3–10 km units effectively operated as autonomous judicial units. Each *plebs* had its own panel of 'suitable' men who could be called on to act as impartial witnesses and thereby

---

[41] Charles the Bald granted immunity from secular jurisdiction to the men living on Redon's lands, thereby theoretically putting Redon outside local process (*CR* A28); he ordered that no-one should enter the monastery's estates to hear cases and give judgement, and no-one should distrain upon nor take sureties from the men living on the monastery's lands ('iubentes . . . ut nulli fidelium . . . liceat praescripti monasterii ingredi villas vel agros sive silvas . . . ad causas audiendas . . . aut iudicium saecularia diffinienda; neque praesumat quislibet iudiciarum exercentium potestatem homines eorum . . . super ipsius monasterii terram commanentes distringere aut inquietare, vel fideiussores tollere'). This seems to have happened in some respects (see *CR* 32, 124, 185, 201 for the abbot taking action against 'invaders') although local courts continued to function within the *seigneurie* of Redon. The immunity may also have given the monastery a right to hold a court, although there are also cases of others presiding within the *seigneurie* (*CR* 124). Certainly in Bains, in 892, the abbot presided at a local court (*CR* 271).

provide the repository of local knowledge on which virtually all decisions were based. These people were certainly male, free and propertied but they were not wealthy men and their property interests were in most cases limited to the *plebs* in which they resided. Their reputations as trustworthy, knowledgeable men often seem to have stretched to more than their own *plebs* and normally they might be expected to attend business in an adjacent community as well as in their own – but no farther. The local men called to serve on panels of judges had essentially the same characteristics, but the range of their reputations tended to be wider, sometimes as much as three or four *plebes*, 20–25 km, and they therefore attended business over a larger area than either impartial or ordinary witnesses. There is nothing that explicitly suggests that this greater range of the judges depended on wealth, although it may have done. Behaviour in the *seigneurie* of Redon differed from that in the surrounding countryside for here four *plebes*, rather than one or two, served as a basic unit within which judges and impartial witnesses performed their judicial rôles and it looks as if the 'panel' from which they were drawn was a panel for the whole block.

In the absence of seventh- and early eighth-century evidence it is impossible to comment convincingly on the origins of these practices. They are unlikely to be of Carolingian origin for practice deviated from that recommended in Carolingian legislation more than might be expected for a recent introduction: the smallest unit to have a court was really very small and panels of law-worthy men tended to serve one or two village communities rather than some wider community of hundred or county. Judgement was certainly found by people called *scabini*, but also by others, including *boni viri*; these *scabini* give no indication that they were skilled in 'law', as required by the legislation and perhaps suggested by the well-known charter from Digne, and they were not usually priests; they did not go on tour[42]; and all available judges were not used for every case, as the Renac meetings demonstrate, so they were not in that sense 'permanent'. Moreover, plaintiffs did not travel long distances to go to court, as the Carolingian bishop Theodulf implied, and courts were often held in or near churches[43]. On the other hand, there is nothing especially Celtic in these Breton practices and there are some obvious points of contact with practice in other parts of Francia. It is therefore more likely that the machinery was of pre-Carolingian origin, and indeed this material may provide a glimpse of the late Roman heritage – much devolved – or at least of the continuation of the *in pago* justice evidenced by the formularies for sixth- and seventh-century Francia[44]. Whether this area of Brittany was distinctive in its rich provision of judicial machinery for peasant

---

[42] *Cartulaire de l'abbaye de Saint-Victor de Marseille*, ed. B. Guérard, vol. 1, pp. 43–6; for doubts about touring see also Estey, 'Scabini', 125f.
[43] Theodulf, 'Versus contra Iudices' in *Poetae Latinae Aevi Carolini*, ed. E. Dümmler, vol. 1.
[44] See Wood above, pp. 20–2; and see Nehlsen-von Stryk, *Boni Homines*, pp. 256–344, for a thorough examination of the relationship between *boni homines* of early medieval Francia and those of late Antiquity.

communities in the ninth century is difficult to ascertain, but it was not necessarily so. *Centenarii* courts, which were presumably smaller than county courts, are mentioned in Carolingian sources and the 16–20 km range of the Mâcon and Nimois *scabini* is comparable to the range of judges from the Redon area[45]. East Breton practices could well have been paralleled in other well-worked parts of continental Europe, and the vociferous peasantry and strong sense of community so well evidenced by the Redon cartulary may have had their counterparts in other regions.

[45] Cf. Estey, *'Scabini'*, 123–6. Estey's comments about the Redon material need some revision, and the significance he attributes to the property qualifications of these men is questionable – a high proportion of peasants owned property and so a property qualification does not in itself imply social distinction from the majority of the community. However, Estey's suggestions for the limited geographical range of *scabini* in southern France are strikingly consistent and his observations about the *local* interests and knowledge of these people are surely right.

VIII

SURETYSHIP IN THE *CARTULAIRE DE REDON*

In the village communities surrounding Redon, in eastern Brittany, the mechanisms of suretyship were used for a range of normal social processes during the ninth century, and there is much practical detail in the earliest Cartulary from Redon about the people who served as sureties and the contexts in which they did so. Since our knowledge of such process in the early middle ages is so often derived from legal tracts, codes and formularies, rather than from cases, this evidence of practice is particularly important, although it has attracted rather less attention from scholars than has the vernacular terminology associated with it.[1] It is therefore my intention to indicate the range of information provided by the Cartulary about the occurrence and behaviour of ninth-century sureties in this region and to investigate the social role and status of the persons chosen to act as such.

The monastery of Redon was founded in AD 832, and had the patronage of the Carolingian emperor Louis and of his representative in Brittany, Nominoe. It was endowed with many small grants of property in its neighbourhood in the decades following its foundation, and it purchased and leased others; records of the grants and sales, together with documents arising from previous transactions, were copied in the eleventh century into the *Cartulaire de Redon*.[2] This collection includes 283 charters of the ninth and early tenth century, and a further sixty-two, which may not have been included in the medieval cartulary, are known from early modern transcripts.[3] Three quarters of the total relate to the forty years following the foundation and constitute — for the ninth century — a remarkable number of documents concerning a limited area. Further, since many properties came to Redon together with extant documentation about them, the collection includes material from at least one generation previous to 832 and material about transactions to which Redon was not party. The importance of the corpus for European history in the early middle ages cannot be overemphasized, quite apart from its long-recognized importance for Celtic studies: since most documents record small-scale, private transactions, it provides a very considerable body of detailed, localisable information about individuals and personal relationships in a peasant society, some two centuries before the record-making revolution of the central middle ages.

VIII

SURETYSHIP IN THE *CARTULAIRE DE REDON*

Eastern Brittany (the counties of Vannes, Rennes and Nantes, that is modern Morbihan, Ille-et-Vilaine and Loire-Atlantique), together with Anjou and Maine to the east of it (modern Maine-et-Loire and Mayenne), is a zone of fluctuating cultural and political status, and this was never more so than in the early middle ages. Often claimed as an integral part of the vast Frankish state, it was sometimes clearly ruled by the Franks; equally clearly sometimes it was not, as was nearly always the case with the lands to the west; at other times it was politically dominated by the aristocratic families of north-west France. The ninth century was a period in which there were some obvious changes in political status: early in the century the Franks, under the Carolingian dynasty, took control of the whole peninsula of Brittany and between 820 and 832 appointed a Breton (Nominoe) as their representative in the area; this meant some level of political unification for the peninsula, for the first time; by 842 Nominoe had revolted, and he and his successors (the *principes*) ruled Brittany (and sometimes the lands to the east of it) as a single unit, more or less independently, for much of the ninth century. The area that is covered by the Redon material (the whole of south-eastern Brittany) includes much of the intermittently Frankish counties of Rennes and Nantes, and also much of the rarely Frankish county of Vannes, which lay west of the River Vilaine (sometimes cited as a boundary) (see fig. 1). The entire area, then, might be expected to show some traces of institutions introduced by the Carolingians in the ninth century, and/or institutions associated with the *principes*, and the eastern part of it might have had traces of Frankish institutions of longer standing. These possibilities have to be borne in mind when considering the suretyship material and its parallels.

Redon itself actually lies on the River Vilaine. The area surrounding it, the subject of the charters, was an area of mixed farming practices and was — for the ninth century — intensively exploited. At the beginning of the century many of the farmers were independent peasant proprietors, with plots of up to sixty hectares, and they often had associated dependent serfs; there were few large-scale landowners until the extension of Redon's interests. Although much settlement was dispersed, agrarian society was composed of village-based units, known as *plebes*, and each *plebs* had its focal nucleated settlement and church. The peasant community regulated its own business and relationships within the *plebs*, often under the chairmanship of a distinctive 'officer', the machtiern. He was a man who might, for example, initiate dispute settlement proceedings (although he did not himself serve as judge) and might preside over the performance of transactions in which sureties were used (but only rarely served as such himself). Machtiernships were often hereditarily transmitted, through families whose property interests spanned two or three *plebes* — a wider area, that is, than the peasant norm; machtierns do not appear to have been appointees of government, neither Frankish nor Breton; and, though some aspects of the exercise of their office was clearly proprietary, their responsibility seems essentially to have been to the village community.[4]

* * * * *

Breton suretyship has traditionally been viewed in Irish terms. The model of early Irish suretyship devised by Thurneysen, and more recently discussed by Professor Binchy, depends on the identification of three distinctive functions for sureties, with distinctive persons to perform them: the *naidm*, the binding surety who witnessed a contract, enforced what had been contracted and distrained on the property of a guilty party — by physical compulsion if necessary; the *ráth*, the paying surety who made good any deficit — from his own property; and the *aitire*, the hostage surety who guaranteed the enforcement of an obligation with his own person. The relative importance of each function (and person) is supposed to have changed over time (with a trend away from physical compulsion towards payment) but *ráth* and *naidm* could each still play a part in one transaction at the time that the classical Irish law tracts were compiled.[5] Breton terms have been supposed to indicate equivalents to the first and second Irish functions, and possibly the third. It has therefore been argued that the *dilisidus* of the Redon Cartulary was the equivalent of Irish *ráth*, and that 'machtierns' in the same text performed the binding and enforcing role of the Irish *naidm* (earlier *macc*); hence, two distinctive types of surety are supposed to have existed in the ninth century, exercising two different functions.[6] I shall begin consideration of the problems of Breton suretyship with an outline of the material that occurs in the Cartulary, paying particular attention to evidence that the texts themselves provide about function and refraining from arguing by analogy, Irish or otherwise. Thereafter I shall proceed to the social and political questions with which this paper is primarily concerned.

Two terms for surety are constantly used in the Redon charters: the Latin *fideiussor* and — less frequently — a Latinised vernacular word, *dilisid(us)* (occasionally *dilisit*). *Fideiussor* is the classical Roman legal term for one of the accessories undertaking to pay if a principal debtor did not, guaranteeing any kind of obligation.[7] It was also used in a variety of early medieval contexts for those who put down pledges (gages), who guaranteed other people's debts to creditors, who guaranteed other people's pledges in default (appearing for them in court) or who acted as oath-helpers.[8] *Dilisidus* presumably stands for a vernacular equivalent to *fideiussor*, since *dilis* means 'sure' and its Irish and Welsh cognates (*díles* and *dilys*) were used with reference to property that was 'outside legal process' (because ownership was total) and therefore secure.[9] The two Redon terms are sometimes used together in the charter texts and sometimes separately. Hence, 'et obligamus (sic) vobis fideiussores vel dilisidos in securitate ipsius terrae, his nominibus...' (CR 91); or 'et dederunt fideiussores iiii in securitate...' (CR 73); or 'et dederunt dilisidos in securitate...' (CR 132). I see no substantive significance in the recorder's preference for one or other or both terms, and the differences are probably to be explained by differences in record-making habits rather than by intrinsic differences in the transactions.[10] Very occasionally, a third term, *securator*, was employed but no distinction is implied in the nature of the sureties so designated (CR 63, 118, 271). No common Latin words are used for any pledge although the *pignus* of classical Roman terminology is reflected in *pignoratio* and *terra pignorantiae* (CR 86, 193). The Latinised Frankish *uuadio* and *uuadiatio* and the vernacular Breton *aruuistl* each occur once; the contexts clearly indicate 'pledge' or 'gage' put down, the former case in Guérande (near the mouth of the Loire) in 870, the next in Bains in 833 and the last in Molac (west of the Vilaine) in 849 (CR 234, 182, 251).

There are eighty-seven charters that mention sureties in the Redon collection; since two are doublets of the same transaction, one pertains to the eleventh century and another to the twelfth, there remain eighty-four records of ninth-century business using sureties, and my subsequent comments will be confined to these. 292 sureties are cited in the course of these transactions.[11] Of the eighty-four occasions, nine fell before 832 (the foundation date of Redon); 73 per cent fell in the thirty years between 840 and 870, and 31 per cent in the decade 860-870. These proportions reflect the survival of charters in the ninth century and make no particular point about suretyship. The second proportion also reflects the fact that many tenancy disputes were resolved and new tenancies created in the 860s.

The surviving corpus of Redon charters records transactions that took place throughout south-east Brittany — a distance of 100km east-west — but by far the greater proportion of properties lay within 40km of Redon itself, most of these lying to the north of Redon and west of the River Vilaine (see fig. 1). Sureties were named for transactions performed in all parts covered by the charters as also for properties distributed throughout the area. (Although transactions concerning any named property were sometimes performed on the land in question, more frequently they were transacted in some appropriate village meeting-place; sometimes they occurred at a distance from the relevant *plebs*, in Redon or some other monastery or

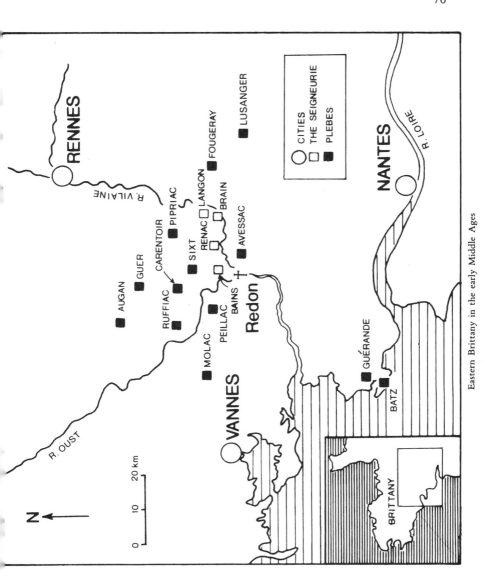

Eastern Brittany in the early Middle Ages

aristocratic residence. For analytical purposes, place of performance needs to be distinguished from the location of the property in question.) Remarkably, 37 per cent of the transactions naming sureties relate to the *plebes* of Ruffiac and Carentoir and, less remarkably, 21 per cent relate to the four *plebes* surrounding Redon (Bains, Brain, Langon and Renac).[12] Admittedly, a quite disproportionate number of charters refers to Ruffiac and Carentoir (22 per cent), but it is an unusually high proportion of these charters that records the use of sureties. It is also notable that nearly all transactions involving saltpans had sureties named (eight of eleven). The apparent preponderance of sureties in some parts is curious and it is also curious that only one of the Langon transactions names sureties (this *plebs* was not far from Redon and the scene of much judicial business) and none of the early Lusanger sales does so. Although these oddities in the distribution pattern cannot at the moment be explained, it is important to observe that the use of sureties was almost as characteristic of the eastern parts of the area as of the western. Although there are considerably fewer surety transactions recorded east of the Vilaine, the proportion is only slightly less than the proportion of eastern records.

Different occasions and transactions provoked the use of sureties in ninth-century Brittany, although it is notable that all concern land transactions and not exchanges of movables: there are thirty-seven cases of sale, twenty of 'pledge' or 'landgage',[13] sixteen of dispute settlement (especially when sureties were given for the future payment of render by the loser), four of agreement to future payment of render with no dispute noted (though possibly implied), and seven miscellaneous occasions. 67 per cent of transactions naming sureties, then, occurred in straightforward cases of the exchange of landed property rights, either fully or partially, for money. Sureties were only rarely used for ordinary *grants* of property; although they were not invariably named in sales they were nearly always characteristic of pledges.

Here is a typical example of the use of sureties in a sale; for ease of comprehension, here and subsequently, I summarise the charter text rather than give a literal translation: Couuetic sold one of his properties, Ranscaman Baih [in Ruffiac], together with its serf, to the smith Carantcar and his wife Uuentamau for 17 *solidi* 4 *denarii*, totally, with full powers of alienation; he assigned Catuuotal, Haeldifoes and Omnis as sureties for the security of the land; if he or his coheirs or relations should contravene the sale, he should pay 34 *solidi*. [There follows a list of twenty-one witnesses, including the vendor, but neither the purchaser nor the sureties.] It was performed on the land in question, on Tuesday, the kalends of March, in the reign of King Charles, with Nominoe holding Brittany and Susannus as bishop [1 March, 847]; Abbot Haeldetuuid made the record (CR 64).

The money sanction is not an invariable aspect of these records, although it is common; when it does occur it is nearly always twice the value of the price paid, or thereabouts.[14] The role of the sureties is never explicitly stated but CR 259 specifies that five sureties were assigned to ensure that land purchased by the abbot for 8 *solidi* would never revert to the vendors nor their descendants (871-77, unlocated). In another case, in Ruffiac in 866, the four sureties of a sale that took place in 857 were produced in court to testify to the validity and totality of the sale when the vendor disputed it. Here the testimony of the sureties was distinguished from that of the witnesses to the original transaction and must be presumed to have had a special status (CR 139).

Transactions of pledge (or 'landgage') are those in which property rights were handed over, for a limited term, for payment; at the end of the term the period could be extended but ultimately both property and payment were due to return to their original owners.[15] When the payment was *not* repaid then the property did not revert either and the transaction effectively constituted a sale on rather light terms. This is a typical example: Iuduuallon gave 20 *solidi* to Iarncon for one and a half parcels of land, *pars* Roetanau and *pars* Eusirgid [probably in Carentoir], and the three men on them, Tiarnoc and his sons Couualin and Uuorethemel; Iarncon gave Iuduuallon three sureties, Iarnbud, Mertinhoiarn and Tanetuuallon. This was for seven years and a week, and thereafter another seven years and a week, and thereafter a third seven years and a week. It was performed on Saturday after Christmas Day in the year that the Emperor Charles died, before [eleven named] witnesses [30 December 813]. If Iarncon and/or his children had not redeemed the land after three times seven years and a week, then Iuduuallon and his wife Ibiau and son Uuallon should own it fully, with powers of alienation and without obligation to pay render to anyone. Lathoiarn recorded this (CR 135).

The way in which these transactions are recorded suggests that usually land was handed over as security for the loan of money; the land was the pledge (gage) and the reason for the transaction seems to have been the pledgor's need for cash.[16] Indeed, the vernacular term *aruuistl*, 'pledge, gage', was explicitly used in this sense.[17] The Latin word *venditio* was also sometimes employed to describe pledge transactions although they are clearly to be distinguished from real sales: the sums of money that changed hands were lower, often no more than the value of rent expected during the term of the pledge; pledged land was sometimes subsequently sold to the pledgee for a further payment (cf. CR 182 and 181); and pledged land might well be redeemed at the end of the specified term. There can have been little long-term benefit to the lessor/pledgor for at the end of the term he may have received his land back but he had lost the income from it during the period of the pledge.[18] It is extremely difficult to see why landowners should have entered into such arrangements except under local political pressure or a short-term need for cash, as once explicitly occurred (CR 234).

The precise actions that sureties were to take in pledge transactions is nowhere specified. However, since the sureties in these transactions were named by the man who provided the land and not by the man who provided the cash there is some suggestion that their role was an enforcing one: it was not their job to pay up if the deal failed but rather to make sure that use of the land was secured to the man who had paid for it, the pledgee.[19] This is, in fact, virtually explicit in the example cited above.

A fifth of the eighty-four cases using sureties are cited in the context of procedures following the settlement of disputes, often to ensure the enforcement of the terms of the settlement. In seven of these, sureties were named for the regular payment of render from tenants; the disputes that these settlements followed were either of the type in which owner A maintained that tenant B's payments had lapsed or of the type in which ownership had been disputed between two proprietors, C and D. In the former type, B agreed to pay regularly in future; in the latter type, it was agreed that C should own the disputed property but D should hold it from him and pay rent. So, for example, between 836 and 842 the abbot and monks of Redon accused Anauhocar and his family of wrongly farming a virgate called Puz, and appealed to the ruler of Brittany, Nominoe, to intervene; Nominoe ordered that the case be heard locally and six men testified against the laymen; thereafter three sureties were given by Anauhocar to Redon both for the land (*in securitate supradictae terrae*) *and* for subsequent annual payment (CR 61). Here the sureties performed two potentially separable functions: they both secured the land to Redon and they also guaranteed the payments. The few records that detail the provision of sureties for payment of future rent, without reference to previous disputes, may in fact have followed comparable settlements: for example, in 868 Maenhoiarn and his brother provided Redon with two sureties for the payment of 2 *solidi*, every Martinmas, for a parcel in Carentoir (CR 134).

In one of the records about rent it is specified that sureties were assigned by the tenant against future claims by his family: in Carentoir, in 863, two sureties were named for payment of the rent and a further four for the security of the property. (*Et dedit Uuruueten duos fideiussores ad supradictum abbatem . . . ut omnibus annis redderet censum ad kalendas octobris, id est, duos solidos, sine repugnatione; et dederunt supradictus Uuruueten et Pivetat iiii fideiussores in securitate ut nec ipsi nec parentes eorum nec filii eorum post eos dicant accepisse se in hereditate illam supradicta*[*m*] *partem.* CR 63) On another four occasions sureties were explicitly assigned after dispute settlement in order to guarantee that the loser and his progeny would not bring another case.[20] In Renac in the late 850s the abbot of Redon and Torithgen, son of Houuen, settled that some disputed properties should be split between the two; Torithgen gave six sureties that neither he nor his progeny would bring another case against the abbot over these lands, and also that — in that event — his share would be forfeited to the abbot (CR 29).[21] All of these cases suggest that one role of the sureties was to enforce: their function was to persuade the man who had named them to keep the terms of the settlement (and, at least once, it was to oversee, and presumably effect, forfeiture). Sometimes, by contrast, it is suggested that they guaranteed payments; when this happened sureties for the payment are often distinguished from others in the same transaction. In cases where no rent was due, however, an enforcing role must be implied: in Pipriac in the very late ninth century the line of the abbot's boundaries was questioned; when the bounds were agreed, sureties were given to the abbot by the peasants that they would stick to the agreed line (CR 47). In a different type of case, c.863, Cunatam handed over a serf to Redon, in recompense for raiding, stealing and causing havoc in Redon property; he assigned two sureties for the serf (CR 32, cf. 163). In practical terms, this presumably meant that they guaranteed that the serf's produce went to Redon and not to Cunatam.

The most detailed comments on the functions of sureties occur in a record of 858 about the consequences of assault. A cleric, Anau, tried to kill the priest Anauhoiarn (a priest attached to Redon); Anau gave his vineyard in Ruffiac to Redon in compensation for the assault, and named three sureties for the security of the grant. Thereafter, he named those three and a further three men as sureties that he would do no wrong to Redon's men in the future; if the sureties came to hear of any bad intention of his, they were to warn the abbot; and if Anau actually committed any further offence they were to give his worth (*precium*) to the abbot and pursue him to death. These men had more than a paying and distraining function: in effect they were to adopt a policing role and administer punishment (CR 202). In this case the social function of the sureties is quite explicit: they were the means by which stability and security in this society was maintained, for they constituted the machinery to check and balance the interests of individuals and particular families. It is a nice indication of the fact that the surety system could be fundamental to social order in a world in which the notion of order was not the monopoly (nor even the preserve) of the state.

There is no further detail on the functions of sureties in this material. In most cases the sureties in these Breton villages were personal guarantors that the legal obligations of others would be fulfilled, as sureties were everywhere. There is really very little detail of how this was done, although payment from the sureties' own property and physical compulsion are both implied. Clearly both did occur — and both might occur with reference to the same transaction, either with one set of sureties or with more. It therefore looks as if a surety might perform his guaranteeing role in a number of ways: he presumably used the method that fitted the particular circumstances and did not follow a rigid system. As a comment on practice this makes sense and is what we might expect from records of practice; it is therefore particularly inappropriate to force the material to fit the formulations of lawyers.

* * * * *

The charters themselves include some information about the social and economic status of the people who served as sureties in these transactions. The number of sureties used on each occasion varied: usually two, three or four, it was exceptionally one, five or six and very exceptionally eight, nine or twelve. Where property was sold or pledged, there is only one type of correlation between the number of sureties and the size or value of the property, or the length of the pledge (landgage) transaction: if the property was *very* small, valued at less than 10 *solidi*, there were usually two sureties. Otherwise, valuable properties might have few sureties, like two for a sale worth 29s.3d., in 856 (CR 172), and less valuable ones might have many, like twelve for a sale worth 16s. 6d., in 849 (CR 58). Nor is there any obvious distinction between numbers used in different decades of the ninth century. As one might expect, then, the reasons for the variation in numbers presumably lay in the status and economic resources of the sureties and in the particular social circumstances that attended each case; possibly, since it was a peasant community, they had to cover the obligation between them — in a society of small proprietors this may sometimes have involved several people of moderate means.[22]

Direct information about the status of the sureties is infrequently recorded, but occurs sufficiently often to be interesting. Of 292 citations of sureties, and about 200 different individuals, a small number were local office holders, either lay or clerical.[23] At least nine of the people used as sureties also served as *scabini* in their localities, that is they served on the panels of judgement-finders used in court cases — free, local, respectable, propertied men, such as Arthbiu of Bains or Uuolethec of Augan.[24] At least eight were people called upon to give evidence, as impartial witnesses, in court cases — again, these were local, respectable men, usually referred to as *seniores* of their respective *plebes*.[25] A couple also served as *mair*.[26] On three occasions the sureties were machtierns. This very limited occurrence is particularly interesting in view of the probable meaning of the element *mach* in the word 'machtiern' — 'surety', like Welsh *mach*: if machtierns had originally been *distinguished* by functioning as sureties, they had clearly lost the distinction by the ninth century. Use of machtierns for these purposes was clearly exceptional and only seems to have occurred for special types of case, as in the settlement following the assault by Anau on a Redon priest (CR 202).[27] Clerics also sometimes functioned as sureties, but not very often: there were certainly two priests and a deacon, and maybe twice that number, but not more.[28] In fact, overall, it is the low proportion of lay and clerical office holders that is striking; 20 per cent at most. Clearly persons of special standing in the village community were sometimes used as sureties but much more often less distinctive members were chosen.

Indeed, although some people stood as sureties for several transactions in their local communities, it was much more characteristic to do so once only: of the 200 individuals used as sureties, less than 20 per cent stood more than once. Now it was characteristic, with a few notable exceptions, for surety transactions (like most others) to be performed in the *plebs* in which the property lay: Guérande transactions took place in Guérande, Augan transactions in Augan, Fougeray transactions in Fougeray, and so on.[29] The norm, then, was that surety transactions were narrowly local affairs that were particular to a particular local group of people.[30] Moreover, the people who served as sureties were men of very limited geographical range. Where people served on more than one occasion, they normally did so in the same *plebs* (or within the block of *plebes* near Redon that constituted the *seigneurie*); the only possible exception to this concerns Iudlin, who served in Batz and neighbouring Guérande in the 850s and 860s (CR 60, 95).[31] So, Catbud served four times in Carentoir between 833 and 866 and Maenuili served a most unusual six times in Ruffiac between 821 and 848; Loieshoiarn served twice in Carentoir, Nominoe and Noli twice in Ruffiac, Breselan twice in Guérande, Iunetmonoc twice in Renac, and so on. The same type of observation may be made of those who only served once as surety: we do not often find them doing business outside their own *plebs* (unless within the *seigneurie*), and if we do, then usually that business did not take them beyond the neighbouring *plebs*. Hence, Christian was surety and sometimes witness in Peillac, *c*.867; Finitan in Molac, *c*.820-27; Greduuocon in Sixt, and (called *senior* of Sixt) gave evidence as impartial witness in Bains, all between 834 and 851; Rethuualart was surety and witness at least ten times in Ruffiac, and witness possibly in Augan and Guer, between 832 and 866 — he was also called as witness for one party in dispute in Ruffiac in 846. Iudrith (of the *seigneurie*) served three times as surety in Renac, Bains and

Brain between 832 and 870, and witnessed at least eight times in those *plebes* with reference to properties in the *seigneurie*.[32]

As for the economic status of the sureties, it is sometimes made clear that they were propertied men. They appeared as donors, vendors, purchasers and pledgors of land in their own right. Uuordoital was a donor of property in Ruffiac, as well as a surety and frequent witness there.[33] Kinetuuant was a pledgor of property in Guérande as well as surety and witness there, 859-66. Cathoiarn was vendor of property in Carentoir as well as witness there, and three times surety and frequent witness in Ruffiac.[34] Tiarnan was donor of property in Bains, a judgement-finder in Langon, surety in Renac and Brain and witness throughout the *seigneurie*.[35] Nothing, however, suggests that these were the properties of great aristocrats: they consisted of small units, a few 10 or 20 hectare parcels at most, and they were not widely scattered. Usually they lay in the *plebs* in which the owner served as surety. The only consistent exceptions to this pattern relate to the *seigneurie*, as in the case of Tiarnan above: here men might well have property in one *plebs* of the group and serve in another. All these people, then, were well-off peasants; they were neither great lords nor country gentlemen and nothing suggests that they had either military capacity or interests. Quite often, by the 860s, they were the men who had made grants to Redon and then taken tenancies on the lands they formerly owned.

There is another characteristic of those who served as sureties that may incidentally throw some light on the way they performed their role. Sometimes the close family (brothers or sons) of one party to a transaction was named as surety; and in one case local elders stated, in a judgement, that it would be most suitable if an accused man's brother stood as surety for his agreed settlement (CR 264). On other occasions people who were themselves liable to make future payments (in a joint transaction) stood as surety for each other: for example, four men from Peillac (A, B, C, D) defaulted on dues owed to Redon; the agreement was renewed in 867, with the new abbot, and they all gave sureties for payment of the render in the future; A gave B and D, while B gave A, D and another (X); C gave X and two others (Y and Z), and the last, D, gave Z (CR 96). This may well suggest that one function of many of the sureties was to resign their own personal interests in the property transferred, whether they had family or other involvements. If a man named his brother, or another potentially interested person, as surety for a sale then the surety was directly committed to the totality of that sale and — in agreeing to stand — publicly resigned his own interest.

* * * * *

The Redon material nicely demonstrates the use of sureties in eastern Brittany in different types of land transaction during the ninth century. Nothing suggests that the practice was exclusive either to Frankish or to Breton parts. When property rights were transferred for money, sureties are recorded often enough to suggest that their use was a norm. They were provided by the vendors or pledgors of land, to guarantee that the property rights really would change hands and that the original owners would neither work nor take profits nor renders from the lands they had alienated. Sureties were also sometimes used to guarantee payment of regular rent from tenants to landlords, particularly when the rents had been disputed between the parties but possibly in other circumstances too. Further, as might be expected, they were used to guarantee that the terms of a settlement arrived at after dispute would be respected by all parties, especially by any loser, whether or not the settlement involved subsequent regular payments. On occasion great care was taken over the selection of sureties, and decisions over appropriate people to carry out the task were sometimes a part of settlement proceedings. On others, small payments might be made to them (CR 111, 136) and they were invariably distinguished from ordinary witnesses to business, who themselves had to be of suitable standing. They did, then, have a special, and valued, role to play. Practical detail of what this role involved is rare, although both enforcing and paying activities are sometimes indisputable and the sureties named after Anau's assault also had a punishing function. We should not forget, however, that several aspects of the operation of suretyship remain uncertain: as well as the lack of precise description of action taken, or envisaged, by the parties to an agreement, we lack evidence of the machinery for implementing the *stipulatio* (sanction); and, apart from the pledge transactions themselves, we do not know if pledges were sometimes put down in the course of action by sureties, as part of the enforcing process, for example.[36] Usually the people chosen to act as sureties were free, male, respected members of the local village community, although we lack evidence on the manner of their selection and on the qualifications for eligibility;[37] they seem to have been reasonably well propertied peasants, with limited interests; they sometimes held some local lay or clerical office but they were not rich or powerful men and they were not the representatives of any higher level of government. Suretyship was essentially a village-based business and the sanctions which the institution imposed operated within communities in which reputation was of importance to individual and to family and essential to the viability of working relationships.[38]

In many ways these Breton practices were not at all distinctive: the use of sureties was widespread in early medieval Europe, in continental as well as insular regions, as it also had been in the ancient world, and the contexts in which sureties were principally used involved debt and court procedure. Payment of fines and compensations by a guilty man — especially composition for homicide — was often treated like contract and sureties were therefore used to guarantee the contractual obligation; a similar approach influenced the use of sureties for appearance in court by an accused man and for future good behaviour of a guilty one. The use of pledges (landed and movable) was also widespread on the continent, both to guarantee obligations in dispute settlement procedure and — as in the Redon cases — to establish security for raising a loan.[39] Pledging (*rewadiare*) and the use of *fideiussores* were established Frankish practices, both Merovingian and Carolingian, but were also common in Byzantine and Lombard Italy and in Visigothic Spain as well as in Anglo-Saxon England.[40] None of this is very surprising, especially when we recall the Roman law of contract — particularly with respect to debt and loan — and the emphases it received in the late Empire: the *Digest*, quoting late commentators, is explicit on the appropriate use of pledge *and* surety in raising loans; the *Theodosian Code* often notes the particular significance of pledging for those who took leases on imperial property; and at least once, in language reminiscent of the Redon material, the *Code* specifies the need for tenants of imperial property to provide sureties for the payment of their rent.[41]

There are two aspects of Breton suretyship in the ninth century which are relatively uncommon: the use of sureties in transactions of sale (of land) and the use of sureties for 'policing'. With reference to sale, three contexts provide apparently close parallels. The legal text known as *Excerpta de libris Romanorum et Francorum*, of pre-ninth-century Breton or near Breton origin, includes a provision that unless something acquired by purchase has *fideiussores*, or the *auctor* (former owner) to answer for it, it could be regarded as stolen; in other words, it requires sales to have guarantors.[42] Secondly, the early eighth-century Irish canonical collection known as *Collectio Canonum Hibernensis* includes a chapter on *fideiussores* and *stipulationes*, mostly with reference to debt. Section 6, *de eo, quod aliquis non debet emere aut vendere sine ratis et stipulationibus*, appears to have precisely the same requirement in mind: sales should not take place without guarantors as well as sanctions, and the section goes on to cite the authority of Jerome, Augustine and an (?) Irish synod.[43] Thirdly, Anglo-Saxon legal codes, especially of the tenth century, constantly repeat the requirement that every man needs a guarantor for his transactions; no-one could buy or exchange without surety *and* witness.[44] The *Excerpta*, the *Collectio* and the Anglo-Saxon codes seem to be articulating principles that were actually implemented in the transactions recorded in the Redon corpus, although they sometimes explicitly refer to exchanges of movables.[45] The *requirement* that sureties be available for goods sold looks like a northern European application of trends visible in Roman Vulgar Law: the legal evidence suggests increasing emphasis on the need for witnesses when titles were transferred by sale, and the need for sureties in some circumstances was also occasionally specified.[46]

It is extremely difficult to parallel — precisely — the policing function of the sureties of CR 202 although late tenth-century English legislators seem to have envisaged a very similar financial role for sureties for a guilty man.[47] The detail of the 'policing' of 202 is unusual, however, for the sureties' capacity to punish seems to have been viewed as an entirely private matter between the contracting parties and the guarantors of their contracts. In the several early medieval contexts in which citizens formed bands for the pursuit of bad men — sixth- and ninth-century Francia, tenth-century England — the bands were mobilised because of state direction and interest, and they were sometimes accompanied by an appropriate officer such as a *comes* or *grafio*.[48] The Breton material suggests unusually private machinery for mobilising the band that was to ride out in pursuit.

* * * * *

The Breton practice evidenced in the ninth century does not look entirely distinctive, and it certainly does not look distinctively Celtic, although there are points of contact with both Welsh and Irish practice. The contexts in which sureties were used, especially since they refer to landed property, are often as reminiscent of late Roman, Visigothic, Lombard, Frankish and even Anglo-Saxon practice, if not more so; it is therefore strained to force the Breton evidence exclusively into a native Irish model. It is also strained to suppose the Breton terms refer to persons of distinctive function: enforcing and paying both clearly occurred and both methods could be employed by a single *fideiussor*.[49] However, what is most interesting in all of this is not so much the parallels here and there, since suretyship was common in European societies, but the differences of emphasis and the possible social and political explanations for those differences. Use of sureties in the sale of landed property seems to have been a local intensification of a general trend in post-Roman Europe rather than a totally distinctive practice. It presumably reflects a society in which the number of transactions was limited and their security potentially fragile. It might well be pointing to the limited occurrence of sale and to the limited mobility of property, rather than — as might at first appear — to the contrary; it might therefore be effectively pointing to the strength of family interests, operating as a restraint on freedom of alienation.

Use of sureties for policing, to constrain and punish bad men, is an interesting extension of the machinery of suretyship, personal guarantors of contract between individuals operating as a means of guaranteeing order in the community. The absence of state interest is very marked, by contrast with the use of comparable machinery elsewhere in Europe in the early middle ages, and suggests an absence of state institutions. It serves to reinforce the impression, also conveyed by other aspects of the Redon material, that the affairs of local village communities were regulated by the peasant cultivators themselves, men who had little contact with an outside wider world. By the twelfth century, partly because of the increased power of Redon itself, that was to change; in the mid-ninth century the change was still some time away.

[1] L. Fleuriot, 'Un fragment en Latin de très anciennes lois bretonnes armoricaines du vi siècle', (1971) 78 *Annales de Bretagne* 622-24, 648-54; M. Planiol, *Histoire des Institutions de la Bretagne* (5 vols., 2nd. ed. Mayenne, 1981-4), ii. 72f, 159, 166f.
I am extremely grateful for the comments made on this paper by Julia Smith, Chris Wickham and, of course, the editors. I am also indebted to the staff of the Computer Centre at University College London for their tolerance during my preparation of a Redon database and, in particular, to Chris Horsbrugh for writing the programs which allowed me to interrogate it. The section of this paper which deals with the characteristics and occurrence of different individuals depends upon a computer-assisted analysis of the incidence of the 6600 personal names and 1100 place-names that occur in the ninth-century charters of the *Cartulaire de Redon*. I shall discuss the technical aspects of this in my forthcoming book *Villages, Villagers and the Structure of Rural Society in Early Medieval Brittany* (Duckworth, 1986). Considerable assistance with clerical support has been provided by the British Academy, to which I owe especial thanks.
[2] *Cartulaire de Redon*, ed. A. de Courson (Paris, 1863), hereafter CR. The manuscript is in the care of the archbishop of Rennes.
[3] Nearly all of these were printed by de Courson in an Appendix to CR and the rest were printed by H. Morice, *Mémoires pour servir de preuves à l'histoire écclésiastique et civile de Bretagne* (3 vols., Paris, 1742-46), i. col. 265, 271f, 295, 297, 308; most of the transcripts from which they were printed are difficult to locate.
[4] For machtierns see my 'On the distribution of political power in Brittany in the mid-ninth century' in *Charles the Bald: Court and Kingdom*, ed. M. Gibson and J. Nelson with D. Ganz, British Archaeological Reports, International Series 101 (1981), 87-107, and J. G. T. Sheringham, 'Les machtierns' (1981) 58 *Mémoires de la Société d'Histoire et d'Archéologie de Bretagne* 61-72. Despite many attempts I have been unable to consult F. Burdeau, 'Les Machtierns', Mémoire, Agregation de Droit Romain, Rennes, 1967. For other aspects of social structure and economy see my forthcoming *Villages, Villagers*. For detailed discussion of dispute settlement procedure see my 'Disputes, their conduct and their settlement in the village communities of eastern Brittany in the ninth century' (1985) 1 *History and Anthropology* 289-312 and my 'People and places in dispute in ninth-century Brittany' in *Settlement of Disputes in Early Medieval Europe*, ed. W. Davies and P. Fouracre (Cambridge, 1986).
[5] D. A. Binchy 'Celtic Suretyship', 355-67; see also *ante*, Stacey.
[6] Cf. L. Fleuriot, 'Fragment' (1971) 78 *Annales de Bretagne* 651.
[7] J. A. C. Thomas, *Textbook of Roman Law* (Amsterdam, 1976) 335.

8 See above, p.85 and nn.39 and 40.
9 Cf. Ior 65/3-6; CG 83f.
10 There are two tendencies: 1) both words tend to be used in first person records and one or other in third person records; 2) both are used up to and including the 840s, while one or other might be used at any time in the ninth century, early or late. This reflects changes in diplomatic practice characteristic of the 840s. There are no apparent regional distinctions in the choice of terms nor do they vary consistently in accordance with the type of transaction to which they refer. (I shall discuss the diplomatic of these charters in *Villages, Villagers*.)
11 See above pp.81-3.
12 These four adjacent *plebes* were controlled by Redon by the 850s, and a fifth — Massérac — was added by 890, forming a compact block of territory (*seigneurie*) over which the abbot and monks had a type of proprietary right (without affecting individual ownership of property within the *plebes*); in practice this meant that the abbot had rights to certain dues and rights of jurisdiction in the area, and that it was immune from state intervention. See further *Villages, Villagers*.
13 See above, p.78.
14 This was common late and post-Roman practice in continental Europe; see E. Levy, *Weströmisches Vulgarrecht. Das Obligationenrecht* (Weimar, 1956) 213-20.
15 The verb of action in these records is usually Latin *pignorare* (sic), 'to pledge, pawn, mortgage', or Latinised Germanic *uuadiare*, 'to give surety'; again, I see no significance in the choice of term except with respect to recording practice.
16 Transactions of this type were not uncommon in late and post-Roman Europe, particularly in order to raise cash; see J. A. C. Thomas, *Textbook of Roman Law*, 330-2; *Digest*, 18.1.81, *Digesta*, ed. T. Mommsen, i (Berlin, 1868; see further below, n. 41); *Les diplômes originaux des merovingiens*, ed. P. Lauer and C. Samaran (Paris, 1908), no. 25, 18 (in which land was pledged to the abbot of St Denis in order raise money to pay a fine in seventh-century Francia). Rather later, the 'beneficial lease' of twelfth- and thirteenth-century England represented a comparable development, and so — occasionally — did the landgage of late medieval Wales, although the latter was more usually associated with a shortage of land rather than a shortage of cash; see H. D. Hazeltine, 'The gage of land in medieval England' (1903-4) 17 *Harvard Law Review* 552f and Ll. B. Smith, 'The gage and the land market in late medieval Wales' (1976) 29 *Economic History Review* 537-50.
17 The word was used in a different sense in Ior 57/3, 65/3; see Glossary.
18 It would be possible to read CR 68 as suggesting that the pledgor received an annual income for twenty-one years of 18*d.*; the text, however, is corrupt and it is by no means certain that this *is* the meaning.
19 The one pledge that has a money sanction attached may imply that if the terms were not met an appeal should be made to the machtiern, who would take action; however, this charter has lacunae and no argument can depend on it (CR 265).
20 CR 29, 118, 127, 180: *pro se et suos semine et omnibus suis ingeniis* (sic) (CR 29).
21 In fact, it is not clear if the half-parcel that he handed over was the subject of the dispute or another parcel, in lieu; neither possibility alters the fact that he was liable to forfeit a share of the disputed parcel.
22 One clause in a Visigothic law tract, however, made the point that *each fideiussor* should have the means to meet the cost, even if there were several of them; E. Levy, *Weströmisches Vulgarrecht*, 201. Such rules might also have been applicable in Brittany.
23 'About 200' since identifications cannot always be certain.
24 Arthbiu (CR 124, 192; 29, 58, 96, 155); Catlouuen (124, 192; 58); Framuual (180); ? Hitin (180); Houuori (147; 146); Iarndeduuid (147; 148, 220); Notolic (192; 29, 132);

Tiarnan (124; 53, 58); Uuatin (124, 192; 58); Uuolethec (147, ?180; 196).
²⁵ Cumiau (CR 106; A17); Greduuocon (106; A17); ?Haeluuocon (106; 96); Hincant (61); ?Houuori (205; 146, cf. 147); Iarnhatoeu (106; 181); Iarnhebet (106; 121, 182); Maenuuoron (106; 181, 199); ? Uuallon (106; 58). Whether or not these men really were impartial is impossible to deduce; functionally, however, they were distinct from partial witnesses; see further my 'Disputes' (1985) 1 *History and Anthropology* 298-300.
²⁶ Cumiau (A17); Uuolethec (111; 196). The precise function of the *mair* is unclear; he may have been a ruler's agent or steward of an estate (cf. Carolingian *maiores*). See further my 'Disputes' (1985) 1 *History and Anthropology* n. 12.
²⁷ Welsh *mach* and Old Breton *meich* would certainly support this meaning, although Sir Ifor Williams suggested that *mach* in 'machtiern' was a cognate of Irish *mass*, 'great, fine'; see further the discussions of Fleuriot and Planiol (above, n.1), Sheringham and myself (above, n.4). The machtierns are Ratfred (105; 202); Ratuili (111, 113, 143; 202); Uuorgost (116; 136); and possibly Catusloiant (198; 172). If *mach* in 'machtiern' means 'surety' it makes much more sense to suppose that machtierns had some responsibility for overseeing suretyship rather than for being sureties themselves, somewhat as sergeants of the peace in late medieval Britain saw that suspects produced sureties for their appearance in court. In the ninth century machtierns may have been involved in transactions that had gone wrong, as one pledge charter clearly implies (CR 265). Hence, although it is imperfect, the material in the Redon Cartulary suggests that machtierns were only rarely sureties themselves, although they might sometimes have had an enforcing role in investigating problem transactions; in the latter, however, they were external to the original contract and not part of the contractual relationship.
²⁸ Priests: Arblant (249); Rihouuen (156; 202); ? Haeluuocon (76; 96); ?Maenuuethen (248; 256); ?Unum (93, 248; 249). Deacons: Loiesuuotal (271); ?Haelhouuen (38; 39, 82).
²⁹ This is true of at least 69 per cent of the surety cases; only 12 per cent *certainly* took place elsewhere; the remainder are unlocated. See above, p.75, for the overall distribution of surety transactions.
³⁰ The chief exception to the predominant geographical pattern concerns Carentoir, for which apparently ordinary property transactions took place in Bains and Renac. Additionally, two Carentoir, one Ruffiac and one Pleucadeuc transaction took place at Lisnouuid, which is unlocated but lay within Ruffiac or Carentoir. At the least, then, in two cases and possibly three this place functioned as a regional centre for Ruffiac, Carentoir and neighbouring *plebes*. Surety transactions performed in Bains and Renac, as might be expected, usually related to the *plebes* of the *seigneurie* (see above, n. 12). Surety transactions only took place at Redon itself in the exceptional case of the settlement following Anau's assault.
³¹ These were not necessarily, however, separate *plebes*. Roenuuallon might possibly be another exception (CR 34, 88, 133, 181, 256).
³² CR 53, 58; 29, 32, 74, 163, 185, 207, 216, 233.
³³ CR 153; 144; 112, 144, 172, 173, etc.
³⁴ Morice, *Preuves*, i. col. 295; CR 151, 160, 171; 8, 9, 155, etc.
³⁵ CR 71; 124; 53, 58; 181.
³⁶ CR 274 states that, after some havoc caused by his tenants in the early tenth century, Bishop Bili and his brother gave security for their good behaviour in the future (*securitatem dare*). The manner of reference certainly leaves open the possibility that some pledge may have been put down, but it might equally indicate that the two men merely gave assurances.
³⁷ Lombard law, for example, specified that sureties needed sufficient property to meet the obligation if necessary to do so and that they should come from the debtor's own district (Liutprand 128, 38); MGH Leges, iv, *Leges Langobardorum*, ed. F. Bluhme (Hanover, 1868), 161, 125.

[38] Suretyship in early medieval Brittany may have been more complex than the processes evidenced in the Redon Cartulary, for there exists in Old Breton a range of words that may relate to suretyship that are not evidenced in this text: *guuistl* (glossing *obses*), *rad* (glossing *stipulationes*) and *meich* (glossing *ratas*). They occur in contexts that do not elucidate precise meaning and do not distinguish between the import of the different words. It is therefore conceivable that some ninth-century people perceived distinctive types of surety, although there are considerable problems with this terminology and although this clearly was not so with the people who drew up the Redon texts. For the problems, see L. Fleuriot, 'Fragment' (1971) 78 *Annales de Bretagne* 648-54 and DGVB 75, 141, 193, 204, 253, 293. *Guuistl* may merely mean 'hostage' and may not imply 'hostage surety', although *aruuistl* clearly does refer to the gage put down and the tenth- or eleventh-century *Vita Gildae*, c.21, seems to refer to hostage sureties: *Nisi enim beatum virum Gildam mihi fideiussorem dederis...*; Gildae. De Excidio Britanniae, ed. and trans. H. Williams, Cymmrodorion Record Series 3 (2 vols., London, 1901), ii.356. CR 105 could be taken to indicate hostage sureties but not certainly so.
[39] See above n. 16; J.-0. Tjäder, *Die nichtliterarischen lateinischen papyri Italiens aus der Zeit 445-700* (Lund, 1955) i.232, where *fideiussores* were appointed in a tutelage case; MGH *Legum*, Sectio v, *Formulae Merowingici et Karolini Aevi*, ed. K. Zeumer (Hanover, 1886) 88 (Marculf II), although pledges were not used, be it noted, in formulas of sales or exchange; cf. the use of *fideiussores* in a variety of contexts in the taking of evidence in court and presenting of cases, ibid. 60, 67 (Marculf I); they were often cited in standard formulas in charter texts, particularly when freedoms were granted in the eighth and ninth centuries, for example MGH *Diplomata Karolinorum*, ed. E. Muhlbacher (Hanover, 1906) i.199 and MGH *Diplomata Regum Germaniae ex stirpe Karolinorum*, ed P. Kehr (Berlin, 1934) i.67; MGH *Leges*, iv, *Leges Langobardorum*, ed. F. Bluhme (Rothari 192, 346, Liutprand 36-41, 108) 46f, 79, 125f, 151. The Lombard laws have much detail (and modifications to it over the years) about surety and pledge procedure, especially in cases of debt.
[40] See further Davies and Fouracre, *Settlement of Disputes*, for discussion of the use of *fideiussor* in a great variety of early medieval contexts. See further below, nn. 44 and 48.
[41] *Digest*, 18.1.81, on whether or not land pledged as security for a loan would become the surety's by purchase if the surety himself paid the loan after the appointed term; *Codex Theodosianus*, 1.11.1, 2.30, 2.31.1, 10.3.4, *The Theodosian Code*, trans. C. Pharr (Princeton, 1952) 23, 60f, 270; J. A. C. Thomas, *Textbook of Roman Law*, 330-35.
[42] *The Irish Penitentials*, ed. L. Bieler (Dublin, 1963) 136-59, clauses A19/P28; cf. A30, on the requirement to pledge for future payment in cases of failure to pay tribute (*pignus det*); cf. A44/P48 on the sacrilege of invoking God as *fideiussor* (although the meaning here is presumably 'oath-helper'). Professor Fleuriot argued that this text was Breton and of sixth-century date, 'Fragment' (1971) 78 *Annales de Bretagne* 612-18; though the argument for the provenance is a strong one and it is very difficult to locate it other than in the east Breton/Anjou/Maine zone the argument for the date is less convincing and I cannot date it more precisely than fifth- to eighth-century inclusive (the manuscript is a ninth-century one and the content would be difficult to explain in a pre-fifth-century context). Although the formulation and terminology is quite different, the Frankish ruling that movables might be regarded as stolen property if witnesses to their transfer could not be provided seems to indicate a comparable pre-occupation and — interestingly — the area north of the Loire is specified in this context; *Pactus Legis Salicae*, ed. K. A. Eckhardt (Göttingen, 1955) clause 47, 292-6.
[43] *Die Irische Kanonensammlung*, ed. F. W. H. Wasserschleben (2nd. ed., Leipzig, 1885), lib. 34, 123. I am here understanding *ratus* as a Latinisation of Irish *ráth* although it may merely

have its common Latin meaning of 'sure'. Although the word *fideiussor* is not used in this clause *ratus* must stand for 'surety'; hence, the requirement that there be sureties and sanction (*stipulatio*) appears to be just the practice used in sale in ninth-century Brittany. Breton manuscripts are the source of much Irish canonical material; cf. Paris Bib. Nat., Lat. MSS 3182 and 12021. The comparability of the material in the *Collectio* is best explained in the context of the establishment of the early Irish church and the accompanying transmission of late Roman ideas; cf. D. Ó Corráin, L. Breatnach, A. Breen, 'The Laws of the Irish' (1984) 3 *Peritia* 382-438 for evidence of the absorption of biblical ideas in native secular material.

[44] I Atr. 3, III Atr. 5 (*The Laws of the Kings of England from Edmund to Henry I*, ed. A. J. Robertson (Cambridge, 1925) 54, 66); I Edw. 1, cf. Hl. and E. 16 (*The laws of the earliest English kings*, ed. F. L. Attenborough (Cambridge, 1922) 114, 22).

[45] Cf., especially, CR 124 where failure to produce sureties in a dispute about ownership provoked a judgement that the property be awarded to the other party. The prominence of the notion of sale in the Breton practice is emphasized by the fact that pledges are sometimes referred to as *venditiones* (although they are to be distinguished from real sales in perpetuity, as indicated above, p.78).

[46] E. Levy, *West Roman Vulgar law. The Law of Property* (Philadelphia, 1951) 129, 160. Cf. E. Levy, *Weströmisches Vulgarrecht*, 222: *Si venditor non fuerit idoneus, fideiussorem dare debet emptori* (Codex Euricianus); and ibid. 233, where Levy cites both Jerome and Augustine on the giving of an *arra* as an earnest in a pledge for sale; even classical Roman lawyers occasionally conceived the possibility of personal sureties being used in sale, *Digest*, 18.1.83; *Codes Theodosianus*, 8.18.1.

[47] I Atr 1.5 and 1.7 (Robertson, *Laws*, 52), in which sureties were to pay the wergeld of the accused to the lord entitled to fines incurred by him.

[48] MGH *Legum*, Sectio ii.1, *Capitularia Regum Francorum*, ed. A. Boretius (Hanover, 1883) 9; MGH *Legum*, Sectio ii.2, *Capitularia Regum Francorum*, ed. A. Boretius and V. Krause (Hanover, 1897) 277f; I Edg. 2, II Cnut 20 (Robertson, *Laws*, 16, 184); cf. I Edm. 7.1, I Atr 1 (Robertson, *Laws*, 10, 52) for sureties for the good behaviour of accused men; perhaps the *gorfodog* of late medieval Wales should be viewed in the same light, Ior 68/17, 70. In fact two of the sureties named in the Anau case (CR 202) were machtierns; however, the case is not comparable to the European examples cited here — even if it were argued that machtierns were representatives of state — since there are two of them, they are not called machtierns in the record and are not cited as leaders; they appear to have been involved by one of the parties to the agreement and not to have acted in any official capacity.

[49] Even where legal tracts from other parts of Europe suggest that payment was the norm, practice often involved more distraint than payment; this is well-evidenced in Lombard Italy. Despite the legislation of Rothari and Liutprand (see above nn. 37 and 39), *fideiussores* in one case of 761 gave a house (from the property of the accused) to the accuser because the pledge could not be found; *Il Regesto di Farfa*, ed. I. Georgi and U. Balzani (5 vols., Rome, 1879-1914) ii. docs.44, 45, pp.51f. (I am grateful to Chris Wickham for making this point to me with some force.)

IX

INTRA-FAMILY TRANSACTIONS IN SOUTH-EASTERN BRITTANY

THE DOSSIER FROM REDON

The source

The monastery of Redon was founded in 832, at the head of the navigable waters of the River Vilaine, in north-west France, in the département of Ille-et-Vilaine and region of Brittany (Bretagne; fig. 1). The source of much of our information about south-eastern Brittany in the central middle ages is a cartulary that was written at Redon in the late eleventh century and maintained thereafter into the mid-twelfth century[1]. It was written in the second half of the eleventh century in the period when Abbot Aumod (1062-?1083) was energetically securing the monastery's interests. This is evident from the fact that the early scripts of the cartulary (to f. 138v) are strongly influenced by those from mid- and late eleventh-century Mont-Saint-Michel – a foundation that we know to have had Breton interests and close contacts with Redon (Abbot Mainard was for a time abbot of both in the first decade of the eleventh century); further, the latest charter written in these scripts is dated to 1081; and Hubert Guillotel has identified the mid-eleventh-century scribe, Iudicael, who completed this first part of the cartulary[2].

There are now 391 charters in this cartulary, but there are at least 46 folios missing and the medieval cartulary would clearly have had well over

---

[1] *Le cartulaire de Redon*, ed. A. de Courson, Paris, 1863 (hereafter CR, cited by charter n°.); and now a new facsimile, *Cartulaire de l'abbaye Saint-Sauveur de Redon*, Rennes, 1998. See H. Guillotel, *Le manuscrit, ibid.*, p. 9-14, for description of the manuscript.

[2] H. Guillotel, *Le manuscrit...*, p. 13-16. Cf. *The Monks of Redon. Gesta sanctorum Rotonensium and Vita Conuuoionis*, ed. and trans. C. Brett, Woodbridge, 1989 (*Studies in Celtic History*, 10), p. 25-27; and also W. Davies, *The composition of the Redon cartulary*, in *Francia*, 17, 1990, p. 69-90.

400 charters[3]. Despite the date of compilation, a high proportion of the charters in this collection relates to the ninth or early tenth century and 246 of the 391 record transactions from the two generations, A.D. 830-880; a further 22 charters pre-date 830. Of 62 additional charters known from early modern transcripts (presumably originally copied from the folios that are now missing), 55 also relate to the period 830-880 and 2 to before 830; and there is an isolated copy of a further ninth-century charter in the Bordeaux Bible (Bordeaux MS 1, f. 259v)[4]. In total, then, we have copies of 302 charters from 830-880 and 24 from pre-830. Over half of the 302 record donations (57%); 18% record sales and 6% record «pledges»[5]; a further 10% record disputes and their outcomes. There is one exchange and the remaining miscellanea include a sworn witness statement, bequests and a genealogy. (Of the pre-830 charters, 12% record donations, 64% sales, 16% pledges, and 4% disputes – a striking difference from the subsequent fifty years.)

Now, these charters only exist in cartulary or later copies. There are no originals. Questions have therefore to be asked about authenticity, especially as we do not know precisely why the initial cartulary was compiled. A small element of falsification is evident in the ninth-century texts where, for example, ecclesiastical rights following a transaction have been amplified (embellishments which appear to have been made in the ninth century not the eleventh)[6]; however, for the most part there is nothing to suggest either tampering with or invention of the ninth-century texts[7]. Moreover, Breton name forms consistently reflect ninth-century

---

[3] See further W. Davies, *The composition...*, p. 70-71.

[4] Most of these additional charters are printed by de Courson in an Appendix to CR (here cited as App.), but all but one of the others are printed by H. Morice, *Mémoires pour servir de preuves à l'histoire ecclésiastique et civile de Bretagne*, 3 vol., Paris, 1742-1746, I, col. 265, 271, 272, 295, 297, 308 (here cited as Addit.). See also H. Guillotel, *Le manuscrit...*, p. 9.

[5] «Pledge» transactions were those in which land was mortgaged to another party for a short, specified period (commonly 3 × 7 years) in return for cash; if the cash was not repaid after the expiry of the term, the land stayed with the pledgee in perpetuity; see further, W. Davies, *Small Worlds. The Village Community in Early Medieval Brittany*, London, 1988, p. 135.

[6] See W. Davies, *Forgery in the Cartulaire de Redon*, in *Fälschungen im Mittelalter. Internationaler Kongreß der Monumenta Germaniae historica, München 16.-19. September 1986*, IV, Hannover, 1988 (*M.G.H., Schriften*, 33-IV), p. 265-274 : p. 272; and below n. 32.

[7] Cf. H. Guillotel, *Le manuscrit...*, p. 18-19.

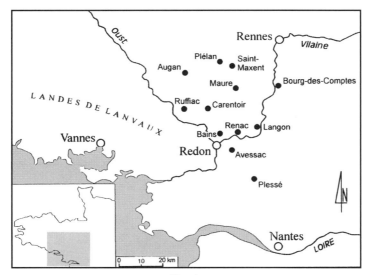

Fig. 1.

rather than later forms of the language and ninth-century orthography is consistently different from that of the eleventh century[8] : indeed consistent changes are determinable between early and late ninth-century practice. The construction of the cartulary can be determined : there are different sets of original material, organized in some cases chronologically and in others regionally – with a major reorganization of the archive taking place in the late 860s under Abbot Ritcant (867-871); different diplomatic practices are evident in the collection and different formulas were consistently favoured by different, named, scribes[9]. Plenty of the material is irrelevant to the interests of Redon in the eleventh century or earlier and there is a mass of local circumstantial detail; indeed, some of the material is patently obviously copied from something ancient and has gaps and errors of transcription. We can therefore be completely confident that the eleventh-century scribes at Redon were working from archaic material and that a high proportion of the ninth-century texts has not been deliberately changed.

---

[8] Cf. B. Tanguy, *Les noms d'hommes et les noms de lieux*, in *Cartulaire de l'abbaye...*, p. 49-69 : p. 49-51.
[9] See further W. Davies, *The composition...*, especially p. 77-78; H. Guillotel, *Le manuscrit...*, p. 19; W. Davies, *Forgery...*, p. 267, 273.

IX

The copyists of the Redon cartulary chose to preserve much of the documentation that pertained to their estates before their acquisition by Redon. The collection therefore allows insights into relationships that were either prior to, or unaffected by, the existence of the monastery, although there is of course plenty about the monastery and its affairs. As it happens, the collection provides a large quantity of case material concerning familial land transactions; this material is very well localized, and – as the figures above make clear – is dense across the two generations of A.D. 830-880.

Contexts

For the most part the charters of the Redon cartulary record transactions relating to the rolling countryside of south-eastern Brittany, a land of good-quality, workable soil and gentle slopes; in the ninth century it was a region of mixed farming, with plenty of cereal growing; however, a few transactions relate to coastal saltpans and to vineyards. This was an area with some estates but also with many small-holdings, worked by free peasant proprietors, by free tenants and by unfree workers; the small-holdings, typically, were of 10-25 hectare size and were known locally as *rannou* (*ran* in the singular). Despite the widespread occurrence of a servile population, there were also vigorous communities of free peasants (who were themselves serf-owners). It is the transactions of these free peasant communities that most frequently form the subject of the charters, although there is also material relating to the dealings of great and of petty aristocrats.

There are differences in the material from east and west of the River Vilaine, both numerically and qualitatively (see fig. 1). That from the west is more plentiful than that from the east. That from the east perhaps indicates larger estates and fewer peasant proprietors than those associated with the many small-holdings that are so evident in the west (although, with less material from the east, one cannot be confident of this distinction). More certain, however, is a linguistic distinction. West and south of the Vilaine the normal vernacular tongue was Breton (a Celtic language still indistinguishable in the ninth century from the Brittonic of south-west Britain [Old Cornish], although it was soon to diverge from insular Brittonic to become Old Breton); this language was sometimes used to record property boundaries and the names of local institutions in the Redon collection and the thousands of personal and topographic names that are recorded are overwhelmingly Breton. To the east of the

Vilaine, and particularly east of a line 8-10 km east of the river, names were much more likely to be Frankish[10].

Rules for the transmission of property

There are no ninth-century collections of property law for eastern Brittany, although one rule is explicitly stated as a preface to a transaction. We therefore do not know – except by processes of deduction – what rules normally guided the inhabitants in their dealings and in inheritance practice. Interestingly, the one rule that is stated is about the free alienability of noble property and the freedom of nobles to adopt an heir[11].

By contrast, the corpus of law from the Celtic cultures of insular Britain and Ireland is vast, with property law and family law a significant part of that material. Irish law especially (which is largely of eighth-century date) has multiple and complex rules for every conceivable situation[12]. There is no need to suppose that Breton law was the same or even similar but, since it was customary law not rulers' law or the product of legislation, scholars have in the past expected that continental Celtic cultures organized their relationships in a manner similar to those of insular Celtic cultures. Rightly or wrongly this has had a profound, and continuing, influence on the historiography of the subject[13].

Without wishing to imply that any of the detail of any insular legal collection is applicable to Brittany, I would nevertheless draw some general points from this insular material: firstly, that one would not expect rules for the transmission of acquired land to be the same as those for inherited or family land; secondly, that the categories of enquiry commonly used to discuss insular norms and procedures can be helpful[14].

---

[10] See W. Davies, *Small Worlds...*, p. 15, fig. 3.

[11] CR 109.

[12] *Corpus iuris Hiberniae*, ed. D. A. Binchy, 6 vol., Dublin, 1979; for a very accessible guide to this difficult material, see F. Kelly, *A Guide to Early Irish Law*, Dublin, 1988. For modern discussion of many of the issues surrounding family relationships in insular Celtic societies, see T. M. Charles-Edwards, *Early Irish and Welsh Kinship*, Oxford, 1993.

[13] For example, A. Le Moyne de La Borderie, *Histoire de Bretagne*, 6 vol., Rennes-Paris, 1896-1904, especially II; R. Largillière, *Les saints et l'organisation chrétienne primitive dans l'Armorique bretonne*, Rennes, 1925; L. Fleuriot, *Un fragment en latin de très anciennes lois bretonnes armoricaines du VIe siècle*, in *Annales de Bretagne*, 78, 1971, p. 601-660; P. Flatrès, *Les anciennes structures rurales de Bretagne d'après le cartulaire de Redon. Le paysage rural et son évolution*, in *Études rurales*, 41, 1971, p. 87-93.

[14] See further, W. Davies, *Small Worlds...*, p. 70-76.

IX

886

Families

If we are to consider family property we need to know how, if at all, the family was defined for purposes of property transmission. In the Redon collection the terminology of family definition and family relationships is unspecific and unstable : there is no word, for example, for the three-generation or the four-generation family group, as there is in Irish law; and although sons, brothers and nephews are regularly identified, there are no words to differentiate first cousins from second or third cousins. Hence, the words *patres, coheredes, consanuuinei* (sic) and *propinqui* all occur for the active and functional family, as for example in the phrase «*Finituuoret cum filiis et fratribus et propinquis*»[15].

Despite the lack of appropriate terms, family interest in the transmission of peasant property is in practice manifest in the evidence of actual cases (where «family» demonstrably means a wider group than the nuclear family). Cases specifying the range of extended family members involved in a transaction constitute no more than 15% of the total corpus of transactions (and they all pre-date 860) but a larger proportion is implied by the use of generic «family» words (again mostly in earlier charters), and by a word commonly used to express the power to be exercised over property conveyed, *di-cofrit*, «land without [the encumbrance of] co-participation»; the latter would perhaps take the proportion beyond 35% to 50%[16].

On the basis of recorded practice, two degrees of kinship (that is the group that includes uncles, nephews and first cousins) were often demonstrably involved in the transmission of landed property. Accordingly, we find a man called Rigun, his son Iargun and his nephew Omnis pledging «their» property in Bains to a wealthy peasant in 833; and when the nephew sold a different property in Bains to a lay couple in 846, that sale was witnessed by his sister, brother and nephew, their relationship to the vendor being carefully and significantly spelled out in the witness list[17]. There are no recorded cases of the involvement of more distantly related kin. I therefore conclude that the three-generation group, that is the descendants of a common grandfather, was the extent of the effective family for these purposes. (Family interest in the transmission of chattels is not demonstrated in this collection.)

---

[15] CR 261.

[16] CR 121, 153, 171, App. 17, etc.; L. Fleuriot, *Dictionnaire des gloses en vieux Breton*, Paris, 1964, p. 112; W. Davies, *Small Worlds...*, p. 50-51, n. 57.

[17] CR 182, 121.

«Family property» does not of course have to imply family co-residence on the land or co-working of it, although both might occur. It does, however, imply that each member of the family group, as customarily defined, had an interest in the management and exploitation of its landed property, and – in effect – a power of veto against its total or partial alienation : since the land was owned by the whole family rather than by individuals, no individual or sub-group had the freedom to dispose of it without the agreement of the family, unless or until a decision for share-out was taken. The use of the vernacular term *cowen-ran*, «shared *ran*», explicitly makes the point[18].

Sibling and cousin transactions

While the total corpus of material implies that siblings often worked together, there are plenty of cases that show them either in dispute or splitting the family property. It appears that it was a normal thing for children either to co-work a peasant family property or to work separate portions within the orbit of the family group; however, it could also happen that one (or more) member of a family insisted that the family property be split so that he could take his portion, as an individual, and go off to a separate and unconnected life. The recorded cases are often about the family member who wished to leave the family and join a monastery but this is not invariably the explanation for the share-out : sometime in the first half of the ninth century Howoret's family shared out its land in Ruffiac, using documents to record the division; in the 840s Howoret sold the share he had received to another peasant and it was only twenty years later that that share was passed on – by a gift – to the monastery[19]. Lalocan's ancestors shared out their land in Plessé round about 830 (a generation before 854); Sulmonoc's ancestors shared out theirs in Bains sometime before the 860s; Agon and his brothers shared out their land in Langon before the 830s (see fig. 1)[20].

Sometimes the decision to share and the terms of the share-out were questioned some years later. In Agon's case, he had in effect bought out the interests of his two brothers, giving them many *solidi* so that he could retain all his father's property himself. His two brothers clearly became dissatisfied with this arrangement for the case and went to court in Langon in the period 832-838; Agon suggested that they should return the *solidi* he

---

[18] CR 6; see further L. Fleuriot, *Dictionnaire*..., p. 112.
[19] CR 220, 221.
[20] CR 92, 162, 192.

had given them and then the land could be redivided, this time equally; the local judgment-finders judged that this was the right way forward; the brothers, Etelfrid and Godun, therefore handed over 30 *solidi* and a barrel of wine to Agon and all were reconciled.

Often it was in the next generation that a share-out would be questioned : it was first cousins and nephews who raised the issues at that time, people who were not party to the original decision but who felt that they had lost some benefit. In order to retrieve what they believed to be their own rightful inheritance, Lalocan's two cousins went so far as to sue the monastery of Redon in 854 for the share that Lalocan had given it; they were thwarted by the elders of the *plebs* (proto-parish, proto-commune), who testified that Lalocan's gift constituted the share which his own father had received in the earlier share-out – and therefore that he was free to give it all away[21]. In Carentoir Iudwallon managed to hold on to a property which his uncle had given to Redon, but he finally had to hand ownership over to the monastery in 866, agreeing to be a tenant and pay an annual rent[22]. A man called Winic actually gave sureties to Redon in 868 that he would not lay claim to a property in Plélan that his uncle had sold to a priest, who had subsequently given it away to the monastery; clearly in this case there were expectations that he might make a claim on his uncle's former land, despite the subsequent transactions[23].

Siblings might buy out each others' shares too, as Agon had tried to do, and this sometimes led to later disputes. In Ruffiac Catweten sold Ran Riantcar to his sister Roiantken with full powers of alienation, for 15 *solidi*, in 821. We do not know why but at some point during the next eighteen years (perhaps because his sister took steps to alienate the land from the family[24]) Catweten tried to revoke the sale; the case went to court but it was judged by the local panel that the sale had been permanent; soon after this Roiantken sold the land[25]. Catweten features as a witness to sales in Ruffiac on at least three occasions between 820 and 830, but we do not know anything about his parents. His sister Roiantken seems to be the same

---

[21] CR 162; cf. CR 29, a different but comparable case. The *plebs* was the primary unit of social organization and it was the predecessor of the fully developed parish; in the ninth century it was usually about 40-50 km² in area, though could be larger or smaller; see W. Davies, *Small Worlds...*, p. 63-67.

[22] CR 56 and 110; Addit. 6 (A.D. 869).

[23] CR 223.

[24] By 839 the land was in the hands of someone else, Haelhoiam, who sold it again; CR 148. We do not know the relationship between Roiantken and Haelhoiam.

[25] CR 146, 145, 147. H. Guillotel, *Répertoire chronologique*, in *Cartulaire de l'abbaye...*, p. 71-78 : p. 74, would date the dispute within five years of the original sale.

Roiantken who married the machtiern Deurhoiarn of neighbouring Augan, acquiring some property from him in Augan as her morning gift[26]. Deurhoiarn and Roiantken were a pious couple, making several grants to Redon from Ruffiac and Augan and finally securing burial within the church at Saint-Maxent, in each case after an elaborate funeral procession. Roiantken seems to have been relatively wealthy and must have come from the well-off peasantry of Ruffiac or the minor aristocracy. She was involved in a number of property deals in her own right – some of which were clearly in order to allow her to make pious donations. Her son Iarnwocon seems to have succeeded to his father's property interests in at least two *plebes* but is not called machtiern in these texts[27].

Disputes inevitably occurred but I would not wish to suggest that they followed each transaction. More importantly, we should consider the possibility that the share-out within the family was a common, if intermittent, process – buying, selling, swapping, and giving; these frequent deals and negotiations between family members were what made a system which transmitted property rights through whole families work. Indeed, it is very difficult to see how such a system could have worked in practice for peasant cultivators without some swapping of portions[28].

Husbands and wives

Husbands and wives often made joint transactions, or consented to each other's transactions; once, in 856, their interest in a transaction was specified as two thirds for the husband and one third for the wife[29]. There is plenty too on the transactions of widows and their sons. However, there is very little in this collection on transactions between husbands and wives, other than those that are a direct consequence of marriage transactions – and these are reserved for a later meeting.

Two sets of transactions nevertheless throw some light on husband/wife deals after marriage, although they have rather different implications. The first is of a recognizable type : some time in the 840s Arthviu sold Ran

---

[26] Machtierns were petty aristocrats and often presided at the performance of village transactions.

[27] CR 79; 173, 174, 175; 236. See W. Davies, *Small Worlds*..., p. 178-179.

[28] There is also evidence of the splitting of land blocks called *hereditates*. In fact these do not appear to have been blocks of family property but the accumulated (sometimes scattered) interests of single individuals : *hereditas Uuorethoc* was thus the property amassed (by purchase and other means) by the man Worethoc; CR 249, 250, 252; cf. W. Davies, *Small Worlds*..., p. 95-97.

[29] CR 193.

Riculf and another property in Bains to his wife Maginsin for over 30 *solidi*, naming six sureties; subsequently she gave the *ran* away to the monastery at Redon[30]. An «elder» of Bains, Arthviu was a well-known local peasant, owner of several properties, a frequent witness of transactions, a surety for some, a man who gave sworn evidence on behalf of a fellow elder and who himself acted on the panel of judgment-finders several times – a notable local worthy[31]. In his recorded transaction with his wife he sold her land that he had acquired from an unredeemed pledge, and which was therefore unencumbered with family restrictions. Since, once she had bought it, Maginsin passed the *ran* on to the church, it looks as if the husband/wife transaction was in fact a mechanism to provide her with some freely alienable property; alternatively, however, Arthviu himself may have been the impetus behind the donation, selling the land to his wife to free it from any possibility of his own family claims. In either case the stimulus seems to have been a desire to acquire freely alienable land, and the consequent freedom to bestow land in perpetuity on the church[32]. The mechanism has parallels with some eighth-century cases from Wales in western Britain : between about 705 and 765 kings of south Wales sold estates to local men who immediately passed on the estates to the church; since, previous to this, permanent alienation of landed property only seems to have been carried out by kings, and since sales are very rare in the Welsh corpus, there is a very strong implication that the sales were in fact a mechanism by which the laity could acquire alienable land[33].

The second case is even more interesting. In April 820 a man called Tethwiu bought Ran Lowinid in Tréal (at that time part of Ruffiac *plebs*) from another called Euhocar; nearly ten years later (829 or early 830) he gave it to his wife Argantan, «knowing that she was a faithful wife», although he reserved an annual payment from it to the very minor local monastery at Quoiqueneuc, in northern Ruffiac, not far from Tréal[34]. Many

---

[30] CR 186.

[31] W. Davies, *Small Worlds*..., p. 93, 126, 155, 157.

[32] Arthviu acquired the land from Moenken, CR 199. This text has been corrupted, apparently in the monastic scriptorium, so that the terms of the pledge to Arthviu are that he acquired very full (in fact, incongruously full) powers of ownership over the pledged land. These phrases appear to have been inserted when the original pledge text was copied in the Redon archives, presumably to make sure that Moenken's family had no possibility of making a counterclaim; see further W. Davies, *Forgery*..., p. 271.

[33] W. Davies, *An Early Welsh Microcosm*, London, 1978, p. 51-54; Id., *Land and power in early medieval Wales*, in *Past and Present*, 81, 1978, p. 3-23 : p. 10-12.

[34] There were at least two such monasteries in Ruffiac, as well as the group of

years later Argantan's son Courantmonoc gave this *ran* to the monastery of Redon, since it had been bequeathed to him by Argantan, and he also gave Redon the annual payment formerly due to Quoiqueneuc[35]. Now Tethwiu appeared several times as a witness to Ruffiac transactions in the 820s; however, when he witnessed in 830 he was called «abbot»[36]. It looks as if he became head of this tiny monastery at Quoiqueneuc round about 829 and, while setting up some benefit for the place, nevertheless took action to keep his acquired land within his family.

These texts are of especial value since they date from the period before the foundation of Redon and show no signs of subsequent Redon tampering. In fact, a cleric called Tethwiu was one of the original group of four that established the monastery at Redon in 832; since the leader of the group, Conwoion, came from this part of south-eastern Brittany, from Comblessac 11 km to the east of Quoiqueneuc, it is plausible that it was indeed the same Tethwiu from Tréal who made up the group of four. If so, he thereby abandoned his family, though still leaving them in possession of the family land, and established himself 20 km away in Redon, witnessing a transaction first after Conwoion in Avessac in 841[37]. In this case the gift from husband to wife looks like a direct strategy to preserve family land; the fact that her son subsequently alienated Ran Lowinid is another, much later, and different, story.

Both cases, incidentally, raise interesting questions about female property rights.

Godparents

There are only four transactions involving godparents – and this is not enough to allow any firm conclusions. However, the cases are intrinsically interesting and if they have parallels elsewhere in Europe in this period may perhaps be understood better.

It appears to have been common in this north-western part of the continent for the godparent (*patronus*) to make a gift of property to the godson (*filiolus*)[38]. Since this was twice linked to a ceremony of hair-

---

priests serving the *plebs* church; everything suggests that this kind of «monastery» was more like a hermitage : a hut, one or two people, some appurtenant land nearby.

[35] CR 151, 152, 154.
[36] CR 146, 196; 155.
[37] CR Ap. 2, 195; cf. *The Monks of Redon. Gesta sanctorum Rotonensium...* cit. n. 2, I.1 and II.8. For Conwoion and Comblessac, *ibid.*, I.1.
[38] CR 45/157; 128, 129, 130; 244; 279.

cutting in this material it may have been part of a wider coming-of-age ritual : alternatively, these particular cases may simply have marked the occasion of becoming a cleric. Hence, some time before 866 Freoc, a cleric, received a *ran* in Ruffiac from his *patronus*, his mother's brother Arthviu (a different man from Arthviu of Bains), on the occasion of his tonsuring[39].

In fact, in two of these transactions (one of which was the Arthviu case above), the *patronus* was the godson's maternal uncle. This might suggest that becoming a godparent was at least in part a mechanism for maternal kin to retain an interest in the offspring of their women. On the other hand, the effect of these godparents' donations was to alienate property from their own kin and put it within the control of their woman's husband's kin. One patronal gift in Bourg-des-Comptes got sold on in 871 by the godson and his mother, with his father's consent – not the godparent's (his mother's brother); in another, much earlier, case, sometime before 834, when the godparent tried to retract his gift in Maure, the godson and his father took the man to court, as a result of which the godparent had to confirm the gift[40]. In effect, then, this became a way for the paternal kin of a boy to acquire an interest in the property of his maternal kin. When the godson was a cleric, the patronal gift in effect became his religious endowment, thereby minimizing the alienation of paternal family land. However, it has to be said that we do not know enough about the individuals involved in these cases and cannot therefore perceive much detail of the dynamics of the social intercourse.

Summing up

The strategies that we can see in this material are practical. What we do not often see are strategies of preservation (perhaps because the successful strategies were undocumented). There is no getting away from the fact that many of the share-outs evidenced in this corpus tended to lead to a diminution of the family's landed property, from family to church. There is little suggestion in this material of any compensating increase in, for example, family influence in the monastic circle or in protection for the family by the abbot; for the most part the protagonists came from too low a social level, and from too far from the monastery (20-40 km), to achieve

[39] CR 45/157.
[40] CR 244; 129.

this. This drain on the family stock may perhaps explain why some of the disputes following such cases seem so bitter : the division was not, on the whole, in the interests of the family.

The transactions between members of the laity that are evidenced in this collection are overwhelmingly about alienability, that is – for whatever reason – they are about acquiring land that was freely alienable and not subject to the encumbrance of peasant family interest and peasant family claims. Hence the pledges and the purchases : buying pledged land (in effect unredeemed mortgaged land) seems to have been a standard way to secure freedom of disposal. There can be no doubt that a primary reason for wanting alienable land was to bestow it on ecclesiastical institutions, whether the local church or a grander one, and whether as outright or precarial gift or endowment to accompany a newly ordained priest; split and share-out occurred in order to release property and bestow it on churches and monasteries. However, not all of the cases of share-out evidenced in this corpus have a religious association – Howoret's family share-out, and Lalocan's and Sulmonoc's did not do so, and only subsequent events introduced a religious interest; even the local abbot Tethwiu took action to keep property in his family and out of the church. We must therefore allow that religious endowment was not the only stimulus to acquiring alienable land.

Most of these cases are too early to investigate the specific reasons behind each action and it is impossible to unravel all that was going on; however, it does look as if some deeper processes were in train. One of the interesting things that this material reveals is the dynamic of property movement within the family : a frequent process of sharing, swapping, and splitting portions of the family land in order to keep it workable; this was what made a system which allowed for joint family ownership work. Nevertheless, though common in the early ninth century, the implications are that splits and swaps were increasing during the century and the reality of joint family ownership was fragmenting, leading to more individually owned land. Family interests had not disappeared by the 880s, but in the period 830-880 we have a window on a gradual change, which was becoming more rapid in the 850s and 860s. Obviously, the establishment of a major property-owning monastic corporation was one factor in increasing the rate of change (and there is plentiful evidence of an aggressive and hard-headed approach to property management coming from Redon in the 860s)[41]. But while the religious pressure to bring freely

---

[41] See W. Davies, *Small Worlds...*, p. 190, 212-213.

alienable land on to the market was therefore immensely important, I suspect that other processes were at work too and several things were happening concurrently : political pressures in the form of fiscal demands and a greater availability of cash[42], to name but the most obvious, must equally have contributed to the forces for change at this particular period.

---

[42] The notable increase in the money element of rents in the central decades of the ninth century in this area and the number of pledge transactions – a major point of which was to generate cash for the pledgor – make the availability of cash point; see W. Davies, *Small Worlds...*, p. 56-58, for detailed discussion.

X

WYNEBWERTH ET *ENEPUUERT* : L'ENTRETIEN DES ÉPOUSES DANS LA BRETAGNE DU IXe SIÈCLE *

Qui fournissait les dots des femmes et quel niveau de contrôle celles-ci pouvaient-elles exercer en ce domaine : ces questions sont aussi difficiles à discuter pour les régions celtiques que pour le reste de l'Europe, étant donné les problèmes causés par l'instabilité de la terminologie médiévale, le caractère partiel des témoignages et l'incohérence des termes employés aujourd'hui pour désigner les institutions et les procédures de la période médiévale. Dans les régions celtiques, comme dans bien d'autres, l'arc de signification du mot *dos* pouvait être large, alors que la série complète de termes utilisés pour les paiements de mariage au haut Moyen Âge était limité – et certaines procédures n'ont pas de désignations conservées pour cette époque.

Dans les lignes qui suivent, je compte explorer ce que le témoignage de Redon, donc de la Bretagne orientale du IXe siècle, peut nous apporter sur les arrangements matrimoniaux et sur les intérêts fonciers des épouses; j'y ajouterai des témoignages bretons et quelques autres comparatifs provenant du Pays de Galles et de l'Irlande, où des institutions similaires à celles de l'Europe occidentale étaient exprimées dans un cadre conceptuel différent.

Les textes

Le cartulaire de Redon est un cartulaire du XIe siècle qui mentionne un grand nombre de chartes du IXe siècle, 246 pour les deux générations des années 830-880 et 22 datant d'avant 830, c'est-à-dire des documents d'origine locale précédant la fondation du monastère de Redon en 832 – un groupe particulièrement important[1]. Si l'on y

---

* Traduction de Pierre-Yves Le Pogam.

[1] A. de Courson, *Cartulaire de l'abbaye de Redon en Bretagne* (Collection des documents inédits sur l'histoire de France, 1re s., *Histoire politique*), Paris, 1863 (ci-après : *CR* avec le n° de l'acte); existe aussi en fac-similé : *Cartulaire de l'abbaye Saint-Sauveur de Redon*, Rennes, 1998. Cf. H. Guillotel, *Le manuscrit*, dans *Cartulaire de l'abbaye...*, p. 9-14, pour une description du manuscrit.

ajoute les chartes connues uniquement par des transcriptions modernes, on aboutit à un total de 302 documents pour la période 830-880 et de 24 pour les années 800-830[2]. La plupart des textes se rapportent à une petite zone du sud-est de la Bretagne, grossièrement une zone de 40 km sur 30 du bassin de l'Oust et de la Vilaine et, par conséquent, ils couvrent de manière intensive cette région sur deux générations. Les acteurs sont le plus souvent des paysans, même si nous apercevons aussi parfois les activités et les négociations de quelques aristocrates. La plupart étaient bretons; autrement dit, ils parlaient une langue – le vieux breton – qui ne se distingue guère, à cette époque, du gallois du Pays de Galles. Cependant, il y avait également des Francs sur la rive orientale de la Vilaine et leur négociations sont également mentionnées dans les documents (voir carte)[3].

On devrait noter ici qu'il n'existe pas de collections de lois pour cette période de la Bretagne. Plus exactement, il n'y a qu'un seul texte, bref, du haut Moyen Âge, de caractère semi-législatif, sans provenance et sans datation, les *Excerpta de libris Romanorum et Francorum* (ci-après : *ELR*)[4]. Ce texte est très probablement originaire de la Bretagne orientale, mais il pourrait également provenir de régions plus à l'est, l'Anjou ou le Maine. Bien que considéré traditionnellement comme datant du VIe siècle, il pourrait bien être du VIIe ou même du VIIIe siècle. Il est de caractère composite, comme l'indique le titre du manuscrit, et, quoiqu'il contienne des matériaux qui possèdent d'étroits parallèles au Pays de Galles ou en Irlande, il est clair qu'il renferme également des matériaux d'origine franque[5]. Par conséquent, ce n'est pas un très bon témoin de la théorie et de la pratique juridiques bretonnes.

Ainsi, ce sont les chartes qui fournissent la majorité écrasante de nos informations. Elles nous offrent des vues sur les caractères

---

[2] La plupart de ces chartes supplémentaires sont éditées par A. de Courson dans un Appendice à *CR* (ci-après : *App.*) et toutes les autres, sauf une, sont éditées par H. Morice, *Mémoires pour servir de preuves à l'histoire ecclésiastique et civile de Bretagne*, I, Paris, 1742, col. 265, 271, 272, 295, 297, 308. Cf. aussi H. Guillotel, *Le manuscrit...*, p. 9.

[3] Pour une discussion plus détaillée de ces documents, cf. H. Guillotel, *Le manuscrit...* et Id., *Répertoire chronologique*, dans *Cartulaire de l'abbaye...*, ainsi que W. Davies, *The composition of the Redon cartulary*, dans *Francia*, 17, 1990, p. 69-90; pour une discussion sur la société locale, Id., *Small worlds. The village community in early Medieval Brittany*, Londres, 1988. Cf. Id., *Intra-family transactions in South-Eastern Brittany*, dans *MEFRM*, 111, 1999, p. 881-894.

[4] Édités avec une trad. anglaise dans *The Irish Penitentials*, éd. L. Bieler, Dublin, 1963 (*Scriptores Latini Hiberniae*, 5), p. 136-159.

[5] Cf. L. Fleuriot, *Un fragment en latin de très anciennes lois bretonnes armoricaines du VIe siècle*, dans *Annales de Bretagne*, 78, 1971, p. 601-660; D. N. Dumville, *On the dating of the early Breton lawcodes*, dans *Études celtiques*, 21, 1984, p. 207-221.

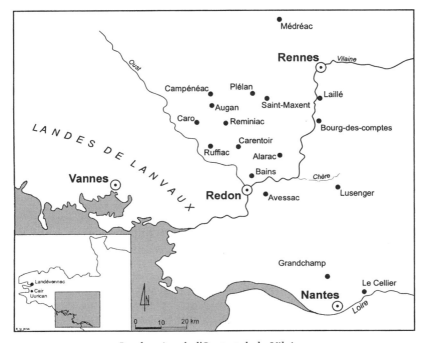

Les bassins de l'Oust et de la Vilaine.

spécifiques des négociations et des relations entre les individus : en d'autres termes, c'est de la pratique qu'elles nous parlent. Par conséquent, nous en savons bien peu sur les principes ou sur les normes coutumières, en dehors de ce que l'on peut déduire de la pratique. C'est pourquoi, on ne peut pas détecter, dans ce matériel, les contradictions entre les règles et la pratique; mais on rencontre quelques témoignages indirects sur le processus d'établissement des normes[6].

LES DROITS DE PROPRIÉTÉ DES FEMMES DANS LES DOCUMENTS DE REDON

Les femmes figurent dans 20% des 267 actes du IXe siècle conservés par la collection de Redon. Je vais esquisser rapidement la nature de leur activité, en commençant par les filles, puis en étu-

---

[6] Cf. ci-dessous, p. 423-425.

diant les épouses agissant en lien avec leurs maris, ensuite les épouses agissant seules, enfin les veuves.

1. *Les filles*

On déduit très clairement de notre matériel que les filles, qu'elles soient paysannes ou nobles, qu'elles soient bretonnes ou franques, pouvaient hériter des propriétés foncières de leurs pères et/ou de leurs mères. Elles pouvaient aliéner ces terres si elles le voulaient (on cite diverses objections contre ces aliénations, mais aucune d'entre elles n'est mentionnée comme l'ayant emporté); et elles pouvaient les transmettre à leurs enfants. Ainsi, la fille de Dorgen réussit à donner la petite *hereditas* de son père à Alarac au monastère de Redon, malgré les oppositions de ses cousins; en 869, la noble femme Roiantdreh choisit comme héritier le prince breton Salomon pour la terre qu'elle a héritée de sa famille, citant sa généalogie sur huit générations masculines pour montrer la force de ses droits sur ce bien et proclamant fermement qu'elle était libre d'en disposer à sa guise (même si elle en réservait des portions pour ses filles); en 850, Bernegarda vendit des terres à Laillé qu'elle avait héritées de son père et de sa mère; et, en 840, un homme, Catuuoret, donna sa terre à Campénéac qu'il avait héritée de sa mère – *ex parte matris meae*[7]. Avec une telle capacité pour aliéner, les filles pouvaient certainement exercer, en certaines circonstances, le contrôle sur les terres familiales, en vertu de leur droit propre – un contrôle parfois commun aux membres de la famille et parfois exercé à titre individuel. Ces terres pouvaient être de taille substantielle.

2. *Les femmes mariées et leurs époux*

Dans l'état de mariage, les femmes pouvaient, conjointement avec leur mari, acquérir de nouveaux biens fonciers, en général, dans nos textes, par achat. Cela est vrai aussi bien chez les paysans que chez les nobles, chez les Bretons que chez les Francs. Ainsi, en 808, Renodo et sa femme Uuinuanau achetèrent ensemble une église à Grandchamp; en 813, Iuduuallon et sa femme Ibiau prirent des champs à Carentoir comme choses en gage[8]; en 847, le forgeron Carantcar et sa femme Uuentamau achetèrent quelques champs à

---

[7] *CR*, nos 29, 109, 125, 194.

[8] Les négociations de mises en gage étaient celles où une terre était hypothéquée à une autre partie pour une courte période, fixée à l'avance (en général trois fois sept ans) contre de l'argent comptant; si l'argent n'était pas remboursé à l'expiration du délai, la terre restait aux mains du créancier. Cf., pour plus de détails, W. Davies, *Small worlds...*, p. 135.

Ruffiac; en 846, Mainhoiarn et son épouse Latmoet achetèrent une pièce de terre à Bains, la sœur du vendeur servant de témoin; dans les années 840, Risuueten et sa femme Uuenuuocon achetèrent un champ à Ruffiac[9]. Beaucoup de ces exemples eurent lieu au début du IXe siècle et se rapportent à des propriétés très médiocres; ils semblent refléter les négociations ordinaires, à petite échelle, de cette société paysanne avant la fondation et les répercussions subséquentes du riche et puissant monastère de Redon.

Les femmes mariées pouvaient aussi aliéner des biens fonciers conjointement avec leur mari, que ce soit par don, par vente ou par mise en gage. Bien que la plupart des témoignages concernant ces aliénations se rapportent à des Francs et à la petite aristocratie, les Bretons Bili et Morliuuet donnèrent au monastère de Redon une pièce de terre située à Augan, quelque part dans les années 860[10].

Il est bien rare que nous sachions comment un couple avait acquis la propriété qu'il aliénait, bien que la terre située sur la rivière Chère et donnée à Redon en 864 par Austroberta et Wandefred ait été achetée par eux en 830[11]. Il est très possible que toutes ces aliénations portaient comme dans cet exemple sur des propriétés acquises après le mariage et ne comprenaient pas directement de portions des dots ou des dons effectués à l'occasion du mariage. Cependant, même si tel est bien le cas, il est néanmoins significatif que les maris et leurs épouses agissaient en commun lors de l'acquisition et de l'aliénation des terres et qu'ils étaient mentionnés comme agissant en commun – et, pour qu'il en soit ainsi, c'est bien qu'ils devaient avoir utilisé des ressources partagées ou communes.

3. *Les épouses agissant séparément*

Dans leur statut d'épouses, les femmes pouvaient également, semble-t-il, agir seules. Elles peuvent ainsi consentir explicitement à des transactions effectuées par leur mari, comme Odana le fit pour la vente de terre à Lusanger faite par son époux Gundouuin en 819[12]. Et elles peuvent consentir implicitement aux transactions de leur mari, en étant mentionnées comme témoin, comme la femme du prince Salomon à Plélan en 863[13]. Cela se produisait aussi bien dans les milieux bretons que francs et était plutôt le fait des aristocrates que des paysans.

En revanche, il arrive qu'un époux consente explicitement à une

---

[9] *CR*, n°s 33, 135, 64, 121, 198.
[10] *CR*, n° 99.
[11] *CR*, n°s 57, 229.
[12] *CR*, n° 226.
[13] *CR*, n° 78.

négociation faite séparément par sa femme. En 816, Acfrudis vend une terre située à Lusanger, qu'elle avait héritée de son père, mais elle le fit avec l'accord de son mari Arluini; citons encore Godildis, qui vend des terres familiales situées à Bourg-des-Comptes en 871, avec l'accord de son mari[14]. Ce sont des cas intéressants, puisqu'ils montrent que ces femmes avaient apporté des terres à leur foyer et qu'elles conservaient une certaine forme de contrôle sur elles après le mariage; mais leurs maris avaient établi une sorte d'intérêt sur ces propriétés, ne serait-ce que par leur pouvoir sur leur épouse. Le même point est établi par le texte incomplet du IXe siècle qui rappelle explicitement que Menion possédait des propriétés dans les environs de Bains, que sa femme avait héritée de son père Anauuocon[15]. Par conséquent, le degré de contrôle que pouvait exercer une femme sur les biens provenant de sa famille reste une question ouverte (aucun témoignage ne nous permet de considérer qu'elle ait possédé aucun droit d'usufruit).

4. *Les veuves*

Au cours de leur veuvage, les femmes pouvaient se remarier, échanger des propriétés et céder ou vendre des propriétés provenant de leur mariage : en 837 ou 838, Uuinanau vendit une vigne à Grandchamp qui avait appartenu à son mari et à elle-même (*in rem proprietatis meae uel conjugalis mei*)[16]. Elles pouvaient également racheter des biens mis en gage par leur famille, c'est-à-dire reverser l'argent reçu et recouvrer la terre familiale, comme Argantlon le fit en rachetant le bien mis en gage par son frère à Carentoir, dans les années 820[17]. Quelquefois elles engagèrent ces actions avec leurs fils, mais pas toujours; une seule fois c'est une fille de la donatrice qui consent à une transaction de ce type[18]. On voit aussi une veuve témoigner lors de l'aliénation faite par sa fille Roiantdreh à Médréac[19]. En ce qui concerne l'aliénation des biens du couple, dans deux cas au moins on peut démontrer que la propriété avait été acquise par le couple dans le mariage, mais, dans un autre cas, à Avessac, un de ses fils fit un procès à une veuve – et obtint gain de cause – pour obtenir le partage de l'héritage de son père : visiblement, cette veuve tentait de contrôler l'héritage de son feu mari, héritage sur lequel on ne pouvait pas s'attendre à ce qu'elle eut d'intérêt légitime[20].

[14] *CR*, n°s 227, 244.
[15] *CR*, n° 184.
[16] *CR*, n° 210.
[17] *CR*, n° 131.
[18] *CR*, n° 214.
[19] *CR*, n° 190.
[20] *CR App.*, n° 20

Comme on l'a mentionné ci-dessus, la riche Austroberta, une femme d'origine franque, acquit et aliéna des propriétés conjointement avec son mari Wandefred. En réalité, Wandefred était son second mari et le groupe de chartes qui détaille les actes d'Austroberta contient plusieurs aperçus importants sur le contrôle qu'elle exerçait sur les terres de son premier mari. Dans les années 860, elle donna au monastère de Redon non seulement des propriétés qu'elles avait acquises avec son second mari, mais également des propriétés qu'elle avait acquises avec son premier époux, Agenhart, ainsi que d'autres provenant de ses propres terres familiales, les terres du père d'Agenhart, Agon[21]. Selon les documents, les propriétés d'Agon furent acquises par les fils d'Austroberta issus de ses deux mariages, de la sœur d'Agenhart, Acfrudis, et de sa nièce, Agonildis; le fils issu du premier mariage acquit des terres en 816 et celui issu du second en acquit d'autres en 831 et 833[22]. Bien que les documents mentionnent ses fils comme les acteurs principaux de ces transactions, de fait, c'est Austroberta elle-même qui disposa finalement de ces terres – pour les donner au monastère de Redon. D'ailleurs son second fils ne peut pas avoir été en âge de faire une transaction en 831, étant donné qu'Austroberta ne contracta pas son second mariage avant la période 819-830 (et son second mari était encore vivant en 831)[23]. Alors que les chartes présentent ses fils comme les acteurs principaux, en réalité c'est Austroberta elle-même qui a dû en être le véritable acteur – un aperçu précieux à la fois sur les conditionnements de ceux qui rédigeaient les chartes à l'époque antérieure à la fondation de Redon et sur la pratique réelle. Encore plus intéressant, dans ce contexte, est le fait qu'Austroberta, en tant que veuve remariée, conservait effectivement le contrôle d'une partie des terres familiales paternelles de son premier mari.

Ainsi, non seulement on peut démontrer que les veuves pouvaient être actives par rapport aux propriétés acquises avec leur mari dans le cadre de leur mariage, mais, en pratique, elles pouvaient aussi exercer leur contrôle sur la terre familiale de leur défunt mari. Par conséquent les veuves, qu'elles fussent bretonnes ou franques, semblent avoir exercé un degré de contrôle considérable sur la propriété.

J'ai cité ces témoignages afin de fournir une manière de contexte pour les actions des femmes concernant la propriété, mais aussi parce que cela possède une influence sur les contrats matrimoniaux et leurs conséquences. Dans bien des cas, on peut démontrer que les

---

[21] CR, n°s 229, 230, 217, 57, 225.
[22] CR, n°s 227, 231; cf. n° 230.
[23] Cf. CR, n°s 226 (de 819, une transaction conjointe avec son premier mari) et 229 (de 830, avec son second mari).

actions des femmes, que celles-ci les effectuent conjointement avec leur mari ou non, se rapportaient à des propriétés acquises après le mariage. De tels cas n'avaient nécessairement aucun rapport avec les arrangements matrimoniaux eux-mêmes, bien qu'il soit vraisemblable que la capacité du couple à acquérir des terres reposait en dernier ressort sur les arrangements matrimoniaux, même indirectement. Quelques cas, cependant, se rapportent à des biens provenant de la femme et attestent clairement, par voie de conséquence, que le contrat de mariage pouvait impliquer, aussi bien dans la culture bretonne que dans la culture franque, une contribution de la part de la famille de l'épouse – l'équivalent de la «dot directe» («dowry» en anglais). Les nombreux exemples prouvant que les filles pouvaient hériter renforcent cette affirmation.

Ce qui est frappant, globalement, c'est l'aptitude des femmes à agir. Certes, beaucoup des cas d'achat et de vente se rapportent à l'action de couples aristocratiques : bien entendu, étant donné qu'ils étaient plus riches, ils étaient plus enclins à engager des négociations foncières. Mais ce n'est aucunement le cas de manière exclusive et nous trouvons des femmes de la paysannerie également impliquées dans des négociations foncières, sur une petite échelle, comme cela est clairement démontré par les acquisitions faites dans le cadre du mariage citées ci-dessus[24].

Les contrats et paiements de mariage

Dans notre collection, les témoignages explicitement consacrés aux arrangements matrimoniaux sont peu nombreux. Malgré tout, il existe quelques chartes qui portent plus directement sur le contrat de mariage. Un texte définit les parts relatives du couple : en 856, Gredcanham et sa femme Uuiuhoiam mirent en gage une petite propriété dans la *plebs* de Caro au prêtre local Hinuueten et à son neveu, ecclésiastique lui aussi, pour vingt et un ans[25]. Le couple, qui n'apparaît pas ailleurs dans la collection de chartes, céda la petite exploitation de Botriuualoe située à Réminiac (comprenant une maison et quelques terres annexes) contre 10 *solidi* 6 *denarii* en argent comptant. Ce type habituel de transaction concernant une mise en gage, en établissant en fait un prêt gagé sur la propriété, comme d'en bien d'autres transactions comparables, venait de la capacité des prêtres à disposer de capitaux liquides pour fournir de l'argent comptant. Bien que nous ne sachions pas comment Gredcanham et sa femme étaient venus en possession de la terre mise en

---

[24] Cf. ci-dessus, p. 410-412.
[25] *CR*, n° 193.

gage, il est frappant de noter que leurs intérêts sont spécifiément comme étant deux tiers et un tiers, la portion d'argent reçue par le mari s'élevant à nettement plus de deux fois celle de sa femme : 8 *solidi* 6 *denarii* contre 2 *solidi*. Par conséquent, le mari nomma deux garanties pour la négociation et sa femme un seul (un homme qui possédait une propriété voisine). Cela implique qu'au moins dans cette famille paysanne, la femme se voyait reconnaître des droits sur a priori un tiers de la propriété commune.

> «...Gredcanham et la femme Uuiuhoiam ont mis en gage une petite pièce de terre appelée Botriuualoe, située dans la *plebs* appelée Caro, dans la zone appelée Réminiac, Gredcanham mettant en gage les deux tiers contre la somme de 8 *solidi* 6 *denarii* et Uuiuhoiam mettant en gage le tiers contre la somme de 2 *solidi*, au prêtre Hinuueten et son neveu, le clerc Trihuueten, pour le terme de 7 ans... [jusqu'à un total de] 21 ans... qui possède comme limite au nord le bord de l'alleu du prêtre Hinuueten... et au sud jusqu'au lieu de Driuuolou, le long du chemin qui sert de limite entre la terre de Loieshoiarn et la terre mise en gage... [et] par la route publique et par une autre route conduisant à l'alleu de Hinuueten. Voici les garanties pour Gredcanham : Iarnhoiam et Driduualt; et pour Uuiuhoiam : Loieshoiarn. Cela fut fait en présence du prêtre Louuian, Diloid, Uuincar... Cela fut fait sur la terre mise en gage le samedi 15 des calendes de février [18 janvier], sous le règne du seigneur roi Charles, Erispoe possédant la Bretagne, avec le comte Deurhoiarn et l'évêque Rethuualatr...» (cf. annexe 1).

Un autre texte est très précis sur une question d'origines. Quelque temps avant 875, Roiantken, femme du «machtiern» Deurhoiarn, acquit une propriété à Augan de son beau-père Riuualt en tant que son *enepuuert*, c'est-à-dire son «don du matin» (la dot indirecte)[26]. En 875, elle donna cette terre à l'église et au monastère de Saint-Maxent, à 20 km au nord-est d'Augan, afin de s'assurer un lieu de sépulture prestigieux à l'entrée de l'église[27]. Elle doit avoir été âgée à cette époque : son mari, qui donna également une autre propriété, mourut aussitôt après, et elle mourut peu de temps après lui; et nous possédons des mentions d'actes accomplies par elle plusieurs décennies auparavant (elle et son mari avaient fait diverses donations pieuses[28]). Avant sa mort, elle confirma, avec son fils Iarnuuocon, le don fait par son mari. Cette Roiantken, qui provenait

---

[26] *CR*, n° 236.
[27] Cf. la contribution de Régine Le Jan sur la propension des femmes de Quedlinburg à utiliser leur *dos* pour s'assurer un emplacement pour leur sépulture.
[28] *CR*, n°s 173, 174, 175; cf. *CR*, n° 79.

probablement d'une riche famille paysanne, originaire de Ruffiac, s'était mariée dans la famille de «machtiern» de Riuualt dans la localité voisine d'Augan (les «machtiern» étaient des aristocrates de rang inférieur, qui possédaient une sorte de présidence de la *plebs*, au IXe siècle par droit héréditaire[29]). Elle semble avoir été la même Roiantken qui eut une dispute avec son frère, au sujet de la propriété de Ruffiac, plusieurs décennies auparavant[30]. Roiantken reçut des réserves foncières, au moment de son mariage, de la part du père de son époux. Elle semble avoir joui d'un contrôle indépendant de celles-ci tout au long de sa vie de femme mariée; et, à l'approche de la mort, elle paraît toujours en avoir le contrôle, avec le plein pouvoir de les aliéner : l'*enepuuert* était sa dot, au moment du mariage, provenant de la famille de son mari.

> «... le 3 des calendes de juillet [mercredi 29 juin], épacte 22, Pas-[c]uueten et Uuorhuuant dirigeant la Bretagne, Deurhoiarn et sa femme Roiantken... demandèrent aux moines de leur montrer [un emplacement] où leurs corps pourraient reposer après leur mort. L'abbé Liosic, avec ses moines, leur montra un emplacement pour leur corps dans le vestibule de Saint-Maxent. Plus tard, ils vinrent ensemble à Saint-Maxent et déposèrent un manteau sur l'autel. Deurhoiarn a donné l'«Aethuric»[31] du clerc Freoc à Saint-Maxent et aux moines qui y servent Dieu, comme don pour sa sépulture; et sa femme Roiantken a donné l'«Aethurec» de Milcondoes, situé à Augan – que Riuualt lui avait donnée en tant qu'*enepuuert* –, comme don pour sa sépulture. Plus tard Deurhoiarn mourut le 2 des ides de janvier, épacte 11 [vendredi 12 janvier 876], et son fils Iarnuuocon et sa femme Roiantken amenèrent le corps avec une grande foule et ils invitèrent les moines à venir les rencontrer sur la route pour recevoir le corps... Et aussitôt après son mari mourut Roiantken, et les moines

---

[29] Cf. W. Davies, *Small worlds*..., p. 108, 178-179 sur Roiantken et Deurhoiarn et p. 138-142, 175-183 sur les «machtierns».

[30] *CR*, n°s 145, 146, 147; cf. W. Davies, *Intra-family transactions*..., p. 888-889.

[31] Le mot Aethuric/Aethurec est extrêmement peu courant. Étant donné la localisation de l'un d'entre eux à Augan, il semble se rapporter à quelque type d'unité foncière. Je remercie John Koch et Paul Russell pour les suggestions suivantes : si nous segmentons en *aeth-urec/uric* – cf. le gallois *eithin*, «ajonc» et le gallois *gwrych*, «haie, clôture» – le sens global, s'il est exact, pourrait être «l'enclos, limité par des ajoncs, de N». L'association des deux occurrences avec un nom de personne («l'Aethuric de Freoc, l'Aethurec de Milcondoes») semble être parallèle avec l'expression «*ran* de N», d'un usage extrêmement répandu pour les unités foncières; cf. «Ran Etcar, Ran Iaruualt, Ran Iuduuallon, Ran Ronhoiarn», etc. Une personne appelée Milcondoes apparaît comme témoin à Ruffiac en 867 et à Augan dans les années 850 (*CR*, n°s 150, 175), ce dernier acte étant une donation par Roiantken; le clerc Freoc était témoin à Ruffiac en 866 et à Augan en 867 et il fit une donation d'un bien à Ruffiac en 866, qu'il avait reçu quelque temps auparavant (*CR*, n°s 67, 68; 66; 45).

la traitèrent comme ils l'avaient fait pour son mari, l'ensevelissant à côté de lui avec beaucoup d'honneurs...» (cf. annexe 2).

Le mot breton pour «don du matin» apparaît également dans une autre collection de chartes, dans le cartulaire de Landévennec, provenant de l'extrémité de la côte ouest de la Bretagne[32]. Il s'agit d'une collection du milieu du XIe siècle, composée en grande partie de documents des Xe et XIe siècles[33]. Dans les textes en question, une femme, Alarun, donne au monastère de Landévennec une propriété qu'elle a reçue de son mari *in ditatione*[34]. La charte n'est pas datée mais semble être de la fin du Xe siècle et provient d'un groupe de chartes comtales de la fin du Xe-début du XIe siècle; son époux, Diles, était presque certainement le Diles qui fut comte de Cornouailles, dans le Finistère, juste avant le comte Budic III au début du XIe siècle; le père de Diles, Alfret, avait été comte avant lui[35]. La propriété – Caer Uurican, une *villa* qui comprenait peut-être trois ou quatre établissements – se trouve probablement à 20 km au sud de Landévennec.

«Ces lettres racontent qu'Alarun a donné à saint Winwaloe, pour le salut de son âme, la pleine propriété d'une *villa* à perpétuité, à savoir Caer Uurican, qu'elle avait accepté comme dot (c'est-à-dire : *enep guerth*) de la part de son mari Diles, fils d'Alfrett. Cette disposition devait rester à jamais, aussi longtemps que la foi chrétienne subsisterait sur terre. Quiconque voudrait briser ou diminuer [ce don]...» (cf. annexe 3).

Les mots *in ditatione* sont glosés par : *id est enep guerth*, «c'est-à-dire don du matin». L'hypothèse que *ditatione/dotatione* signifiait le douaire direct, comme on pourrait s'y attendre, est démentie par le fait que le don provenait de l'époux. Dans ce cas, à nouveau, une partie au moins de la dotation de la femme au moment du mariage provenait de la famille de son époux. Elle possédait visiblement un plein contrôle sur ce don matrimonial.

Une autre charte de Redon, d'une période comparable mais se rapportant à une terre située bien plus à l'est et au sud, se réfère également à la dotation fournie à l'épouse par son mari, nommée cette fois *dos* : quelque temps avant l'an 1050, Odelina conserva la *dos* qui provenait de son premier mari, un «don du matin» consistant en

---

[32] *Le cartulaire de l'abbaye de Landévennec*, éd. A. de la Borderie, Rennes, 1888 (ci-après : *CL*, avec le n° de l'acte).

[33] W. Davies, *Les chartes du cartulaire de Landévennec* et H. Guillotel, *Les origines de Landévennec*, ces deux contributions dans M. Simon (éd.), *Landévennec et le monachisme breton dans le haut Moyen Âge*, Landévennec, 1986, p. 85-95 et 97-114.

[34] *CL*, n° 44.

[35] Cf. W. Davies, *Les chartes du cartulaire de Landévennec*..., p. 91-92.

une terre à Le Cellier, près de la Loire, lorsqu'elle épousa son second mari (un «machtiern», comme le premier), bien que son fils eût contrôlé cette terre après la mort de son mari[36]. En tout cas, le fait que le pouvoir d'en disposer lui revenait en dernier ressort fut démontré lorsqu'elle la donna en fin de compte au monastère de Redon.

Par conséquent, nous possédons des témoignages évidents, provenant aussi bien de la Bretagne orientale que de la Bretagne occidentale, au cours du IXe et de la fin du Xe siècle, de la dotation des femmes, par la famille de leur mari, de biens fonciers, pour leur propre usage et avec le plein pouvoir d'aliénation.

Il existe également une attestation un peu plus ancienne d'un autre type de payement pour le mariage, fait par la famille du marié à la famille de l'épouse, mais elle vient de la collection de lois sans provenance des *ELR*. Ici, on affirme que la *dos* devrait être payée au père d'une femme, comme faisant partie de l'arrangement matrimonial, ou bien à ses fils, s'il s'agit d'une veuve qui se remarie (ou à son père si elle est veuve et n'a pas d'enfants)[37]. *Dos* peut se traduire ici par «prix de la fiancée» («brideprice» en anglais) ou «richesse de la fiancée» et cette clause trouve des parallèles dans d'autres clauses, avec des significations similaires de *dos*, qui se trouvent dans des documents pénitentiels anciens provenant aussi bien d'Irlande que du Pays de Galles. Le document irlandais du VIe ou VIIe siècle dit «Premier synode de saint Patrick» prescrit une pénalité pour l'homme qui accepte un «prix de la fiancée» de quelqu'un d'autre que le fiancé de sa fille[38]; et le document gallois du VIe ou VIIe siècle dit «Livre de David» prescrit une pénitence et le payement du «prix de la fiancée» à sa famille pour l'homme qui couche avec une femme en dehors du cadre d'un arrangement matrimonial[39]. Ces témoignages possèdent également un reflet dans le canon irlandais du VIIIe siècle déjà discuté par Patrick Corbet[40]. Malgré ses analogies patristiques, la formulation de ce canon, en tant que triade (cf. ci-

---

[36] C'est-à-dire le fils de son second mariage; *CR* 303.

[37] *ELR* A47 : «Si quis filiam marito tradiderit, legitimam dotem accipiat. Quod si cassus mortis illum demisserit et ipsa alteri uiro nubere uolerit, filii dotem accipiant. Quod si hos non habuerit, patri dari iubetur», *Irish Penitentials*, éd. Bieler, p. 144.

[38] Ch. 22 : «Si quis tradiderit filiam suam uiro honestis nuptis et amauerit alium et consentit filiae suae et acceperit dotem, ambo ab aecclesia excludantur», *Irish Penitentials*, éd. Bieler, p. 56.

[39] Ch. 6 : «Qui autem cum uirgine uel uidua necdum disponsata peccauerit, dotem det parentibus eius et anno uno peniteat», *The Irish Penitentials*... cité n. 4, p. 70.

[40] Cf. la contribution du même dans le présent volume.

dessous), possède un fort caractère irlandais et d'autres documents irlandais, aussi bien juridiques qu'anecdotiques, mettent en valeur l'importance du «prix de la fiancée» (*coibche*, ou parfois *tinnscra*) dans les négociations matrimoniales irlandaises des VIIIe et IXe siècles[41].

Le terme ENEPUUERT

Enepuuert signifie littéralement «valeur» (*werth*) de la «face» (*enep*), autrement dit «la valeur de l'honneur ou de la réputation d'une personne». Le payement qui allait à la nouvelle épousée de la part de la famille de son mari dans la Bretagne des IXe et Xe siècles était une sorte de compensation pour le dommage porté à son honneur, c'est-à-dire pour la honte d'aller dans la couche de son mari. Le mot continua d'exister en moyen-breton plus tardif (*enebarz*), où il se rapportait toujours à un payement pour le mariage (en se différenciant d'*argobrou*, «douaire»), et même en breton moderne où – selon Marcel Planiol – il dénotait un présent offert à la fiancée, en reconnaissance de sa virginité, au début du XXe siècle[42]. Dans cette société, le «présent du matin» ne disparaît pas aussi rapidement que cela semble avoir été le cas dans d'autres sociétés européennes et nous devrions être prudents en mettant l'accent de manière appuyée sur les douaires directs pour la Bretagne du Moyen Âge central.

Les termes vernaculaires utilisés ici pour rendre la notion de payement à la nouvelle épousée de la part de la famille de son mari reposent sur des notions de réputation et d'honneur, de valeur et de compensation, et non sur la notion de don si familière dans les langues vernaculaires germaniques. On trouve des analogies à ces concepts dans d'autres sociétés médiévales celtiques. En gallois apparaît exactement le même mot qu'*enepuuert*, sous la forme *wynebwerth*. Bien que le mot, avant le XIIe siècle, ait une signification générale de «prix de l'honneur» (rendu littéralement par *pretium faciei suae*, «valeur de sa face», dans un texte latin du Xe siècle[43]), c'est-à-

---

[41] F. Kelly, *A guide to early Irish law*, Dublin, 1988, p. 71-72; *Bethu Brigte*, éd. D. Ó. hAodha, Dublin, 1978, p. 5, traduit p. 23; cf. T. M. Charles-Edwards, *Early Irish and Welsh kinship*, Oxford, 1993, p. 464.

[42] L. Fleuriot, *Dictionnaire des gloses en vieux breton*, Paris, 1964, p. 160; M. Planiol, *Histoire des institutions de la Bretagne*, II, Mayenne, 1981, p. 177-178.

[43] *The text of the Book of Llan Dâv*, éd. J. G. Evans avec la collab. de J. Rhys, Oxford, 1893, n° 233. Des textes irlandais du VIIIe siècle, possèdent un équivalent direct avec *log n'enech*, littéralement, «dignité de la face». Cela apparaît fréquemment dans l'abondant matériel législatif, par exemple : «Il existe dans la loi irlandaise sept femmes qui n'ont pas droit au payement ou prix de l'honneur (*log nenuch*) de la part de quelqu'un : une femme qui vole, une femme qui se moque de toutes les classes de la société, une conteuse dont la parenté paye pour ses his-

dire la compensation légalement due pour toutes sortes d'insultes, au cours du XIIIe siècle *wynebwerth* en gallois n'en vint à se rapporter qu'à un type particulier d'insulte, à savoir la compensation due à une femme pour l'adultère de son mari. Une triade législative – un procédé littéraire utilisant des groupes de trois choses pour classer les informations – spécifie cette compensation à côté des autres propriétés qui devraient lui rester : le « don du matin » et le douaire[44]. « Il y a trois choses qui ne peuvent être enlevés à une femme, même si elle est abandonnée à cause de sa mauvaise conduite, ce sont son *cowyll*, son *argyfreu* et son *wynebwerth* lorsque son mari a des relations avec une autre femme »[45]. Comme dans les documents bretons antérieurs, le mot se rapporte au payement fait à une femme de la part de la famille de son mari, même si le contexte particulier est assez différent. Ce qui est plus important encore, les deux cultures conceptualisent ces payements en terme d'honneur et de honte, les textes gallois mettant l'accent en particulier sur l'idée de honte : une autre triade législative à propos des « trois hontes d'une jeune fille » rappelle que la seconde honte a lieu quand « elle va pour la première fois dans la couche de son mari... pour sa virginité [est payé] son *cowyll* »[46].

Bien que ces témoignages vernaculaires gallois proviennent de la législation courante du Moyen Âge tardif, ils possèdent des éléments archaïques et ils sont par conséquent, à certains égards, pertinents pour notre période. Aussi, on peut à juste titre noter leurs prescriptions concernant l'échange de propriétés lors du mariage, en particulier dans la mesure où les textes législatifs gallois impliquent

toires mensongères, une prostituée qui travaille dans les buissons, une femme qui blesse, une femme qui trahit, une femme qui refuse l'hospitalité aux personnes respectueuses de la loi. Telles sont les femmes qui n'ont pas droit au prix de l'honneur (*log neneach*) ». Heptade 15, F. Kelly, *A guide...*, p. 348-349; cf. p. 8-9.

[44] Pour les triades comme genre littéraire et juridique, cf. M. E. Owen, *Functional prose : religion, science, grammar, law*, dans A. O. H. Jarman et G. R. Hughes, *A guide to Welsh literature*, I, Swansea, 1976, p. 271-273; cf. aussi *Trioedd Ynys Prydein*, éd. R. Bromwich, Cardiff, 1961.

[45] « Tri pheth ny dygir rac gureic kyt gatter am y cham, y chowyll, ae hargyfreu ae hwynebwerth pan gyttyo y gwr a gureic arall », *Welsh medieval law*, éd. A. W. Wade-Evans, Oxford, 1909, p. 93; traduit par M. E. Owen, *Shame and reparation : women's place in the kin*, dans D. Jenkins et M. E. Owen (éd.), *The Welsh law of women*, Cardiff, 1980, p. 66. Comparer avec la version latine : *Tria sunt que non possunt mulieri auferre, licet ob suam dimitatur culpam : scilicet,* c o w y l l h ; *et* a r g u e r e u, *id est, animalia que secum a parentibus adduxit; et animalia que redduntur pro* u y n e b w e r t h *si maritus eius aliam cognoverit* » (*The Latin texts of the Welsh laws*, éd. H. D. Emanuel, Cardiff, 1967, p. 145).

[46] M. E. Owen, *Shame and reparation...*, p. 49.

qu'il y avait trois types de payement : l'*amobr* ou «prix de la fiancée», qui allait au seigneur de la fiancée ; le *cowyll* ou «don du matin», qui allait à la fiancée elle-même de la part de son mari ou de sa famille ; et l'*argyfrau* ou douaire (direct), qui allait de la famille de la fiancée au couple, au nouveau foyer[47]. Ce triple aspect de l'accord matrimonial était la norme pour les esprits juridiques gallois – les légistes professionnels – de la fin du Moyen Âge, bien qu'il ait certainement cessé d'être en pratique avant le XIVe siècle ; à cette époque le *cowyll*, le «don du matin» semble avoir déjà disparu aux Pays de Galles (il n'y a pas de témoignage comparable dans la pratique du XIIIe siècle)[48]. Par conséquent ce modèle au caractère triple semble pouvoir s'appliquer à des contextes plus anciens, antérieurs au XIIIe siècle. Il existe certainement un bon témoignage, dans une charte latine, du payement du «don du matin» (ici appelé *dos*) au milieu du VIIIe siècle dans le sud-est du Pays de Galles[49].

* * *

Quelle perspective le cartulaire de Redon nous offre-t-il donc sur les négociations matrimoniales et sur les participations des épouses aux questions de propriété ?

En règle générale, il démontre de manière très claire, par des cas individuels nombreux et variés, le rôle actif et les pouvoirs des femmes par rapport à la propriété. Elles étaient actives à la fois conjointement avec leur mari et séparément. Bien qu'il soit clair que l'objet de beaucoup de leurs actions communes ne dérivaient pas directement de l'arrangement matrimonial, néanmoins, souvent elles peuvent avoir été une conséquence indirecte de celui-ci. Parfois aussi l'action commune était clairement engagée en rapport avec la propriété apportée au foyer par l'épouse. Mais, en tant que veuves, les femmes pouvaient effectivement contrôler les propriétés du couple et même parfois l'héritage familial de leur défunt mari, bien qu'elles pussent s'attendre à ce que celui-ci leur soit contesté par leurs fils. Par conséquent, l'étendue du contrôle d'une femme était variable du vivant de son mari, bien que l'on ait des indications qu'elle ait eu un degré de contrôle plus grand sur le «don du matin» (la dot indirecte) que sur le douaire (la dot directe). Cependant, son contrôle paraît avoir été extensif en pratique, lorsqu'elle était veuve : lorsque Roiantdreh choisit Salomon comme héritier, elle proclamait sa li-

---

[47] D. Jenkins, *Property interests in the classical Welsh law of women*, dans *The Welsh law of women...* cité n. 45, p. 73-86.

[48] R. R. Davies, *The status of women and the practice of marriage in late-medieval Wales*, dans *The Welsh law of women...*, p. 93-114.

[49] *The text of the Book of Llan Dâv...* cité n. 43, n° 207.

berté complète d'aliéner la terre de sa propre famille. Ce cas nous rappelle aussi utilement que, si les églises furent souvent les bénéficiaires des aliénations féminines, cela n'était pas obligatoire; de plus, à la différence d'autres parties de l'Europe occidentale, insulaire et continentale, il n'y avait pas d'établissements religieux féminins en Bretagne dans le haut Moyen Âge. La distraction du patrimoine familial en faveur de leurs moniales n'était pas une stratégie en usage dans la région.

Les femmes pouvaient apporter des propriétés à leur foyer dans la Bretagne du IXe siècle, une dotation qui correspond au «dowry» en anglais (la «dot directe»), bien qu'il n'y ait pas de terme spécifique utilisé pour ce type de dotation, en latin ou en langue vernaculaire, dans les textes bretons de cette période (le mot *argobrau*, cependant, c'est-à-dire le même mot – *argyfrau* – que l'on retrouve en gallois pour «dowry», apparaît dans les textes médiévaux bretons tardifs). Le mariage pouvait aussi impliquer, aux IXe et Xe siècles, de fournir un «don du matin» (la dot indirecte) à l'épouse de la part de son mari. Il y avait, par conséquent, deux types de dots. Ces deux types de payements/dons peuvent bien avoir été courants; mais nous ne pouvons pas savoir s'ils étaient «normaux». L'association du concept d'honneur et de honte avec la dotation de l'épouse par son mari et la famille de celui-ci sert à différencier nettement la provision du «don du matin» de celle du «douaire». Bien que la signification primaire du terme *enepuuert/wynebwerth* puisse bien avoir été déjà perdue dans la Bretagne des IXe et Xe siècles, l'utilisation continue de ce terme spécialisé – dans les textes latins de notre période – met en valeur le fait que pourvoir aux nécessités du nouveau foyer incombait aux deux parties.

En allant un peu plus loin, si nous gardons en tête les témoignages sur le «prix de la fiancée» dans le texte précoce des *ELR*, à savoir d'un don ou d'un payement fait à la famille de la promise par celle du fiancé, il n'est pas impossible qu'un troisième payement puisse aussi avoir eu lieu; s'il a été courant aux IXe et Xe siècles, il aurait correspondu au modèle (quelque peu archaïque) illustré plus tard par les textes législatifs gallois.

Pratiquement tous les éléments mentionnés ci-dessus se rapportent à des propriétés foncières; seuls les textes législatifs gallois du XIIIe siècle nous rappellent qu'une dotation pouvait consister en biens meubles[50]. À cause de la nature de nos textes bretons, qui

---

[50] La loi et la pratique juridique galloises de la fin du Moyen Âge mentionnent plus souvent les biens meubles que les propriétés foncières en rapport avec les payements pour les mariages; cf. D. Jenkins, *Property interests...* cité n. 47 et R. R. Davies, *The status of women...* cité n. 48, p. 77-78 et p. 109.

concernent au premier chef des affaires de transferts fonciers, nous pouvions nous attendre à entendre parler de propriétés foncières. Il ne s'ensuit pas que les dons de biens meubles n'aient pas eu lieu. Seulement, nous n'en entendons pas parler.

Si l'on considère les processus qui étaient en jeu plus que les cas individuels, il est difficile de détecter une différenciation significative entre les comportements franc et breton. Tandis que les dons importants faits par un petit groupe de femmes de l'aristocratie franque leur confère une certaine prééminence, les femmes d'origine bretonne firent également des dons – prenons l'exemple de Roiantdreh, une Bretonne puissante et très indépendante. Et la conservation même du terme breton *enepuuert* met en valeur le fait que l'épouse d'origine bretonne possédait sa dotation propre. En un certain sens, la meilleure preuve de l'activité importante des femmes mariées d'origine bretonne provient des achats et des ventes de champs à petite échelle entre des paysans libres bretons au tout début du IXe siècle, à un moment qui n'est pas compliqué par la présence d'un monastère important en tant que puissant seigneur, patron et bénéficiaire potentiel.

Par conséquent, il est possible de distinguer différents types de dotations matrimoniales courantes dans la Bretagne du IXe siècle et de faire quelques commentaires raisonnables quoiqu'incomplets sur le niveau de contrôle d'une femme sur cette dotation. Il n'y a pas de preuve directe pour savoir si ces dotations constituaient ou non l'essence même de l'union; cependant, étant donné que des formulations juridiques telles que celles que nous possédons prescrivent effectivement qu'une union *de facto* devait être suivie d'un don, cela doit signifier que le don (et spécialement le don de la famille de l'homme à celle de la femme) était vu – au moins par les clercs – comme légitimant l'union[51].

Il est également possible de faire une tentative de commentaire sur le processus d'établissement des normes. Plusieurs textes de la collection de Redon suggèrent que ceux qui faisaient les rédactions luttaient contre la transmission de propriété à travers les femmes : Roiantdreh citait sa généalogie sur huit générations mâles pour «prouver» son droit à disposer de ses biens; la transmission d'une terre à Bains depuis les frères Aetlon et Arthuiu à travers l'arrière-petite-fille d'Aetlon et la «concubine» d'Arthuiu nécessita une notation spécifique; le groupe de transactions se rapportant à Austrober-

---

[51] Cf. T. M. Charles-Edwards, *Early Irish and Welsh kinship...* cité n. 41, p. 462-465. La signification du don en Bretagne s'oppose à la loi laïque irlandaise, où le don n'était visiblement pas essentiel : différents types d'union, avec ou sans transfert de propriété, étaient reconnus, cf. T. M. Charles-Edwards, *op. cit.*, p. 463.

ta engendra une notation spécifique sur ses deux époux[52]. Cela est extraordinairement important : alors qu'il est clair que les rédacteurs se trouvèrent en difficulté dans la formulation des documents, et par conséquent que la dévolution à travers les femmes n'était pas une norme attendue, néanmoins il est tout aussi parfaitement clair que dans les faits ces femmes exerçaient des pouvoirs considérables. Il semble que la pratique était en train d'évoluer, au cours du milieu et de la fin du IXe siècle, et que les normes étaient vraiment sous pression. Le fait même que certaines des négociations d'Austroberta fussent attribuées à ses fils met nettement cette perspective en valeur.

En tout cas, les trois types de don («prix ou richesse de la fiancée», «don du matin», douaire) étaient-ils ou non courants dans la Bretagne du IXe siècle et le «prix de la fiancée» était-il réellement payé, ces questions doivent rester ouvertes. Cependant, en comparaison des témoignages des VIe-VIIe siècles et des témoignages insulaires, cela n'est pas impossible (et certainement pas aussi invraisemblable que certains voudraient le suggérer). Bien qu'il y eût de nombreuses différences entre le Pays de Galles et la Bretagne, les documents législatifs gallois explicitent sans ambiguïté le fait que les légistes pouvaient encore concevoir une négociation matrimoniale comme possédant trois éléments de dons jusqu'au XIIIe siècle et les témoignages de la pratique juridique galloise au XIVe siècle montrent amplement la réalité de l'obligation de payer l'*amobr*, c'est-à-dire une sorte de «prix de la fiancée», bien qu'il ait été transformé, dans cette société médiévale tardive, de payement au père de l'épouse en payement à son seigneur[53]. La négociation à caractère triple est donc bien une possibilité réelle pour le Moyen Âge central.

Le «prix de la fiancée» – appelé aussi *dos*, de manière révélatrice, dans le latin des pays celtes – peut bien avoir contribué à la dotation d'une femme, comme Jack Goody l'a rappelé[54], et il est probable que c'était le cas lorsque les femmes restaient pour une raison ou une autre dans leur famille natale. Il ne faudrait pas l'oublier. Il est, en fin de compte, quelque peu déplacé de discuter de la dotation des femmes, en l'isolant des autres transactions qui avaient lieu lors du mariage : se concentrer sur la *dos*, qu'elle soit directe ou indirecte, distrait notre attention de la série de relations qui étaient inaugurées ou poursuivies lors du mariage, lorsqu'un complexe système de négociations sur les échanges, matériels ou non, prenait

---

[52] *CR*, n°s 109, 184, 231.
[53] Cf. R. R. Davies, *The status of women...* cité n. 48, p. 103-104.
[54] J. Goody, *The development of the family and marriage in Europe*, Cambridge, 1983, p. 240-261.

place entre les familles. Là où disparut le «prix de la fiancée», contrairement au cas de la Bretagne pour quelques siècles, cela impliquait au moins une évolution des rapports entre la femme et sa famille natale.

ANNEXE

1 – Reminiac, 856, 18 janvier

Gredcanham et sa femme Uuiuhoiam mettent en gage auprès d'un prêtre et de son neveu, clerc, une pièce de terre à raison de deux tiers pour lui et un tiers pour elle; ils obtiennent un prêt à sept ans, renouvelable deux fois.
B. Cartulaire de l'abbaye Saint-Sauveur de Redon, XIe siècle, Rennes, bibliothèque de l'archevêché, f. 102r.
a. A. de Courson, *Cartulaire de l'abbaye de Redon en Bretagne*, Paris, 1863 (*Collection des documents inédits sur l'histoire de France*, 1re s., *Histoire politique*), n° 193.

Noticia in quorum presentia pignoraverunt Gredcanham et Uuiuhoiam femina petiolam de terra nuncupante Botriuualoe, sitam in plebe nuncupante Caroth, in loco nuncupante Ruminiac, Gretcanam, duas partes super solidos viii et denarios vi et Uuiuhoiam terciam partem super solidos ii, in manibus Hinuueteni presbyteri et nepotis sui Trihuueteni clerici, usque ad caput... vii annorum. Et si tunc redimerint, redimant, et si tunc non redimerint, fiat iterum ut supra usque ad caput aliorum vii annorum, hoc est xiiii annorum; et si tunc redimerint, redimant, et si tunc non redimerint, fiat iterum ut supra usque ad caput trium vii annorum, hii sunt xxi annorum. Et si tunc non redimerint, fiat ipsa terra in alode comparato ab ipso die, sine redempsione, finem habens a fine porte alodis Hinuueteni presbyteri, a sinistra parte ad perarium, ad roborem, ad alium perarium, ut simul dividant et ligna et fructus eorum; ad dextera parte usque ad villarem Driuuolou per semittam, hoc est, confinium inter terram Loieshoiarni et terram pignorantiae et confinium menehi Sancti Petri apostoli; et inde per fossellam usque ad terram pignarantia Louuuian presbyteri, per viam publicam et per aliam viam usque ad alodem Hinuueteni presbyteri. Et isti sunt fideiussores vel dilisidi pro Gretcanham : Iarnhoiam et Driduualtum; et pro Uuiuhoiam : Loieshoiarnnum. His presentibus actum fuit : Louuianus presbyter testis, Diloid testis, Uuincar testis, Rithoiarnus testis, Iunham testis, Haelhoiarnus testis, Loiesuuetenus testis, Uuorhatoeu testis, Hirdmarcocus testis, Clotuuious testis. Factum est hoc super ipsam terram pignorantiae, die sabbato, xv kal februarii, regnante domno Karolo rege, vel Erispoe possidente Brittanniam, et Deurhoiarno commite, et Rethuualatro episcopo. Ego Haeldetuuido, clericus, scripsi; Doithanu testis.

2 – Augan, 875, 29 juin; 876, 12 janvier; 878, 14 mai

Deurhoiarn et sa femme Roiantken ayant obtenu de se faire ensevelir à Saint-Maxent, ils ont fait diverses donations «pour leur corps» à cette église, dont l'enepuuert de Roiantken. Avec leur fils Iarnuuocon, celle-ci a confirmé la donation de son époux après son décès; puis, après le décès de sa mère, Iarn-

uuocon a donné deux autres biens, l'un pour l'âme de Roiantken, l'autre pour celle «de ses pères».

B. Cartulaire de l'abbaye Saint-Sauveur de Redon, XIe siècle, Rennes, bibliothèque de l'archevêché, f. 116r.

   a. A. de Courson, *Cartulaire de l'abbaye de Redon en Bretagne*, Paris, 1863 (*Collection des documents inédits sur l'histoire de France*, 1re s., *Histoire politique*), n° 236.

Mundi termino adpropinquante, malis crebrescentibus, petierunt Deurhoiarn et uxor sua Roiantkent Sanctum Maxentium, in festivitate apostolorum Petri et Pauli, iii kalendas iul, l(una) xxii, regnante Pasuueten et Uuorhuuant Brittanniam, monachos rogaverunt ostendere sibi [...]^{a)} ubi corpora eorum requiescerent post obitus illorum. Et ostendit abbas Liosic, cum monachis suis, locum corporum eorum in vestibulo Sancti Maccentii. Et postea simul perrexerunt ad Sanctum Maxentium et posuerunt suam manicam super altare. Et dedit Deurhoiarn Aethuric Freoc, clericus, in dono corporis sui, et uxor eius Roiantken dedit Aethurec Milcondoes, in Alcam, quam dedit illi Riuualt in enepuuert, in dono corporis sui, Sancto Maccentio in honore Salvatoris atque monachis in illo loco Deo servientibus. Et posta defunctus est Deurhoiarn, ii idus ianuarii, luna xi, et filius eius Iarnuuocon et uxor sua Roiantken detulerunt corpus simul cum omnibus, et invitaverunt monachos obviam sibi in via accipere corpus. Et cito ut adierunt, monachi exierunt obviam corpori cum reliquis suis, et simul detulerunt corpus ad monasterium Sancti Maxentii, et sepelierunt eum secundum dignitatem, ut moris est christianorum. Et postea invitavit filius eius Iarnuuocon, una cum matre sua et cum multis nobilibus hominum, abbatem Liosic nomine, cum suis monachis, in quadam exhedra iuxta basilicam Sancti Maccentii et illas donationes quas dederunt pater, matre vivente, in dono corporum suorum firmavit coram multis testis; hii sunt : Ratfred testis, Inhoc testis, Maenuuallon testis, Nominoe testis, Catuueten testis, Uuoetuual testis, Iedicahel testis, Euuen testis, Uuinkalon testis, Riscaham testis, Uuorlouuen presbyter testis, Finithic presbyter testis, Scuban presbyter testis, Marcoc testis, Iacu testis, Seder testis, Iarnuuoret testis. Et cito Roiantken defuncta est post virum, et sic monachi fecerunt illi sicut viro suo, iuxta illum sepelierunt illam cum magno honore. Et venit Iarnuuocon filius eius, in prima dominica post sepulturam eius, visitare sepulcra patrum suorum; et post missam invocavit abbas Liosic cum suis monachis, adstetit inter templum et altare, posuit manicam suam super altare et dixit : Villam Eneuuuor do Maccentii et monachis, pro anima matris meae, in hereditate perpetua, in honore Salvatoris; et postea, in die dominico, venit Iarnuuocon visitare sepulcra patrum suorum et post missam perrexit, stantibus monachis, presente populo, dedit partem Kethic Sancto Maccentio et heres illius Suluuoion nomine, pro animabus patrum suorum, coram multis testibus : Iarnuuocon testis, qui dedit hanc donationem, Uuincalon testis, Bleidbara testis, Comhael testis, Arbidoe testis, Conglas testis, Katic testis, Suluuoion testis, Tanetuuotal testis, Idon testis, Tutuuoret testis, Loiesuuoret testis, Uurliuuet testis, Tanetlouuen presbyter. Ista donatio fuit ii idus maii, luna viii.

   ^{a)} *Mot gratté.*

3 – Plonévez-Porzay, [fin du Xe siècle]

Alarun a donné à l'abbaye de Landévennec la villa *de* Caer Uurican, *qu'elle avait reçue de son époux, Diles, en* ditatio, *«c'est-à-dire en* enep guerth*».*

B. Cartulaire de l'abbaye de Landévennec, XIe siècle, Quimper, Bibliothèque municipale, ms. 16, f. 160v.

a. A. de la Borderie, *Cartulaire de l'abbaye de Landévennec*, Rennes, 1888, n° 44.

Hae literae narrant quod Alarun dedit unam villam sancto Uuingualoeo, pro anima sua, in dicumbitione atque in hereditate perpetua, id est, Caer Uurican, quae accepit in ditatione[a], a viro suo Diles, filio Alfrett. Et idcirco aeternaliter hoc permaneat quandiu christiana fides in terra servabitur. Et qui frangere aut minuere voluerit, sciat se alienum fore a liminibus sanctae Dei aecclesiae, et pars ejus cum Dathan et Abyron, et ira Dei incurrat super eum hic et in futuro. Amen.

[a] *En glose* : id est enep guerth.

XI

A note on *ville* names and settlement development in the Morbihan

In the course of nearly twenty years of working in the Morbihan, and particularly in doing fieldwork with my colleague Grenville Astill of the University of Reading, I noticed a tendency for settlements with *ville* names to be located in areas which had plentiful potsherds of the fifteenth and sixteenth centuries but very few of the thirteenth and fourteenth centuries. In view of the literature associating *ville* names with new settlement ("colonization") of the central middle ages, that is of the twelfth and thirteenth centuries, this observation was of some interest[1]. Since M. Chédeville has used place-names in a very productive way in writing early Breton history, I therefore thought it appropriate to offer this short note in his honour. What follows is a detailed look at the evidence in a limited part of the eastern Morbihan; although the area is small (128 km²), it is one that we have studied systematically, over a long period, both on the ground itself and in surviving archives[2].

Introduction: the survey context

Our project in the eastern Morbihan was about changing land-use in the historic past, that is in the period since records began in northern Europe; it was also about the organization of human settlement in relation to land-use; and about the relationship between what changed and what did not change. We looked – at micro-level – at the Oust-Vilaine watershed, focussing on the four communes of Ruffiac, Tréal, Saint-Nicolas-du-Tertre and Carentoir, as a core for intensive study, with the communes

---

1. The classic approach to *ville* names in France is summarized in G. Duby, *Rural Economy and Country Life in the Medieval West*, London, Edward Arnold, 1968, p. 76-98: new villages were established in the eleventh to thirteenth centuries, especially 1150-1200, slowing down thereafter, with *villeneuves* created up to the second third of the thirteenth century and some dispersed settlement thereafter (original, French, edition p. 154-64). Both Chédeville and Tanguy comment on the great increase in name-forms of *ville* type in the eleventh to thirteenth centuries: A. Chédeville and N.-Y. Tonnerre, *La Bretagne féodale XIᵉ-XIIIᵉ siècle*, Rennes, Ouest-France, 1987, p. 295, 300, 306-310; B. Tanguy, "Toponymie et peuplement en Bretagne. Le recul de la frontière linguistique du Vᵉ au XVIᵉ siècle", *in* M. Mulon & J. Chaurand (ed.), *Archéologie, Toponymie. Colloque tenu au Mans (mai 1980)*, Paris, 1981, p. 166; B. Tanguy, *Dictionnaire des noms de communes, trèves et paroisses des Côtes d'Armor*, Douarnenez, Ar Men – Le Chasse-Marée, 1992, p. 12.
2. For detail of the fieldwork, see W. Davies and G. Astill, *The East Brittany Survey. Fieldwork and Field Data*, Aldershot, Scolar Press, 1994; for interpretation, see G. Astill and W. Davies, *A Breton Landscape*, London, UCL Press, 1997 (we hope to publish the latter in French).

surrounding the core sampled to take in the whole of the watershed *(fig. 1)*. This is an area of dispersed settlement and densities of population in the 1990s are low, at between 33 and 43 inhabitants per km². The land surface is well-used, in no way "marginal" or "peripheral" in the archaeological sense, and there is plenty of arable land.

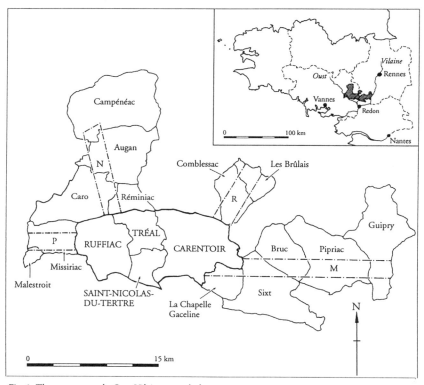

Fig. 1. The survey area: the Oust-Vilaine watershed.

The fieldwork aspect of the project included the systematic fieldwalking of ploughed fields in order to note features and collect material from the surface; walkers picked up all material that did not occur naturally: that is, sherds of modern as well as prehistoric, Roman and medieval ceramic; fragments of modern brick as well as earlier tile; and samples of slate and stone that had been introduced on to the fields.

Five years of fieldwalking demonstrated that a very high proportion of ploughed fields in the survey area have a scatter of introduced material – principally pottery, tile and stone – on the surface. Many fields have small quantities of sherds and of building material, evenly or haphazardly distributed across the surface of the field. These scatters are in marked contrast to the few which cluster densely on the surface and which can be shown to lie directly above or near structural remains. The lighter scatters must ultimately derive from refuse disposal: such material decreases with depth in the plough soil, and is not associated with sub-surface features; it was clearly introduced from the surface. Everything suggests that the refuse was disposed of in the context of agricultural activity, with broken sherds distributed in the course of manuring the arable fields: the arable was fertilized by the distribution of stable dung, as well as by allowing animals to graze on the fallow; sherds of pottery and other household waste became mixed with farmyard piles of dung before it was spread on the fields. The light scatters of pottery therefore denote the arable that was manured from settlements, while the dense clusters constitute a tool for indicating settlement location.

The quantities of central medieval and late medieval material on the fields are such that a high proportion of the debris from settlements must have been spread on them. The frequency of late and some post-medieval sherds in the plough soil of some fields suggests that this medieval habit of distributing refuse on arable fields continued through the sixteenth and at least part of the seventeenth century too, after which there was a change in refuse disposal practice.

The most widely occurring of pottery fabrics of all periods in our whole survey area is a ware that we termed "Fabric 1", a soft brown coarseware of local origin used both for tableware and cooking vessels in the thirteenth and fourteenth centuries, and perhaps beginning as early as the eleventh[3]. It occurs exceptionally frequently. So common is it that it was found on the surface of just over half of all fields walked in the initial fieldwalking programme in the core (52% of records). Its frequency is especially striking.

This material occurs throughout the survey area, though less densely in the centre of the core than in Carentoir and in western transects of Ruffiac *(fig. 2)*. Although widespread in its occurrence, it is nevertheless absent from some discrete zones, like the areas north of Les Vignes and around Le Bois Faux (Carentoir) and south of La Ville Robert (Ruffiac) *(fig. 3)*. It occurs across the whole contour range, though more frequently than the norm on steep slopes and more rarely in low wet valley bottoms and on high flat ridges.

Although some of this material occurs in dense clusters on the fields, most of it is lightly and evenly or haphazardly distributed across the surface, thereby denoting arable manured with farmyard waste of the thirteenth and fourteenth centuries. Normally six or seven fields with this type of light scatter surround one field with a dense cluster, the field with a settlement: settlements were therefore isolated and dispersed, then as now, and arable fields surrounded each settlement. Other wares of the same period do occur in the clusters and on the arable fields, but they are very rare by comparison with Fabric 1 (for example, Fabric 5 occurs in only 10% of all records, Fabric 7 in 2%, Fabric 58 in < 1% and Fabric 309 in < 1%).

The distribution of Fabric 1 is therefore an important tool for defining the arable fertilized from the twelfth to fourteenth centuries. The distribution pattern is distinctive and period-specific. The occurrence of the pottery on steep slopes implies some pressure on land for cultivation in this period, as does its association with the stoney land indicated by *friche/roche* names. Interestingly, zones which do have Fabric 1 include all the settlements with relatively early "wood" names, such as *La Touche*: all eleven of these settlements in the core have a preponderance of fields with Fabric 1 surrounding them; by contrast, none of the eight (later) *Bois* settlements has a preponderance of Fabric 1 in the surrounding fields *(table 1)*. The contrast is stark and absolutely explicit.

---

3. Davies and Astill, *East Brittany Survey*, p. 189-194, for detail of the fabric; *ibid.*, p. 194-203 for other medieval fabrics.

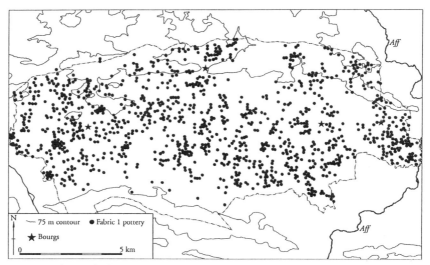

Fig. 2. Distribution of Fabric 1 pottery in the core of the survey area.

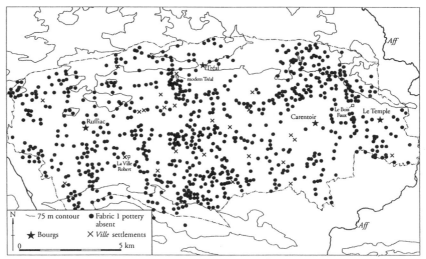

Fig. 3. Location of settlements with ville *names in the core of the survey area, compared with location of fields devoid of Fabric 1 pottery.*

The same approach can be applied to widely occurring fabrics of other periods, for example to Fabric 4, a fifteenth- to early seventeenth-century fabric used initially for bowls and subsequently for cooking ware that could be brought to table. This material occurs on the surface of less than half of fields walked in the core (38% of records), and is rather more common in Carentoir than in Ruffiac. Like Fabric 1 it occurs across the

XI

Place-name	Commune	Predominance of Fabric 1
Bostubois	Tr	No
La Métairie du Bois	Car	No
Le Bois Brassu	Car	No
Le Bois Brun	Tr	No
Le Bois Faux	Car	No
Le Bois Guillaume	Car	No
Le Bois Robert	S-N	No
Le Bois By	Car	No
La Touche	Tr	Yes
La Touche à l'eau	Ruff	Yes
La Touche Aga	Ruff	Yes
La Touche au Roux	Car	Yes
La Touche Caro	S-N	Yes
La Touche du Mur	Car	Yes
La Touche ès Huët	Car	Yes
La Touche ès Rageard	Car	Yes
La Touche Fion (sic)	Tr	Yes
La Touche Gourelle	Ruff	Yes
La Touche Peschard	Car	Yes

Table 1. Bois *and* touche *names in the core of the survey area.*
Predominance or otherwise of fields with Fabric 1 in the areas surrounding bois *and* touche *place-names in Carentoir, Ruffiac, Saint-Nicolas-du-Tertre and Tréal.*

whole survey area, but although common, its scatters are less common and less dense than those of Fabric 1: unlike the earlier period, it is quite clear that other fabrics were also in wide use during the currency of Fabric 4. Its distribution does not therefore *define* the land-use/settlement pattern as the earlier fabric does. The other widely occurring fabrics of this later period are Fabrics 6 and 23, fifteenth-/sixteenth-century tablewares: Fabric 6 occurs in 30% of fields walked in the core, and is more common in Ruffiac than in Carentoir, while the regional import Fabric 23 occurs in 37% of fields walked in the core. Quantities per field of all these fabrics are very much smaller than those of Fabric 1; however, the pattern of settlement and land-use remained the same: a field with a dense cluster surrounded by six or seven (or more) arable fields with a light manuring scatter is again the norm; settlement therefore remained dispersed, with arable close to settlements.

The distribution of the fifteenth-/sixteenth-century ceramics Fabrics 4, 6 and 23 is similar to that of the thirteenth-/fourteenth-century Fabric 1, and occurs in similar types of location. However, it is not identical. Many fields with small quantities of Fabric 1 also have small quantities of Fabrics 4, 6 and/or 23; the implication is clear: arable of the thirteenth century was still being cultivated in the sixteenth. However, there are cases of fields with Fabric 1 that lack any Fabrics 4, 6 or 23 (22% of Fabric 1 fields), and correspondingly cases of fields with Fabrics 4, 6 or 23 that lack any Fabric 1 (32% of Fabric 4/6/23 fields). Again, the implication is clear: some fields went out of cultivation between the thirteenth and sixteenth centuries, probably in response to demographic decline, and some came in afresh. The overall increase over the area of thirteenth-/fourteenth-century arable by the late sixteenth century was 15%[4].

---
4. See Astill and Davies, *Breton Landscape*, p. 119-137 for full detail on these points.

143

If we compare the thirteenth-/fourteenth- with the fifteenth-/sixteenth-century patterns of land-use and settlement, we immediately become aware of continuities and discontinuities. Most of the arable worked in the central middle ages was still worked in the late middle ages; but some went out of cultivation and some new land was taken in. The land that went out of cultivation was sometimes high (20% of these fields were above 70m, whereas only 11% of all the Fabric 1 fields lie above this height), and sometimes on north-facing slopes (29%, as against the all-Fabric-1 mean of 23%). The land that came into cultivation anew was more likely to lie at 200-400m from water than the "all-fields" norm and included land that subsequently reverted to *lande*. The changes were not major: some retreat from exposed high land; then later some 15% expansion on the earlier arable maximum; and some tendency to choose new land to exploit, especially land farther from water.

These changes must reflect responses to two major phases of social change: firstly, as epidemics took their toll and population dropped by over 30%[5], a retreat in the late fourteenth century from the unkind, steep and stoney lands exploited during the period of high demographic pressure c. 1300; and then, secondly, the piecemeal extension of the arable, in new zones, as demographic pressures began to build again and as – especially – new nobles looked for economic opportunity. A significant proportion of the noble farms of the fifteenth and sixteenth centuries were on newly exploited lands. A good 40% of them had no, or negligible, Fabric 1 on the surface of surrounding fields, and no central medieval exploitation in the neighbourhood.

The distribution of settlements with *ville* names

After a necessarily long introduction and explanation of context, we come to *ville* names. Within the core of the survey area (that is the present communes of Ruffiac, Tréal, Saint-Nicolas-du-Tertre and Carentoir), twenty-four settlement names which include the element *ville* are recorded on the *ancien cadastre* of 1825-1829; all but three of these names are still in use and many are also found in seigneurial archives of the fourteenth century onwards (especially those from the monastery of Redon's Priory at Ruffiac) and in parish records of the sixteenth to nineteenth centuries *(table 2)*[6]. At least a further seven such names are known from archive sources but, since these cannot be located precisely, they are not usable in the present exercise[7]. Of the twenty-four, four are of the *Villeneuve* type[8], two are of *-ville*, one is of *La Ville-au*, thirteen are of *La Ville* + a proper name or other noun and the remaining four are of *Ville/La Ville* + a descriptive term or adjective (only two of the latter with *La*).

---

5. By 1430 there were clear population reductions. This is demonstrated by the several *Réformations* of the *fouage*, adjusting the number of fiscal units down to the reduced population size. The 1426-1430 *Réformation* specifies the numbers of "old" *feux* (the fiscal units used in the late fourteenth century) for Ruffiac, Carentoir, Tréal and Le Temple parishes (Le Temple was a tiny parish within Carentoir at that time; Saint-Nicolas-du-Tertre was still a part of Ruffiac parish); secondly, the data specify a reduction of 175 *feux* c. 1430, a 38% reduction overall; see Astill and Davies, *Breton Landscape*, p. 134-135, for references and detail.
6. See Astill and Davies, *Breton Landscape*, p. 10-15, 26-7, for discussion and list of relevant archive material.
7. *Ville Briend, Ville Fier, Ville Gario, Ville Giehare*, all evidenced in 1480 (Archives d'Ille-et-Vilaine, 3H 193), the first of these clearly being near Ruffiac Priory and the rest probably so; *Ville Blanche*, near La Ville Marie (Ruffiac), from 1636 in Baptêmes, Marriages, Sépultures for Tréal, and also in Archives d'Ille-et-Vilaine, 3H 188 (liasse 5), in 1669; *Ville Morin*, Tréal BMS from 1627; *Vieux Ville*, Tréal BMS 1735.
8. Villeneuve in southwestern Carentoir (just east of La Rincelaie) is recorded as "La Villeneufve" in the 1427 *Réformation des feux* and "Villenave" in the 1536 *Montre* (Cte R. de Laigue, *La noblesse bretonne aux XVe et XVIe siècles, Réformations et montres*, 3 vol., Rennes, Plihon et Hommay, 1902, p. 134, 147).

A NOTE ON VILLE NAMES AND SETTLEMENT DEVELOPMENT IN THE MORBIHAN

When fields were walked in the neighbourhood of these *ville* places, fifteen of the twenty-four places were surrounded by fields that had no Fabric 1 at all or were surrounded by a large majority of fields without Fabric 1, the thirteenth- and fourteenth-century ceramic which is normally so common *(fig. 3)*[9]. Were this pottery not so common, its rarity in the neighbourhood of 63% of settlements with *ville* names might not be significant; but Fabric 1 is the commonest of all wares of any period to be found in the survey; its absence is significant and implies that fields were not being cultivated in the neighbourhood of these settlements in the thirteenth and fourteenth centuries. Indeed, since settlement and arable fields commonly go together, it implies that rather few of the *ville* settlements were located there in the thirteenth and fourteenth centuries. To reinforce the point, fields in the neighbourhood of 96% of these same *ville* settlements had scatters of Fabrics 4, 6 and/or 23, material which is in fact much less common than Fabric 1. This makes it clear that these same fields *were* being cultivated in the fifteenth and sixteenth centuries and implies that the settlements were in existence at that time. Many of the *ville* names must therefore denote new settlements that were established in the fifteenth and sixteenth centuries.

Place-name	Commune	Fields with Fabric 1	Fields with Fabric 4/6/23
La Grand'ville	Car	No	Yes
Malleville	Car	No	Yes
Ville de bas	S-N	Yes	Yes
La Ville Chapelle	Car	No	Yes
La Ville David	Tr	Yes	Yes
La Ville Daval	Car	Yes	Yes
La Ville Daniel	S-N	No	Yes
La Ville Hoyard	Ruff	Yes	Yes
La Ville Hatte	Tr	No	Yes
La Ville Héleuc	Car	No	Yes
La Ville Jeanne	Tr	Yes	Yes
La Ville Lio (Villio)	Tr	No	Yes
Villeneuve	Car	Yes	Yes
(La) Villeneuve	Car	Yes	Yes
Villeneuve	Ruff	No	Yes
Villeneuve	S-N	No	Yes
La Ville Marie	Ruff	No	Yes
La Ville Mariée	Car	No	Yes
La Ville Noël	Ruff	No	Yes
La Ville au Noël	Car	Yes	Yes
La Ville Ouie (Louis)	Car	No	Yes
La Ville Régent	Tr	Yes	Yes
La Ville Robert	Ruff	No	Yes
Ville Verte	Car	No	No

Table 2. Ville *names in the core of the survey area.*
Columns 3 and 4 show where fields with Fabric 1 and fields with Fabrics 4/6/23 predominate in the areas surrounding ville *place-names in Carentoir, Ruffiac, Saint-Nicolas-du-Tertre and Tréal.*

---

9. By "in the neighbourhood" I mean fields within 500m of the *ville* settlement, at extreme limits; in practice, virtually all of the fields were within 200m of the settlements. Not surprisingly, therefore, excluding all beyond 200m makes no difference to the proportions of fields with and without Fabric 1.

XI

If we try to differentiate between types of *ville* name, we find no significant difference: the one case of *La Ville-au* does have Fabric 1 nearby; two of the *Villeneuve* names do and two do not; two of the four *(La) Ville*+other do and two do not; and four of the thirteen *La Ville*+name/noun do and the rest do not. If we look at the incidence of *La* it again makes no difference: 63% of *ville* place-names with *La* have significantly little Fabric 1 in the surrounding fields, and 50% of those without *La* have significantly little.

As indicated above, much of the new arable of the late middle ages is associated with new noble establishments in new zones of the survey area – and often with new *métairies* exploiting the lands for noble landlords. Such are the fields west of Gravaud; fields by Le Bois Brassu; fields by La Gélinais (all Carentoir); fields by Les Landes du Houssa (Ruffiac). In fact, recorded noble properties of the fifteenth century have a distinctive distribution: most lie in the centre of the survey area; 71% in eastern Ruffiac, Tréal, Saint-Nicolas, and western Carentoir; and a third lie in the very small central communes of Tréal and Saint-Nicolas. In other words, they tend to be sited away from the old-established parish centres of Ruffiac and Carentoir. Most strikingly, fields in and around the present commune centre of Tréal, the location of La Ville Lio, a *métairie* first mentioned in 1427, are largely devoid of Fabric 1 but have plenty of fabrics of the later middle ages and sixteenth century[10]. Of thirty fields walked in and around Tréal centre, only nine had any Fabric 1 (and that in very small quantities), whereas twenty had Fabrics 4, 6 and/or 23. This stands in contrast to fields near the parish centre of Tréal of that time, now known as Le Vieux Bourg.

Of course, although some of the *métairies* that are first recorded in the sixteenth century (for example, La Ville Régent, La Ville Marie), have *ville* names, these figures do not imply that all *ville* settlements lay outside the areas of arable worked in the thirteenth and fourteenth centuries. Some of them – La Ville David (Davy), La Ville Hoyard, the (La) Villeneuve in southwestern Carentoir – are surrounded by fields with Fabric 1 and are clearly in areas that were heavily cultivated in the central middle ages. This is what we would expect, given the much discussed evidence of names of this type occurring at the earlier period[11]. But what is significant is the fact that the name type was still clearly being used for new settlements in the very late middle ages and early modern period. This is in any case the implication of M. Le Moing's work on Haute-Bretagne, with his strong evidence that *ville* names were being coined by non-Breton speakers after the thirteenth century[12].

Ville names, as such, cannot therefore be used as an indicator of "new settlement" or "colonization" in the central middle ages – much less of *grands défrichements* at that time. Forming names with this element was current for several centuries longer.

---

10. Often *La Villio* in seventeenth- and eighteenth-century texts; in 1427 the form was *La Ville Guehioc* and in 1513 *La Villegleio* (de Laigue, *Noblesse bretonne*, p. 828, 830).
11. Cf. Tanguy, *Dictionnaire*, p. 350, for example; F. Falc'hun, *Nouvelle méthode de recherche en toponymie celtique*, Plabennec, Éditions Armoricaines, 1978-1979, p. 34; A. Vincent, *Toponymie de la France*, Brussels, 1937, reprinted Brionne, Montfort, 1988, p. 290-294; A. Dauzat and Ch. Rostaing, *Dictionnaire étymologique des noms de lieux en France*, Paris, Librairie Guénégaud, 1963, revised ed. 1978, p. 718-23.
12. J.-Y. Le Moing, *Les Noms de lieux bretons de Haute-Bretagne*, Spezed, Coop Breizh, 1990, p. 276-9 and maps 28, 29.

Bibliography

Astill, G. and Davies, W., *A Breton Landscape*, London, UCL Press, 1997.

Chédeville, A. and Tonnerre, N.-Y., *La Bretagne féodale XIe-XIIIe siècle*, Rennes, Ouest-France, 1987.

Dauzat, A. and Rostaing, Ch., *Dictionnaire étymologique des noms de lieux en France*, Paris, Librairie Guénégaud, 1963, revised ed. 1978.

Davies, W. and Astill, G., *The East Brittany Survey. Fieldwork and Field Data*, Aldershot, Scolar Press, 1994.

de Laigue, Cte R., *La noblesse bretonne aux XVe et XVIe siècles, Réformations et montres*, 3 vol., Rennes, Plihon & Hommay, 1902.

Duby, G., *Rural Economy and Country Life in the Medieval West*, London, Edward Arnold, 1968.

Falc'hun, F., *Nouvelle méthode de recherche en toponymie celtique*, Plabennec, Éditions Armoricaines, 1978-1979.

Le Moing, J.-Y., *Les noms de lieux bretons de Haute-Bretagne*, Spezet, Coop Breizh, 1990.

Tanguy, B., « Toponymie et peuplement en Bretagne. Le recul de la frontière linguistique du Ve au XVIe siècle », in M. Mulon & J. Chaurand (ed.), *Archéologie, Toponymie. Colloque tenu au Mans (mai 1980)*, Paris, 1981.

Tanguy, B., *Dictionnaire des noms de communes, trèves et paroisses des Côtes d'Armor*, Douarnenez, ArMen – Le Chasse-Marée, 1992.

Vincent, A., *Toponymie de la France*, Brussels, 1937, reprinted Brionne, Montfort, 1988.

Résumé

La recherche microtopographique sur le terrain (« *fieldwalking* » et fouilles) et aux archives, concentrée sur l'est du Morbihan, a montré que quelques noms de lieux en « ville » ont été créés aux XVe-XVIe siècles, pour désigner de nouveaux établissements associés à des terres labourées pour la première fois. Par conséquent, on ne peut pas utiliser les toponymes en « ville » comme des indices de la nouvelle colonisation des XIIe-XIIIe siècles.

XII

FIELD SURVEY AND THE PROBLEM OF SURFACE SCATTERS OF BUILDING MATERIAL : SOME EAST BRETON EVIDENCE

Résumé : L'observation minutieuse et systématique des fragments de roche recueillis à la surface des champs labourés et lors de fouilles montre que, dans les zones étudiées en Bretagne orientale, on peut distinguer la roche importée de la roche locale. La roche importée se compose essentiellement d'ardoise de couverture d'origine proche mais, dans la surface étudiée, de la pierre de construction a aussi été apportée, en provenance de couches de pierres plus dures situées à moins de dix kilomètres au nord et au sud. La roche importée est parvenue sur les champs pour deux raisons principales, *bien distinctes* : ou elle a été répartie au cours du fumage au moyen des ordures de ferme, ou elle reflète la dispersion de matériaux provenant de constructions antérieures. L'attention portée aux fragments de roche de surface est donc un moyen d'étude utile. Quelques distinctions chronologiques apparaissent également : les constructeurs romains utilisaient les roches les plus dures de la région et très peu de schistes briovériens ou de roches silteuses cambriennes utilisés plus tard ; les ardoises de couverture noires ont été employées dans des contextes médiévaux.

Quite early in the programme of fieldwork associated with the East Brittany Survey - a study of landscape, land-use and settlement that I run with Grenville Astill - we came up against a problem concerning building material, a problem that could not be ignored in a project which has a major interest in settlement evidence (Astill and Davies, 1984-7). It is the main aim of this Survey to determine in detail how human communities used land in the relatively small area of the communes of Ruffiac, Tréal, Saint-Nicolas-du-Tertre and Carentoir (192 km^2) in the last two thousand years, as also to establish how and when the process of exploitation changed during that period and the effects of such changes on social groupings and labour patterns (fig. 1). It is therefore concerned with the complex of spatial and social relationships arising from exploitation, and hence with the particulars of settlement history.

THE PROBLEM

The Survey methods include work on archival material up to the nineteenth century (including estate documents and demographic data), a survey of all standing buildings in the four communes, systematic fieldwalking of available ploughed fields in those communes and sampling beyond this core, together with geochemical and geophysical surveys and small-scale excavation of selected fields. The building problem arose as follows : our programme of fieldwalking involved the systematic collection of surface material, since this is a prime indicator of agricultural, occupational and other human activity. This material consists most obviously of sherds of pottery - Iron Age, Roman, medieval, post-medieval - as also of fragments of brick and tile, the latter often in direct relationship to settlement sites : Roman tile

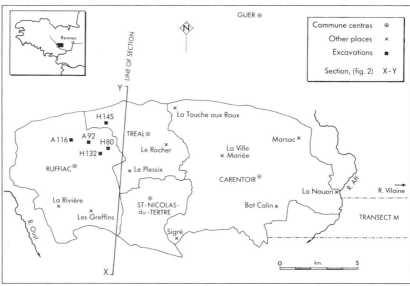

Fig. 1 : Location of study area.

scatters, for example, are sometimes dense and discrete enough to pinpoint Roman-period settlements. However, at least between the sixteenth and early twentieth centuries, the standard building material used in this area has been the local *schiste*. When launched on the fieldwalking programme we realized that we were ignoring a potentially significant source of evidence in the *schistes* also lying on the surface of the fields. Building debris of the last few centuries might include a little brick and tile but it will overwhelmingly be composed of fragments of local stone ; there is no reason why this might not be just as true of earlier centuries as more recent ones. Any scatter of stone on the surface of the fields, then, is potentially just as significant an indicator of human activity as are potsherds. To ignore such an obvious pointer to former structures would be blinkered, to say the least. However, since the rock in this area usually lies within 50 cm of the surface - and sometimes much closer - it is normal to find plenty of fresh or worn fragments of local bedrock on the surface. The problem, then, was to devise a method of distinguishing rock fragments that were imported and utilized by man from those that were local ; and further to find a method of so doing efficient and consistent enough to produce usable results. It is a type of problem that is particularly tricky for the archaeologist, accustomed as he is to think in terms on the one hand of artefacts and on the other of "natural" ; here we have material that, although "natural", nevertheless has cultural significance - it is not man-made nor even necessarily man-fashioned but it *is* man-used.

LOCAL GEOLOGY
AND BUILDINGS STANDING NOW

In Brittany the oldest rocks are the soft-weathering Brioverian (Precambrian) which characterizes much of the peninsula, later intruded by granites and then overlaid with the shales and sands of younger sediments like the Grès Armoricain, subsequently toughened into slates and quartzites in the Armorican folding of 300 million years ago ; later intrusions of granite and deposits of Carboniferous slates and shales completed the rock succession. Today the folds and outcrops of the granite run largely along west-east alignments, accentuated by the ridges of harder grès and slate, the depressions which separate them being floored with the softer-weathering *schistes*.

Ruffiac, Tréal, Saint-Nicolas-du-Tertre and Carentoir lie on the Brioverian (b2-3) - by far the most frequently occurring natural rock type - and this normally presents itself as a soft silty shale, which breaks and decomposes easily, and is characterized as much by its cleavage and fissility as by its softness. However, there are sandier areas within the Brioverian (*zones gréseuses*), as well as areas of harder Brioverian and quartzose and conglomeratic outcrops. To north and south, near the commune boundaries, the Brioverian is framed by narrow bands of harder rocks, those of the Réminiac Syncline to the north and the Malestroit Syncline to the south. These structures are constituted, successively, of the blue/pink siltstones of the Cambrian Formation de Pont-Réan (K-01), the yellowish sandstones of the Ordovician Grès Armoricain (02), the fine, hard, black siltstones of the Ordovician Formation de Traveusot (03-4), the talcy siltstones (with thin sandy layers intercalated) of the Ordovician Formations de Riadan and Saint-Marcel (05-6), and then the pale quartzites, reddish-yellow sandstones and sandy siltstones of the Silurian formations (S1, etc.). Moving 3-4 km farther south into the Anticline of the Landes de Lanvaux one travels through the silty/quartzitic/greywacke shales and arkoses of the Bains-sur-Oust group (b-o2) to the granite massif of the Landes de Lanvaux itself (Babin, 1976) (fig. 2). Slates of the Bains group and the fine black siltstones (**Schistes d'Angers**) to the south and east have been exploited by the roofing industry for distribution for at least four centuries (Chaumeil, 1938 ; Soulez-Larivière, 1975-6) ; by contrast, the local versions of all of these harder bands, as also Brioverian, though not high quality building stone, have long been used for building in their immediate localities, with little or no large-scale quarrying for wider distribution. Although there are some larger quarries on the periphery of the communes (like that in the woods behind Sigré) stone for local use was usually quarried in neighbouring fields (Meirion-Jones, 1982 : p. 46-7 ; Musgrave, 1988 : p. 240-5). This means that there is a proliferation of small quarry holes throughout the four communes and beyond; and accordingly there are sufficient exposures to determine natural rock types throughout the area.

The present array of standing buildings in this area, which from the late sixteenth century to the 1930s number 4589, characteristically uses a mixture of the harder (but not usually finely dressable) stones - sandstones, quartzites, the Cambrian siltstones, the harder Brioverian - together with soft Brioverian and (sometimes large) conglomerate and quartz blocks for strengthening and for foundations (fig. 3). Granite was *not* used until very recently, and is only present in small quantities. Characteristically, construction is of a very roughly coursed inner and outer face, with a rubble core of smaller pieces bonded by a mud slurry (*pisé*) (fig. 4); door and window jambs and the corners of walls usually have more dressed and squared blocks. Until the early twentieth century the *rangées* of peasant houses and other buildings in the study area, as also in surrounding communes, normally used stone in one of two related ways :

1 - Most commonly they used a great mixture of local stone, drawn from their immediate neighbourhood or from the harder bands to north or south of the communes : K-01M from **Malestroit** *and* **Réminiac Synclines**, harder and softer Brioverian, 03-4, grès, conglomerate, quartz and thin slivers of black roofing slate ; in this extremely common mixture the proportions of each stone type vary in apparently random fashion, with the core composed of the same mixture but smaller fragments ; jambs and corners often use a high proportion of K-01M (fig. 5). One collapsed house at Bot Colin, for example, reuses a K-01M mullion in its wall face, and this is by no means unique. Variants of this build include some quartzite too, like houses at Marsac, Le Rocher and La Rivière, and very occasionally incorporate some tile (Marsac).

2 - The second common method is to use less of a mixture of stones, and to use narrow blocks of very fissile material, in layers, almost giving the impression of regular coursing ; indeed, in general these buildings look much less irregular and they use predominantly K-01M,

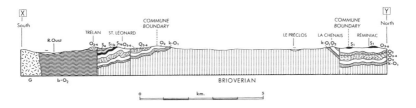

Fig. 2 : Diagrammatic section through the solid geology of the study area.

or local soft Brioverian interleaved with K-01M (fig. 6). This build is especially characteristic of the outbuildings of *petits châteaux* (like Préclos, La Ruée, and the surrounding walls of La Rivière and Les Greffins) but can be found in other types of settlement too (like Le Plessix in Tréal).

As for the *châteaux* themselves, and *métairies*, their stone fabric has often been rendered, but where it is visible it is usually of the same type of construction as the first method outlined above : this is true of La Nouan, La Ruée, La Rivière, Les Greffins, La Touche aux Roux (which has notable proportions of quartzite too). In other words, near contemporary *petit château* and peasant *rangée* use much the same walling technique despite the larger size and more elaborate design of the former (fig.7).

Local roofing practice did not so much utilize the fine quality slates of the established industries but local, coarse, black 03-4 and the coarse pink/purple siltstones of the **Pont Réan Formation**, especially from quarries to the north of the four communes, in bands of K-01 near Guer (fig. 8). These "pink" slates can still be found *in situ* from Malestroit to Carentoir, and sometimes they still lie in piles beside the collapsing buildings that are so characteristic of the area ; however, during the last century they have usually been replaced on occupied houses by the much finer, machine-cut, black slates of mass production and distribution.

Collapsed and collapsing buildings are characteristic of the area now. It is of no little importance to note that their particular type of construction allows for easy disintegration : once the roof has gone the mud slurry bonding does not hold well ; the walls are an easy quarry for nearby builders ; bushes quickly become established in them ; and the structure can be reduced to a heap of stones, mud and vegetation in a matter of years (fig. 9). However, it is extremely common to see new houses standing beside collapsing ones ; everything suggests that the mixture of old but still used, redundant and new buildings which is characteristic of this area has been a norm for centuries (fig. 10).

ROCK FRAGMENTS FROM EXCAVATIONS

In order to deal with the problem of distinguishing between local and imported fragments at present on the

Fig. 3 : *Rangée* at La Touche Aga, Ruffiac.

Fig. 4 : Rubble core of a house at La Hardouinaie, Carentoir.

Fig. 5 : Walling (I) at La Ruaudaie, St-Nicolas-du-Tertre.

Fig. 6 : Walling (II) at La Ruaudaie, St-Nicolas-du-Tertre.

fields, it was decided to begin a systematic programme of careful observation and examination of residual rock fragments, both in sub-surface structures and generally in the plough and stratified soils. This was sustained both in surface collection and in excavation. In selected cases all stone above a given minimum size (sometimes as low as 1g, depending on circumstances) was collected, washed, weighed and classified. (The fragments are easy to classify, with experience, because of the ease of taking natural samples from the many small local quarries.) Excavation produced especially useful results, and these results are essential for the interpretation of the very large corpus of surface observations.

Firstly, it is absolutely clear that imported material can easily be distinguished from local. Non-local fragments in and on the soil are overwhelmingly roofing material (both black and pink, often with nailholes) together with smaller quantities of K-01M, grès and quartzite from the bands immediately to north and south of the four communes, that is within 2-3 km of the periphery of the study area and within 2-9 km of its four centres ; they are often associated with fragments of Brioverian, conglomerate and quartz of more immediately local provenance.

Secondly, it is clear that fragments distributed in the course of manuring - that is yard refuse - are distinguishable from fragments derived from nearby collapsed buildings, and the latter are - as one might expect - distinguishable from wall collapse itself. (Of course, yard refuse includes building scatter, but this is building scatter that has been redistributed at least once after collapse.) It is evident that the ubiquitous scatters of roofing material in fact arrived through manuring.

Stone distribution that derives from manuring is characterized by its even distribution over the field - it does not cluster. It contains relatively high proportions of roofing material and little building stone. The same distributional pattern is also characteristic of sherds deriving from manuring, the dates of which suggest that farmyard manure was spread on the fields at least from the twelfth until the nineteenth century. The high proportion of roofing fragments in the manuring distribution is presumably to be explained by the short life of a roof in relation to that of a wall and the need to renew every three or four generations. Just as slates now lie around in piles in farmyards, presumably they have done so for centuries and have been duly cleared after disintegration and spread with associated muck and debris. Excavation (T1) through a lynchet near field A116, near Les Viviers in Ruffiac, provided a good example of manuring scatter : the lynchet itself lies on the edge of arable associated with the château of Coetion in the early nineteenth century ; it was formed by repeated agricultural activity at least since the twelfth century and provides an accumulation of more than 1m of soil beneath the modern ploughsoil - 1.8 m from subsoil (which lies on the Brioverian) to the crest of the lynchet; this buildup was almost entirely (97 %) associated with medieval pottery (Astill and Davies, 1985 : p. 90-5). All visible fragments of rock were collected throughout the excavation, in a meticulous piece of work whose excavators deserve handsome tribute. Classification of rock fragments in this lynchet revealed high proportions of (probably natural) Brioverian and of introduced black roofing material, with smaller proportions of K-01M and grès.

		Black roofing	Pink roofing	Brioverian	K-01M	Grès	Quartzite	Conglomerate	Quartz	Total kg
H145	: T9	6,9	7,6	59	2	4,7	1,8	16	-	20,374
	: T10	4,5	6,2	42,1	12,7	6,7	11	14	-	22,183
A92	: T28[1]	0,1	0,04	12,2	1,9	16,3	48,5	16,5	2,2	322,39
	: T28[2]	-	-	1,9	1	19,2	54	14,1	9,7	355,468
	: T29	1,6	-	16,8	15,9	15,7	32,1	14,6	1,8	3,57
H80	: T15	12,2	14,4	44,9	7,1	8,2	1,6	11,6	-	5,455
	: T16[7]	-	-	17,6	73,8	3,4	-	4,8	-	1,491
	: T16[8]	-	0,7	48,6	5,5	37,1	4,5	3,1	-	0,705
	: T21	-	5,7	27,3	3,6	7,5	44,1	5,6	6,1	0,898
	: T22	1	1	43,6	37,9	2,2	-	13,4	-	3,011
A116	: T1	30	4	31,6	17,3	4	0,6	0,4	-	5,129
	: T2	9,3	9,8	33,6	36,2	2,4	-	-	-	6,735
	: T3	17,8	6,7	32,3	29,1	3,9	1,3	1,5	-	9,285
	: T4	10,2	5,1	36,3	27,5	6,3	1	2,1	3,5	12,62
	: T5	10,7	3,5	60	19,3	2,5	-	2	-	5,12
Cf : H132	: surface	2,1	0,04	27,2	10,7	4,7	27,2	8,1	20,3	588,28

Table 1 : Percentage of rock types from excavations.

N.B. The tables in this chapter use the continental convention of commas in the place of decimal points.

Fig. 7 : Old roof at Le Cleu, Tréal.

Fig. 8 : Seigneurial building at La Herblinaie, Carentoir.

Fig. 9 : Collapsing house at Courrouet, Tréal.

Fig. 10 : Mixed build of *rangée* at Le Plessis Payen, Carentoir.

Black Roof	Pink Roof	Brioverian	K-O1M	Grès	Total kg
30 %	4 %	31,6 %	17,3 %	4 %	5,129

The grès and siltstone here are likely to have derived ultimately from building debris, although there is relatively little of it. The shallower ploughsoil (30 cm) excavated in the western end of field H80, just east of La Hattaie, was similar in its rock composition. It again lay on the Brioverian. Classification of fragments in the ploughsoil of 6 x 6 m square T15 on H80 produced comparable results to that of the lynchet, with similar proportions of roofing material, relatively much Brioverian, and only a fifth harder stones (Astill and Davies, 1987 : p. 113-17). Again, this is best explained as manuring scatter.

All Roofing	Brioverian	Conglomerate	Grès	Total kg
26,6 %	44,9 %	11,6 %	8,2 %	5,455

By contrast, the scatter deriving from a building is distinguished by its *range* of types of (largely introduced) stone ; and by the inclusion of a notable proportion of the harder stones - grès, quartzite, harder and altered Brioverian, and sometimes K-01M ; it may well have quite large fragments of imported stone - of 150-200 g, as occurred in the ploughsoil of field H145 - and fragments of semi-dressed grès ; moreover, its distribution on the surface of the field is discrete - it clusters and varies in density. Excavation in H145, to the south of Quoiqueneuc, gave results that clearly relate to a collapsed building at the corner of the field ; this is now the weedy, brambly heap of a clearance mound but in the 1820s there were two occupied buildings on this site, as the *ancien cadastre* makes clear. Here the local rock is altered grès but the stone scatter in the first 30 cm of plough soil of excavated 6 x 6 m square T9, 60 m from the mound, and throughout the fill of a pit in the 4 x 4 m square T10, 20 m from the mound, has a high proportion of Brioverian, significant proportions of grès, quartzite and conglomerate, and rather small proportions of black and pink roofing material. The mixture recalls the makeup of standing buildings ; quantities were high.

	Black Roof	Pink Roof	Brioverian	K-O1M	Conglom.	Grès	Quartzite	Total kg
T9 :	6,9 %	7,6 %	59 %	2 %	16 %	4,7 %	1,8 %	20,374
T10 :	4,5 %	6,2 %	42,1 %	12,7 %	14 %	6,7 %	11 %	22,183

Likewise, excavation (T2) of a low bank near Les Viviers, 130 m east of the lynchet excavation T1, is strikingly different in its stone composition from that of the clearly agricultural T1. This bank now lies in an area of meadow which was uncultivated in the early nineteenth century, although it is likely to have marked the edge of a cultivated area in earlier centuries. Its context is therefore less consistently agricultural. In it there was much K-O1M, from both Synclines, again Brioverian and some grès, and as much pink as black roofing material :

Black Roof	Pink Roof	Brioverian	K-O1M	Grès	Greywacke	Total kg
9,3 %	9,8 %	33,6 %	36,2 %	2,4 %	1,8 %	6,735

Though the bank itself may well have been originally constructed in relation to agricultural use to the north of it, its makeup seems to reflect scatter from buildings of the deserted settlement 50 m to the south rather than manuring activity alone. This settlement is now ploughed out but was indicated by irregular quartz and conglomerate blocks in the excavated 6 x 6 m square T3 of A116 and by a discrete surface distribution of medieval pottery. Indeed, the breakdown of rock fragments in the ploughsoil of T3 echoes that of T2 (Astill and Davies, 1986 : p. 116-19) :

Black Roof	Pink Roof	Brioverian	K-O1M	Grès	Greywacke	Total kg
17,8 %	6,7 %	32,3 %	29,1 %	3,9 %	1 %	9,285

As a further constrast, undistributed wall collapse is evident from the quantity, size and distribution of blocks. Excavation of the 6 x 6 m square T28 in the field A92, which lies on the Brioverian beside Les Landes de la Ruée, produced evidence of a collapsed Roman-period structure, associated with very large quantities of tile, and first- and second-century pottery. The stone included substantial quantities and proportions of hard stone - grès, conglomerate and quartzite - some of which was dressed, with relatively little Brioverian ; there were absolutely minimal proportions of roofing material in the plough soil and none at all in the layer beneath it (context 2). (However, the plough soil (context 1) produced comparable *amounts* of roofing material to that in the same area of plough soil in H80.) It is of considerable interest to note that the building scatter in the plough and lower soil of T29, a 6 x 6 m square opened 15 m from the collapse, where there was a far, far smaller quantity of stone, almost precisely reflected the proportions found in the collapsed wall. It suggests that other scatters may similarly reflect the stone composition of the structures from which they ultimately derive (Astill and Davies, 1987 : p. 118-21) :

	Black Roof	Pink Roof	Brioverian	Conglomerate	Grès	Quartzite	Total kg
T28[1] :	0,1 %	0,04 %	12,2 %	16,5 %	16,3 %	48,5 %	322,39
T28[2] :	-	-	1,9 %	14,1 %	19,2 %	54 %	355,468
T29 :	1,6 %	-	16,8 %	14,6 %	15,7 %	32,1 %	3,57

DATING

The Roman context of the latter excavation makes its distinctive mix of stone types datable. This signals a further potential of this investigation : the possibility that some features can be dated by their associated stone scatter. Work done so far in the study area indicates that Roman building practice of the first and second centuries relied heavily on use of the harder stones largely found 1-2 km north of the core communes - grès and quartzite especially - with more immediately local conglomerate. Quantities of Brioverian and roofing material are noticeably minimal. The ditch fill (8) in square T16 and the collapsed walling of a firing pit in square T19 on field H80, which lies south east of A92 and has features associated with late Iron Age pottery, had proportions of stone of comparable types. Large flat slabs of K-O1M - notably rare at the Roman A92 nearby - were also excavated in the pit fill (context 22) in T16 on H80, which was also associated with much Iron Age pottery. This is the only apparent case of early use of K-O1M and I would not wish to argue from it to exploitation of the K-O1M bands in the late Iron Age : context 22 is not necessarily a purely Iron Age context, and overall quantities of stone from H80 were extremely small. It is notable that Roman sites throughout *avoid* the southern part of the communes, that is the area farthest from the Roman road but closest to the heavily quarried bands of K-O1M of more modern periods.

Although other contexts produce different stone mixtures in association with material of different date range, in no case other than the Roman is it possible at present to associate a practice characteristically and exclusively with one narrow period. The manuring scatter of T1 was associated with twelfth- to fifteenth-century medieval pottery and the harder fragments of stone of that scatter tended to occur more than 40 cm beneath the plough soil, in the least recently disturbed parts of the lynchet ; this presumably reflects one medieval usage. In field A116, 250 m away, excavated soil in T3 produced less roofing material but otherwise comparable proportions of introduced stone ; this scatter included some large (over 100 g) and some roughly dressed pieces. Fragments in excavated soil of T4 and T5 of the same field were in similar proportions (Astill and Davies, 1986 : p. 116-19). All this was associated with medieval pottery and again presumably reflects medieval stone usage. Refinement of the chronology of stone usage in the medieval and early modern periods may ultimately be possible with further work, just as we are slowly refining the chronology of coarse wares used in the region (Giot and Querré, 1986 ; Giot and Querré, 1987).

It is also possible to make some observations about the dated contexts of roofing material. In a number of cases fragments of black roofing material appear in contexts which clearly pre-date those with pink. In the lynchet in T1, with its close association with twelfth- to fifteenth-century pottery, there occurred vastly more black than pink roofing material (30 % : 4 %) ; the pink material almost invariably occurred in the upper 20-30 cm of the deposit, while the black occurred well down to 50-70 cm, and sometimes below. So also the pit in T10 in field H145, which had a fill of building collapse again associated with medieval wares, had black roofing fragments at the bottom of the fill (context 5) ; whereas the pot in the pitfall was consistently medieval that in the 40 cm of ploughsoil above was medieval *and* post-medieval, and it is therefore difficult to see the fill itself as other than medieval, deriving from manuring after blocks had been thrown into the pit. By contrast, the modern treehole in T21 (context 46) on field H80 had relatively large quantities of pink material in its fill and no black. The results are consistent with the suggestion that black roofing material was in use at an earlier date than pink and that pink material was sometimes overwhelmingly predominant in more recent times. However, both black *and* pink material were notably absent in clear Roman contexts in A92. So also the pitfill 7 and ditchfill 8 in square T16 on field H80 contained no black material in layers that had large quantities of Iron Age pottery.

It is therefore evident that medieval contexts contain both black roofing material and fragments of building stone. This must imply some building *and roofing* in stone during the medieval period, even if other materials were also in use ; and this must suggest that there was no complete change in building tradition in the fifteenth and sixteenth centuries as has sometimes been assumed from the date of standing buildings. It would be unreasonable at present to propose a characteristic medieval mix of stones beyond significant proportions of Brioverian and K-O1M, and small proportions of hard stone. After the Roman period, it looks as if people used whatever stone was to hand, locally, from collapsed buildings or from neighbouring fields ; hence buildings near former Roman settlements tend to have higher proportions of quartzite - like those at Marsac, Le Rocher or La Touche aux Roux. The mix in any single case was likely to be comparable to, but not identical to, others. The appearance of roofing material in medieval contexts must imply that black slate was being used on a reasonable scale from the central or later middle ages. (We know that the Angers slate quarries were being worked at least from the twelfth century (Fourcault and Pré, 1975) ; there is no need to suppose that slates from this particular source reached this inland locality - indeed it is most unlikely ; however, the Angers references do make it entirely credible to suppose local exploitation of local resources at a comparable date.) We do in any case have dated references to the renewal of slate roofing on peasant housing in this area from the early sixteenth century onwards - the *bourg* of Ruffiac, Lodineu, Le Cleu, Chêsne Davy, Les Abbayes are all mentioned, quite apart from the ubiquitous *métairies* (Archives Départementales d'Ille et Vilaine 3H188, 3H193 ; Arch. Dép. du Morbihan G981 ; Arch. Dép. de Loire Atlantique B1999).

ROCK FRAGMENTS IN SURFACE SCATTERS

Information gathered during excavation is not only useful in itself but allows some interpretation of surface scatters. It is abundantly clear that both building scatters and manuring scatters can be identified on the surface of fields and are thus highly useful indicators of past human activity.

Stone fragments that derive from collapsed buildings in the immediate locality are identifiable by the range of types of stone on the field surface, by their distinct character by comparison with the local bedrock, and by the discrete nature of the scatter. Hence, even before excavation, it was obvious that surface fragments on field H145 were not entirely local but were derived from the previously collapsed buildings at the edge of the field. To the south west another such scatter was noted on field H132, beside La Ruée, a field without any trace of collapsed buildings and with notable quantities of surface medieval pottery ; the scatter was in a discrete area which coincided with a clustering of that pottery. All fragments larger than 10 cm across were collected, in units of 5 m squares over an area of 20 m x 45 m, then weighed and classified. Types and relative proportions by weight were as follows (total weight 588.28 kg) :

Black Roof	Pink Roof	Brioverian	K-O1m	Conglomerate	Grès	Quartzite	Quartz
2,1 %	0,04 %	27,2 %	10,7 %	8,1 %	4,7 %	27,2 %	20,3 %

There is nothing in this collection that is not consonant with debris from a building constructed in the manner of those still standing in the locality. Such a building does not feature on the *ancien cadastre* (locally of the 1820s) and cannot therefore have been in existence, inhabited or deserted, in the early nineteenth century ; neither curtilage nor garden areas are indicated on the *cadastre*, as is usually the case with inhabited, deserted or recently collapsed buildings. Its mix of stone types would not suggest a building after this period (nor would it be likely to have completely disappeared) ; equally its mix of stone types would not suggest an entirely Roman-period build (there is not enough hard stone and too much soft Brioverian), though there could be Roman-derived material here, perhaps from robbing of the structure nearby to the north in A92. Here then surface evidence indicates the presence of a former building (it lies near a still surviving track), constructed at some point during the middle ages, but collapsed without trace by the early nineteenth century.

Evidence of regular past manuring is clearly indicated by scatters of roofing material on the surface of fields, either in association with fragments of local bedrock, where soil is shallow and ploughing deep, or with negligible quantities of other stone. These roofing scatters are so very common that they can only derive from farmyard heaps spread on the fields ; they are widespread throughout the locality. Three broad patterns are discernible : there are fields with no roofing material at all, zones with black/grey and pink roofing material, and zones with black and grey roofing material only (Astill and Davies, 1985 : p. 97-8). For example, some fields near La Ville Ouie and La Ville Mariée, in Carentoir, have none ; most of the basin south of Ruffiac has black (and grey) roofing material only ; however, north of that area, fields near Le Bignon and Bergottais have black, grey *and* pink.

The former must represent areas that have only very recently been brought into cultivation, in a period when chemical fertilisers are used and farmyard manure is not spread on the fields. Such areas are usually demonstrably of very recent ploughing : for example, fields classified as woodland on IGN maps of this century but now cleared and turned to arable use.

Zones with black/grey and pink roofing material are presumably zones of long, continuous arable use, the scatters reflecting the decomposition of the slates used at various periods. As demonstrated above, pink material tends to occur in later stratified contexts : on H145 there was black and pink material in the plough soil, with slightly more pink ; but very little pink in the earlier pitfill. The ploughsoil above the curving ditch of T15 on

H80 was similar. Where old roofing slates still lie in piles in farmyards, they are very frequently of the pink type - they seem to represent the last phase of use before the advent of machine-cut slates. Zones *without* pink roofing material may well therefore in many cases equally be zones of long agricultural use, but with little continuous building or re-roofing. Whereas black/grey roofing is a norm and is used over long periods from the middle ages onwards, material from the more recent pink quarries did not get so widely distributed. Hence, for example, large zones of the sample Transect M, which ran due east for 20 km from south-east Carentoir to the river Vilaine, have no pink roofing material at all although it does sometimes occur in the immediate neighbourhood of villages like Pipriac : despite the broad regional difference, it seems that there was more building in the villages, more renewal, and therefore a wider range of materials used. In other words, the significance of this distribution is as much for local building as for manuring practice.

****

There is still fieldwork to be done, more data to be gathered and more testing of existing hypotheses to be undertaken ; excavation of field H132 and its stone scatter, for example, is crucial. However, even at this stage one can clearly observe that it *is* possible to distinguish local from introduced material and that this can be done quite easily by eye. Indeed distinctions can be made in the field, with experience and with training in careful observation, without the need to collect, weigh and classify - procedures which can therefore be reserved for critical cases. Not only can basic distinctions be made but it is possible firstly to identify areas that have been manured between some point in the middle ages and the advent of chemical fertilisers ; and secondly to identify areas which have previously had stone standing structures. Both types of information are of crucial importance to a study such as East Brittany Survey and provide information that cannot be supplied from other sources. It is therefore vital to exploit them.

The technique used in this study is applicable to other areas which have a comparable building tradition and could certainly be more widely used. Since it is relatively easy to make the essential observations in the field, without the very time-consuming and labour-intensive need to collect and classify, it is a viable procedure. Its success essentially depends on good training in careful observation. If it be used, of course, it is important to establish the basic geology, and its micro-variations, from the outset : recognized rock units often change character along their outcrop, if only subtly, and some assessment of the range of changes is a necessary prerequisite for successful observation. But, once done, there is certainly as much potential here for contributions to long-term settlement and land-use history as there is in the familiar Roman tile scatter.

Acknowledgements

My thanks are especially due to Dr Grenville Astill of Reading University Archaeology Department both for years of collaboration and for his particular comments on an earlier draft of this paper ; to Dr Eric Robinson of University College London Geology Department for much assistance with my discussion of the basic geology and for advice on building stone in general ; and to Dr Elizabeth Musgrave for the generous access she allowed me to her recent thesis and many of her notes. Pete Addison took the photographs, for East Brittany Survey. Needless to say, I have for many years benefitted from the advice of Pierre-Roland Giot on numberless aspects of the archaeology and history of Brittany.

BIBLIOGRAPHY

ASTILL G. and DAVIES W., 1984 - Prospections archéologiques dans l'est de la Bretagne : le bassin de l'Oust et de la Vilaine. *Dossiers du Centre Régional Archéologique d'Alet*, n° G, 1984, p. 251-9.

ASTILL G. and DAVIES W., 1985 - Prospections archéologiques dans l'est de la Bretagne ; mars-avril 1985. *Dossiers du CeRAA*, vol. XIII, 1985, p. 85-98.

ASTILL G. and DAVIES W., 1986 - Prospections archéologiques dans l'est de la Bretagne ; mars-avril 1986. *Dossiers du CeRAA*, vol. XIV, 1986, p. 111-120.

ASTILL G. and DAVIES W., 1987 - Prospections archéologiques dans l'est de la Bretagne ; septembre 1986 et Pâques 1987. *Dossiers du CeRAA*, vol. XV, 1987, p. 109-27.

BABIN C., 1976 - The Ordovician of the Armorican Massif (France). M.G. Basset. *The Ordovician System : Proceedings of a Palaeontological Association Symposium, Birmingham, September 1974*, Cardiff, 1976.

CHAUMEIL L., 1938 - *L'Industrie Ardoisière en Basse Bretagne*, Lorient, 1938.

FOURCAULT V. and PRE J., 1975 - Les ardoisières de Renazé de 1450 à 1928. *La province du Maine*, vol. LXXVII, 1975, p. 2-10.

GIOT P.-R. and QUERRE G., 1986 - Les poteries Armoricaines à spicules. *Dossiers du CeRAA*, vol. XIV, 1986, p. 1-12.

GIOT P.-R. and QUERRE G., 1987 - Quelques productions céramiques médiévales de Bretagne. *La Céramique (Ve-XIXe s.). I Congrès International d'Archéologie Médiévale. Paris, 1985*, Caen, 1987, p. 149-56.

MEIRION-JONES G.I., 1982 - *The Vernacular Architecture of Brittany*, Edinburgh, 1982.

MUSGRAVE E., 1988 - *The building industries of eastern Brittany, 1600-1789*. University of Oxford D. Phil., 1988.

SOULEZ-LARIVIERE M.F., 1975-6 - Angers et ses ardoisières. *Mémoires de l'Académie d'Angers*, vols. IX and X, p. 63-75.

XIII

SURFACE SCATTERS OF BUILDING STONE: ENHANCING FIELD SURVEY WORK

INTRODUCTION

In field survey work it has been traditional to pay considerable attention to surface collection of pottery and ceramic tile, with — over the past ten years especially.— greater and greater refinement of approaches to surface collection. It is the purpose of this paper to demonstrate the value of paying comparable attention to the surface occurrence of building stone, and to extend my published comment on the subject (Davies 1990).

The work discussed here was undertaken during the fieldwork programme of the East Brittany Survey, a multi-disciplinary study of land-use and settlement directed by Grenville Astill and myself; fieldwork was carried out in the period 1982−8 and detailed results published after each season (Astill and Davies 1982; 1983; 1984; 1985; 1986; 1987; 1989). This Survey is concerned with the way human communities used land in the past two thousand years, with the relationship between settlement and land-use, and with changes in practice and in the relationship, as also with the reasons for those changes. It depends on the analysis of textual and field data, and has therefore drawn upon written archive material as well as fieldwork, the latter involving a survey of all pre-1920s standing buildings, systematic fieldwalking of all available ploughed fields, and selective excavation. The study is focussed on the

SURFACE SCATTERS OF BUILDING STONE

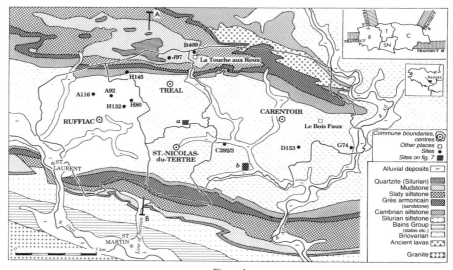

Figure 1
The area of the East Brittany Survey.

communes of Ruffiac, Tréal, Saint-Nicolas-du-Tertre and Carentoir (192 km^2), with sample transects to north, east and west of this core (Fig. 1).

There are noticeable quantities of 'foreign' stone lying on the fields of this area. Careful identification of stone types, very careful field observation, and judicious small-scale excavation, makes this material usable in ways which can considerably enhance our understanding of past settlement and land-use patterns.

By 'foreign' stone, I mean stone which does not derive from the immediately underlying bedrock, but stone which has been carried some distance, by human agency, to the place where we find it on or below the ground surface. The core communes of this Survey area lie on Brioverian rock (b_{2-3}), a soft-weathering PreCambrian silty shale, which breaks and decomposes easily. The tectonic movements that saw the introduction of granite intrusions into the Brioverian and later sediments in south-east Brittany also folded some of those sediments, throwing up ridges of conglomerate, and toughened some of the siltstones and sandstones into slates and quartzites. The predominating Brioverian stone of the core communes is therefore sometimes punctuated by quartzose and conglomeratic outcrops, and its soft shaley character is sometimes hardened into a less flakey rock. To the north and south, near the commune boundaries, the Brioverian is framed by the narrow bands of later, harder, folded sediments of the Reminiac Syncline to the north and the Malestroit Syncline to the south. These structures are constituted, successively, of the blue/pink/purple siltstones of the Cambrian Formation de Pont-Réan (k-o_1), the sandstones of the Ordovician Grès Armoricain (o_2), the hard, black, slatey

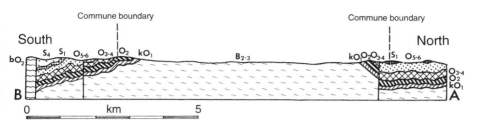

(for legend see Fig.1)

Figure 2
Diagrammatic section through the solid geology of the study area.

siltstones of the Ordovician Formation de Traveusot (o_{3-4}), the talcose siltstones of later Ordovician formations (o_{5-6}) and then the quartzites and sandstones of the Silurian formations (S_1, etc) (Carte Géologique 1981). 2 km to the south lie the shales and black slates of the Bains group ($b-o_2$), and 2 km farther south the granite massif of the Landes de Lanvaux (Figs. 1, 2) (Davies 1990, 322−3).

It is, in fact, exceptionally rare to find granite in the study area, except when a granite lintel occurs in a nineteenth- or twentieth-century building. Instead, you can see plenty of Brioverian lying around or in structures, as one might expect; there are also very large quantities of Ordovician and Cambrian siltstones distributed *throughout* the study area and not confined to the borders (o_{3-4}, $k-o_1$), with some smaller quantities of Ordovician and Silurian sandstones and quartzites (o_2, s_1); slate from the Bains group is also common. In other words, in the past the people of this region were using and moving stone from a zone of about 300 km², and using it in all parts of the region; this means that, in practice, people may have travelled up to 5 km to collect stone for building. With the exception of some of the roofing slate, which was imported from the large Angers and Rochefort slate industries to the east and west (Chaumeil 1938; Soulez-Larivière 1975−6), it is most unusual to find stone in this area which comes from farther afield. The entire study area constitutes a discrete stone-using zone, within which local stone circulated and was widely used.

In the core communes there are over 4000 standing buildings which date from sixteenth to early twentieth centuries, and a few whose fabric is clearly late medieval; many have lintels bearing seventeenth- and eighteenth-century dates (Fig. 3). Most of these buildings are south-facing *rangées* of peasant farm dwellings, usually single-storeyed with storage lofts above, but there are about 100 more substantial structures in the *petits châteaux* and associated farms (métairies) of the local nobility (see Fig. 9). Characteristically, wall construction is of roughly coursed inner and outer faces, with a rubble core of small stone fragments bonded by mud; door and window jambs are often made of dressed and squared blocks, using Cambrian siltstones especially ($k-o_1$). Most of these standing structures are built of a mixture of the harder stones — sandstones, quartzites, Cambrian siltstones, thin slivers

339

SURFACE SCATTERS OF BUILDING STONE

Figure 3
Dated lintel in a house at Galny, Carentoir.

of black roofing slate, conglomerate and quartz blocks — together with some proportion of soft Brioverian shale; proportions vary from building to building in accordance with the availability of stone from nearby fields, collapsed buildings and any other source (see Figs. 5, 6, 9). There are also some structures, particularly the outbuildings of *petits châteaux*, which use less of a mixture of stone types and instead use narrow slabs of extremely fissile material — k-o$_1$M and soft Brioverian especially — thereby giving an impression of regular coursing. Perhaps surprisingly, both seigneurial *petit château* and peasant *rangée* use essentially the same walling technique, although the château walls have often been subsequently rendered. Nowadays, both grand and peasant houses tend to be roofed with composition tiles or machine-cut black slates from the established industries of the late twentieth century, but slates from an older tradition can still be found on some roofs (see Fig. 6): these older slates are principally made from local coarse black o$_{3-4}$ and the coarse pink/purple siltstones of the Guer quarries to the north (k-o$_1$) (Davies 1990, 323).

STONE IN EXCAVATED SITES

Excavation has demonstrated the changing use of stone over time. While it is perfectly clear that slabs of blue/pink/purple siltstone of the Pont Réan formation (k-o_1) were used in the Late Iron Age, neither siltstones nor Brioverian feature significantly in the well-built Roman villa. For example, investigation of a complex mass of pits, ditches and structural remains associated with Late Iron-Age pottery in field H80 (La Hattaie) revealed a siltstone path or series of stepping stones (T16:C22); 73% of the stone in the intercutting pits (T16:C7), which contained Iron-Age pottery, daub, and tile, was Cambrian siltstone (Astill and Davies 1987, 115−16; Davies 1990, 326). The Roman villa not far away at A92 was quite different (Les Landes de la Ruée): its walls and wall collapse had an overwhelming predominance of the hardest, best building stones — sandstones, quartzites (especially) and conglomerate — with ceramic tile for roofing (Astill and Davies 1987, 118−19; Astill and Davies 1989, 45−6). Its 678 kg of wall collapse consisted of 7% Brioverian, 1.5% Cambrian siltstones, 18% sandstone, 52% quartzite, 15.5% conglomerate, and 6% quartz (T28: C1, 2). Both black and pink/purple roofing slate were strikingly absent from the lower (Roman) contexts.

Medieval practice was quite different. In 1988 excavation of part of a very substantial seigneurial structure revealed foundations of the massive walls (1 m wide at widest) of a building of the central middle ages, overlaying some earlier ditches and post-holes; associated pottery would suggest an eleventh- to fourteenth-century date.[1] The substantial foundations lay on a soft Brioverian shale bedding and had a base of huge blocks of quartz and very hard altered shale; the surviving walling (348 kg)

Figure 4
Foundations of a medieval structure in field H132, La Ruée, Ruffiac.

comprised 24% Brioverian, 39% altered shale, 27% quartz, 6% conglomerate, 2% quartzite and 2% sandstone; its rubble core included tiny proportions of Cambrian siltstone and black roofing slate amongst the other stones (Fig. 4). Extensions to the original building used similar materials. This building lies in the mixed stone tradition of standing buildings of the sixteenth to early twentieth centuries, except that proportions of Cambrian siltstone in the walling are very small. However, within the building a 1 × 2 m hearth had been constructed of pink siltstone (k-o_1). Further, the site had been levelled subsequent to occupation and a series of alterations; in the building's destruction layer lay a dump of roofing slate, some of which appears to have been roof collapse *in situ*; all of these slates were of blue/pink/purple siltstone, k-o$_1$ (Astill and Davies 1989, 51−5).

Broadly, then, we may note these distinctions in the use of stone at different periods: Roman-period stone building used large proportions of quartzite and sandstone, very little soft shale, and negligible amounts of slate; stone building of the central middle ages used plenty of shale, such hard stones as were easily available (hence little quartzite and sandstone), with siltstones — especially Cambrian siltstone — for special features and roofing; building of the early modern period essentially continued the medieval tradition, but used considerably more Cambrian siltstone and often used black slate (from several sources) for roofing.

SURFACE SCATTERS OF STONE

As indicated above, there are large quantities of imported stone to be found in the study area, quite apart from the material evident in standing buildings and retrievable through excavation. This is the 'foreign' stone that lies on the surface of fields today. Surface scatters of imported stone either derive from structures formerly on or near the findspot; or they derive from the manuring of arable fields with farmyard waste — a practice that appears to have been normal in this area at least in the mid- to late Roman period and in the period from eleventh/twelfth to eighteenth centuries inclusive. Building collapse *in situ* is a striking feature of the present landscape (Fig. 5). The piles of rubble ultimately disintegrate and are distributed through the plough soil. There are, for example, building scatters in plough soil up to 80 m from a collapsed structure on the edge of field H145 (Quoiqueneuc) and in the lynchet T2, 80 m from the site of a former structure on field A116 (Les Viviers) (Astill and Davies 1987, 110−11; Astill and Davies 1985, 92−5). Manuring scatters may well contain fragments of stone deriving from building collapse on or around the farm site — i.e. a displaced building scatter — but they more characteristically contain large quantities of roofing slate, deriving from the piles of replaced and discarded slates that tend to lie around farmyards, as can still often be seen today. Although it may sound difficult, it is in fact quite easy to distinguish by observation between (I) scatters from former structures near the scatter and (II) manuring scatters, since the former tend to cluster while the latter are more evenly distributed. When the carefully observed and meticulously collected cluster of stone on field H132 was investigated (La Ruée), it was found to lie immediately above the substantial structure subsequently excavated in 1988 (just as brick and tile cluster above Roman villa sites, like the site excavated at field A92). By contrast, the deep lynchet T1 had accumulated over many centuries of repeated fertilising and ploughing; despite its very obvious agricultural origin, this lynchet included a scatter of roofing slate, siltstone, shale and sandstone (Davies 1990, 326; Astill and Davies 1989, 52−4, 44−6; Astill and Davies 1985, 92−4).

(I) Building scatters

Building stone scatters usually go through the plough soil, as demonstrated by excavation in fields A92, A116 and associated lynchets, H80, H132, D153, H145, and B409 (in all of which fragments were systematically collected and analysed). These plough soils have varying proportions

Figure 5
Collapsing house and piles of building rubble at La Basse Roche, Carentoir.

of black slate, Cambrian siltstone, Brioverian shale, local sandstone, local quartzites, and often conglomerates and quartz, despite the fact that nearly all lie on the Brioverian bedrock (the exceptions are H145, which lies on the Cambrian siltstone/sandstone interface (k-$o_1 m/o_2$), and B409, which lies on degraded Ordovician mudstone (o_{5-6})). Whatever the particular proportions of different rocks at any one site, wherever they have been investigated the proportions in the plough soil reflect the proportions of stone in the walls from which they derive: the stone in the 20 cm of plough soil investigated 15 m from the Roman villa of A92 roughly reflected the stone of the collapsed stucture (T29:C3):

o_{3-4}	k-o_1	b_{2-3}	Altered	o_2	s_1	Conglom	Quartz
2%	7%	4%	15%	14%	41%	11%	0

The high proportion of very hard stones (o_2, s_1, altered shale and conglomerate) is very striking. That plough soil also, correspondingly, contained an overwhelming proportion of Roman sherds (31, with 2 pre-Roman) with only 1 medieval and 4 post-medieval (Astill and Davies 1987, 118–19). Similarly, although we cannot test the stone composition of the ploughed-out structure in A116, we can note that the small quantities of very hard stone and relatively high proportions of shale and siltstone in the surrounding plough soils are consistent with those of the medieval and later building tradition. The stone in the 30 cm of plough soil in the field was:

	o_{3-4}	$k\text{-}o_1$	b_{2-3}	o_2	s_1	Conglom	Quartz
T3:	20%	36%	33%	4%	1%	2%	0
T4:	14%	32%	36%	6%	1%	2%	4%

This plough soil correspondingly had a predominance of medieval pottery: in the case of T3 and T4 the pottery was largely (74%) of the central middle ages, together with some fifteenth or sixteenth century sherds (13%); in the case of the nearby lynchet T2, which had similar proportions of stone, 86% of the pottery was of the medieval, or immediate post-medieval, period (Astill and Davies 1986, 116–18; Astill and Davies 1985, 95).

As I have indicated, building scatters can occur in the plough soil of arable fields as a result of secondary distribution. The lynchet T1, 300 m from the ploughed-out site in A116 and 350 m from the nearest standing structures, provides an example of building material distributed in the course of manuring and then accumulated down hill. We have no knowledge of any structures nearer than 300 m, and indeed, since the lynchet lies in a valley bottom beside a stream, in an area of long-used arable, it is extremely unlikely that there were any closer settlements in the historic period. The lynchet is large, with a buildup at its crest of 1.8 m of soil above the subsoil; pottery, half pre-medieval, half medieval (67 sherds), was distributed throughout the loam (C2), but most of the building stone occurred in the top 50 cm:

o_{3-4}	$k\text{-}o_1$	b_{2-3}	o_2	s_1	Conglom	Quartz
32%	21%	23%	4%	0.5%	0.5%	0

This mixture of stones, directly above the Brioverian bedrock, can only ultimately derive from some structure; but the long agricultural use of this zone is obvious from the lynchet. Quantities are small (5 kg). The building stone must therefore have arrived in the course of manuring — and, given its confinement to the top 50 cm, presumably in the course of more rather than less recent manuring. Apart from the high proportions of black slate, proportions of stone here are comparable with those on and by A116 itself — plenty of siltstones, very little hard stone — and accord well with the predominance of medieval pottery in the upper part of the lynchet (Astill and Davies 1985, 92–4). I suspect that the large proportion of black slate (o_{3-4}) reflects repeated manuring activity: if black slate be disregarded in T1, T2, T3, T4, then the proportions of other stones are broadly comparable at all four sites.

Another field, D153 (Bot Colin), which was meadow in the early nineteenth century and is now pasture, nevertheless has two intercutting lynchets; their excavation revealed three successive, differentiated plough soils (T35); despite its recent exploitation, the field clearly has a long history of arable use. It lies on the Brioverian. The uppermost plough soil had a weak building scatter of siltstones, sandstone and quartzite — less than 1 kg per cubic metre — and two-thirds of the pottery belonged to the immediate post-medieval centuries (sixteenth-seventeenth centuries). This scatter seems to derive from manuring in the immediate post-medieval period. The plough soil below it contained some medieval and a little Roman and Iron-Age pottery, but very little stone. The lowest soil had neither stone nor pottery (T35:C3). This complicated excavation provides a nice example of successive ploughsoils, of which only the latest (post-medieval) showed significant traces of building scatter (Astill and Davies 1989, 59–62).

The plough soil at T36 in field B409 (Le Bois Guillaume) contained disproportionately high quantities (31%) and very large lumps of black slate (o_{3-4}). B409 lies on a degraded Ordovician mudstone (o_{5-6}), and at T36 had an exceptionally high buildup of soil above natural, over 1 m. Its upper 40 cm of plough soil contained 112 medieval out of 127 sherds, with the remainder being Iron-Age, Roman and post-medieval. Both the pottery and the rock fragments of this plough soil were completely distinguished from the contents of the soils beneath, where the pottery was exclusively Iron-Age and stone was very scarce, with negligible quantities and proportions of o_{3-4}. In the upper, medieval/modern plough soil, apart from the black slate, proportions of siltstones were low and quartzite high (Astill and Davies 1989, 41–4). These features were most unusual and initially puzzling. However, there is a large Roman villa site 150 m away from T36 and it is notable that proportions of very hard stone on B409 (quartzite and sandstone) reflect those at the Roman villa site at A92:

o_{3-4}	$k-o_1$	b_{2-3}	o_2	s_1	Conglom	Quartz
31%	3%	14%	5%	37%	1%	9%

It must therefore be very likely that the stone in the upper plough soil derives from collapse of a nearby building that had re-used stone from the Roman site. Quartzite is still very prominent in the collapsing walling of the early modern structure at nearby La Touche au Roux, an extremely unusual feature in standing buildings of the area. The quantities of stone in the upper plough soil of B409 were also extremely large — 188 kg in 14 cubic metres. In view of the fact that the field was meadow in the 1820s,[2] that the amount of stone in the upper plough soil was enormous (while there was virtually none in the plough soil beneath), and that there were also unusually large amounts of medieval pottery in the plough soil and on the surface of the field, it must be likely that the building collapse in the upper plough soil derives from a medieval building, demolished before the construction of the modern farm 70 m away.

(II) Manuring scatters

The vast majority of arable fields in the study area has no obvious scatter of building stone on the surface, but does have clearly visible scatters of roofing slate. These scatters can only have arrived on the fields as a consequence of agricultural activity: they are evenly distributed; quantities are strikingly high; they are normally associated with small quantities of pottery; they do not derive from sub-surface features (neither natural nor man-made); and quantities of material decrease from the surface through the plough soils, as demonstrated, for example, in excavation of field G74 (La Métairie au Joly) (Astill and Davies 1989, 55–6). In the four core communes, this roofing material comes overwhelmingly from the hard black siltstones of o_{3-4} (sometimes fine, sometimes coarser) and the blue/pink/purple siltstones of $k-o_1$ (Fig. 6); for ease of reference I shall refer to these as black and pink roofing slate respectively.

Manuring scatters are distinguishable by eye. Observations were made in fieldwalking from 1984 to 1988 for just under 1000 fields, and recorded on standard fieldwalking forms. More recently, spot checks have been made of these initial observations, and data added

XIII

SURFACE SCATTERS OF BUILDING STONE

Figure 6
Houses at La Touche Aga, Ruffiac, with roofing of (from left to right) modern composition, modern machine-cut, and old local slates.

for transects not initially observed. Results have been incorporated in a database of all surface fieldwalking data. Analysis of the occurrence of this material, particularly in the context of its relationship to surface pottery scatters, is extremely interesting.

There is far more black than pink slate on the fields of the four communes. There are (a) fields with none, (b) fields with both black and pink, and (c) fields with black roofing only. Fields with pink roofing only do occur, but are exceptionally rare in the study area; however, to the north of the four communes, in sample transect N, there are zones with pink only (Astill and Davies 1986, 116).

There is also some occurrence of grey roofing slate (o_{5b-6}), from bands to the north, in parts of the study area, but quantities are negligible.

(a) *Fields with no slate* The modern arable fields *without* roofing material of any sort tend to lie on cadastral *lande*, that is on land that was uncultivated in the 1820s; this is the case for 60% of these fields, in striking contrast to the 25% mean on cadastral *lande* for all fields walked, and the 12% of fields with Fabric 1 (medieval arable) that lie on cadastral *lande* (see Table 1). Many lie at higher altitudes, 52% being over 50 m and

TABLE 1
CADASTRAL LAND-USE

	Arable	Lande	Meadow	Other
All fields	64	25	6	5
Fabric 1	78	12	7	3
No slate	35	60	5	0

Percentage of fields in principal categories of 1820s land-use

23% over 70 m (see Table 2). Most (82%) have no (or negligible) pottery on the surface (70%, 12%). The small amount of pottery found on these fields does not include any Roman fabrics at all and includes only 3 Iron-Age sherds, although it does have the complete range of medieval and post-medieval fabrics found in the area. In other words, there must have been some very occasional agricultural use of some of these fields in the period AD 1000–1900, but the accent is on occasional. Fields with no roofing material seem therefore to be fields that have only very rarely or very recently been used for arable cultivation. Virtually all are high or waterlogged or obstructed by outcropping rock, and this presumably explains why they were usually passed over for agricultural purposes.

(b) *Fields with black and pink slate* Modern arable fields that have pink as well as black roofing material on the surface occur in discrete areas and are often near settlements (although by no means all settlements have pink material in their vicinity) (see Fig. 7). They are much more likely to have medieval and immediate post-medieval fabrics on the surface than is the norm in the study area, that is Fabrics 1, 4, 5, 6, 8, 23 and 48, eleventh to sixteenth centuries; this is especially notable of Fabrics 4, 5, 6 and 48 (see Table 3).[3] Moreover, fields with pink slate tend to have, or be near, relatively large accumulations of Fabrics 4 and 6 (fifteenth-early seventeenth century) and are often, but not invariably, near fields with relatively large quantities of Fabric 1 (eleventh-fourteenth century). This must be significant, since it is demonstrable that fields with more than 50 g of Fabrics 1 or 4 or 6 or 8 reflect the nearby presence of former settlements; they are usually surrounded by a cluster of fields with smaller quantities of the fabrics, representing the arable worked from the settlement. Fields with pink and black slate are also often near locations occupied by nobles in 1536 (de Laigue 1902, 145–8, 677, 831–2). It would therefore appear that pink roofing material was being spread on arable fields in the neighbourhood of sites occupied in late medieval/early modern times, fifteenth and sixteenth centuries especially.

(c) *Fields with black slate* Modern arable fields that only have black roofing slate are widely distributed throughout the study area and are very common. They are much *less* likely to have medieval and immediate post-medieval fabrics on the surface than is the norm across the study area (see Table 3): only 44% have Fabric 1, as against the mean of 52%, and only 15% have Fabric 8, against the 21% mean; moreover, salt-glazed fabrics of seventeenth-nineteenth centuries are unusually common (Fabrics 29, 34, especially). Black slate therefore often occurs in areas where there is no Fabric 1, the

TABLE 2
HEIGHT ABOVE SEA-LEVEL

	< 30m	30–50	50–70	> 70m
All fields	7	39	35	19
Fabric 1	16	42	28	13
No slate	10	38	29	23
Black/arable/no pot	18	50	32	15
Black/lande/no pot	5	16	42	37

Percentage of fields, by height band

347

SURFACE SCATTERS OF BUILDING STONE

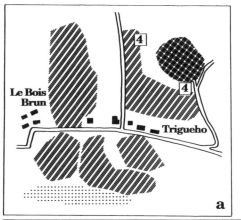
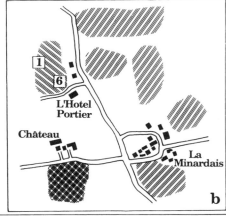

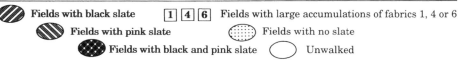

Figure 7
Surface distribution of black and pink slate at
a) Trigueho, Tréal.
b) L'Hotel Portier/La Minardais, Carentoir.

TABLE 3
INCIDENCE OF MEDIEVAL, IMMEDIATE POST-MEDIEVAL AND
SALT-GLAZED FABRICS

Fabric No:	1	5	8	6	4	23	48	29	34
All fields	52	10	21	30	38	37	14	7	14
Black/pink	62	13	25	41	51	44	21	8	20
Black only	44	7	15	25	34	30	12	9	13

Percentage of fields with each fabric

commonest of all pottery fabrics and commonest medieval fabric, eleventh-fourteenth centuries: this is true of more than half 'black only' fields, and is strikingly so in the area near Le Bois Faux in the commune of Carentoir. Fields with black slate virtually always have post-medieval fabrics; they often do not have central/late medieval fabrics. This must suggest that, although some black slate could well have been put on the fields in the medieval and immediate post-medieval periods, this material was not spread on all medieval arable; by contrast, it *was* spread on most fields of post-medieval exploitation, and almost invariably occurs on post-medieval fields that have no medieval background.

We can take the latter analysis a stage further: there is a small proportion of fields with black roofing material but no pottery at all on the surface; some of these were (i) arable in the 1820s, and some were (ii) uncultivated. (i) The fields that were arable in the 1820s, as we know from the cadastral survey of that date, must have been fertilized, but it is clear that pottery did not get into any

TABLE 4
DISTANCE OF FIELDS FROM CADASTRAL SETTLEMENTS

	<50m	<100m	<200m	<400m	>400m
All fields	23	37	66	93	7
Fabric 1	17	31	59	91	9
No slate	8	17	47	87	12
Black/arable/no pot	18	32	77	96	4
Black/lande/no pot	11	11	26	79	21

Percentage of fields, by distance band

manure that was spread. (In this context it is worth noting the modern village of Tréal, an unusually late, post-1820s, bourg: it has very little surface pottery in and around its houses and gardens, unlike other settlements. The same point is made by localizable written descriptions of eighteenth-century land-use: land that we know was arable in the eighteenth century sometimes has no or very few sherds on the surface today.) All of this combines to suggest that domestic refuse disposal practice had changed since the early eighteenth century; although fields continued to be manured, discarded pottery did not find its way into the manure. The 1820s arable fields with black slate and no pottery are sometimes in unfavourable topographical positions: waterlogged, or high, or on a north-facing slope; if they have none of these unfavourable characteristics, they are likely to be more than 225 m from a settlement and/or more than 350 m from water (see Tables 2, 4, 5, 6). These must be fields brought into arable use only in the eighteenth or early nineteenth centuries, worked at that period under pressure to increase the cereal crop. (ii) The fields with black slate and no pottery that were *un*cultivated in the 1820s are more obviously high or steep or on north-facing slopes or a very long way from water. They must be land brought into arable cultivation only in the later nineteenth or twentieth centuries, with the development of modern farm machinery and mechanized transport; they can be as much as 575 m from a settlement and 1200 m from a stream — in striking contrast to pre-industrial arable, which tends to be within 200 m of a settlement and 400 m of water.

CHRONOLOGY

In an attempt to identify the period when black slate began to be widely used in this

TABLE 5
DISTANCE OF FIELDS FROM A STREAM

	<50m	<100m	<200m	<400m	>400m
All fields	12	22	43	73	27
Fabric 1	15	28	48	78	19
No slate	14	24	42	78	24
Pink/black	7	16	36	72	28
Black/arable/no pot	9	22	39	70	30
Black/lande/no pot	5	11	21	42	58

Percentage of fields, by distance band

XIII

SURFACE SCATTERS OF BUILDING STONE

TABLE 6
SLOPE OF FIELDS

	flat	east	west	north	south
All fields	23	8	5	26	38
Fabric 1	23	9	5	23	39
No slate	25	8	4	34	29
Black/arable/no pot	9	9	9	26	50
Black/lande/no pot	26	11	0	32	32

Percentage of fields, by slope

area, I have looked carefully at fields that were put down to meadow in the sixteenth and early seventeenth centuries. At that period some of the nobility of the area made major changes to the management of their lands, creating large square arable fields, planting woodland, constructing avenues to their houses, diverting streams, and increasing meadow land near their houses. This usually involved conversion of arable to meadow and woodland. Black slate virtually always occurs on the fields whose use turned from arable to meadow in the early modern period, for example, J97, B409, C292/3, H132. This must mean that black slate was getting on to the fields before the change in land-use, that is before (at least) the early seventeenth century. We also never find pink slate without black on these managed landscapes.

It is quite clear from the excavation of structures and of plough soils that both o_{3-4} and k-o_1 (sediments that supply black and pink roofing slate) were used from early times. Late Iron-Age contexts in H80 had plenty of pink Cambrian siltstone and there was black siltstone packing in a pre-twelfth-century posthole in H132. However, the excavation results suggest much greater use of Cambrian (pink) than of Ordovician (black) siltstones in medieval contexts; indeed, the whole of the collapsed roof of the H132 building was made from that material.

Moreover, there was vastly more pink material than black in the ploughsoil of the lynchet T2, which contained scatter from the medieval structure on A116; the medieval upper pitfill (T10:C3) of a pit in H145, which contained blocks from a dismantled structure, had four times as much pink material as black; and proportions of pink material in the plough soils of A116, H80 and H145 were greater at 10−20 cm than at 0−10 cm and on the surface. All this is consistent with the proposition that the majority of pink material was spread on the arable before the majority of black material, and that the mass of pink material derives from walling, roofing and other dismantled structural features, whereas the mass of black material simply derives from disused roofing slates. One can still occasionally find these pink siltstones used for structural features, like partitions, in standing buildings (Fig. 8). The associated pottery, in particular, suggests that the pink material was getting on to the fields in the late middle ages and early modern period, when that pottery was being discarded, whatever the date of the original structures. One can envisage buildings being refurbished and renewed with the multiple changes of the late fifteenth and sixteenth century: new men were coming into the local nobility, some grander houses were built, and new approaches to land management started to make an impact on the landscape (Fig. 9). The associated pottery also correspondingly suggests that black material was being distributed on the fields in the sixteenth, seventeenth, eighteenth and nineteenth centuries.[4] Indeed, the black material is so prevalent, that I am inclined to wonder if it was deliberately spread on the fields: quantities in the plough soil of B409 are enormous, some of it occurring in large lumps, and it is very prominent in the lynchet of the long-used arable by T1.

Figure 8
Cambrian siltstone orthostats in a deserted house at La Certenaie, Carentoir.

CONCLUSION

Looking at stone has its uses. It is essential to do some systematic collecting, weighing and classifying, and some basic preparation on the local solid geology, if observations are to be usable. But, once done, one can make observations that extend and enhance the information derivable from other aspects of field survey and from other types of data, and can do so economically.

Analysis of the occurrence of stone allows us to differentiate the use of building stone by period. Since surface scatters of building stone are observable in surface fieldwork, they are an extremely useful pointer to the location of former structures, as happened in the classic case of H132, a medieval structure which lies 150 m from the seventeenth-century *petit château* which (presumably) succeeded it. Further, the occurrence of pink roofing material in manuring scatters in the four communes seems to point to the nearby location of medieval settlements that used building stone — in this area a characteristic of noble rather than peasant settlements. These are very useful tools, particularly for locating the medieval settlement pattern.

Identification and analysis of manuring scatters can also be of enormous value in identifying arable land of various periods: whereas pottery scatters can define the arable

Figure 9
Seventeenth-century *petit château* ('le manoir de Balangeart') at La Rivière, Ruffiac.

of the central middle ages, black roofing slate on fields without pottery, in association with cadastral data, can define (and distinguish) the arable of the eighteenth and nineteenth centuries, and the absence of slate can define the arable of the late nineteenth/twentieth century only. When we find arable fields in this area *without* slate, these fields are unlikely to have been worked in the historic period unless very recently. These manuring scatters of slate are therefore an exceptionally useful tool for mapping the changing pattern of land-use during the historic period and the changing relationship between settlement and arable. With the necessary training and preparation, it is possible to make observations on this relationship across a wide area in a short period.[5]

NOTES

1. See Astill, forthcoming, for detailed analysis of pottery fabrics.
2. See p. 350.
3. See Astill forthcoming for detailed consideration of the fabrics.
4. Note: H132 was meadow by 1609, and has little black slate; there is far less black slate in T2, by the meadow A116, than in T1, by long-used arable.

5. I am most grateful to my colleague Grenville Astill for his comments on this paper, and to Dr Eric Robinson of UCL for assistance with geological problems. Diagrams were prepared by Colin Stuart, of UCL Geology department; photographs of buildings were taken by Pete Addison, and of excavations by Pat Foster, both for the East Brittany Survey. Records of standing buildings, and an extensive photographic collection of buildings, are archived at University College London.

REFERENCES

ASTILL, G.G. and DAVIES, W. 1982: Un nouveau programme de recherche sur le terrain dans l'est de la Bretagne. *Archéologie en Bretagne* 35, 29–42.

ASTILL, G.G. and DAVIES, W. 1983: Recherche sur le terrain dans l'est de la Bretagne (EBS) 1983. *Archéologie en Bretagne* 39, 13–23.

ASTILL, G.G. and DAVIES, W. 1984: Prospection dans l'est de la Bretagne; la campagne de mars-avril 1984. *Dossiers du Centre Régional Archéologique d'Alet* 12, 49–59.

ASTILL, G.G. and DAVIES, W. 1985: Prospections archéologiques dans l'est de la Bretagne; mars-avril 1985. *Dossiers du Centre Régional Archéologique d'Alet* 13, 85–98.

ASTILL, G.G. and DAVIES, W. 1986: Prospections archéologiques dans l'est de la Bretagne; mars-avril 1986. *Dossiers du Centre Régional Archéologique d'Alet* 14, 111–20.

ASTILL, G.G. and DAVIES, W. 1987: Prospections archéologiques dans l'est de la Bretagne; septembre 1986 et Pâques 1987. *Dossiers du Centre Régional Archéologique d'Alet* 15, 109–27.

ASTILL, G.G. and DAVIES, W. 1989: Prospections archéologiques dans l'est de la Bretagne; septembre 1988. *Dossiers du Centre Régional Archéologique d'Alet* 17, 41–63.

Carte Géologique 1981: *Carte Géologique de la France à 1/50,000: Feuille X-20, Malestroit* (Ministère de l'Industrie, Bureau de Recherches Géologiques et Minières, Service Géologique National, Orléans).

CHAUMEIL, L. 1938: *L'Industrie ardoisière en Basse Bretagne* (Lorient).

DAVIES, W. 1990: Field Survey and the Problem of Surface Scatters of Building Material: some East Breton Evidence. In *La Bretagne et l'Europe préhistorique. Mémoires en hommage à Pierre-Roland Giot* (*Revue archéologique de l'Ouest* supp. 2), 321–32.

DE LAIGUE, R. 1906: *La noblesse bretonne aux XVe et XVIe siècles, Réformations et montres* (2 vols, Vannes).

SOULEZ-LARIVIERE, M.F. 1975–6: Angers et ses ardoisières. *Mémoires de l'académie d'Angers* 9–10, 63–75.

XIV

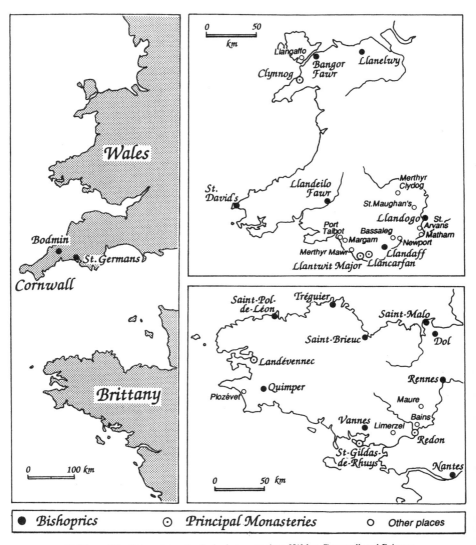

48. Maps of the bishoprics and principal monasteries of Wales, Cornwall and Brittany.

XIV

Ecclesiastical centres and secular society in the Brittonic world in the tenth and eleventh centuries

The material evidence that survives today at Govan would point to the existence of a substantial cemetery in or near the area of the present church, during the late ninth, tenth and eleventh centuries, a cemetery that was patronized by wealthy people. My task is to describe the social and ecclesiastical context of comparable sites in some other parts of the Celtic world, in order to provide some possible models for early medieval Govan. Although it could be just as fruitful to look at Ireland, I shall focus on the Brittonic world of Wales and Brittany, since comparative material is plentiful, with an occasional glance at Cornwall. Both Welsh and Breton tradition pay some attention to Strathclyde: Saint Cadog is said to have visited Scotland and Saint Gildas is said to have come from Strathclyde (VC 26, VG 1); whatever the truth of these stories, there certainly seems to have been some transmission of Strathclyde material to North Wales in the late ninth century (Miller 1975, 275–9). There is good reason, then, to suppose that southern Scotland shared in the literary culture of the Brittonic world in the early middle ages.

Where would we find large and well-furbished cemeteries in the Brittonic world in this period, and how would we explain their occurrence? We might find such a cemetery at a large monastery (which may or may not have been episcopal). We might also find such a cemetery near any ecclesiastical foundation, be it large or small, monastic or not, which had wealthy and powerful patrons. And we might find such a cemetery at any site distinguished by the presence of a notable holy cult. Monastery, wealthy patronage, and cult do not have to be alternatives; a large cemetery might be attached to a monastery that was a cult site, or to a small church that had wealthy patrons because it was a cult site, or to a monastery with wealthy patrons and a famous founding saint. It is conceivable that a religious community associated with the site might not have been monastic, that patronage occurred for some reason other than cult, and that there were patrons who were ecclesiastical rather than secular. Such theoretical possibilities seem, however, less likely. Let me, then, say something about ecclesiastical communities, about relations between church and laity, and about cult and burial.

Ecclesiastical communities

By the tenth century there were several types of religious community in Brittonic areas: episcopal communities, large and small monastic communities, and protoparochial churches served by small groups of clerics, to name the most obvious.

There were just over a dozen bishoprics in Wales and Brittany, and certainly one, sometimes two, in Devon/Cornwall.[1] The bishops exercised their authority within reasonably well defined exclusive territories and had powers of inspection over monasteries and churches. They usually resided in communities, which were sometimes known as 'monasteries' and sometimes not: the seat of the bishopric of St David's was called *monasterium* by Asser in the late ninth century, as was that of Saint-Pol-de-Léon by Wrmonoc and that of *Dinuurrin* in Cornwall by an anonymous writer. Episcopal communities were relatively large and relatively complex, whatever they were called, with different functions performed by different people. Most, if not all, would have had some daily observance of prayer and worship, although we need not suppose that observance was distinctively ascetic. The bishop was the source of ecclesiastical authority for the region surrounding his bishopric, an area often in the order of thirty to forty miles radius; he would therefore be used to travelling and used to receiving visitors. The income reaching his community would be high relative to that of other types of community, deriving from the rents and profits from properties owned, from free offerings from the faithful, and from dependent churches, be they *all* the churches of the locality or merely those with an especially close relationship with the bishopric. It is therefore reasonable to emphasize that authority was focused in bishops, although the bishop's relationship with local churches varied from one locality to another; this was not yet a world with a fully functioning parochial system.

The bishops of St David's, St Andrews and Dol were occasionally referred to as *arch*bishop but this term did not have the institutional significance in Celtic parts that it had in other parts of Europe by this time; it was an honorific term. No archiepiscopal provinces were recognized in these areas until Pope Gregory VII recognized the archbishopric of Dol in 1076; there were consequently no regular gatherings of bishops, although there were certainly some meetings of bishops in eastern Brittany in the mid-ninth century (Smith 1982; Davies 1992, 14).[2] The absence of an archiepiscopal hierarchy and of regular synods served to emphasize the power of individual bishops.

The community of a large monastery might look very like that associated with a bishop: there would have been a large group of people, whose functions were differentiated (scribe, steward, teacher, cook, doctor, doorkeeper), who were active and busy, and who travelled and received visitors. It is these major monasteries that are the 'mother houses' of the Welsh law texts. Monasteries owned properties, including river rights, sea rights and harbours, as well as land; they received rents and renders; they had interests in lesser churches, either through their power to appoint priests and priors or through direct rights to a proportion of income earned (Davies 1978, 124–5; 1982a, 155–6, 165–6; 1988, 189–92). Hence, by the eleventh century, and probably long before, Llancarfan in Glamorgan (south Wales) had established a household at Bassaleg in Gwent to gather renders due to it, just as Redon in south-east Brittany had a 'receiving' place at Maure by 871 (see illus 48). When clergy from these large foundations were travelling, they could expect to call at a string of reception points and find plentiful food and drink. Llancarfan accordingly had a network of properties and dependent churches in south Wales in the tenth and eleventh centuries, including isolated churches, monasteries whose leaders (*princeps* and *praepositus*) were appointed by the abbot of Llancarfan, and small monasteries which sent up a good share of their income to the mother house (VC 59, 28, 54, 40, 63; Davies 1982a, 148–9). In western Brittany, Landévennec had a network of similar size at this period, running through Trégourez to Landrevarzec, Lanriec to Lanrivoaré and then Beuzit (Davies 1986, 93–4) (illus 49).

The relationships in these cases, that is those between a major monastery and its surrounding churches and religious communities, were essentially the same from north to south, although Redon

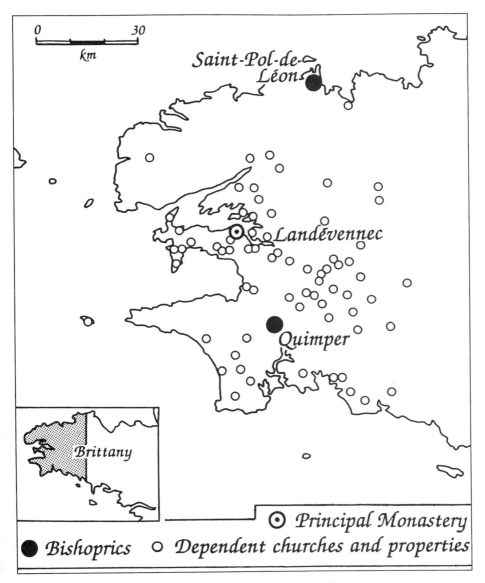

49. Map showing dependent churches and properties of Landévennec.

was a different sort of monastery, in a different sort of area, from Llancarfan. Further, although these major monasteries shared many characteristics with episcopal communities (property interests, specialization of members' functions, and so on), they were not identical. They were different because the scale of their property interests tended to be smaller, and their leaders lacked the sacerdotal (and therefore wider) authority of the bishop; they did not ordain priests or consecrate churches; they could not create clerics. It is true that they too were managers, but they were managers of a smaller range of activities.

Now, although I have stressed the similarities between Llancarfan, Landévennec, Redon, St David's, and so on, in their relationships with neighbouring religious communities, I would not want to stress internal similarities: inside the communities there were differences. It is unlikely that any Brittonic area saw the extremes of ascetic practice that characterize our image of the earliest monasticism or of the monasticism that developed in western Europe in the late eleventh century, but there were certainly variations in observance. It might vary from the modest diet, simple clothing, times of silence, long periods of prayer, and manual labour of the St David's tradition ('each his own ox') to the more varied food and greater level of material comfort that characterized the Welsh monasteries of the South East (Davies 1982a, 154). Monastic rules, and the approach to regular life, also varied. In some monasteries the pattern of daily life was strictly determined in accordance with a rule; in others it was only loosely so determined. In some monasteries the rule itself was prescriptive, and detailed; in others it was just a guideline. 'Best practice' might also be conveyed anecdotally in stories of good behaviour, as practised by the real or supposed founder. From the ninth century, the Rule of Benedict was common (though not exclusively used) in Breton monasteries: it was a major influence at Landévennec, alongside the Rule of Winwaloe, and it was the sole guide at Redon (Smith 1985, 61–2). It does not appear to have been a feature in Welsh monasteries at all at this period.

There would also have been differences in the composition of monastic communities. By the tenth century the southern Welsh monasteries were dominated by priests;[3] this seems also to have been the case in Cornwall, where there were at least twenty monasteries by the eleventh century (Olson 1989, 105–6). But although there were many priests in the Breton communities that we know about, and although communities of priests feature in the Breton hagiographic tradition, the proportion of priests in monasteries was certainly not so high there by the eleventh century. Nor do we find much reference to hereditary priests in these Breton monasteries, though hereditary priestships certainly occurred in the rural churches.

All monasteries were not large, and there appear to have been many small communities in extensively exploited agricultural areas, sometimes as many as one every three or four miles. The number of monks could be as small as three; they had little in the way of property; and they were often dependent on a larger foundation (Davies 1982a, 144). Although there were small monasteries both in Brittany and Wales, in Brittany there were also non-monastic rural churches. Many of these churches were served by groups of three or four priests by the late ninth century; they performed pastoral functions for the lay community, each community (*plebs*) having its church (Davies 1983; cf Blair and Sharpe 1992). These priests had a focal role in peasant villages, in secular as in spiritual society, buying and selling property, making loans, acting as scribes and sureties, carrying messages and working as representatives of women and aristocrats.

ECCLESIASTICAL CENTRES AND SECULAR SOCIETY

Relations between church and laity

Although wealthy patrons do not have to be members of the laity (in theory, at least, wealthy monasteries could have buried their abbots at Govan), it must be likely that some laymen used the site. It is therefore useful to look at lay/ecclesiastical relationships.

Rulers tended to be patrons of powerful religious houses in the early middle ages, and religious houses often became powerful because of ruler patronage (cf Smith 1986); the relationship was symbiotic. However, that relationship worked in different ways at different times and places.

In Wales rulers sometimes made grants to major churches and monasteries in the tenth and eleventh centuries, but when they did so, the records suggest that it was nearly always for penitential reasons (and certainly more so than at earlier periods): grants were made in penance for murder, for selling a dependent church, for imprisoning an enemy in a monastery (LL 223, 244, 239, etc). When rulers made grants in Brittany in this period, they often did so when they or their relatives were sick – to Redon, to Saint-Malo, to Landévennec – although there were also some outright grants in the tenth century (CR 4, 49, 85, 235, A52; CL 45; VM 18). In both cases, rulers were potentially patrons; whether or not they actually became patrons depended on local and personal circumstances. Connections could, however, be very close in specific cases: in tenth-century Brycheiniog, bishops acted as intercessors for kings; and a mid-tenth-century bishop of Saint-Pol drafted documents for the Breton ruler, Alain Barbetorte. Indeed, relationships between bishops and rulers were so close in western Brittany that Count Budic was the father of an eleventh-century bishop of Quimper (LL 237b; CL 25, 46).

Local aristocrats, as well as rulers, were also sometimes patrons but we hear much more of conflicts than of collaboration with them. There was the Breton machtiern, Ratfred, and his brothers who threatened burning in order to force grants of property to themselves in Bains and Sixt, and there were others who stole cows and pigs from monastic lands in the 860s; later, others injured the monks of Saint-Gildas at Plozévet, in disputes over control of land (CR 105, 32; VG 27). Men from a royal retinue invaded church sanctuary at St Arvans in Gwent and killed a deacon, round about 955; a local aristocrat, Rhiwallon ap Rhun, fought with the bishop's household, c 1033, and wounded a member of it; and there was King Caradog's retinue, whose members rode up to St Maughan's, where food was collected ready for the bishop to arrive and feast, and ate and drank themselves to a state of stupor, c 1072 (LL 218, 257, 272).

These stories were not recorded in order to make a point about enmity but to send out warnings: it had to be demonstrable that local aristocrats who stole, raided and assaulted always came unstuck; they were punished, either through the divine retribution that characterizes hagiographic punishment or through the formal judgements of rulers, clergy and locals that are recorded in charter collections. The punishment of blinding, for example, is especially characteristic in Brittonic hagiographic material. A man (usually a ruler) attacks the protective power of a church – he may assault a cleric, abduct a holy girl, attack a church building, or steal church goods. He thereby infringes the privilege of the church and is consequently blinded; horrified, he comes and prays for forgiveness, promising to heap gifts on the church; the blindness is then lifted and he makes thankful grants to God and the saint. So, the wicked ruler Hailoch tried to destroy St Machutes's church (at or near Saint-Malo); the wicked King Maelgwn sent his retinue across the boundary of the monastery of Llanelwy (St Asaph) in north Wales, where Cedig Draws had fled for protection to St

XIV

Kentigern after drawing blood from Maelgwn's son in a drinking quarrel;[4] and the wicked King Tudwal turned St Ninian off his land (Whithorn in Galloway) (Davies 1981, 524).

These are stories whose historicity is very questionable; however, they are stories told to explain how lands held at the time of telling were acquired, and told in order to inculcate and reinforce respect for the immunity of ecclesiastical property. Whether or not *most* aristocrats actually were hostile to their local ecclesiastical foundations (some clearly were – there are plenty of well-evidenced cases), we do not know; however, if they were hostile, the church could ultimately be a *beneficiary* of such hostility. Clerics could benefit as much from penitential and compensatory grants as from gifts made for pious reasons. The most striking characteristic of relationships between clergy and laity, then, is that – although they may often have had conflicts – laymen (and this is true of peasants as well as aristocrats) were major benefactors. There is no doubt that churches and monasteries acquired very significant property holdings over the course of the early middle ages. The prevailing trend was for the transfer of property rights from secular into ecclesiastical hands.

Cult and burial

Lay participation in the cult of saints is another aspect of the relationship between clergy and laity. In Wales, Cornwall and Brittany, there is plentiful evidence of the elevation and veneration of local saints in the early middle ages, sometimes very small-scale local saints, like Dingad and Clydog, Just and Gerent (Davies 1982a, 174; Olson and Padel 1986). By the ninth century, textual statements that the burial places of saints were regarded as especially important are plentiful; they occur in Breton Saints' Lives, like those of Paul and Machutes, and Welsh charters and narratives such as the *Historia Brittonum*. This is scarcely surprising and would be true of many other parts of western Europe at this period (cf Thomas 1971, 137–66). Early in the tenth century, the bodies of many Breton saints were removed to safer parts, as communities fled from the Viking onslaught, but some were soon returned while corporeal relics of others eventually made their way back to Brittany (Merdrignac 1986, 171; Smith 1990; Blanc 1992, 128). In the tenth and eleventh centuries, we hear of the miracles performed at the tombs of St Gildas's three brothers, in southern Brittany; of visits of local people to a saint's church on the day of his festival, like those made to St Cadog's church at Llancarfan; of the power of relics, like those of St Tudwal, to extinguish fire; and of major cemeteries associated with the real or supposed burial places of famous saints, particularly the cemeteries at the places called *merthyr* – Merthyr Clydog, Matharn (Merthyr Tewdrig) and, by implication, Merthyr Mawr (Mimor). *Merthyr* is a Welsh borrowing from Latin *martirium*, the place of burial of a saint; in Brittany the form is *merzer*, as found in Limerzel (cf Thomas this volume).

It was usually an association with a particularly famous saint that endowed a site with a reputation for especial holiness. By the mid-tenth century we read of the laity's interest in burial in especially holy cemeteries, the holier the cemetery the more desirable the place for lay burial. There is a characteristic sanction attached to Landévennec charters in the mid-tenth century: 'terra sancta cymiterii non recipiat eos'; those who do not respect the grant recorded in this text, will not be buried in the holy ground of a cemetery (CL 24, 25, 40, 42). In parallel fashion (though the culture has many different aspects by this time), *c* 950, one Bledrys ap Gwollwyn gave property in south Wales in order to secure his burial beside an episcopal church (LL 221). Not surprisingly, rulers wanted burial at places connected with the most famous saints. Alain Barbetorte, who died in 952, was initially buried at a major cult site in Nantes, the burial place of 'les enfants nantaises', Saints Donatien and Rogatien, although he was later exhumed; Count Budic made a grant of property in the early eleventh century to Landévennec so that he might be buried there; and Count Benedict did likewise slightly later (CL 46, 47). By the eleventh century it was believed that eighth-century kings of Brycheiniog and a seventh-century king of Glywysing were buried at St Teilo's cult site at Llandaff; and rulers of southern Glamorgan were believed to be buried at St Cadog's site at Llancarfan (LL 149, 146; VC 28). In Wales the physical evidence above ground is rarely striking, although there is a growing corpus of excavation data on special graves and surrounding burials, with radiocarbon dates that span the early middle ages (James 1992). For Landévennec, however, there is plentiful visible evidence: the ninth-century church was repaired when the monastery was 'refounded' in the mid-tenth century, to be replaced by the great romanesque church begun in the late eleventh century. The tomb of 'Gradlon' — traditionally believed to be an early king and major benefactor of the monastery — was prominent in the great church, and second only to that of the founding saint; there are burials beneath and around the successive churches, and a large collection of medieval and later tombstones (little studied) (Simon 1985, 199–228; Barral I Altet 1986; Bardel 1991; Blanc 1992; cf Guigon *et al* 1987, for other cemeteries).

Rulers (and others) made grants in order to secure burial at their preferred famous place, like Bledrys, Count Budic and Count Benedict above. By the late tenth century, some form of payment seems to have been common in order to arrange burial at a religious place. By the eleventh century such payments must have constituted a significant aspect of income for major religious houses (CL 13, 24, 28; VC 28, 53). In other words, people were prepared to pay for burial in an especially holy place. By the eleventh century it is likely that the machinery of the parish was fairly well established in Brittany (though not in Wales); hence, most laymen must have been buried by or through the agency of their parish church, but powerful people with the means to do so were buried, and continued to be buried, at major cult sites.

A context for Govan

Is there anything in this material which might help us understand the collection of stones at Govan? If the analogies are useful, they would suggest that this is a burial place for aristocrats and/or rulers in the tenth and eleventh centuries. They would also suggest that the place is likely to have been favoured by powerful laymen because it was a prominent cult site (cf Macquarrie 1990; Macquarrie this volume). And, further, they suggest that by the eleventh century it is likely that some ecclesiastical community was benefiting from the site's popularity and might well be adjacent, drawing income from the whole region through a network of dependencies as well as from control of the burial place. (At Llancarfan, burial of the local aristocracy was within the walls of the monastic precinct.)

The secular aristocracy that came to Govan for burial was surely likely to have come from very mixed cultures, given the location of the place – Irish, Scandinavian, Pictish, British, even English. Govan is well placed to draw interest from all directions and could have drawn local leaders from 50–60 miles all round, including eastern Scotland and Anglian parts to the south. It is therefore not surprising that the surviving material evidence should have mixed cultural origins (Higgitt 1990; cf Bailey, Lang, this volume). Correspondingly, the somewhat later Kentigern dossier from nearby

XIV

Glasgow is also a cultural mix, drawing from Wales, Cumbria, Strathclyde, and St Serfs/Loch Leven to the east (Jackson 1958; Radford 1967b; Macquarrie 1986).

There are no precise parallels in the Brittonic world of this period. However, there are one or two sites that have comparable features. The foundations that produce the most striking physical parallels are the sites of Llantwit Major and Merthyr Mawr in Glamorgan, for they both have notable collections of inscribed stones of the tenth and eleventh centuries (Nash-Williams 1950, nos 220–26, 238–47, 255, cf 270a; Knight 1984, 382–5). So, to a lesser extent, do the bishopric of St David's and the church of Llangaffo on Anglesey (Merthyr Caffo, a dependency of Clynnog in the late middle ages), and SS Donatien and Rogatien in Nantes (Nash-Williams 1950, nos 370–83, 14–24; Cahour 1874) (see illus 48). Llantwit was a major pre-Norman monastery, with a long history of powerful abbots, at least from the eighth century, and it was explicitly a place of royal burial. One long inscription records a cross set up for the soul of King Ithel and a large disk-headed cross names Hywel ap Rhys, a king of the late ninth century, as the erector (Nash-Williams 1950, nos 223, 220, cf 222; Davies 1978, 124). We have some narrative detail of the workings of the monastery in the century or so after its foundation, in the Life of Samson, but no narrative from these later centuries (VS).

The ten tenth-/eleventh-century stones collected at Merthyr Mawr and neighbouring Ogmore seem to derive from an important early medieval cult site. The designation 'merthyr' would itself suggest that it was believed to be a saint's burial place. Round about 935 it was known as the merthyr of an otherwise unknown saint Miuor/Mimor. At that time the record of a grant of land in the locality referred to another merthyr, Merthyr Glywys, i.e. the burial place or *martirium* of (Saint) Glywys (LL 224). Now Glywys is the eponym of Glywysing, the name of the principal kingdom of south-east Wales prior to its renaming as Morgannwg in the late tenth century. Two of the Merthyr Mawr inscribed stones also refer to Glywys, and one of them explicitly refers to him as a saint: for the soul of 'St Glywys'; the other records a grant made to God, Glywys, Nertat and the bishop (Nash-Williams 1950, nos 239, 255). It therefore looks as if, in the tenth and eleventh centuries, there was a cult site near Merthyr Mawr which was the real or supposed burial place of Glywys, the supposed founder of the local kingdom, who was by then regarded as a saint (Davies 1978, 99).[5] (Mar of nearby Margam was a supposed son of Glywys, who was also the supposed grandfather of St Cadog.) We no longer have Glywys's tomb but this situation must remind us of Gradlon, the royal benefactor from Cornouaille, whose memory was perpetuated by his prominent tomb in the church at Landévennec.[6] It must also remind us of the Govan sarcophagus. If this sarcophagus did once hold the bones of St Constantine (Radford 1967a, 176; cf Thomas pp. 20–1), as seems a reasonable suggestion, then the analogies would suggest that Constantine was another royal benefactor, notable for his real or supposed political activity but subsequently sanctified (cf Macquarrie 1990, 13–14; cf Spearman pp. 33–45, Craig, p. 81). Its unweathered state must suggest that – like Gradlon's tomb – it once lay within the medieval church.

The number of stones now at Merthyr Mawr is small by comparison with the number at Govan.[7] However, there are collections of more stones ten miles to the north west at Port Talbot and Margam, many of which are made from Bridgend sandstone, like the Merthyr stones (Nash-Williams 1950, nos 229–36, 258–64). Since Margam was an important Norman Cistercian house, it is possible that stones were moved there from Merthyr Mawr in the Norman period (cf Knight 1984, 374); the Merthyr collection could therefore originally have been more of the Govan size.

We do not, however, know much about what went on at Merthyr Mawr/Glywys in the tenth and eleventh centuries, apart from burial. Nor do we have much detail about what went on at Llantwit by this date. Although the physical parallels are less precise, if you want detail of people and relationships and powers to clothe the analogy, you have to turn to the two places that I have mentioned so frequently in this paper: Llancarfan, not far from Llantwit, and Landévennec, the one in south Wales, the other in west Brittany. There are some things about Landévennec by the eleventh century that would have made it somewhat different from Govan – the predominance of the Rule of Benedict, for example – but even so its combination of 'royal' tomb, monastery, cult site, and lay burial place must make it the closest single investigable parallel. The early medieval site has also benefited from sustained excavation over the last decade (Bardel 1990; 1991). In both cases, those of Llancarfan and Landévennec, there is considerable eleventh-century written material and for Landévennec ninth- and tenth-century material too. If, then, you want to give Govan some social and ecclesiastical context, you could do a lot worse than read the Life of St Cadog and the Cartulary of Landévennec (VC; CL).

Notes

1. Bangor, St David's, Landeilo Fawr (later replaced by Llandogo and Llandaff), and possibly Llanelwy; Nantes, Vannes, Quimper, Saint-Pol-de-Léon, Tréguier, Saint-Brieuc, Saint-Malo, Dol, and Rennes; Exeter (soon replaced by Crediton) and Lanalet (St Germans) (preceded by *Dinuurrin* (?Bodmin) in the ninth century (Olson 1989, 51–6, 60–6, 75)) (see illus 48).
2. The Breton ruler Salomon requested the *pallium* from Pope Nicholas I for Bishop Festinian of Dol, *c* 865–6; this request was not granted, but the church of Dol often seems to have regarded its head as archbishop during the succeeding two centuries, and others in tenth-century Brittany sometimes seem to have agreed. At times, then, Dol was functioning as an unacknowledged archbishopric for some parts of the Breton church during the tenth and eleventh centuries (Smith 1982, 66–7).
3. It is these priestly communities that may be supposed to have constituted the *clas*, a Welsh word which means no more than community but which was characteristically applied to property-holding religious communities in Wales, under an abbot, in the period of the Norman Conquest; some priests had offspring who succeeded them (Evans 1992).
4. This story, in which firstly the riders' horses are blinded and then Maelgwn himself, occurs in the Welsh text about Kentigern and Maelgwn that is copied into the fifteenth-century St Asaph text, Alter Liber Pergameneus; there is a different version in the Red Book of St Asaph. The story appears to be of Welsh origin (Davies 1982b, 271).
5. NB the form *Mimor/Miuor* (i.e. the saint's name) is soon replaced by the similar sound *mawr* ('great'). Cf LL 212, *c* 862, where we find the form *mimor*, as also the bounds of Merthyr Mawr (which included Ogmore). The form *mimor* continues through into the twelfth-century papal bulls; however, LL 212 is glossed 'now called merthyr *mawr*'. Dr Diane Brook has pointed out to me that the true reading of Nash-Williams no. 255 may well be 'filie sua' rather than 'fili epi'; see Brook 1992b for consideration of this and related issues.
6. Annie Bardel suggests that this tomb could in fact have been the tomb of a twelfth-century Abbot Gradlon from the comital family (1991, 76–7).
7. See Brook 1981 for a very thorough consideration of the siting of inscribed stones in relation to early ecclesiastical sites in south Wales.

BIBLIOGRAPHY CHAPTER XIV

Barral I Altet 1986. X. Barral I Altet, L'abbaye médiévale de Landévennec. Architecture et sculpture: bilan et perspectives de recherche, in Simon 1986: 189–205.
Bardel 1990. A. Bardel, Landévennec, *Gallia Informations*, 24–6.
Bardel 1991. A. Bardel, L'abbaye Saint-Gwénolé de Landévennec, *Archéologie Médiévale*, 21, 51–101.
Blair and Sharpe 1992. *Pastoral Care before the Parish*, ed. J. Blair and R. Sharpe. London: Leicester University Press.
Blanc 1992. M.-L. Blanc, Les sépultures de l'abbaye de Landévennec, *Chronique de Landévennec*, 72, 127–32.
Cahour 1874. A. Cahour, R. Kerviler, L. Petit, P. Anizon, Compte-rendu des fouilles faites à St-Donatien en 1873, *Bulletin de la Société archéologique de Nantes et de la Loire-Atlantique*, 13, 19–130.
CL: *Cartulaire de l'abbaye de Landévennec*, ed. A. de la Borderie. Rennes: Société archéologique du Finistère, 1888.
CR: *Cartulaire de l'Abbaye de Redon*, ed. A. de Courson, Collection de documents inédits sur l'histoire de France. Paris: Ministre de l'instruction publique, 1863.
Davies 1978. W. Davies, *An Early Welsh Microcosm*. London: Royal Historical Society.
Davies 1981. W. Davies, Property rights and Property Claims in Welsh 'Vitae' of the Eleventh Century, in *Hagiographie, cultures et sociétés*, ed. E. Patlagean and P. Riché, 515–33. Paris: Études Augustiniennes.
Davies 1982a. W. Davies, *Wales in the Early Middle Ages*. Leicester: Leicester University Press.
Davies 1982b. W. Davies, The Latin charter-tradition in western Britain, Brittany and Ireland, in *Ireland in Early Mediaeval Europe*, ed. D. Whitelock, R. McKitterick, D. Dumville, 258–80. Cambridge: Cambridge University Press.
Davies 1983. W. Davies, Priests and Rural Communities in East Brittany in the Ninth Century, *Études Celtiques*, 20, 177–97.

Davies 1986. W. Davies, Les chartes du cartulaire de Landévennec, in Simon 1986: 85–95.
Davies 1988. W. Davies, *Small Worlds. The Village Community in Early Medieval Brittany*. London: Duckworth.
Davies 1992. W. Davies, The Myth of the Celtic Church, in Edwards and Lane 1992: 12–21.
Edwards and Lane 1992. *The Early Church in Wales and the West*, ed. N. Edwards and A. Lane. Oxford: Oxbow Monographs 16.
Evans 1992. J.W. Evans, The survival of the *clas* as an institution in medieval Wales: some observations on Llanbadarn Fawr, in Edwards and Lane 1992: 33–44.
Guigon, Bardel, Batt 1987. P. Guigon, J.-P. Bardel, M. Batt, Nécropoles et sarcophages du haut moyen âge en Bretagne, *Revue archéologique de l'Ouest*, 4, 133–48.
Higgitt 1990. J. Higgitt, Early Medieval Sculpture at Dumbarton, *Proc. Soc. Antiq. Scotland*, 120, 139–42.
Jackson 1958. K. Jackson, The Sources for the Life of St Kentigern, in N. Chadwick et al, *Studies in the Early British Church*, 273–357. Cambridge: Cambridge University Press.
James 1992. H. James, Early medieval cemeteries in Wales, in Edwards and Lane 1992: 90–103.
Knight 1984. J. Knight, Glamorgan AD400–1100: Archaeology and History, and Sources for the Early History of Morgannwg, in *Glamorgan County History*, vol. 2, ed. H.N. Savory, 315–409. Cardiff: Glamorgan County History Trust Ltd.
LL: *The Text of the Book of Llan Dâv*, ed. J.G. Evans with J. Rhys. Oxford: published privately by Evans, 1893.
MacQuarrie 1986. The Career of Saint Kentigern of Glasgow: *Vitae*, *Lectiones* and Glimpses of Fact, *Innes Review*, 37, 3–24.
MacQuarrie 1990. Early Christian Govan: the Historical Context, *Records of the Scottish Church History Society*, 24, 1–17.
Merdrignac 1986. B. Merdrignac, Judicaël et Josse, in *Histoire des saints et de la sainteté chrétienne*, vol. 4, *Les voies nouvelles de la sainteté 605–814*, ed. P. Riché, 168–76. Paris: Hachette et Cie.
Miller 1975. M. Miller, Historicity and the Pedigrees of the Northcountrymen, *Bulletin of the Board of Celtic Studies*, 26, 254–80.
Nash-Williams 1950. V.E. Nash-Williams, *The Early Christian Monuments of Wales*. Cardiff: University of Wales Press.
Olson and Padel 1986. B.L. Olson and O.J. Padel, A Tenth-Century List of Cornish Parochial Saints, *Cambridge Medieval Celtic Studies*, 12, 33–71.

Olson 1989. B.L. Olson, *Early Monasteries in Cornwall* (*Studies in Celtic History*, 11). Woodbridge: The Boydell Press.

Radford 1967a. C.A.R. Radford, The Early Church in Strathclyde and Galloway, *Medieval Archaeology*, 11, 105–26.

Radford 1967b. C.A.R. Radford, The Early Christian Monuments at Govan and Inchinnan, *Trans. Glasgow Arch. Soc.*, 15, 173–88.

Simon 1985. M. Simon, *L'abbaye de Landévennec de Saint Guénolé à nos jours*. Rennes: Ouest-France.

Simon 1986. *Landévennec et le monachisme breton dans le haut moyen âge*, ed. M. Simon. Landévennec: Association Landévennec, 485–1985.

Smith 1982. J.M.H. Smith, The 'Archbishopric' of Dol and the Ecclesiastical Politics of Ninth-Century Brittany, *Studies in Church History*, 18, 59–70.

Smith 1985. J.M.H. Smith, Celtic Asceticism and Carolingian Authority in Early Medieval Brittany, *Studies in Church History*, 22, 53–63.

Smith 1986. J.M.H. Smith, Culte impérial et politique frontalière dans la vallée de la Vilaine: le témoignage des diplômes carolingiens dans le cartulaire de Redon, in Simon 1986: 129–39.

Smith 1990. J.M.H. Smith, Oral and Written: Saints, Miracles, and Relics in Brittany, c. 850–1250, *Speculum*, 65, 309–43.

Thomas 1971. C. Thomas, *The Early Christian Archaeology of North Britain*. London: Oxford University Press, for the University of Glasgow.

VC: Vita Cadoci, in *Vitae Sanctorum Britanniae et Genealogiae*, ed. A.W. Wade-Evans, 24–140. Cardiff: University of Wales Press Board, 1944.

VG: Vita Gildae, auctore monacho Ruiensi, in *Gildae De Excidio Britanniae*, ed. H. Williams, vol. 2, 322–88. London: Cymmrodorion Record Series 3.

VM: Prima Vita Machutis, in F. Lot, *Mélanges d'histoire bretonne*, 294–329. Paris: Honoré Champion, 1907.

VS: Vita Samsonis, in *La vie de S. Samson*, ed. R. Fawtier. Paris: Honoré Champion, 1912.

XV

'Protected Space' in Britain and Ireland in the Middle Ages

This is a discursive and speculative paper, intentionally so, since I aim to ring bells in your heads and encourage you to think about possibilities. It does, however, take its starting point from a detailed analysis that I have discussed elsewhere (Davies 1995).[1]

The notion that some clearly defined spaces are places of protection, places where people can be safe, is a familiar one. It is probably best exemplified by the Christian idea of sanctuary (still invoked, for example, by illegal immigrants to Britain) but it is in no way confined to Christian contexts: there are the ancient Greek sanctuaries associated with Diana at Ephesus or Minerva at Sparta, for example, and there are the Levitical cities of refuge of the Old Testament (Timbal Duclaux de Martin 1939: 18-19), while the idea remains common in children's play; even the despised Violet Elizabeth had to be protected by William Brown and his friends when she 'took sanctuary' with them.

In this paper I want to draw your attention to the act of protecting as well as to the places where people could feel protected, although - as we shall see - the two came together in the later middle ages. My comments will relate to Britain and Ireland, and largely to the central middle ages, but I will make some reference to later periods.

Protection

The idea that an individual can legitimately afford protection to another was a norm in early medieval European societies, continental as well as insular. By 'legitimately' I mean that it was a power, and a right, acknowledged by the society surrounding the individual and in several cases articulated in legal collections; Anglo-Saxon law codes offer a good insular example. It was usual for a man's power to protect to be related to his status: the higher his status, the greater that power. This finds its most concrete expression in the graded penalties for breach or violation of protection that feature in many early medieval legal texts: if you killed a man in a bishop's house, the penalty was greater than if you killed him in a priest's house; the offence to the bishop was greater, because his status was higher; and you owed compensation to the bishop for violating his protection in addition to the compensation you owed for the deed itself to the dead man's kin or lord.

So much is standard; it is familiar and well-known. Before going further, I will take a few minutes to consider words for 'protection' and their semantic ranges, since they are important for our understanding of early medieval approaches. In Germanic languages the word for protection is *mund* and in Celtic languages there are words related to the root *snãd-*, words like modern Welsh *nawdd*, Old Irish *snádud*, Old Breton *nodet*. The meaning at the core of *mund* is 'hand', and hence its secondary sense of 'protection', taking into the hands of someone. At the core of *snãd-* seems to be the meaning 'to bind', and hence its sense of being attached to someone. Both groups of words were used to express the reciprocities that underlie the power and responsibility of the head of a household in the early middle ages: he protects and guards the members of the household, and so they are in his hands and are thereby bound to him; they are in his power; as protector, he receives compensation for offences committed against them. The seventh- and eighth-century Lombard law on *mundium* (the sphere of someone's protection) is prominent: for example, a widow may return to the *mundium* of her near relatives, from that of her husband's relatives, in certain circumstances, and a girl can return to the *mundium* of her relatives if he who holds her *mundium* attacks her (Fischer Drew 1973: 79-80, 85-92, for example). Even in England in the early seventh century, the consequences of infringing protection were explicitly set out in the Laws of Æthelberht, 75 and 76 (Attenborough 1922: 14).

By extension, therefore, the household was a 'safe' place; it was safe because it was protected. It was (or should have been) inviolable.[2] Attacks on or in a household struck at the householder's power of protection and therefore struck at the heart of his own honour and identity. 'Household' here was often explicitly both house and the land around it: to early Icelanders safety extended to the land 'within the fence [round the house]' (Gourevitch 1987: 529); and in Irish secular law, the precinct round the dwelling was explicitly included in the inviolable area - *maigen dígona* (Binchy 1941: 83). Valuing the inviolability of the household was not peculiar to the early middle ages: we still think of an Englishman's home as his castle; the 'homestead' is not just the place where you live but it is the place where you are safe (owning, as I do, a garden across which my neighbours have the only available access to their property, I am often conscious of a deep-seated sense of outrage when strange vehicles encroach: this is not merely proprietary: I feel threatened and fearful, I start to feel unsafe); and in the *genre* of the Western, the 'bad' men are always the ones who attack the 'good' homesteaders. In the classic film of the early '50s, *Shane*, whenever the bad men cross the stream and enter the protected area around the hero's house, the tension mounts -the music changes - we can read the visual signals - we know that the crossing is a threat to the safety of the hero's family.

In the early middle ages, by a different extension, a man might stretch his power of protection to people beyond the homestead. In England, as late as the early tenth century, a secular man could offer protection to a thief for a limited period, for three days if the protector was a thegn, for nine if he was a king (IV Æthelstan 6 (Attenborough 1922: 148, 150)); if violated, the value of his *mundbyrd* was due to the protector for breach of protection. In Ireland a protector could give legal freedom from distraint (*snádud*), a power for which there were elaborate, status-related rules: protection from distraint could last for fifteen days from one sort of noble (*aire ard*) but only for ten days from a lesser noble (*aire tuíseo*), just as the extent of the *maigen dígona* also varied with rank. So intrinsic was the notion of protection to the fabric of Irish society, that these powers still existed in Ireland, and were exercised, in the late sixteenth century (Kelly 1988: 140-1).[3]

On the continent, by yet another early medieval extension, the word *mundbyrd* in Carolingian Francia came to refer to a special royal protection, given by the ruler to some selected individuals and to monasteries, such as Lorsch: the beneficiary was protected from all harm by the king; if he was harmed, then the guilty one was subject to pay a fine. This case involves an extension of the king's personal power of protection, an extension that reinforced his distinctively royal status (Ganshof 1965: 46).

In the early middle ages the power to protect was an aspect of the status of free men. Its application says much more about the power, privilege and independence of the protector than it does about the status or condition of the individual who came within the sphere of his protection. Hence, in our texts breach of protection attracts far more attention than respect for it. It did so because being able to sustain protective power was essential for the public recognition of status and therefore for the maintenance of social and political order in that world.

4

The territorialization of protection

There are, of course, other types of 'safe place' than the household and the proximity of a protector; such are the meeting places protected by early Kentish law in England, or the safety of the Icelandic *thing*, or the quiet and order of an Irish court (*airecht*) meeting for judicial business - no anger or incitement was allowed. The reasons for these kinds of safety are different from the safety that derives from a protector and they do not primarily arise from a person's status;[4] rather, they are to do with a community's need to meet and conduct its business without fear of attack. Hence, characteristically, weapons had to be put down by those arriving at the meeting, and drawing a weapon when the meeting was in progress was a particularly serious offence. In early English law these concepts are more frequently expressed by the word *frið* than by *mund*, where *frið* is 'peace', 'security', 'freedom from fighting', and secondarily, 'truce', 'agreement'; *friðstow* is therefore the 'peace-place', the refuge or place of safety. The ideas are distinct from the act of protection inherent in the notion of *mund*.

The power to protect was not without limits, and - at least until the tenth century - there was a tendency to express its extent in temporal terms when it stretched beyond the household; hence, we find protection for thirty days, or whatever period was appropriate.[5] What is so interesting in insular areas is the fact that in certain contexts the power to protect became territorialized beyond the homestead: power to protect could be expressed in relation to a defined space. Hence, in Welsh, *nawdd*, 'protection', gave the word *noddfa*, 'place (*ma*) of protection'. And accordingly offences committed in the *noddfa* brought compensation to the protector as well as to the damaged party. This is most explicitly set out in the southern Welsh, late twelfth-century, Cyfnerth Redaction of the laws: the payments due for offences in the *noddfa* (outside the cemetery) were to be split 50:50 between the abbot and 'learned youths' of the church (Pryce 1993: 180). There are tenth- and eleventh-century cases of compensatory payments of this type being made to clerics - in material from the church of Llandaff, from the South East (Davies 1995: 138-40); and there are many twelfth-century references to the use and violation of specific *noddfeydd* (Pryce 1993: 170-3). There are also examples of apparently comparable compensation being paid to churches in Ireland, as to Armagh for 'outrage' in the late tenth century (Ó Corráin 1978: 22). It is usually assumed that the *termonn* lands that surrounded Irish churches and monasteries marked the physical extent of protected space (Hughes 1966: 148-9; Lucas 1967: 203-4), although the *termonn* is more explicitly associated with refuge and with the limits of the 'holy' in the seventh and eighth centuries (Doherty 1985: 56-9). Armagh, Clonmacnoise, Kildare and Scattery Island certainly had locatable *termonn* lands by the ninth century. Hogan (1910) listed 32 *termonn* names for early Ireland - often associated with a saint's name, like *Termonn Brígte* or *Termonn Ciaráin*. Where these names refer to ecclesiastical space, the space may, as Ann Hamlin has suggested, have been marked out by cross-inscribed stones (Hughes and Hamlin 1977: 80-1).

Now, the territorial expression of protection has a very strong ecclesiastical flavour once it gets beyond the limits of the freeman's homestead. The idea of the protective power of the saints is particularly strong in Old Irish material - witness Colman's Hymn invoking John the Baptist as protection (*snádud*), the early poems from Iona invoking Colum Cille as protection (*snádud*) and the developed analogies of the saint as *lorica*, breastplate (Stokes and Strachan 1903: ii.301; cf. Clancy and Márkus 1995: 153-4, 170). Many of the examples of protected space for which we have good recorded evidence, like Llanbadarn Fawr and Llanddewibrefi in 1109, relate to monasteries and churches.[6]

It could be that we should add to these Welsh and Irish cases the further ecclesiastical examples of the so-called 'chartered sanctuaries' of northern and western England - Hexham, Beverley, Durham, Ripon, St Buryan, and Padstow. Beverley, like several others, had graded penalties for the violators of its 1½ miles of protected space in the late middle ages, increasing as they approached the church (Cox 1911: 126-7); Durham and Hexham had similarly graded penalties at least by the late eleventh century - marked out by crosses (Hall 1989: 426-7). St Buryan and Padstow were both noted for their 'privileged' sanctuaries (Olson 1989: 72, 79). These chartered or privileged sanctuaries look like Welsh protected space because they are significantly different from 'ordinary' sanctuary as we find it in English churches. Their special status was known, and remarked upon by late medieval and early modern travellers like Leland, and some northern cases had special powers in relation to unemendable offences (Hall 1989: 433). The extent of their special space tended to be marked out physically, often by crosses (four at Beverley and Hexham, six at Wetherhal (Cox 1911: 128, 155, 175)); the areas were large - 1-2-3 miles in diameter; and penalties for offences within tended to be graded (as they were in Irish canon and Welsh secular law). Given the English legislation which territorialized

6

protection in the tenth and eleventh centuries (see further below), we should perhaps *expect* them to be comparable. It does not follow that they had all the characteristics of the Welsh *noddfa* (in particular we do not know about the range of punishable offences in the crucial period of the tenth and eleventh centuries) but they are sufficiently similar to be considered in the same light; and sufficiently unlike sanctuary as it is commonly found. We should note that the areas around the salthouses in eleventh-century Nantwich and Middlewich were also especially protected: specified offences committed within a league of the two places attracted fines, although there were no penalties beyond the league (*Cheshire Domesday*, S2 (i.268r)). The latter material, which happens not to be ecclesiastical, provides us with clear evidence that protection was territorialized in practice, and not just in theory, in eleventh-century England.

We should also think of the girths of Scotland, like that mentioned at Luss in 1315 (*RRS* 5: no. 55); Lesmahagow, Innerleithen, Tynninghame and Wedale church (Stow) all have much earlier references, although these earlier, twelfth-century, references use Latin words for the girth (Lawrie 1905: no. 172, *RRS* 1: no.219, *RRS* 2: no.68).[7] 'Girth' is a metathesized form of the late Old English word *grið*, where *grið* is a borrowing from Scandinavian *grið*, whose early semantic range (though not root) was very close to that of *mund*: it had a primary meaning of 'home', 'abode', extended to 'peace', 'truce', 'pardon', and so on; it often meant 'safe conduct' in Old Icelandic (Sørensen 1993: 159). By the eleventh century it could mean in English both 'protection' and also a specific 'peace' or 'truce', limited in space or time. *The Oxford English Dictionary* (*s.v.* grith) cites these meanings of peace and protection but also cites the use of girth for 'place of protection' (both general and specific) from 1300 until the nineteenth century. A high proportion of *OED* citations of this latter usage are in Scottish contexts. Not only do we find 'girth' as the word for ecclesiastically protected areas in Scotland; we also find grithcrosses at Tynemouth; and grithmen attached to northern English church areas, such as Ripon, in the later middle ages (the grithmen may or may not have sought protection - in Scandinavia grithmen were members of the household, whether permanent family members or servants on short-term contracts (Sørensen 1993: 159)). Just as Beverley and Tynemouth had crosses to mark the limits of the protected area, so Lesmahagow had four such crosses by 1144 (Lawrie 1905: 136) and the monastery of Applecross in western Scotland had stone markers to lay out its protected territory - a place to this day known as a'Chomraich in Gaelic, the 'protected place' (MacDonald 1985: 179).[8]

As Professor Barrow pointed out at the conference, it may also be the case that Scottish placenames in *tearmann* - as in Tillytarmont and Drummietermont - point to Gaelic versions of the same phenomenon, given this use of the Irish word *termonn*; hence Clach an Tearmainn, the *termonn* stone, marking the limits of Oronsay Priory in the strand separating Colonsay and Oronsay (Watson 1926: 259). I am not confident, however, that all *termonn* names denoted 'protected' space in the sense used here, particularly in the earliest Christian centuries.[9]

Sanctuary

Whatever its origin, the spatial dimension of extended protection looks largely, though not entirely, ecclesiastical; it is both a reflection of, and a contributor to, the status of specific churches.

By the eleventh century space protected by ecclesiastical bodies in Britain and Ireland also looked like 'sanctuary'; and in part it was. But, it involved a lot more than sanctuary and the reasons for its existence were quite different. Firstly, the physical scale of insular protected space was altogether different from the 'ordinary' sanctuaries we find in Britain and from sanctuary on the continent. In the case of protected space, we are dealing with zones that could be as big as one, two or three miles in radius in Wales, Scotland, and England, as also in some Breton cases: St Asaph reputedly had a mile square (Pryce 1993: 171n); Applecross was twelve miles across (Watson 1926: 125) and Luss three miles 'around' (*RRS* 5: no. 55); Hexham and Ripon were two miles across, Beverley three miles, and St Buryan and Padstow perhaps the same (Cox 1911: 215, 223); and the original *minihi* of Gouesnou in western Brittany was about 1.3 square miles, though later doubled (Tanguy 1984: 15). This contrasts with the classic 30-35-40 metres (*passus*) of sanctuary land around churches on the continent and with the tiny '*sauvetés*' of southern France.[10] Secondly, the nature and scale of the consequences of violation of protected space were altogether different: if an offence was committed in a protected space (theft, abduction, arson, assault, homicide), then it occasioned significant financial compensation to the protector (as well as to the damaged), a compensation supported by secular law, as befitted an issue of personal status. Violation of sanctuary might well require penance, in recognition of the affront to the church, but that was essentially a spiritual matter and did not have to have material consequences; hence, excommunication was a common penalty for breach of sanctuary. Although the canonists began to discuss the application of secular penalties for breach of sanctuary in the eleventh century, Timbal Duclaux de Martin knew of no actual cases of secular penalties being applied at that time (1939: 207-8; 185, 237).[11]

This difference is hardly surprising given that sanctuary is in essence to do with asylum - refuge. It is a mechanism for ensuring the safety of life and limb for fugitives: at its heart is the legal and social position of the person seeking protection, not the status of the protector. From at least the time of the *Theodosian Code*, churches had provided a place of asylum for fugitive slaves and others (as the Levitical cities of refuge had provided asylum for homicides (Numbers 35)) (Timbal Duclaux de Martin 1939: 83-4). These ideas were quite clearly taken into Irish ecclesiastical thinking by the eighth century, for canons explicitly refer to Old Testament cities of refuge (*Hibernensis* XXVIII; cf. Doherty 1985: 57); as they also reached England by the late seventh century (Laws of Ine 5, Attenborough 1922: 38). Refuge for criminals could certainly be subject to restrictions: there were early medieval distinctions between the refuge rights of accused and condemned criminals. Nevertheless, sanctuary was essentially for fugitives, although ultimately the type of fugitive who could expect to be protected came to be severely limited (thieves and brigands were excluded in the thirteenth century and fifteenth-century papal bulls exempted further categories of offender).

The restrictions of the later middle ages followed an extension of the scope of local sanctuaries on the continent in the years round about AD 1000, in the context of the Peace of God movement: there should be a special peace for a church and the houses around it, like the Catalan precincts known as *sagreres*, sacred places (Head and Landes 1992; Martí 1988). What this meant in practice was a right to freedom from molestation for church property and often, given the prevailing political context, for the poor and defenceless or unarmed. In other words, it meant extending the right of asylum from fugitive criminals to the poor. The movement was taken to extreme lengths in some parts: in north-west Herefordshire (Leominster and neighbourhood) 'refuge cemeteries' were consecrated in the mid twelfth century, which had no associated rights of burial at all; these were places 'for the refuge of the poor in time of hostility' - a sacred refuge without an associated holy focus (Kemp 1988: 86, 89); at the same period Bishop Stephen of Rennes blessed a cemetery 'for the refuge of the living, not the burial of the dead' in the parish of Marmoutiers (Timbal Duclaux de Martin 1939: 230). Although, therefore, sanctuary was often expanded in western Europe in the eleventh and twelfth centuries, it was not expanded to become protected space after the sense of *nawdd* or *mund*. The idea of asylum remained central.

The chronology of territorialization

This spatial expression of protection does not look especially ancient. I doubt that it started much before the tenth century in Britain. Although the *Hibernensis* and other seventh-/eighth-century Irish texts go to some length to discuss marking out the bounds of holy places (XLIV), by the sign of the cross, they are more concerned with refuge (canonical sanctuary) than with protection (Lucas 1967: 184; Doherty 1985: 56-7).[12]

My preference for the relatively late development of protected space arises for the following reasons. Firstly, it is extremely difficult to find strong and well-evidenced suggestions of the practice before about 900. Secondly, there is a coalescence of English cases of 'chartered sanctuary' attributed to the period of Æthelstan: rightly or wrongly people tended to believe that it was Æthelstan who had confirmed or established the areas. Thirdly, the English legislation on *mund* became noticeably more territorial during the tenth century, and by the time of Æthelred and Cnut was strongly so: Alfred's stress on *periods* of protection gave way to Æthelred's stress on the violation of protected *space* (VIII Æth. 1, 4) (cf. Hall 1989: 431); all churches were in the protection (*grið*) of God and Christ (VIII Æth. 1, I Cnut 2 (Robertson 1925: 116, 154)); while the penalties due to churches for violation of their protection varied since, though all had the same sanctity, all did not have the same status (VIII Æth. 5) - an important clause, emphasizing status and differentiating the authority that derives from status from the authority that comes with holiness. Fourthly, none of the Irish cases of compensation for infringement comes till the late tenth century. Fifthly, as I have argued elsewhere, there are special reasons for believing it to be a tenth-century development in Wales (Davies 1995: 163-4). It is also likely that the change to a territorial approach was influenced by the - intrinsically territorial - canonical law of sanctuary. However, it may be as important that the change was a part of a general shift in attitudes to physical space: land became something to be delimited, ridden around, and physically dominated, rather than a generalized source of sustenance or a distant source of goods to be plundered and vacated; property literally had to be encompassable.[13]

I would also reinforce the chronological point by focussing on the borrowing of *grið* into English. This is a tenth-century borrowing. In tenth- and eleventh-century English royal legislation *grið* was used in parallel to *mund*: this is quite explicit in the Laws of Cnut, where 'mundbreach' in Wessex is 'grithbreach' in the Danelaw (although the usages are not always so regionally distinctive) (II Cnut 12, 15; Robertson 1925: 180). In fact, by the year 1000 *ciricgrith* was a more common term than *mund* for the protection afforded by the church, whatever the region - and a more common term than the *frið*, peace, of the church, though the terminology is not stable (by the eleventh and twelfth centuries Latin *pax* could refer both to a specifically given protection and to a general peace). It looks as if English ideas began to change round about 900: it has been argued that the Laws of Alfred started to equate church peace with house protection (Riggs 1963: 34); and in Edward and Guthrum's Peace (2.1) *ciricgrið* was to be as inviolate as the specific protection given by the king (the king's *handgrið*). The earlier 'peace' (*frið*) was becoming the 'protected area'; the protected area was more than a refuge for criminals (ie more than sanctuary): penalties for violation of the ecclesiastical protected area in the tenth and eleventh centuries could be heavy; and perhaps some special protected areas, of considerable size, were marked out on the ground.

****

We have come a long way from the simple sphere of a freeman's protection, his 'home'. Quite different ideas like canonical sanctuary (the consecrated refuge) came to Britain and Ireland and influenced approaches to church territory; moreover, approaches to protected space continued to change and develop. In England, Scotland and Wales, over time, the protected space could become an immunity (an area exempt from the demands of others, such as demands for taxes or to inspect) or could even become a *seigneurie* (an area which a lord set out to dominate, over which he pro-actively established control, by exercising judicial powers and setting up monopolies). This *could* happen to the *noddfa*, though it did not necessarily do so. It is true of Llandaff by the early twelfth century, with its royal exemptions, and its rights to hold courts, market and mint (Davies 1995: 150-2). It is true of Beverley and Ripon by the thirteenth century (and possibly even by the late eleventh century), with their extensive jurisdictional rights and powers (Lobel 1934: 126); it is true of the late medieval *minihi* in Brittany (Chédeville and Tonnerre 1987: 354, 358) and it is true of Luss by the early fourteenth century, with its rights of criminal jurisdiction (*RRS* 5: no. 55). In other words, the protected space so contributed to the status of some particular institutions that it became the core of wider powers; and of the successful attempts of some lords to turn power over land into power over people.

Protecting space gave considerable financial and practical powers to some major religious bodies in the tenth and eleventh centuries - the period at the heart of the development. We do not need to explain these newly acquired powers in terms of the devolution and fragmentation of royal or imperial power (as historians are prone to do for the continent). Indeed, in some insular cases new ecclesiastical powers seemed to develop as a response to increasing rather than decreasing ruler power: in Wales it was a defensive reaction against ruler aggression; in England the church's power to protect became in part an expression of ruler power, for each reinforced the other.

****

It was my purpose in giving this talk to draw attention to protecting space in Britain and Ireland and stimulate some further thought. The phenomenon is a commonplace for historians of early medieval Ireland and Wales. It looks as if it may be as characteristic of England in the tenth and eleventh centuries, particularly in view of the framing of English legislation and the evidence of *Domesday Book*; and perhaps it may not be quite so characteristic of Ireland as is commonly assumed - at least at the early, seventh- and eighth-century, period. The same does not appear to be true of the continent, with its much greater emphases on ecclesiastical immunities. The use that insular ecclesiastical bodies initially made of protected space had some of the same consequences for them as the early immunity had for Frankish churches - additional income (Fouracre 1995); in political terms it was the functional equivalent of the Frankish immunity.

What is significant about this institution is not the mere delimitation of a special space but the distinctive nature of the powers exercised within the space. It is these that differentiate protection from sanctuary. The subject could tolerate a much lengthier investigation, particularly with reference to what happened inside the English chartered sanctuaries, but also with reference to continental similarities and divergences; and indeed with some detailed attention to the Scottish and Irish *termonn* - the word itself has a quite different range of reference from Welsh *noddfa* (borrowed from Latin *terminus*, boundary) and we should perhaps be looking at *comrach* rather than *termonn* for close parallels. I hope others will pursue the trail: not only does it look rich; but it lies at the heart of strategies for establishing and sustaining power, both personal and corporate. And that is central to our understanding of social and political development in the early middle ages.[14]

Appendix

A note on ecclesiastical immunities

By the tenth century the continental immunity (a privilege which freed the holder of immune lands from various kinds of public intervention in those lands, especially with regard to taxation and public systems of justice) was largely an ecclesiastical phenomenon - one that had points of contact with 'protected space'. If the immunist took fines for offences committed within the immunity, this must have looked rather like the consequences of violation of 'protection'. However, although some control of judicial process might lie in the hands of an ecclesiastical immunist lord, the process still in theory remained public and there is no reason to believe that offences committed in the immunity but outside the sanctuary (eg theft between lay persons) carried *additional* compensations to the ecclesiastical lord over and above the 'public' fine. The pre-twelfth-century immunity is therefore very different from 'protected space'. In any case, at least in the Carolingian period, those guilty of major crimes had to be handed over to public authority by the immunist. And, further, we have reservations nowadays about the power of the immunist even in relation to minor offences (Fouracre 1995: 58-68). By the twelfth century, canonists began to apply penalties for violation of immunity to violation of sanctuary and this made the distinction between sanctuary right and ecclesiastical immunity less clear than it had been before (Timbal Duclaux de Martin 1939: 147-58, 185-96); these are late developments, however, and do not affect the clear distinctions of the seventh to eleventh centuries.

There is another type of immunity, sometimes called the 'narrow immunity' by continental scholars, which also has features which resemble insular protected space. The twelfth-century canonists argued that *every* church had a *special* immunity stretching for 30 (and in some cases 40) paces (*passus*); if anyone committed sacrilege by injuring or stealing from clerics within this area, then they were liable to pay a money fine (Gratian *Decretum*, C.17, q.4, c.21). Although the size of this zone was similar to the 30-40 paces of the sanctuary zone, the offence committed was quite distinct from violation of sanctuary; both were sacrilege, but damaging clerics near the church was a different kind of sacrilege. The special immunity was therefore different from sanctuary right in canonist thinking. This special immunity was also differentiated from 'protected space' by its small size and by the absence of secular enforcement of its provisions; and, in any case, the extent to which the canonists' theory was put into practice is very uncertain (and would repay some examination).

There were, then, two different kinds of immunity in canonist thinking, and each was different from sanctuary. I would argue that all three were different from pre-twelfth-century 'protected space', although the 'ordinary' immunity could be comparable in size and the 'special' immunity could in theory involve payment of fines to a church. The similarities are such that, despite the differences, it seems reasonable to propose that the Frankish immunity performed much the same function for continental churches as protected space did for insular churches; and that by the twelfth and thirteenth centuries protected space could easily become the core of an insular immunity.[15]

Abbreviations

Cáin Adamnáin: ed. K. Meyer, Anecdota Oxoniensia, Medieval and Modern Series 12, Oxford 1905.

Le Cartulaire de Redon: ed. A. de Courson, Paris 1863.

Cheshire Domesday: *Domesday Book*, vol. 26, *Cheshire*, ed. P. Morgan (general editor J. Morris), Chichester 1978.

14

Decretum Magistri Gratiani: in *Corpus Iuris Canonici*, ed. E. Friedberg, 2 vols., Leipzig 1879-81.

Hibernensis: *Die irische Kanonensammlung*, ed. H. Wasserschleben, 2nd edn Leipzig 1885.

RRS 1: *Regesta Regum Scottorum*, vol. 1, *The Acts of Malcolm IV King of Scots 1153-65*, ed. G. W. S. Barrow, Edinburgh 1960.

RRS 2: *Regesta Regum Scottorum*, vol. 2, *The Acts of William I King of Scots 1165-1214*, ed. G. W. S. Barrow, Edinburgh 1971.

RRS 5: *Regesta Regum Scottorum*, vol. 5, *The Acts of Robert I King of Scots 1306-29*, ed. A. A. M. Duncan, Edinburgh 1988.

References

Attenborough, F. L. (ed. and trans.) 1922, *The Laws of the Earliest English Kings*, Cambridge.

Binchy, D. A. (ed.) 1941, *Críth Gablach*, Dublin.

Chédeville, A. and Tonnerre, N.-Y. 1987, *La Bretagne féodale XIe-XIIIe siècle*, Rennes.

Clancy, T. O. and Márkus, G. 1995, *Iona. The Earliest Poetry of a Celtic Monastery*, Edinburgh.

Cox, J. C. 1911, *The Sanctuaries and Sanctuary Seekers of Medieval England*, London.

Davies, W. 1995, 'Adding Insult to Injury: Power, Property and Immunities in Early Medieval Wales' in W. Davies and P. Fouracre (eds.), *Property and Power in the Early Middle Ages*, Cambridge, pp. 137-64.

Davies, W. and Fouracre, P. (eds.) 1995, *Property and Power in the Early Middle Ages*, Cambridge.

Doherty, C. 1985, 'The monastic town in early medieval Ireland' in H. B. Clarke and A. Simms (eds.), *The Comparative History of Urban Origins in Non-Roman Europe*, British Archaeological Reports International Series 255(i), pp. 45-75.

Edwards, N. 1990, *The Archaeology of Early Medieval Ireland*, London.

Fischer Drew, K. (trans.) 1973, *The Lombard Laws*, Philadelphia.

Fouracre. P. 1995, 'Eternal light and earthly needs: practical aspects of the development of Frankish immunities' in W. Davies and P. Fouracre (eds.), *Property and Power in the Early Middle Ages*, Cambridge, pp. 53-81.

Ganshof, F. L. 1965, *Frankish Institutions under Charlemagne*, trans. B. and M. Lyon, New York 1968.

Gourevitch, A. J. 1987, 'Semantics of the medieval community: "farmstead", "land", "world" (Scandinavian example)' in *Les communautés rurales*, pt 5, *Recueils de la société Jean Bodin pour l'histoire comparative des institutions* vol. 44, Paris, pp. 525-40.

Hall, D. 1989, 'The Sanctuary of St Cuthbert' in G. Bonner, D. Rollason, C. Stancliffe (eds.), *St Cuthbert, his Cult and his Community to AD 1200*, Woodbridge, pp. 425-36.

Head, T. and Landes, R. (eds.) 1992, *The Peace of God: Social Violence and Religious Response in France around the Year 1000*, Ithaca and London.

Hogan, E. 1910, *Onomasticon Goedelicum Locorum et Tribum Hiberniae et Scotiae*, Dublin.

Hughes, K. 1966, *The Church in Early Irish Society*, London.

Hughes, K. and Hamlin, A. 1977, *The Modern Traveller to the Early Irish Church*, London.

Kelly, F. 1988, *A Guide to Early Irish Law*, Dublin.

Kemp, B. 1988, 'Some aspects of the *parochia* of Leominster in the twelfth century' in J. Blair (ed.), *Minsters and Parish Churches. The Local Church in Transition*, Oxford, pp. 83-95.

Lawrie, A. C. 1905, *Early Scottish Charters*, Glasgow.

Le Moing, J.-Y. 1988, 'Toponymie bretonne de Haute-Bretagne', Thèse de Doctorat, Université de Rennes 2, 2 vols.

Le Moing, J.-Y. 1990, *Les noms de lieux bretons de Haute-Bretagne*, Spezed.

Lobel, M. D. 1934, 'The ecclesiastical banleuca in England' in F. M. Powicke (ed.), *Oxford Essays in Medieval History presented to Herbert Edward Salter*, Oxford, pp. 122-40.

Lucas, A. T. 1967, 'The plundering and burning of churches in Ireland, 7th to 16th century' in E. Rynne (ed.), *North Munster Studies*, Limerick, pp. 172-229.

MacDonald, A. D. S. 1985, 'Iona's style of government among the Picts and Scots: the toponymic evidence of Adomnán's Life of Columba', *Peritia* 4, pp. 174-86.

Martí, R. 1988, 'L'Ensagrerament: l'adveniment de les *sagreres* feudals', *Faventia* 10, pp. 153-82.

Ó Corráin, D. 1978, 'Nationality and kingship in pre-Norman Ireland' in T. W. Moody (ed.), *Nationality and the Pursuit of National Independence*, Belfast, pp. 1-35.

Olson, L. 1989, *Early Monasteries in Cornwall*, Woodbridge.

Pryce, H. 1993, *Native Law and the Church in Medieval Wales*, Oxford.

Riggs, C. H. 1963, *Criminal Asylum in Anglo-Saxon Law*, University of Florida Monographs 18, Gainesville.

Robertson, A. J. 1925, *The Laws of the Kings of England from Edmund to Henry I*, Cambridge.

Sørensen, P. Meulengracht 1993, *Fortælling og ære. Studier i islændingesagaerne*, Aarhus.

Stokes, W. and Strachan, J. (eds.) 1901-3, *Thesaurus Palaeohibernicus*, 2 vols., Cambridge.

Tanguy, B. 1984, 'La troménie de Gouesnou. Contribution à l'histoire des minihis en Bretagne', *Annales de Bretagne*, 91, pp. 9-25.

Timbal Duclaux de Martin, P. 1939, *Le droit d'asile*, Paris.

Watson, W. J. 1926, *The History of the Celtic Place-Names of Scotland*, Edinburgh.

Notes

[1] I owe thanks to Professor Richard Bailey, whose comments in a coach on a trip to Luss first stimulated me to think about these issues.

[2] Note that even in late eleventh-century Cheshire offences in the homestead - *in domo* - carried a special fine (*Cheshire Domesday*, C4 (i. 262v)).

[3] Violation of the legal protection of a freeman by killing or injuring someone under protection was the offence known as *díguin* in Irish law. Binchy (1941: 83) points out that the meaning of *díguin* extended to include 'breach of house-peace', where the 'house-peace' encompassed the surrounding precinct as well as the house.

[4] Although, if a king presided at a meeting, it would of course reinforce the safe status of the occasion.

[5] In Ireland, at least, the limits also included certain types of person; some could never be protected - a runaway slave, a runaway wife, a killer, a son who failed to look after his father; this clearly distinguishes the rules about protection from those about sanctuary (Kelly 1988: 141).

6 Breton *minihi* (< Latin *monachia*, monastic land) may have been used in a fashion similar to *noddfa*, although its usages were clearly various (Chédeville and Tonnerre 1987: 354-8). The vernacular term was in use already in the mid-ninth century (*Cartulaire de Redon* nos. 141, 142, 181, 193), although it is not clear that it had any meaning at that period beyond 'monastic land' - some of which was already in lay hands. From the later middle ages the term meant sanctuary, in the conventional sense (Tanguy 1984: 24). The place-name *minihi* tends to occur in western Brittany and also in the North East (Le Moing 1988: ii.78; Le Moing 1990: 234; Tanguy 1984). Most frequently of parish size (eg Gouesnou, Locronan), a few *minihi* were enormous (more than eleven parishes round Tréguier) and some were very much smaller than the parish (eg Gouézec); they were sometimes marked out by crosses. Given the parish size of the majority, it is worth considering the possibility that the *minihi* took on the meaning of ecclesiastical protected space in the tenth and eleventh centuries; the Life of St Goulven emphasizes the inviolability of the saint's space at Goulven, Finistère (Tanguy 1984: 21-2).

7 I am extremely grateful to Professor Geoffrey Barrow for supplying me with references to girths and *tearmann* names after the February conference.

8 For the anglicized Irish word *comrick*, 'legal protection', which was used in English official documents in Ireland in the late middle ages and early modern period, see Kelly 1988: 141n; also Binchy 1941: 107, on different Irish words for 'protection'. (Irish *commairce*, and other words for protection, seem to have replaced *snádud* in the later middle ages.)

9 It is also unlikely that monastic *valla*, earthworks delimiting an area around a monastery, as identified in Ireland, were to delimit 'protected space': they define much smaller areas than the protected spaces we know about (Edwards 1990: 106-12).

10 However, unusually, St Denis claimed a large area (Timbal Duclaux de Martin 1939: 160).

11 Of course, continental ecclesiastical immunities may have *looked like* 'protected space' in the insular sense in the tenth and eleventh centuries, but they were different in their operation (Davies and Fouracre 1995: 12-16, 256-8); see further, Appendix.

12 There is a germ of the protective notion in *Hibernensis* XLIV.8, with its warnings against the violation of holy places by homicide and theft, but the starting point is different - pollution of the holy - and at this stage the penalties appear to be purely ecclesiastical (ie penance). There is another germ of comparability in that penances were graded in accordance with the status of the sanctuary as well as the nature of the offence - a recognition of the importance of status (cf. Doherty 1985: 57-8). Within another couple of centuries some churches were claiming a right to secular penalties (*díre*) - not just penance - for offences committed by laymen within the *termonn*, enforced by secular rulers (*Cáin Adamnáin*, 36). Though the conceptual approach is different here, the application of such claims must have had effects which were indistinguishable from the effects of violation of protected space; in other words, when such claims came to be acknowledged, the *termonn* became like the *noddfa*.

13 There were strong feelings at the conference that the Irish and western Scottish development must have been earlier. The Irish development could of course have been precocious; but the signs are that (i) the Irish *termonn* in the seventh and eighth centuries essentially marked out a place of refuge, safety and safe-keeping, as it continued to do in the central and later middle ages (Lucas 1967); (ii) some of the *termonn* lands took on the attributes of a protected area in the ninth/tenth centuries (see also above, n. 12). Apart from the claims of seventh-century Armagh to an unbelievably large area within its *terminus*, we have little idea of the size of the *termonn* in the early middle ages. All this would benefit from a much closer and more systematic examination - and a closer look at what happened inside a *termonn*.

14 I understand that Dr Brian Golding, of the University of Southampton, is currently working on a book on English sanctuary; this will be a very welcome addition to the existing literature.

15 I am very grateful to my colleague David d'Avray for assistance with canonist texts.

XVI

CELTIC KINGSHIPS IN THE EARLY MIDDLE AGES

There is an eighth-century Irish law text about status which—in discussing the status of the king (*rí*)—explains what a king does on each day of the week: Sunday for beer-drinking, Monday for dealing with disputes between peoples, Tuesday for board games, Wednesday for following the hounds, Thursday for marital intercourse, Friday for horse-racing, Saturday for judgments.[1] In other words, it defines the royal function as judgment, foreign policy, playing games and getting drunk; the king has very limited practical functions and is *conspicuously* idle; he is a person of leisure; indeed, earlier in the text, he loses status if he does manual work.[2]

The image of kingship that we find in this and related Irish texts has often been used as a stereotype for 'Celtic' kingship: a small-scale ruler with no regulatory powers and with very little experience of, or aptitude for, government; whose office symbolized the identity of the group he led; whose inauguration was accompanied by bizarre ceremonials that symbolized his mating with the land (or the tribal goddess); who did extraordinarily little, but by his very being guaranteed both security and good fortune for the group. This is the king called sacral and tribal by many modern scholars, and—more graphi-

---

[1] *Críth Gablach*, edited by D. A. Binchy, Mediaeval and Modern Irish Series, 11 (Dublin, 1941), c. 41. See the comments of Thomas Charles-Edwards, 'A Contract between King and People in Early Medieval Ireland? *Críth Gablach* on Kingship', forthcoming; I am most grateful to Dr Charles-Edwards for allowing me to see this paper in advance of publication.

[2] *Críth Gablach*, c. 40.

cally—the 'priestly vegetable' by Patrick Wormald.[3] It is a kingship which is pre-eminently passive, non-bureaucratic, and charismatic.

The ideology that we find in this and related texts is clear enough; the texts are well placed in time and space and relate to Ireland in the seventh and eighth centuries. But even in seventh-century Ireland, one can find alternative images and there are certainly plenty of alternatives to be found in other Celtic areas; hence, it must at the outset be questionable whether the passive, charismatic model of kingship is applicable to all—or any—Celtic areas in the historic period. Consider, for contrast, some of these alternative images. There is, for example, the tyrant king Benlli of Powys in north Wales, who used to kill anyone who did not arrive for work before sunrise, as related by the early ninth-century *Historia Brittonum*.[4] The image of rulership here is overwhelmingly one of power and maleficence: the ruler interferes in the private lives of his subjects; the ruler causes trouble; the ruler is pre-eminently *active*.

Or, a story from the earliest (ninth-century) Life of Machutes (Saint Malo), of a common type: the ruler of northern Brittany, Hailoch, tried to destroy Saint Malo's monastic church; he was therefore blinded; but he went to seek pardon for his dreadful deed, and gave the saint some excellent and fertile lands as well as gold and silver; the blinding was then miraculously lifted. This is a type of story repeated in many later Welsh Lives, and other texts: rulers raided, rounded up cattle, burnt barns, and pursued and attacked those who opposed them. The climax of the stories usually demonstrates

---

[3] For the 'priestly vegetable', see P. Wormald, 'Celtic and Anglo-Saxon Kingship: Some Further Thoughts', in *Sources of Anglo-Saxon Culture*, edited by P. E. Szarmach with V. D. Oggins, Studies in Medieval Culture, 20 (Kalamazoo, 1986), pp. 151–83, at p. 153. The most frequently cited inauguration ceremony is the supposed bathing in mare's broth reported by Giraldus Cambrensis; see F. J. Byrne, *Irish Kings and High-Kings* (London, 1973), pp. 17–18. For the stereotype, see D. A. Binchy, *Celtic and Anglo-Saxon Kingship* (Oxford, 1970), pp. 8–11. Other texts: *Audacht Morainn*, edited by F. Kelly (Dublin, 1976), and discussion at pp. xiii–xvi.

[4] *Historia Brittonum*, cc. 32–3, in *Chronica Minora Saec. IV. V. VI. VII.*, III, edited by T. Mommsen, *MGH AA*, XIII (Berlin, 1898), 111–222, at pp. 172–5.

that when the ruler (or his men) entered ecclesiastical property, terrible disasters struck: they were blinded; the earth swallowed them up; the stolen cattle would not cook when put in the pot, and so on.[5] The principal purpose of telling such tales is to make a point about ecclesiastical immunities, but what is interesting in the present context is the emphasis on the king as enemy (arch enemy); kings are raiders, thieves, destroyers; they are people to be feared, people of power again, and also—explicitly—of violence. When the hagiographers wanted to typify a raider, again and again they chose a king as their example.

Or a last example, from Adomnán's Life of Columba, written c. 700 by an Irish abbot on a Scottish island, about people in Scotland: some of Saint Columba's disciples set sail on spiritual journeys, they knew not whither; fearing for their safety when they landed, Columba went to the great king Brude (a Pict) and told him to instruct the king of the Orkneys, whose hostages Brude was holding, to safeguard the lives of the saint's disciples if they should land on the islands. A certain Cormac *did* land on the Orkneys and he was preserved from death because of Columba's intervention with Brude, Adomnán would have us believe. Here again is an image of power, but effective power, used for beneficent purposes.[6]

Images of kingship will vary in accordance with the type of text and perspective of the author, in Celtic areas as in any other parts—even though they are all in some way Christian and are all subject to the influence of biblical models. There are many different images of Celtic kingship to be found, and many of them are extremely unlike the *Críth Gablach* view of the king's week with which I began. In many parts the stereotype of royal behaviour was more likely to stress the activity of the king, his power, and his propensity to command, than the passive, sacral character of a man who guaranteed good fortune.

---

[5] *Prima Vita Machutis*, c. 19, in F. Lot, *Mélanges d'histoire bretonne* (Paris, 1907), pp. 294–329, at pp. 318–19; cf., *passim*, *Vitae Sanctorum Britanniae et Genealogiae*, edited by A. W. Wade-Evans, Board of Celtic Studies History and Law Series, 9 (Cardiff, 1944).

[6] *Adomnán's Life of Columba*, edited by A. O. and M. O. Anderson (London, 1961), II, 42.

The differences between images do not have to be confusing and can, indeed, be useful; they remind us that perspective varies with the eye of the beholder and they alert us to the possibility, indeed likelihood, of differences between the kingships of different Celtic areas. In what follows, I want to develop your appreciation of the differences between political institutions in Celtic areas in the early middle ages, and then go on to consider their significance for our understanding of the nature and working of Celtic societies and the roles of the king in those societies.

My concern is with the six Celtic countries of Ireland, Scotland, the Isle of Man, Wales, Cornwall/Dumnonia and Brittany; and it is with the early middle ages, that is the period before the impact of the several Norman conquests and infiltrations. Normans were influencing Brittany by the early eleventh century, Wales and Scotland by the late eleventh century, and Ireland by the mid-twelfth. Dumnonia had already been conquered by the English in the late ninth/early tenth century; and the Isle of Man, about which very little evidence survives, was politically dominated by Norse rulers from about the middle of the ninth century. These countries are 'Celtic' because their vernacular languages were Celtic during the early middle ages (and in parts remain so to this day), although the vernaculars were increasingly interpenetrated with English, French and Norse as conquests introduced the settlement of foreigners and involved the areas in wider political cultures. However, even in the very early middle ages the commonness of Celtic was itself diverse: there are two broad linguistic divisions, that between Gaelic (or Q-Celtic), the language of Ireland and western Scotland, and Brittonic (or P-Celtic), the language group of the rest; by the eighth century the separate Brittonic languages of Cumbric, Welsh and Cornish/Breton were distinguishable.[7] We should therefore remember that people did not all speak the same language in Celtic areas, even in the early middle ages, and only a few of the Celtic languages were mutually intelligible.

Although my concern is with the early middle ages as a whole, in

---

[7] K. Jackson, *Language and History in Early Britain* (Edinburgh, 1953); Cornish and Breton were interchangeable at this date and not distinguishable as separate languages before the eleventh century.

the broad sense of the sixth to the eleventh centuries inclusive, it is essential to point out that the source material available for Celtic areas is varied in quality and non-existent at some periods in some places. On the whole, Irish material is plentiful from the seventh century, and of varied types, both in Latin and the vernacular; Welsh material is extremely unevenly distributed, and fuller for the South East than for other parts; Breton sources are exceptionally rich for the ninth century but almost non-existent for seventh, eighth and tenth centuries; Cornish and Scottish sources are very thin; and Man sources barely exist at all before the late eleventh century. This makes comparison difficult, and always tends to make the Irish perspective the most prominent.

Whether the sources are rich or scanty, times change and 600 years is a very long time. Quite apart from the impact of foreign invasion and infiltration of foreign influence, it is only reasonable to suppose (and indeed it is often demonstrable) that these societies changed between 500 and 1100 AD, and between 500 and 800, 700 and 900, and so on. While remaining aware of developments within the longer term, I shall therefore focus this paper on the century round about 800–900 AD, a time for which there is reasonably comparable source material for all areas except the Isle of Man and Cornwall, and a time removed both from the impenetrably obscure relationships and institutions of the sixth century and from the rapidly increasing cross-cultural interchange of the eleventh. Although a full study would involve consideration of inauguration, income, succession, and so on, I shall focus on issues of scale, political system and royal function, since comparison is particularly instructive in these respects. My interest, of course, is primarily in the broad lines of comparative analysis rather than in the particularities of detail in any one area.

Scale

Whether we are considering the year 500 or the year 1100, Ireland was a land of many kings and thereby of exceptionally small kingdoms—the land of *rí* and *tuath*, 'king' (cognate with *rex*) and 'people'.[8] Estimates of the number of *tuatha* vary between 80 and 150, often calculated by reference to later baronies, for we have no way of making a precise calculation at any point in the pre-Norman period.[9] However, it must be relevant that references to different peoples in the sixth, seventh and eighth centuries are many and are consistent with estimates in the order of 100 *tuatha* round about 800 AD.[10] Given the size of Ireland, here is a political structure whose basic units were of the order of 10–12 miles radius and 375 square miles in area. In fact, the political structure was more complex than this, since there were overkings (*ruirí*) as well as kings, and over time the range and powers of overkings developed and increased. Over time the number of *tuatha* seems to have declined somewhat, as also the independence of some of the *rí*, and by the middle of the eleventh century the classic pattern of many small kingdoms with some fluctuating overkingships was obviously changing. However, even at that date kingship was still conceptualized in terms of *rí* and *tuath* and there remained many small, sometimes independent, political units.[11]

---

[8] See F. J. Byrne, 'Tribes and Tribalism in Early Ireland', *Ériu*, XXII (1971), 128–66, for a very helpful discussion of the range of reference of the word *tuath* in the early middle ages.

[9] But see A. P. Smyth, *Celtic Leinster* (Blackrock, 1982), for a very imaginative attempt to reconstruct some; see especially 'Historical Atlas', pp. 139–57.

[10] Cf. the 50 or so kings named in the list of those agreeing to Cáin Adomnáin, kings who came from the orbit influenced by Iona; M. Ní Dhonnchadha,'The Guarantor List of *Cáin Adomnáin*, 697', *Peritia*, I (1982), 178–215, at pp. 180–1.

[11] See below, pp. 110–12, for further discussion of overkings. See D. Ó Corráin, 'Nationality and Kingship in pre-Norman Ireland', in *Nationality and the Pursuit of National Independence*, edited by T. W. Moody (Belfast, 1978), pp. 1–35, for a useful discussion of the changing pattern of kingship, especially at pp. 9–11. He is right to point out that there is occasional reference to the leaders of some *tuatha* as *duces* rather than *reges* from 756, but the proportion of cases is tiny and the change in terminology was not always sustained. Compare the eleventh-century Kells charters, which list local rulers and refer to each as *rí*; *Notitiae as Leabhar Cheanannais*, edited by G. Mac Niocaill (Dublin, 1961). Further, though a few *tuatha* were clearly 'taken over' by others from the mid-eighth century, what is significant is that their independent identity continued—for centuries: when an Uí Néill ruler

The political language of the Annals up to the early twelfth century is still overwhelmingly dominated by the words *rex* and *rí*, although *toísech* (leader) and *tigerna* (lord) undoubtedly sometimes occur in eleventh- and twelfth-century texts. Kingship continued to be defined at the small-scale base level.

By the eleventh century—indeed by the tenth—the political structure of Scotland was quite different; but its earlier background was also different and reflected the presence of different linguistic groups. While it is not impossible that there were three or four Irish-type *tuatha* in the Irish-settled parts of south-western Scotland in the sixth century, what we know of other parts suggests larger units at that early date. British kingdoms of the Lowlands were in the order of 40 miles across, 1250 square miles in area; while, if Pictland to the east and north comprised the seven regions of tradition, as it may have done, then those regions were of a comparable or larger size. It is difficult to be certain about this background because of problems of evidence. What *is* clear is that by the eighth century an extremely powerful single Pictish kingdom had been established, of vastly greater size, and that in the middle of the ninth century a single monarchy of a larger kingdom of Scotland came into being. Over the tenth and eleventh centuries this kingdom had a complex relationship with resident and attacking Scandinavians but it came to absorb the last remaining British kingdom, Strathclyde, and came to acquire a size and shape comparable to that of modern Scotland. Even by 900, however, its size was of the order of 20,000 square miles.[12]

Brittany looks in some ways similar to Scotland, since a wide-ranging single monarchy was established in the peninsula in the mid-ninth century. However, its background was quite different: there had been several, independent regional rulerships in the area, of a scale comparable to the British kingdoms of early Scotland, but these were not normally described as kingdoms; I know of no surviving ideology

---

took over the Corco Sogain *tuath* in 816, he became *rex Corco Sogain*. Byrne, *Irish Kings and High-Kings*, cc. 1–3, remains an exceptionally good overview of Irish kingship.

[12] See A. A. M. Duncan, *Scotland, the Making of the Kingdom*, Edinburgh History of Scotland, I (Edinburgh, 1975), for a good general survey.

of kingship from early Brittany.[13] The establishment of the ninth-century monarchy arose in response to the very particular circumstance of Carolingian conquest. The Breton Nominoe took responsibility for the whole peninsula in the 830s, initially as an agent of the Carolingians. His successors Erispoe and—especially—Salomon acted more independently and were usually referred to as *principes*, and occasionally *reges*.[14] Though relationships with Frankish rulers fluctuated in the later ninth century, this period was crucial to the formation of the political identity of Brittany; the Breton *principes* behaved as independent rulers and dealt with Brittany as if it were a separate state. This was short-lived as a *royal* monarchy for the rulers of Brittany became known as dukes of the west Frankish kingdom in the tenth century. The extent to which they were independent of the French monarchy in the period before their full integration with France in the late fifteenth century varied with French, English and Norman politics, but was often considerable. However, the events of the ninth century still remained significant since centralized institutions of government for the peninsula had been established then and continued thereafter, whether they were termed royal or ducal. Brittany took its shape from the ninth-century developments, and became a state of about half the size of Scotland (13600 square miles).

Dumnonia is also similar, in the sense that we have no knowledge of any political unit other than the single relatively large monarchy evidenced in the early sixth century; nothing suggests the existence of any other political units. This unit initially comprised much of the

---

[13] See W. Davies, *Small Worlds* (London, 1988), pp. 13–24, for a summary of developments; for longer discussions, A. Le Moyne de la Borderie, *Histoire de Bretagne*, 6 vols (Rennes, 1896–1904), I–II, and A. Chédeville and H. Guillotel, *La Bretagne des saints et des rois, v^e–xe siècle* (Rennes, 1984). There is one reference to a ruler as *rex* in the pre-ninth-century period, and that is in a Frankish source; *The Fourth Book of the Chronicle of Fredegar*, translated by J. M. Wallace-Hadrill (London, 1960), c. 78, at p. 66. There is a gloss (*ri* on *regie*) which implies that the vernacular language of kingship remained in use—at least among scholars; L. Fleuriot, *Dictionnaire du vieux breton*, Collection Linguistique, 62 (Paris, 1964), p. 296.

[14] See now J. M. H. Smith, *Province and Empire* (Cambridge, 1992) for a detailed analysis of the Frankish relationship.

Celtic Kingships

south-western peninsula of England—Cornwall, Devon, and parts of Somerset and Dorset—and was half the size of Brittany. Over the course of the seventh century English conquest confined this kingdom to the area of modern Cornwall, something in the order of 1350 square miles; the English sustained their interest in the county and filtered first into east Cornwall and finally by the early tenth century into the far west. The last king of Cornwall drowned in 875; there is no trace of any later Cornish rulers, either dependent or independent. The West Saxon king Egbert made grants of Cornish property in the early ninth century and King Alfred included Cornish lands in the bequests detailed in his will; King Athelstan seems to have crushed any outstanding resistance in his campaigns of 927.[15]

The scale and relationships of kingdoms in Wales provide a different pattern. In the early centuries Wales was essentially a land of small independent kingdoms, sometimes shared between brothers, and uncomplicated by overkingship structures. In the late sixth century in the South East there are hints of the existence of small kingdoms on the Irish scale but in other parts there is only reference to larger kingdoms, comparable to the British kingdoms of the Scottish Lowlands. Over time some kingdoms thrived and absorbed others, so that the number of units declined and the size of the remaining units grew; by the tenth century Wales was a land of three principal kingdoms, Gwynedd, Dyfed and Morgannwg, as it remained until the Norman Conquest. These are kingdoms of the order of 29 miles radius, 2700 square miles area.[16]

In all areas structures changed over time, and scale was not therefore a constant. It is not the purpose of this paper to investigate the different reasons for change but it is relevant to its subject to be aware that each area had a different starting point and that the structures changed in different ways. Wales, Dumnonia, and Brittany all had a background of government through the provincial structure of the Roman Empire, as did the Scottish Lowlands for a time; the kingdoms that emerged in these areas commonly (though not invari-

---

[15] Susan M. Pearce, *The Kingdom of Dumnonia* (Padstow, 1978).
[16] W. Davies, *Wales in the Early Middle Ages* (Leicester, 1982), pp. 85–120, for a general survey.

ably) took their shape from Roman *civitates*; so, insofar as there is a commonness in their initial size and shape in the early middle ages, that is strongly influenced by their Roman backgrounds. The Irish model, conveyed so powerfully in *Críth Gablach* and other texts, relates to institutions on an entirely different scale from those that we find in other Celtic areas, with the exception of the Isle of Man:

	Ireland	*Scotland*	*Brittany*	*Dumnonia*	*Wales*
700AD	375	375/13200	2700	1350	1250
900AD	375	21600	13600	—	2700
i.e.	1	1 / x35	x 7	x 4	x 3
	1	x 58	x 36	—	x 7

(These figures do not pretend to offer a precise definition of territory in each case, for they are estimates designed to emphasize the order of difference.)

For Man, one can only make flimsy guesses about the early political structure: the Welsh collection of genealogies in BL MS Harleian 3859 includes the genealogy of a Brittonic Man dynasty, whose kings peter out at a period consistent with the eighth century, while later Welsh collections claim a royal female from Man as an ancestor of the Gwynedd kings.[17] If there is anything in this, it suggests Man was a tiny British kingdom, about half the size of the Irish *tuath*. Certainly, much later, there were kings of Man who ruled this small province together with the Western Isles of Scotland, although often subject to the domination of Norwegian rulers.[18]

Political Systems

Overkingship was fundamental to the Irish political system, as much in 1100 as in 500 or 800 AD. Ireland was a region characterized by a complex multiplicity of overkingships: some kings were

---

[17] P. C. Bartrum, *Early Welsh Genealogical Tracts* (Cardiff, 1966), p. 10. However, note Mr Bartrum's warning that these kings may have been of Galloway origin (p. 126).

[18] R. H. Kinvig, *The Isle of Man* (Liverpool, 3rd edn, 1975), pp. 58–66. Godred Crovan, of uncertain origin, established the kingdom in 1079.

Celtic Kingships

overkings as well as being kings, and some were overoverkings (or overkings of overkings (*rí ruirech*)). What this meant in practice was that the more powerful kings established relationships outside their own *tuatha*: they made less powerful kings their dependents, establishing client relationships with them and expecting military support and tribute from them. Thereby, some kings became clients of other kings, and powerful kings could harness military support from lesser kings (as well as from their non-royal clients). These relationships of royal dependence did not alter the fact of *rí* and *tuath* and the relationship between them: most peoples continued to relate to their kings, who continued to defend and protect them and guarantee their good fortune; the overking had a relationship with his client king, and only had a relationship with that client's people in limited and occasional circumstances.[19] In practice the *rí* did not become the agent of a powerful ruler in a more complex state.

In the early centuries overkingships were not institutionalized: their existence depended upon personal capacities of the moment and this made for extreme political instability at any level above the single *tuath*. But between 700 and 1100 AD several overkingships did become institutionalized—principally, the overkingships associated with the kingships of Tara (for the North) and Cashel (for the South), and those of Connacht (northwest) and Leinster (southeast). And in the eleventh century, some overkings levied exceptional taxes, using agents to collect them, and some attempted to enforce general laws on groups of *tuatha*. It is quite clear that the 'traditional' political

---

[19] This issue lies at the heart of the problem of characterizing the Irish political system. The identity of *tuatha* was extremely persistent, and the association of *rí* and *tuath* was exceptionally strong in Old Irish material. There were still many kings in eleventh-century Ireland. If a *tuath* lost its *rí*, however, it might in practice relate to an overking, and even *Críth Gablach* allows for the possibility in the eighth century of overkings ruling those not subject to any other ruler, and for overkings forcing *tuatha* to make agreements (*Críth Gablach*, cc. 33, 38). The critical issue is the extent to which an overking might relate to his client king's people, in normal circumstances, both in the eighth and in the eleventh centuries. Although it is perfectly clear that overkings *might* do so, at both periods, it is exceptionally difficult to ascertain the *normal* situation—at either period.

system was changing.[20] However, this did not prevent the continuing creation of other, more fragile and ephemeral, overkingships; and even in the institutionalized cases families and individuals competed for succession. Hence, Uí Briúin septs competed for the overkingship of Connacht; and Uí Dúnlainge for that of Leinster, till the Uí Cheinnselaig returned in 1042. Donnchadh and his brother Tadg fought for the kingship of the Dál Cais after their father Brian Boru's death in 1014; Muirchertach Ua Briain and his brother Diarmait fought for the overkingship of Munster in the 1080s, and so on. So, there were undoubtedly changes from the 'classic' Irish system of the eighth century during the pre-Norman period: the institutionalization of some overkingships, the increasing geographical scale of the major overkingships, the disappearance of some *tuatha*; nevertheless, many individual *tuatha* did continue, as did the multiplicity of kings and the variability of overkingship patterns.[21]

In other Celtic areas, the exercise of kingship was much less complicated by overkings. I know of no hints of overkingship within Brittany or Dumnonia, either early or late. There were counts and there were rulers' agents to carry out the rulers' business; by the late ninth century the rulers of Brittany also had some vassals; but the agents and vassals were not themselves rulers of independent peoples.[22] Although it is not impossible that both Irish and Picts in early Scotland knew overkings—the sixth-century Brude incident cited above certainly suggests that this is what Adomnán expected c. 700, from his Iona perspective—by 800 (and for most of the eighth century) the large Pictish kingdom seems to have been organized as a monarchy.[23] The Pictish king had his agents, as had his Breton

---

[20] Ó Corráin, 'Nationality and Kingship', pp. 20, 23.
[21] Ó Corráin, 'Nationality and Kingship', pp. 9–10, 25–6.
[22] Davies, *Small Worlds*, pp. 184–6, 201–07. I am *not* considering here the intermittent relationship between Breton rulers and Frankish kings in the ninth century, which—when it existed—could be deemed a type of overkingship, though an overkingship *external* to Brittany; for this, see Smith, *Province and Empire*, especially pp. 108–15.
[23] *The Annals of Ulster (to AD 1131)*, edited by S. Mac Airt and G. Mac Niocaill (Dublin, 1983), *s.a.* 739: the king of Athol was drowned by the king of the Picts; this is a unique reference, but it must imply the existence of at

Celtic Kingships

counterpart, and some agents may have had regional responsibilities.[24] It looks as if the expanded Scottish kingdom of the later ninth century and later—again a monarchy—took over the administrative institutions of the developed Pictish state: by the eleventh century we certainly find royal agents (defined by a Brittonic term, *mormaers*) with regional responsibilities.[25] There was undoubtedly development in Scotland just as there was in Ireland, but the Scottish development neither built upon nor utilized overkingly relationships.

Although it is quite reasonable to suggest that some early kings of Wales were more prominent, and therefore more powerful than others, I know of nothing which suggests that overkingship was a significant institution in Wales before 900. The early kings were independent. However, in the later ninth, tenth and eleventh centuries power relationships changed: firstly, the interest expressed by Engish kings in Wales led to the creation of dependent relationships between Welsh kings. The English kings from Alfred to Edgar expected 'submission' and occasional attendance at their courts in England, and they sometimes demanded military assistance and tribute; they did not, however, interfere directly in Welsh affairs. In effect, the English became overkings of many of the Welsh kings. Although the English relationship with Wales weakened considerably from the 950s, it is quite clear that the experience had repercussions within Wales: the leading Welsh kings of the later tenth and eleventh centuries sought the submission of their weaker neighbours. Overkingship therefore *became* prominent in Wales, where once it had been insignificant.[26]

There is therefore a further striking contrast between kingship in Ireland and in other Celtic areas: whereas overkingship was charac-

---

least some regional kings. Such traces, and ambiguities, disappear by 800. *Historia Brittonum*, c. 57, and *Bede's Ecclesiastical History of the English People*, edited by B. Colgrave and R. A. B. Mynors (Oxford, 1969), v. 21: king of the Picts.

[24] *Exactatores* (presumably tax collectors) of Nechtan, *Annals of Ulster*, s.a. 729. G. W. S. Barrow, *The Kingdom of the Scots* (London, 1973), pp. 30–68.

[25] Barrow, *Kingdom of Scots*, p. 67; cf. K. Jackson, *The Gaelic Notes in the Book of Deer* (Cambridge, 1972), pp. 19, 101–10.

[26] W. Davies, *Patterns of Power in Early Wales* (Oxford, 1990), pp. 67–79.

teristic of the political structure of Ireland throughout the early middle ages, and indeed became even more prominent in the eleventh century, it was neither characteristic nor even present in some other parts. In Brittany, in particular, and in the developing kingdom of Scotland other means of sustaining wide-ranging power were used. It is easiest to grasp the difference by expressing the two alternatives in an extreme form; on the one hand there were the complex and competing structures of Irish royal clientship, providing power, honour and status, and military support, for the successful overking but scarcely touching the life of the majority of the Irish population; and on the other the Breton or Scottish royal monarchy, with a central ruler controlling a wide area of territory and several groups of people, using royal agents to represent him about the territory and execute his will. This of course oversimplifies; and in practice would-be monarchs were not successful in their attempts to reach to the farthest parts of their kingdoms. However, there remains an essential difference between the man who is both king and client, whose role is to do his own business, and the man who is a royal agent, whose role is to do the king's business. The one succeeds through family rights, the other is appointed. There is also an essential difference between the ruler (overking) whose authority is limited to the inhabitants of a small zone, and a band of personal clients, and the ruler (monarch) who claims authority over all the people in a wide territory. The one deals in small numbers, the other in large; the one can move about his territory of rule on a daily basis if he has a horse, the other cannot possibly do so except at very infrequent intervals; the one can personally be known to all of the ruled, the other can be known to only a tiny proportion of them. Of course, these cases were not in practice so extreme: heredity would hang about the agent and the mechanisms of royal succession were far from straightforward. Any ruler's independence and autonomy were necessarily relative, and circumscribed by the powers of neighbours. And there were places—like Wales—with a complex mixture of systems. But there still remains a difference between the political system (like the monarchies) which begins to think about the government of subjects—however imperfectly—and the system (like the overkingships) which is essentially for the purpose of raising military support for the ruler, to sustain him in power.

Function

What were kings for? What roles were they acknowledged to have, regardless of whether or not they performed them, or performed them well?

For all the differences in political systems, there were some functions that were common to Celtic kings. Both in theory and in practice kings tended to be the representatives of their kingdoms, negotiating with external agencies on behalf of their peoples. They met the first Christian missionaries and permitted them to preach; they wrote to foreign authorities for advice on religious doctrine, like Nechtan of the Picts; they made treaties with foreign rulers—over borders and other matters of common interest; they made alliances with foreign rulers, against enemies like the Vikings.[27] They also almost invariably had responsibility for the physical defence of their kingdoms against enemies, often through their own personal military capacity: these men were fighters, warrior leaders. The Breton ruler Salomon could not go on pilgrimage to Rome, as he wished, but had to stay and defend the Bretons against the Vikings; in Connacht, the Uí Maine king Cathal mac Murchad, and his nobles, fell at the battle of Forath in 818, and two kings of the Uí Briúin were successful (Diarmait mac Tomaltach and Máel Cothaid mac Fogartach); the Gwynedd king Rhodri died fighting the English in north Wales in the late ninth century; the Pictish king Elpin fled the battlefield in 728, and the would-be king Conall escaped the field of battle in 789, after his defeat by Constantine.[28] In these two respects kingship was very

---

[27] For example: Patrick, *Confessio*, cc. 52, 53, in L. Bieler,'Libri epistolarum Sancti Patricii Episcopi', *Classica et mediaevalia*, XI (1950), 1–150, XII (1951), 79–214; *Bede's Ecclesiastical History*, v. 21; *The Text of the Book of Llan Dâv*, edited by J. G. Evans with J. Rhys (Oxford: [published privately by JGE for subscribers], 1893), no. 192; Salomon and Franks against the Vikings, *Annales de Saint-Bertin*, edited by F. Grat, J. Vielliard, S. Clémencet (Paris, 1964), *s.a.* 868, 873 (pp. 151, 193–5); cf. *Bede's Ecclesiastical History*, iv. 26.

[28] *Cartulaire de Redon*, edited by A. de Courson, Collection de documents inédits sur l'histoire de France (Paris, 1863), no. 247; *Annals of Ulster, s.a.* 818; *Annales Cambriae, s.a.* 877, in E. Phillimore,'The "Annales Cambriae" and Old-Welsh Genealogies from "Harleian MS." 3859', *Y Cymmrodor*, IX

similar in all Celtic areas.

However, other royal functions differed, especially in relation to the conduct of business and the regulation of society. Responsibility for the formulation and expression of normative principles—laws—varied considerably and was not necessarily a royal prerogative. However, a case can certainly be made that law-making was a distinctively royal function in Pictland in the eighth and ninth centuries.[29] In Ireland, law-making was distinctively *not* a royal function. Both Ireland and Wales had cultures with powerful bodies of professional lawyers, whose function it was to collect, preserve, remember, declare and formulate (and therefore in practice modify) customary law. In Ireland there were certainly circumstances in which a king might make special commands, new rules, for the good of his *tuath*—in times of plague or invasion, or in support of ecclesiastical regulations (*cána*)—but these were exceptional circumstances requiring an immediate or forceful reaction; they were not the norm.[30] In Wales too kings were expected to make commands for the regulation of their territories by the tenth and eleventh centuries.[31] It may also be observed that one king's name, that of Hywel Dda, has been strongly associated with the collecting of Welsh law texts. Although it is extremely difficult to establish precisely the part that Hywel played in the tenth century, it is by no means impossible that he took some such initiative—perhaps conditioned by his experience at the English court. However, even if this was so, the vast bulk of the law remained customary, the initiative remains exceptional, and

---

(1888); *Annals of Ulster*, s.a. 728, 789.

[29] See M. O. Anderson, 'Dalriada and the Creation of the Kingdom of the Scots', in *Ireland in Early Mediaeval Europe*, edited by D. Whitelock, R. McKitterick, D. Dumville (Cambridge, 1982), pp. 106–32, at pp. 121–3; Wormald, 'Celtic and Anglo-Saxon Kingship', p. 169.

[30] F. Kelly, *A Guide to Early Irish Law* (Dublin, 1988), pp. 21–2; Binchy, *Críth Gablach*, p. 104; the parties to the promulgation of the ecclesiastical law Cáin Adomnáin, c. 697, included over fifty kings (Ní Dhonnchadha, 'Guarantor List of *Cáin Adomnáin*', pp. 180–1). NB: clerics were among the legal professionals and some played a significant part in the preservation and study of the law; see Ó Corráin, 'Nationality and Kingship', pp. 14–15.

[31] See Davies, *Patterns of Power*, pp. 81–3.

the legal profession thrived throughout the middle ages.[32] Brittany is remarkably different in that there is no early medieval evidence of the existence of professional lawyers and very little written law of any type; in view of the wealth of ninth-century evidence, its absence is very striking.[33] Customary principles were obviously followed, but no-one made a business of recording them; and rulers made no show either of innovating or of controlling the process of recording.[34] Rulership was exceptionally dis-associated from rule-making and rule-collecting. In law-making, then, it looks as if Pictish kings might have had a major role, Breton rulers had no role, and Irish and Welsh kings had some role, though a role limited by the expertise and interest of professional lawyers.

Kings also played different parts in 'keeping order' in their societies. In all areas, as in much of western Europe, mechanisms for keeping order were largely private. And so, the use of sureties to guarantee contracts and dispute settlements was widespread.[35] By this means private individuals selected reputable, and acceptable,

---

[32] *Welsh History Review: Special Number on The Welsh Laws*, edited by G. Williams (Cardiff, 1963); D. Jenkins, *The Law of Hywel Dda* (Llandysul, 1986), pp. xi–xx. NB the occurrence of the lawyer Blegywryd in the mid-tenth century, *Book of Llan Dâv*, no. 218.

[33] There were some people interested in law in Brittany, however, since several collections of Irish canonical material have a Breton origin, and some have Breton glosses; at least one collection (Paris, BN lat. 12021) was made in Brittany for an abbot; see *The Irish Penitentials*, edited by L. Bieler, Scriptores Latini Hiberniae, 5 (Dublin, 1963), pp. 12–16.

[34] W. Davies, 'Disputes, their conduct and their settlement in the village communities of eastern Brittany in the ninth century', *History and Anthropology*, I. ii (1985), 289–312, at pp. 306–08. There are a couple of advocates mentioned in the Redon cartulary, but there is no reason to suppose that they were professionals; they were agents who spoke for women: Davies, *Small Worlds*, p. 170.

[35] D. B. Walters, 'The General Features of Archaic European Suretyship', and W. Davies, 'Suretyship in the *Cartulaire de Redon*', both in *Lawyers and Laymen*, edited by T. M. Charles-Edwards, M. E. Owen and D. B. Walters (Cardiff, 1986). I do not know of any early medieval Scottish evidence of the use of sureties, but the lacuna could be explained by the paucity of evidence in general.

members of the community to make sure that arrangements were carried out as agreed; if a problem subsequently occurred the surety might make reparations from his own means or force the defaulting party to meet his obligations. But occasionally an element of the public entered into the treatment of offences to the individual, and kings might then take a role. In Scotland, by the eleventh century, there was a royal officer (*mair*) who arrested those suspected of committing offences; bad behaviour was clearly a royal responsibility, and the king had agents whose duty it was to see that the royal responsibility was carried out.[36] In Brittany in the ninth century, although the ruler would require aristocratic defaulters to answer for their behaviour at his own court—if, for example, they were accused of looting or burning in a locality—at village level the initiatives were local and non-royal. (In other words, it was the status of the person that involved the ruler, *not* the nature of the offence.) Accusations would be made and proceedings started by peasants acting as private, and often aggrieved, individuals; sureties, and occasionally machtierns, would pursue defaulters. There is one famous case in which it is made clear that the sureties were charged to pursue a persistent defaulter and kill him, should he offend again. Neither the ruler nor his agent had a part in these processes.[37] In Wales, there is eleventh-century south-eastern material which makes it absolutely clear that in cases of theft it was the reponsibility of the local community to pursue the thief, like the later English 'hue and cry'. The law tracts suggest that it was the reponsibility of landowners, *qua* landowner, to apprehend suspects. A useful earlier text from the borders of Wales, the so-called 'Ordinance of the Dunsaete', goes some way towards combining the two approaches: when cattle are stolen, the men of the locality take up the trail, but when they cross the river bank it is then the landowner's responsibility to conduct an enquiry (or produce compensation himself). In none of these cases, however,

---

[36] Barrow, *Kingdom of Scots*, pp. 67–8. NB 'mormaer', *Annals of Ulster, s.a.* 1032.

[37] Davies, 'Disputes'; eadem, *Small Worlds*, pp. 146–54. There is only one case evidenced of machtiern responsibility (*Cart. Redon*, no. 265), but this could well have been more common; for machtierns see Davies, *Small Worlds*, pp. 138–42.

Celtic Kingships

does any of this appear to have been a royal responsibility or interest.[38] In Ireland it appears to have been a family responsibility to initiate action and arrest defaulters (sometimes with the assistance of their lord, if they had one). The family might distrain on the property of an alleged offender in order to provoke redress, with the assistance of professional lawyers.[39] Once a settlement had been made the powers of sureties came into play. So, with respect to order, the Scottish king had responsibilities, where the Welsh and Irish did not; and the Breton ruler did, *de facto*, if the offender's status was high enough.

When it came to making judgments about defaulters and about disputes, practice again varied. In Ireland, it was essentially lawyers—professionals, experienced in the law—who made the decisions, although the king might sometimes act as a lawyer and give judgments too and might also declare the lawyers' judgment in a court.[40] In strong contrast, in Brittany the business of making the actual judgment was usually carried out by panels of locals—people

---

[38] *Vita Cadoci*, c. 69, in *Vitae Sanctorum Britanniae*, edited by Wade-Evans, at p. 136; 'Ordinance of the Dunsaete', in *Die Gesetze der Angelsachsen*, edited by F. Liebermann, 3 vols (Halle, 1903–16), I, 374–9. In the tenth and eleventh centuries some punishments for offences against the church were determined in synods, sometimes in a king's presence; it is possible that the king functioned as a guarantor in such cases; Davies, *Wales*, p. 138.

[39] Kelly, *Guide*, pp. 177–86, 215–16. Already in the eighth century there were ideas about that the king should punish, but there is not much evidence that kings *did* so; *Críth Gablach*, c. 30; cf. Ó Corráin, 'Nationality and Kingship', p. 16. By virtue of their nobility, Irish nobles (including kings) had coercive powers and political authority (*flaith*); *Críth Gablach*, c. 23. See also my comments in Davies, 'Clerics as Rulers', in *Latin and the Vernacular Languages in Early Medieval Britain*, edited by N. P. Brooks (Leicester: 1982), pp. 81–97, at p. 90.

[40] Kelly, *Guide*, pp. 51–6, 193–8; R. Sharpe, 'Dispute Settlement in Medieval Ireland', in *The Settlement of Disputes in Early Medieval Europe*, edited by W. Davies and P. Fouracre (Cambridge, 1986), pp. 169–89, at pp. 182–7. NB: *iudex* for *brithem* in Ireland, perhaps emphasizing the judgment function of the lawyer; cf. *Annals of Ulster*, s.a. 802, etc. Cf. *deemsters* in the Isle of Man, whose primary function seems to have closely paralleled that of the *brithem*, i.e. knowing the (unwritten) law and making judgments in some circumstances; A. W. Moore, *A History of the Isle of Man*, 2 vols (London, 1900), II, 744–5, 756–7.

who knew the contestants and the circumstances—although aristocrats were likely to be judged by the ruler.[41] In Wales we know of groups of landowners making judgments in the ninth century, and groups of monks doing so in the eleventh century, and the (later) law texts suggest that landowners—non-professionals—did so in south Wales.[42] All we know in Scotland is that by the eleventh century a royal officer, the *iudex*, gave rulings on behalf of the king and had a prominent role in the administration of justice.[43] With respect to arriving at a judgment (rather than declaring it or assessing the penalty), the Scottish king again appears to have had a prominent role, through his agent; both the Breton and the Irish ruler *could* play a part in judgment, but characteristically it was the role of other people; as it also was in the Welsh case. Whether the king played a role or not, there is a fundamental difference between the judgment-by-professionals system of the Irish and the judgment-by-locals system of the Bretons and Welsh.

Lastly, the king's role in the conduct of business. In these societies transactions were made in public, in the presence of witnesses, so that they might be easily—and personally—verified. In Brittany this happened in village meetings, without any king or royal representative being present, and usually with the presence of a local hereditary 'transaction president', the machtiern.[44] In Wales this would happen in meetings of local elders, without a king unless one happened by chance to be there.[45] But in Scotland the king's repre-

---

[41] W. Davies, 'People and Places in Dispute in Ninth-Century Brittany', in *Settlement of Disputes*, ed. Davies and Fouracre, pp. 65–84; eadem, *Small Worlds*, p. 150.

[42] Davies, *Wales*, pp. 132–3; D. Jenkins and M. E. Owen, 'The Welsh Marginalia in the Lichfield Gospels', parts I–II, *Cambridge Medieval Celtic Studies*, V (1983) and VII (1984), at II, 91–2; *Vita Cadoci*, c. 37, in *Vitae Sanctorum Britanniae*, edited by Wade-Evans, at p. 104; cf. the 'Ordinance of the Dunsaete', above, pp. 118–19 and n. 38. (The professional lawyer, *famosissimus uir Bledcuirit*, who features in a tenth-century charter, is not cited as making the judgment, but as articulating a point of principle about a breach of sanctuary: *Book of Llan Dâv*, no. 218.)

[43] Barrow, *Kingdom of Scots*, pp. 69–82.

[44] Davies, *Small Worlds*, pp. 109–10, 134–8.

[45] Davies, *Wales*, pp. 132–4, and *Patterns of Power*, pp. 27–8; the Welsh

sentatives, the *iudices*, formally witnessed transactions and acted effectively as guarantors, in the king's name; we most frequently find them perambulating, and thereby determining, the boundaries of estates, and thereafter participating in the formal handover of the estate to another party (*traditio*); (in other words, they defined the property, which—once defined—could be handed over).[46] In Ireland business seems to have been done in the public assembly (*oenach*) of the *tuath*, necessarily in the presence of the king. Indeed, by the eleventh century the *oenach* could function as a political assembly, dominated by the king.[47] Kings seem to have played a significant role as guarantors of business and transactions in both Scotland and Ireland, but did not normally do so in Wales and Brittany.

Conclusion

Royal responsibility, then, looks as if it was more developed in Pictland/Scotland than elsewhere but royal responsibility differed widely from area to area, and some regions were similar in some respects, but different in others. Wales and Brittany had similar non-royal institutions for doing business, but were quite different in approaches to law-making; in Ireland and Wales there were similar non-royal approaches to law-making but different ways of making judgments. Kings (or their agents) had significant roles in the conduct of public business in Ireland and Scotland but effectively none in apprehending defaulters in Ireland, as also in Wales.

On the surface, the distribution of responsibility lacks coherence:

Law making	*Judgment*
model 1: Scotland	model 1: Scotland
model 2: Ireland, Wales	model 2: a) Ireland b) Brittany
model 3: Brittany	model 3: Wales

---

eighth-century texts are especially notable.
[46] Barrow, *Kingdom of Scots*, pp. 69–74.
[47] Binchy, *Celtic and Anglo-Saxon Kingship*, p. 19; Kelly, *Guide*, p. 4; Ó Corráin, 'Nationality and Kingship', pp. 20–1.

Law and order	*Public Business*
model 1: Scotland	model 1: Ireland, Scotland
model 2: Brittany	model 2: Wales, Brittany
model 3: Wales, Ireland	

There is, however, a consistency to these patterns and a sense to be made of them. Where neither kings nor their representatives interacted, or scarcely interacted, with local communities at ground level (as in Wales and Brittany) they neither played a major part in public meetings nor in the regular business of making 'everyday' judgments. In other words, kings sat outside local rural communities, which essentially ran themselves. But where kings or their agents interacted with local communities (as in Ireland and Scotland) then they did tend to play a part both in public meetings and in making judgments.

The strength of the king's role can be related to the differences of scale noted initially. There are three broad categories to be distinguished. Firstly, as one might expect, the king who was monarch, and the monarch who had a range of royal agents to execute his will (which was more so in Pictland/Scotland than elsewhere), tended to have more explicit functions and responsibilities, and more role in the regulation of society.[48] Secondly, the king who had kingly clients (the overking) tended to have *fewer* functions and responsibilities, and a smaller role in regulation; he did not systematically use his client kings as royal agents and as governmental machinery (although—pursuing the traditional Carolingian analogy—one might have expected him to do so). I stress this, in order to dispel the temptation to argue that, although Irish kingdoms were small, the overkings of Ireland really behaved like kings of larger kingdoms, using their subject kings as hierarchies of agents. However, thirdly, where royal functions were *most* limited was in those areas of relatively large kingdoms but a minimum of governmental machinery— areas of larger kingdoms but few agents, like Wales and southern

---

[48] Cf. Wormald, 'Celtic and Anglo-Saxon Kingship', pp. 169–70, for comments on the power of the Pictish/Scottish monarchy.

Scotland. In these cases the polity was too large for the machinery that existed and too large for the king to have much social function. The polity did not coincide with any cohesive society.

But it is notable that the Irish *rí* still had political functions, even though he might be a client, had no (or few) officers, and ruled a tiny unit. He had to ensure plenty, peace and victory for the *tuath*; he had to protect it and lead the host; he had to guarantee fertility, good weather and good fortune; he had to ensure justice (in the broadest sense of the word) and maintain his own honour and status. The type of function that this king performed was different in quality from that which a king performed in a larger unit. The king of the small kingdom was part of an organic whole: here the polity *was* society. So, he moved about the *tuath*; was recognized by its members; was conscious of the membership. He was in some real sense their representative, as he was also both external—special—and internal, because part of the organic whole. His governmental function was limited but his representational function was strongly developed. The king of a larger unit, whether his regulatory role was significant or slight, had no such relationship with his populations; there the representative quality was notional rather than actual. There were, then, variations in the *quality* of kingly functions, as well as variations in the quantity of kingly function. Some kingships were moving towards governmental functions; some had social functions; some had a mixture; and some had very few functions at all.

***

If we look at the several, and various, manifestations of kingship in Celtic areas, whether through images or practice or institutions, we can make some general points of wider relevance. The size of a unit of kingship makes a difference to the type and quality of kingship both conceived and practised. Machinery, governmental machinery, can moderate the effects of increasing size, although in a pre-industrial society it tends to change the quality of the relationship between ruler and ruled. So much is scarcely controversial, or newsworthy. But what gives a system its individual character is not just size, or the presence or absence of governmental machinery, but the further variables of political relationships and the distribution of political functions. The relationship between king, or his agent, and people, is one aspect of the former; the relationship between the several powerholders—king, agents, clients—is another. The number of functions attributable to a ruler is one aspect of the latter and the distribution of those functions among the powerholders, if there be several, is yet another. Hence, the political systems of early medieval Ireland and Carolingian Francia may both depend upon complex patterns of dependence, but that does not make them identical systems.

A political system which has a king who presides over transactions in person is a very different sort of system from one where this is done by royal officers, or alternatively by private individuals. A political system where law-making is done by the king, law enforcement by royal officers, and witnessing by a different set of royal officers is very different from one in which law is customary (but susceptible to royal influence), law enforcement is private, and witnessing royal. There were kings who were protectors and those who were rulers, those who were benefactors and those who were exploiters. Even within the narrow confines of the Celtic world in the early middle ages we find a range of systems and a range of types of king. I should like to think that an awareness of such variety on the western periphery will allow us a better understanding of the exercise and development of political function in mainstream medieval Europe. [49]

---

[49] Grateful thanks are due to Jinty Nelson and Andrew Lantry, for their extremely helpful comments on a draft of this paper.

XVII

Alfred's contemporaries: Irish, Welsh, Scots and Breton

On Monday 9 July 871, 'the year that King (*rex*) Salomon wanted to go to Rome but was unable to do so because his chief men (*principes*) would not let him, because of fear of the Northmen', Salomon walked the bounds of St Ducocca's little monastery in the *plebs* of Cléguerec 'down from Cléguerec hill to the great stones, along the public road to the mound at the crossroads below Silfiac church ... down the valley ... to the river Blavet'.[1] This followed the return of the property, which was substantial, to the abbot of Redon, Liosic, in Perret (north of Silfiac), before Salomon, his sons, four counts, the leader (*princeps*) of Poher, a bishop, an archdeacon, another abbot, and many others; it was returned by the 'tyrannical' machtiern Alfrit (*tyrannus et uere tyrannus – tyrannus* is the standard Latinization of 'machtiern' in this collection), who had appropriated the land and constructed a boundary bank or ditch (*fossata* and *finem*) around it; the occasion followed a court case brought by Liosic's recent predecessor Ritcand before Salomon in his court at Retiers, following at least two decades of complaint. Salomon later sent many gifts to St Peter's, in Rome, since his intended visit had been prevented.

Salomon was the ruler of Brittany at the time of Alfred's accession (857–74). He was a ruler who, as can be seen from the charter above, travelled the length of the country (Perret is just about in the middle of Brittany, and Retiers is in the far east of the country, well to the east of Rennes; see Fig. 35); he had defensive responsibility for it, he commanded a court of aristocrats, and he had diplomatic relations with the pope. He was a ruler of power and significance.

In this he was not alone among Alfred's western contemporaries. Alfred was born at a time of hero rulers in north-western Europe. In the mid-ninth century Kenneth (Cinaed) mac Ailpín was renowned in Scotland (843–58); he was not the first to rule Pictland in eastern Scotland and Dalriada in the west together, the two main components of the so-called 'unified' kingdom of Scotland, but he was the significant ancestor – the man regarded in tenth-century and

---

[1] *CR*, no. 247; a *plebs* was the primary unit of social organization and the predecessor of the fully developed parish; in the ninth century it was usually about 40–50 km^2 in area; see W. Davies, *Small Worlds. The Village Community in Early Medieval Brittany* (1988), 63–7.

Fig. 35 Map of Brittany

later tradition as the founder of the kingdom of Scotland.[2] (In fact, the polity was not called 'Scotland' at that stage but continued to be called Pictish in ninth-century sources and then was termed 'Alba' in the early tenth century.[3]) In Brittany in 849 Salomon's predecessor Nominoe was ruling (842–51), the first to rule the whole of Brittany, and ancestor of the dynasty that dominated the country through the ninth century and into the tenth.[4] In Wales Rhodri Mawr was ruling, one of several Welsh rulers at the time, but the only one to attract – at least from the twelfth century – the epithet *mawr*, 'great': a hero of resistance to the Vikings, ruler and extender of Gwynedd (north-west Wales), he was seen as

---

[2] 'Chronicles of the Picts', in *Chronicles of the Picts. Chronicles of the Scots*, ed. W. F. Skene (1867), 8. Cf. D. Broun, 'The origin of Scottish identity in its European context', in *Scotland in Dark Age Europe*, ed. B. E. Crawford (1994), 22–3.

[3] Broun, 'Origin of Scottish identity', 25–6.

[4] A. Chédeville and H. Guillotel, *La Bretagne des saints et des rois, V^e–Xe siècle* (Rennes, 1984), 227–78.

a significant ancestor, at the head of the genealogies of the rulers of Welsh Wales, north and south, for centuries thereafter.[5] And in Ireland, a land of very different political structures, with many kings and complex patterns of overkingship, the southern Uí Néill (that is, midland) ruler Máel Sechnaill mac Máel Ruanaid raided and took hostages across the whole of Ireland, even to the south coast, the first in any real sense to be an 'overking' of the whole of Ireland; emphasizing his political range, he was called 'king of all Ireland' (*ri Herenn uile*) by the Ulster annalist at his death in 862 and, unusually for an Irish overking at this time, he died peacefully.[6]

This, then, was a significant, and formative, period in political development in Celtic areas.

Rhodri Mawr was still ruling when Alfred became king. However, the others had been succeeded by other, but still prominent, rulers: Kenneth's son Constantine in 'Scotland'; Nominoe's brother's grandson Salomon in Brittany; and Máel Sechnaill's northern Uí Néill rival Aed (of the Cenél nEogain branch of the family) in Ireland, called 'king of Tara' by the annalist.[7] Some had direct contacts with Wessex; others did not. Some had courtly relationships with Alfred's world; others did not. They all shared a Viking problem, at different times and in different ways. I intend in what follows, therefore, to give you a brief sketch of the political structures within which Alfred's western contemporaries operated; to make some comments on their interactions with Wessex; and to consider their Viking problems.

Contemporary Polities in the West

Alfred's contemporary Celtic rulers may have numbered as many as one hundred and probably numbered at least fifty, made up as follows: a series of, respectively, single and joint rulers in Brittany, a few contemporary rulers in Scotland, several contemporary rulers in Wales, and many contemporary rulers in Ireland.

Scotland and Brittany were both regions where political developments of the mid-ninth century had, or are seen to have had, long-term consequences leading to the formation of a state, or quasi-state.

Brittany had been politically fragmented before this period, and had been at times notionally subject to Frankish kings, but institutions of government were rapidly developed after Nominoe, the 'originator', particularly under

---

[5] W. Davies, *Patterns of Power in Early Wales* (1990), 44–6; 'Descriptio Kambriae', I.2, I.3. in *Giraldi Cambrensis Opera*, vol. 6, ed. J. F. Dimock, Rolls Series (1868), 166–7; P. C. Bartrum (ed.), *Early Welsh Genealogical Tracts* (1966), 36, 46–7; J. E. Lloyd, *A History of Wales from the Earliest Times to the Edwardian Conquest* (2 vols, 1911), ii. 765–8.

[6] *AU*, AD 862; see F. J. Byrne, *Irish Kings and High-Kings* (1973), 262–7.

[7] *AU*, AD 864.

Salomon and under Alan I, the Great, who was ruling at the time of Alfred's death.[8] Although intermittently acknowledging the superiority of the West Frankish king in the tenth century and thereafter, and dropping the royal title of the later ninth century in favour of the more limited *dux*, Brittany in effect functioned as a separate state, with a very effective fiscal system, until the sixteenth century; since it kept its own laws and its own *parlement* and estates, it was in some respects separate until the French Revolution.[9] Although its rulers' relationship with the Frankish kings varied in the ninth century – sometimes dependents, sometimes allies, sometimes enemies – and although there are some doubts about the effectiveness of their authority in the far west, Brittany provides the best example of ninth-century Celtic political development: there is no hint that there was any Breton authority responsible for the whole country before the ninth century.

The 'origin' of the kingdom of Scotland is traditionally placed in the mid-ninth century, under Kenneth, who united Pictland in the east and Irish Dalriada in the west (although Pictish terminology continued in contemporary texts for some decades). This union certainly seems to have been anticipated by the periodic rule of both elements by a single Pictish or Dalriadic king in the eighth and early ninth centuries; and it is fashionable at the moment to argue that the union involved southern not northern Pictland in the mid-ninth century.[10] In other words, the physical extent of Kenneth's impact in the mid-ninth century is arguable; in any case the early kingdom clearly did not include the whole of present-day Scotland, for there were Scandinavian settlements in the North and Gall-Goídil (Irish-speaking foreigners) in the Hebrides;[11] both northern and western Isles came to be part of the kingdom of Norway in the central Middle Ages (see Fig. 36).[12]

However, despite those doubts, the basis for what would become the kingdom of Scotland appears to have been laid at this time: tenth-century chroniclers saw Kenneth as the significant ancestor.[13] Further, part at least of the British kingdom of Strathclyde seems to have been dominated by 'Scotland' from the late ninth century (that is the area around Dumbarton, near the mouth of the Clyde). By the eleventh century Scotland was a well-founded kingdom, with effective fiscal, judicial, military and administrative institutions.

---

[8] Chédeville and Guillotel, *La Bretagne*, 313–21, 368–74.

[9] Chédeville and Guillotel, *La Bretagne*, 402; J. Kerhervé, *L'État breton aux 14e et 15e siècles. Les ducs, l'argent et les hommes* (2 vols, Paris, 1987); A. Croix, *L'Âge d'or de la Bretagne 1532–1675* (Rennes, 1993).

[10] Broun, 'Origin of Scottish identity', 29; D. N. Dumville, *The Churches of North Britain in the First Viking Age* (1997), 36.

[11] Gall-Goídil, literally 'foreigners' and 'Gaels, that is, Irish'; hence either Irish who behaved like foreigners (Scandinavians) or Irish-speaking Scandinavians; see Dumville, *Churches of North Britain*, 26.

[12] B. E. Crawford, *Scandinavian Scotland* (1987), 51–8.

[13] M. O. Anderson, *Kings and Kingship in Early Scotland* (1973), 77, 196–7; Broun, 'Origin of Scottish identity', 22.

XVII

CONTEMPORARIES: IRISH, WELSH, SCOTS AND BRETON

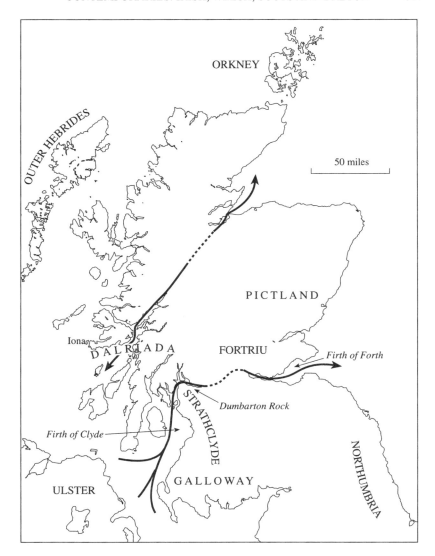

Fig. 36 Map of Scotland (after *Scottish Atlas*)

In Wales there is little to suggest institutional development at this period. There were several separate kingdoms in the region, of which Rhodri's kingdom, Gwynedd, was the largest, probably encompassing the whole of north Wales by 872. But there were at least four other Welsh kingdoms to the south, of which at least two had continuous histories into the late eleventh century; these political

Fig. 37 Map of the kingdoms of Ireland

units were, then, very small. Rhodri, and his son Anarawd especially, seem to have been bent on territorial expansion for Gwynedd, Anarawd raiding the kingdoms to the south (see Fig. 38).[14] While it is reasonable to compare this with the behaviour of Irish overkings – raiding for tribute, taking hostages, seeking submissions – and therefore to see the Gwynedd kings as would-be 'high-kings' of Wales, high-kingship was not the outcome of the raids; those

---

[14] Asser, c. 80, trans. Keynes and Lapidge, *Alfred*, 96.

XVII

CONTEMPORARIES: IRISH, WELSH, SCOTS AND BRETON

who were raided looked outside Wales for protection and soon brought in foreign fighters, both Scandinavian and English, to help their resistance.[15] Although Rhodri's descendants established themselves in south-west Wales (Dyfed) in the tenth century, different branches of his family fought each other and contested for power and control, limiting governmental development in that period. The fiscal system was rudimentary; there was a high degree of anarchy in the tenth and eleventh centuries; powerful ecclesiastical immunities were established; and significant political action was sometimes taken by bands of aristocrats against the interests of kings.[16]

Ireland was again a contrast: in the ninth century it was still a land of many kings and tiny kingdoms (*tuatha*), some of whose kings were overkings, expecting tribute, attendance and (military) assistance from their subject kings, from whom they took hostages and to whom they gave gifts.[17] The overkingships were not – on the whole – institutionalized and were therefore very volatile: some had very short lives and succession was rarely straightforward. The ensuing political climate was consequently dominated by fighting and raiding, conflicts which involved – by the ninth century – some ecclesiastical institutions too. Kings could be abbots, especially in Munster (south-western Ireland): Olchobar, king of a *tuath* and Munster overking in 851, was also abbot of the monastery of Emly.[18] Despite this prevailing volatility, some of the separate kingdoms were absorbed by others and some of the many overkingships came close to being institutionalized: those of the north and middle (Uí Néill), south-east (Leinster), south-west (Munster) and west (Connacht). Moreover, the Uí Néill overkingship exercised by Máel Sechnaill in the mid-ninth century looked beyond the north and centre to the whole of Ireland, taking hostages and securing assistance from the 'provinces' beyond (see Fig. 37).

Máel Sechnaill did not *establish* an all-Ireland overkingship (which was not to happen until the eleventh century), and he did not secure the Uí Néill overkingship for his branch of the Uí Néill family, the Clann Cholmáin. However, he did establish a model – a pattern for other powerful kings to emulate. Many tried, but it took time for them to be consistently successful.

There were different kinds of polity, then, and different patterns of political development in the west, but Alfred's most prominent contemporaries in these four Celtic regions were all powerful men, who could command and control effective fighting forces. Their territorial range – the scale of their active

---

[15] Cf. D. N. Dumville, 'Anglo-Saxon and Celtic overkingships: a discussion of some shared historical problems', *Bulletin of the Institute of Oriental and Occidental Studies, Kansai University*, 31 (1998), 85, on the ninth-century end of Welsh political structures.

[16] W. Davies, *Wales in the Early Middle Ages* (1982), 106–12; Davies, *Patterns of Power*, 35–7, 41–7; W. Davies, 'Adding insult to injury: power, property and immunities in early medieval Wales', in *Property and Power in the Early Middle Ages*, eds W. Davies and P. Fouracre (1995).

[17] Byrne, *Irish Kings*, 41, 196–9; D. Ó Corráin, 'Nationality and kingship in pre-Norman Ireland', in *Nationality and the Pursuit of National Independence*, ed. T. W. Moody (1978).

[18] Byrne, *Irish Kings*, 214.

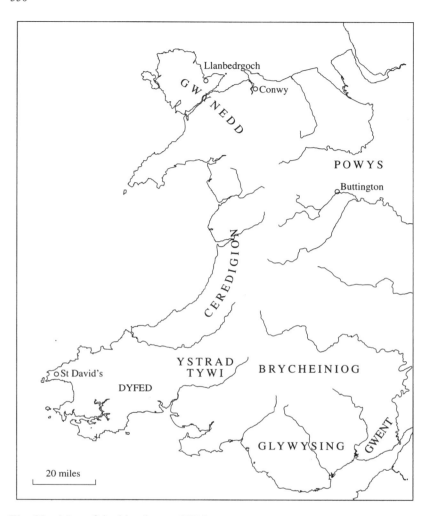

Fig. 38 Map of the kingdoms of Wales

rulership – was in most cases comparable to Alfred's Wessex. Brittany was directly so, being the same size of 'state'; the 'Scotland' of the later ninth century was a little smaller;[19] the overkingship of Ireland stretched even farther, although of course the basic units of kingship there were very much smaller. But

---

[19] Cf. Broun, 'Origin of Scottish identity', 29, who argues that the original Alba was smaller than Pictland.

Gwynedd, the largest kingdom of Wales, even when expanded to include Powys to the north-east and Ceredigion to the south, was clearly not of the same scale. This fact probably had a bearing on Asser's attitude to Alfred: in contrast to his experience at home, Alfred's Wessex was a great kingdom.

Interaction with Wessex

The last known king of Cornwall was drowned in the 870s; Asser was given the monastery of Exeter with a sphere of authority that included Cornwall; some of the inscribed stones of Cornwall commemorate people with English names; and Alfred's will included land in north-east Cornwall.[20] Although it can be maintained that it took Athelstan's campaigns in the south-west in the tenth century to finalize the integration of this country within the English kingdom, in essence the work was done in Alfred's reign. Once the kingdom of Cornwall had been incorporated in Wessex, of the kings of the west it was the Welsh who had the most direct interaction with it.

The elements of the story are well known. First, Alfred's biographer, Asser, was called from St David's in west Wales to Alfred's court. St David's was an ancient, and prestigious, monastic and episcopal house. After Asser came to the West Saxon court, he divided his time between St David's and Wessex, notionally six months on and six months off. In other words, he maintained contact with Wales and was himself a channel for continuing communication between Alfred's court and the rulers of Wales. Simon Keynes has reminded us that he thinks that the *Life of Alfred* was itself written for a Welsh audience.[21] Second, Rhodri, the great king of Gwynedd, was killed by the English in 878; this was presumably by the midland English, who had campaigned in north Wales throughout the ninth century and were defeated at Conwy in 881.[22] Third, according to Asser, the southern Welsh kings – that is, the kings of Dyfed, Glywysing, Gwent and Brycheiniog – sought Alfred's protection, accepted Alfred's *dominium*, and 'submitted' to him round about the mid-880s because they were being harried by the sons of Rhodri on the one hand from the north and by the Mercians on the other from the north-east (see Fig. 38).[23]

I do not think that *dominium* in this account means 'rule' in any practical sense, because there is no reflection in Welsh sources of any kind of English rule on the ground; however, the arrangement must have brought the Welsh rulers into close touch with the Wessex court – a relationship amply demonstrated in

---

[20] S. M. Pearce, *The Kingdom of Dumnonia. Studies in History and Tradition in South Western Britain AD 350–1150* (1978), 168–9; cf. E. Okasha, *Corpus of Early Christian Inscribed Stones of South-West Britain* (1993), 47–8.
[21] Keynes and Lapidge, *Alfred*, 56–7.
[22] Davies, *Patterns of Power*, 69.
[23] Asser, c. 80, trans. Keynes and Lapidge, *Alfred*, 96, and notes at 262–3.

the next two generations by well-recorded appearances of Welsh rulers with the king in England (although this was not sustained into the later tenth and eleventh centuries).[24] Almost certainly as a consequence, Welsh warriors joined the West Saxon troops which followed the Essex host to Buttington on the River Severn in 893, laying siege to the host for several weeks before defeating it; some of the Welsh, then, went to fight for the English. Ultimately Anarawd, Rhodri's son, joined the southern kings and had by 895 secured English assistance against Ceredigion and Ystrad Tywi (in west Wales); at that point English troops were inside Wales, campaigning and ravaging with the north Welsh.[25]

Beyond Wales and Cornwall interaction was not so direct. However, in a sense Breton and Irish rulers belonged to the same courtly world as that of the West Saxons. Just as Alfred travelled to Rome and went to the court of Charles the Bald, subsequently sending for continental scholars for his court, Breton and Irish rulers had comparable diplomatic relationships and scholarly exchanges. Erispoe of Brittany, Nominoe's son and successor (851–57), had his daughter betrothed to Charles's eldest son in 856; Salomon's son (who may have been sponsored by Charles at baptism in 864) swore fidelity to Charles; and Salomon himself received lands in Neustria from Charles.[26] Salomon, as we saw at the start, wished to make the journey to Rome and, though prevented from doing that, sent gifts to the pope. Both Louis the Pious and Charles patronized leading Breton monasteries such as Landévennec and Redon, with a notable consequent impact on their scholarly culture: most notable of all, Carolingian minuscule quickly replaced characteristically Insular forms of writing in Brittany, but favourite Carolingian authors were also copied and Carolingian-preferred texts of the Bible and the liturgy were adopted.[27]

Irish rulers were obviously more distant, but even so Charles the Bald received a delegation in 848, bringing gifts from the *rex Scottorum* (king of the Irish), Máel Sechnaill, and a request for safe passage to Rome for the travellers; Donnacán, the holy scholar, had died in Italy in 843. Irish scholars inhabited the courts, secular and ecclesiastical, of ninth-century western Europe – a marked and distinguished presence – and kept in intellectual touch with their homeland: a group of four such scholars on their way to the Continent were entertained in the Gwynedd court round about 840 and later wrote back to their teacher in Ireland about the cryptogram test they had encountered there. Notably, the three Irish who landed in Wessex in 891 headed straight for Alfred's court; the Irish, of all people, were accustomed to travel and to contacts abroad.[28]

---

[24] H. R. Loyn, 'Wales and England', *Welsh History Review*, 10 (1980–81), 283–301.
[25] *AC*, AD 894.
[26] Chédeville and Guillotel, *La Bretagne*, 288; J. L. Nelson, *Charles the Bald* (1992), 208; *AB*, s.a. 873.
[27] Chédeville and Guillotel, *La Bretagne*, 344; J. M. H. Smith, *Province and Empire. Brittany and the Carolingians* (1992), 162–77.
[28] D. Ó Cróinín, *Early Medieval Ireland 400–1200* (1995), 222–9; *ASC, s.a.* 891.

The northern world seems to have been more distant from Alfred's circle and from the Continent, although this impression may have more to do with the paucity of sources than any real difference. At least we know that the Carolingian scholar Walahfrid Strabo wrote a poem on the violent death of Blathmac, 'holy teacher' of Iona in Dalriada off the west coast of Scotland, and that Abbot Indrechtach of Iona died in England in 854, on his way to Rome.[29]

The Common Problem

All of these western and northern regions experienced Viking raiding in Alfred's lifetime and this caused problems for all of them, to differing extents and with different outcomes.

Raiding was a problem for the Bretons for most of Alfred's lifetime (although to a lesser extent in the late 870s and early 880s), and was often inextricably connected with those experienced by the West Frankish king. The Viking threat actively involved Breton aristocrats, sometimes working in independent groups, in alliance or in conflict, and was perceived as a problem by other Bretons, like those in the monastery of Redon: the abbot sought permission from the bishop to be excused from sending his priests to Vannes for ordination because of the dangers they might encounter on the road. Breton rulers themselves spent a great deal of time on campaign, culminating in the victories of Alan the Great against the Loire and the Seine Vikings in 888–90 both within Brittany and at St Lô in Normandy.[30]

Raiding in Ireland and Wales was problematic until the 870s, and then lessened. In Wales Rhodri won victories in 856, but was forced overseas to Ireland in 877. The problems came from the west and seem largely to have been a backlash of Viking activity in Ireland, where they were seriously disruptive for about forty years from 833, burning monasteries, capturing clerics for ransom and killing warriors. With fleets on the rivers and inland lakes of Ireland, there were many different groups of Vikings, although they were predominantly of Norse origin until the Danes arrived in 849. From 873, however, the so-called '40-year peace' dawned.[31]

From 839 Vikings raided from the west into the Pictish heartland in inland Scotland, killing members of the Pictish ruling family that year. Thereafter raids continued through Alfred's lifetime into the early tenth century, the raiders

---

29 *AU*, AD 825; cf. C. Doherty, 'The Vikings in Ireland: a review', in *Ireland and Scandinavia in the Early Viking Age*, eds H. B. Clarke, M. Ní Mhaonaigh, R. Ó Floinn (Dublin, 1998), 310; *AI*, AD 854.

30 Chédeville and Guillotel, *La Bretagne*, 297–321, 359–68; N. S. Price, 'The Vikings in Brittany', *Saga-Book of the Viking Society*, 22 (1989), 339–55.

31 H. R. Loyn, *The Vikings in Wales* (1976), 4–8; *AU*, AD 856, 877; Ó Cróinín, *Early Medieval Ireland*, 233–55.

sometimes staying for long periods – Olaf (Amlaíb) spent three months in Fortriu in 866 – collecting tribute and causing devastation, and they took Dumbarton, royal focus of Strathclyde, in 870 (see Fig. 36).[32] Some at least of these raiders – like Olaf – were Dublin Norse; it has been argued that he and his allies dominated the kings of 'Scotland' for much of the later ninth and early tenth centuries;[33] indeed, it has recently been suggested that Scotland was the focus of an overkingship of Scottish and Irish Vikings at this time.[34] However, there clearly were other Viking groups involved in Scotland; the Gall-Goídil (Irish-speaking foreigners) came from the Hebrides, and the Danish Halfdan of Northumbria raided Galloway and Strathclyde in 875. Viking activity was politically disruptive in central Scotland for much of the period.

While the pattern of raiding was obviously different for these Celtic areas, so too were their experiences of Viking settlement. In Brittany there is no evidence of any ninth-century settlement. For Wales the evidence is very thin: Asser certainly speaks of Vikings overwintering in the south-west in 878; and for the longer term there are traces of some small-scale settlement in both the south and the north of the country. However, it is extremely difficult to tie any of this down to the ninth century.[35] At Glyn Farm, Llanbedrgoch, on Anglesey, currently being excavated, there are certainly structural phases of this period and indications of strengthening the fortifications and increases in population in the late ninth century. Whether or not any of this represents Viking, as opposed to native, activity is controversial; and, in any case, excavation is not yet finished.[36] By contrast, the heavy Norse settlement of the northern and western isles off Scotland, and northern parts of the mainland, seems to have begun by this time, leading by 1100 to linguistic change, together with the creation of the Scandinavian Earldom of Orkney and incorporation of the isles into the kingdom of Norway.[37] There was significant settlement in Ireland too, but of a quite different kind: a small number of strongpoints was established, controlling the hinterlands around them. Although they did not all survive into the central Middle Ages, several of those in the south of the country did so.[38] By the eleventh century the Limerick

---

[32] *AU*, AD 866, 870; A. O. Anderson, *Early Sources of Scottish History, AD 500–1286* (2 vols, 1922, rev. edn 1990), I, 292–312.

[33] A. P. Smyth, *Scandinavian York and Dublin* (2 vols, Dublin, 1975–79), I, 17–19, 35–6, 62–4, 93–7, 108; cf. Dumville, *Churches of North Britain*, 1–2, 29.

[34] D. Ó Corráin, 'The Vikings in Scotland and Ireland in the ninth century', *Peritia*, 12 (1998), 329–31, 333–7.

[35] Loyn, *Vikings in Wales*, 8–22; Davies, *Patterns of Power*, 51–6.

[36] M. Redknap, 'Glyn, Llanbedrgoch, Anglesey (SH 515 813)', *Archaeology in Wales*, 34 (1994), 58–60; ibid., 35 (1995), 58–9; ibid., 36 (1996), 81–2; ibid., 37 (1997), 94–6; ibid., 39 (1999), 56–61.

[37] Crawford, *Scandinavian Scotland*, 76–9.

[38] H. B. Clarke, 'Proto-towns and towns in Ireland and Britain in the ninth and tenth centuries', in *Ireland and Scandinavia*, eds Clarke, Ní Mhaonaigh, Ó Floinn, 341–68; P. F. Wallace,

Vikings were especially active in the Irish Sea, but more than a century before that the rulers of Viking Dublin were ranging widely over western and northern Britain as well as within Ireland; by the late tenth century Dublin, a Viking foundation, was a thriving urban centre, as the other surviving strongpoints were also to become. This urban development was something new for Ireland, in contrast to the long-established urban trends of southern England. This had important repercussions, both in respect of genuinely urban and commercial development and of the creation of a goal for would-be high-kings of Ireland: control of Dublin became essential for successful overkings in the eleventh and twelfth centuries, and those who contended for the position characteristically headed straight for the city.

Lastly, alliances. Interaction between Celtic rulers and aristocrats and Viking groups is very characteristic of the Viking period in the west. As was the case elsewhere in Europe, the Vikings were not a simple 'enemy'. Breton rulers, and other Bretons, at times allied with Viking leaders, both against other Vikings and against West Frankish rulers. So, Salomon fought *with* the Loire Vikings against Weland in 862 and *with* Haesten when he went to raid Poitou in 866; but he fought *against* Haesten *and* the Loire Vikings in 869 at Avessac, and with the Franks *against* the Vikings in the period 868–73.[39] The presence of active Viking groups on and around the Continent had a direct bearing on the relationship between Breton and Frankish rulers. Irish kings too allied with Viking leaders: Cerball, king of Ossory, allied with Olaf and Ivarr in 859; Aed of the northern Uí Néill allied with the Dublin rulers against the southern Uí Néill in the early 860s; Norse and Irish raided the ancient Irish sites of Knowth and Newgrange together in 863, to cite but a few examples. They intermarried too: Olaf married the daughter of Aed, and Cerball's daughter married a Dublin Viking.[40] This provided at least a complicating factor in Irish politics; though we no longer think that the Vikings destroyed 'classical' Irish society, they certainly fed the volatility of the Irish political process.

Even Anarawd of Gwynedd for a time allied with the Danish king of York – against the English – although Viking alliance is much more characteristic of tenth-century than of ninth-century Welsh history. (Scotland is uncertain: Godfrey of the Gall-Goídil may have worked with Kenneth, but the record is not contemporary.[41]) Alliance with Viking groups was therefore a major factor in determining political trends in the west. This seems to have been much more pronounced than it was in England. However, while there is certainly much less of alliance-

---

'*Garrda* and *airbeada*: the plot thickens in Viking Dublin', in *Seanchas. Studies in Early and Medieval Irish Archaeology, History and Literature in Honour of Francis J. Byrne*, ed. A. P. Smyth (Dublin, 2000), 273.

[39] *CR*, nos 242, 247; *AB*, s.a. 862, 866; Price, 'Vikings in Brittany', 348–53; Smith, *Province and Empire*, 105–7.

[40] *AU*, AD 859, 861, 862, 863; Byrne, *Irish Kings*, 263; Doherty, 'Vikings in Ireland', 301.

[41] Anderson, *Early Sources*, I, 267; Crawford, *Scandinavian Scotland*, 47.

making in the English record than in the Celtic, perhaps this is because the English record was dominated by the interests of the West Saxon court. James Campbell's comments on Viking alliances with the English may perhaps lead to a reassessment in the future.[42]

A Last Word

It is interesting that this Alfredian period was also a period of hero rulers in the Celtic west and north, much more consistently so than at any other period in the early Middle Ages. The rulers of Brittany, Wales and Scotland at this time have all been – and continue to be – heroes of school books, as King Alfred is. It may be suggested that that is more to do with modern myth-making than with ninth-century activity. Modern myth-making certainly plays a part in sustaining it: Breton independence movements since the nineteenth century have used stories of ninth-century rulers to emphasize their separate past; the maintenance and development of Scottish and especially Welsh political identities also draw from time to time on ninth-century heroes. However, the perspective is not merely modern: these rulers of the second half of the ninth century were seen as significant ancestors by medieval kings and their record-makers; and they were regarded as significant people by historians in the Middle Ages. Their fame began early: Rhodri was already 'Great' by the twelfth century, as Gerald of Wales makes clear. Not only that. Contemporary records made them distinctive too, in various ways, as indicated above.[43]

Why is it that the later ninth century provides the great heroes of the past in Celtic areas? It cannot be a reaction to and reflection of King Alfred, since several predated him. Perhaps it is more likely that it was a response to the legacy of Charlemagne. And resistance to the Viking aggressor gave the kings a prominence they would not otherwise have had; the Vikings unquestionably came from outside; the impact of aliens provoked at least the beginnings of a sense of identity.

I hope that this gives some context to Alfred in north-west Europe. While I do not wish to belittle his achievement, Alfred was clearly one of several Insular, western, rulers, of similar-sized polities. These were rulers who inhabited a courtly world where scholarship was valued and whose scholars moved between courts and churches across western Europe. They were rulers who were thrust into prominence by the need to deal with the Viking inrush. While differing in some respects, notably in their access to and control of coinage, these rulers were of the same cultural world as Alfred. Of course, they are not as dominant in the contemporary record as Alfred; but this is because the contemporary record

---

[42] See above, Chapter 1.

[43] See above, notes 5, 6, 13; and for Brittany, R. Merlet (ed.), *La Chronique de Nantes* (Paris, 1896).

in the Celtic west is much more miscellaneous in provenance: it was not so dominated by the ruler's court. I would like you to entertain the possibility, however, that these Celtic rulers were just as significant.

XVIII

On servile status in the early Middle Ages

The origins of serfdom in medieval Europe are inextricably associated with the end of slavery in Antiquity. This is true on many levels – ideological, semantic, historiographical. A transition from 'slavery' to 'feudalism' remains fundamental to Marxist analysis. Words meaning 'slave' in the earlier period come to mean 'serf' in later centuries. And it is a prominent theme of the historiography, both early and more recent, that gang slaves on Roman rural estates were given agricultural tenancies to produce the 'hutted slaves' (*servi casati* or *casarii*) of the late Roman period, retaining their slave status but gaining some economic freedom; thus they became the ancestors of at least some of the later servile population.[1] It is also the case that many social forms of the early Middle Ages were strongly influenced by Roman models (or what people thought were Roman models) – through language and memory, and, ultimately, through perceptions of Roman law. Considering serfdom, therefore, necessarily involves considering slavery, even if – as some modern writers think[2] – our conclusion should be that the decline of one is quite unconnected with the rise of the other.

When modern historians write about slaves and serfs in the Middle Ages, they often have in mind two clear and contrasted models. The archetypical slave is the person who can own no property and has no rights over his own person or children, since he

---

1 For early serfdom, see the collected papers of M. Bloch, *Slavery and Serfdom in the Middle Ages* (Berkeley, 1975), pp. 1–91; L. Verriest, *Institutions médiévales* (Mons & Frameries, 1946), pp. 171–91. For changes in ancient slavery, see A.H.M. Jones, *The Later Roman Empire* (Oxford, 1964), vol. 2, pp. 792–5; C.R. Whittaker, 'Circe's pigs: from slavery to serfdom in the later Roman world', *Slavery and Abolition*, 8 (1987), 89–107; and C.J. Wickham, 'Marx, Sherlock Holmes, and late Roman commerce', *Journal of Roman Studies*, 78 (1988), 187–90.

2 See below, pp. 229–31, on the French model.

(and his labour) are totally controlled by someone else; his family has no legitimated social function and he is not a member of the society in which he lives and works.[3] Hence, his legal status is that of an object and his treatment like that of an animal. The archetypical serf is hereditarily tied to his position, which he cannot change; he is bound to return some of the product of his labour to his lord, and may have other physical or financial obligations to him. Although he may be legally unfree and may lack access to public judicial mechanisms, he is not totally in the power of someone else and by common consent has in principle some, if limited, rights. He will probably have possession of some property and have a household.[4]

Though the models are clear enough, in practice drawing the line between slave and serf is particularly difficult in Europe in the early Middle Ages, and very much depends on the definitions used: there are, for example, persons who have the legal status of an object but who can nevertheless own some property; and persons with functioning households who have no acknowledged rights or community role, and so on. The difficulty of drawing a hard and fast line between the two lies at the heart of much of the debate on servile status in this period and consequently near the heart of the issue of the origins of serfdom.

Problems of text, terminology and numbers

Assessment of the nature and social importance of servile status in the early Middle Ages is hampered by our inability to quantify essentials. Since we lack systematic and comprehensive surveys of whole populations (the English Domesday Book of 1086 is the closest we get to a comprehensive survey, and even that text has stimulated countless differences of interpretation), we simply cannot know how many people fell into one group or another.[5] There are plenty of estimates, based on the more or less convincing guessing of numbers, but in the end we have to admit that we cannot count. This is a fundamental problem, however full, varied

---

3 Orlando Patterson's work, *Slavery and Social Death: a Comparative Study* (Cambridge, MA, 1982), has been especially influential.

4 See, for example, Bloch, *Slavery and Serfdom*, pp. 33–91; R.H. Hilton, *The Decline of Serfdom in Medieval England* (London, 1969), pp. 9–31.

5 A. Farley (ed.), *Domesday Book seu Liber Censualis Wilhelmi Primi Regis Angliae*, 2 vols (London, 1783); since the text is organized with reference to the holdings of principal landholders, it is usually impossible to identify the demographic characteristics of any given region; there is also considerable disagreement among scholars over the precise meaning of terms used; and this is in addition to errors, omissions,

and wide-ranging the texts may be. There are, therefore, always going to be arguments about proportions of freemen and about the *dominant* character of these societies, whether or not we believe that crude numbers determine that character.

There are also terminological problems which are insuperable if we are looking for precise and limited meanings. Words descriptive of status are used inconsistently, even at the same period in the same region, and even more so in different regions, and they may in fact have a very wide semantic range. Hence, to take the most obvious example, a common Latin word for male slave in Antiquity was the word *servus*; but by the late Middle Ages it could denote both 'servant' and 'serf'.[6] When we find it in texts of the early Middle Ages, the context is rarely precise enough to attribute either the firm juridical meaning of slave, the person totally in the power of another, or the meaning of serf, the tied person who has some rights.[7] One word could mean several things; we cannot hope to unravel the social realities of the distant past if we look for simple translations and do not grapple with the deep structures of meaning; and these are going to be debatable.

Single status words are not the only problem. The language of service runs through and through early medieval texts; *servitium* and related words therefore feature in references to obligations between men. But there is no simple key to serfdom here for service could be distinctly honourable as well as neutral or menial; by the tenth century *servitium* could in some regions refer both to the obligations of peasant dependants to their landlords and also to the military obligations of a warrior aristocracy.[8] The truth is that early medieval writers used ideas of service to refer to reciprocal relationships at

duplications, and so on. There are Carolingian estate surveys from an earlier period, which include information on size and composition of the households which had rent or other obligations. See, for example, F. Ganshof, *Le polyptyque de l'abbaye de Saint-Bertin (844–859). Édition Critique et Commentaire* (Paris, 1975); and A. Longnon (ed.), *Polyptique de l'abbaye de Saint-Germain-des-Prés*, 2 vols (Geneva [1885, 1895], 1978); but these deal with particular estates rather than with whole regions; and there is every reason to suppose that the characteristics of these north French estates were not typical of populations in the rest of France, let alone the whole of Western Europe, and that estate households were not representative of free peasant households.

6 See the comments of William Phillips in ch. 4, above.

7 However, plenty of published discussion hinges on attempts to do this. H.-W. Goetz, 'Serfdom and the beginnings of a "seigneurial system"', *Early Medieval Europe*, 2 (1993), 34–46, usefully differentiates the use of *servus* in ninth-century legal and other texts, where the former have the meaning unfree and the latter miscellaneous types of dependant.

8 See J.F. Niermeyer, *Mediae Latinitatis Lexicon Minus* (Leiden, 1984), s.v. *servitium*.

many different social levels. Service could encompass, but did not necessarily denote, servitude.[9] It was not the *fact* of obligations that conferred inferior status, but rather the lack of capacity for independent action.

However, owing service meant being to some extent in the power of someone else. There were varieties of being in power (familial, servile, honourable[10]) and being in power did not of itself bring *menial* status – witness the wives and male children of aristocratic men. Although we can differentiate the power of a head of household over his family from that of a master over his slave and from that of a lord over his vassal, the language of power and of personal relationships can be confusing.[11] Power over people is obviously relevant to this discussion, but it is the amount and quality of power not the mere fact of power that is significant.[12]

The notion of freedom adds a further problem: unfreedom can vary in meaning from the legal status of a Roman slave to exclusion from a particular judicial system; modern discussions of medieval freedom can easily become tautological. Sixth- and seventh-century (and some later) texts clearly differentiate between free and unfree persons; this was a meaningful distinction to the writers of those texts.[13] While slaves would invariably fall into the category of unfree, tied dependants might not. By the eleventh century writers were

9 Some modern writers, however, preference the honourable connotations of the language of service, although this view does not command wide-spread acceptance. For a recent discussion of *servitium* in French contexts, see D. Barthélemy, 'Qu'est-ce que le servage, en France, au XIe siècle?', *Revue Historique*, 287 (1992), 255–60.

10 Compare the comments of Richard Saller in ch. 6, above.

11 We can try to simplify the analysis if, like Pierre Bonnassie, we distinguish between power over a person and possession of him: *From Slavery to Feudalism in Southwestern Europe* (Cambridge, 1991), p. 312; but while that might allow us to isolate the slave it will not allow us to isolate many of those normally classified as serfs. Lords could have considerable power over serfs without possessing them.

12 P. Dockès, *Medieval Slavery and Liberation* (London, 1982), pp. 4–8, has a useful discussion on types of power; he selects power of life and death as the distinguishing criterion of the slave-master's power: the slave is one of the 'living dead', only surviving by the grace of his master.

13 For example, Kentish law from Anglo-Saxon England, Aethelberht 4, 6, 9 etc., in F.L. Attenborough (ed.), *The Laws of the Earliest English Kings* (Cambridge, 1922), p. 4; Lombard law from Italy, Rothari 39–40, 221, 259, 264, 382–3 etc., in *The Lombard Laws*, trans. K. Fischer Drew (Philadelphia, 1973), pp. 60, 95, 104, 105, 128; Visigothic law from Spain, P.D. King, *Law and Society in the Visigothic Kingdom* (Cambridge, 1972), pp. 159–89. The notion of the freeman is still strong in Carolingian *capitula* of the early ninth century; see, for example, in the context of military obligations: 'Capitulare missorum de exercitu promovendo', in *Capitularia Regum Francorum*, vol. 1, ed. A. Boretius, *Monumenta Germaniae Historica LL in quarto*, sectio 2 (Hannover, 1883), no. 50, pp. 136–8. See also the thoughts of Susan Reynolds on this issue, though she is working across a longer period, *Fiefs and Vassals* (Oxford, 1994), pp. 38–45.

more likely to use other forms of distinction between men, such as the tripartite military/religious/labouring classification,[14] perhaps reflecting the fact that the difference between freedom and unfreedom had become less clear-cut and/or was less significant.[15] Later in the Middle Ages, particularly under the influence of Roman law, the concept was revived and applied and debated. The times when notions of freedom were less readily articulated were times when the shape of society, and ideas about membership of society, were changing. Other concepts were used to differentiate between the social and political capacities of different types of men. Though relevant to the wider question of the place of the individual in society, the concept of freedom did not define that place. Hence, too much emphasis on the occurrence of 'freedom' words can lead us to ignore differences (and similarities) in the condition of men. People could be exploited, dominated and brutalized without being classified as unfree.

Recent analyses

The modern study of medieval slavery and serfdom began with Marc Bloch, whose work rightly continues to be exceptionally influential.[16] Put crudely, Bloch's view was that ancient slavery first declined and then subsequently medieval serfdom arose for new reasons, reasons that were to be associated with social and political changes of the tenth and eleventh centuries in Western Europe. Elaborations of this approach remain very much in vogue with French historians and have flourished during the last fifteen years. Essential to the current model is the notion that the eleventh century is the century of the 'Feudal Revolution', a time when petty aristocrats built castles and strove to dominate the peasantries of the surrounding territories. The year AD 1000 features prominently in the model, and the overtones of the Peace movement are marshalled to emphasize the suddenness and violence of the change: peasants openly objected to the depredations of the lay aristocracy, it is said, and church leaders engineered agreements that behaviour would

14 G. Duby, *Les trois ordres ou l'imaginaire du féodalisme* (Paris, 1978).
15 See the discussion of this issue by Ruth Karras, *Slavery and Society in Medieval Scandinavia* (Newhaven, 1988), pp. 164–6; cf. Goetz, 'Serfdom and the beginnings of a "seigneurial system" ', 49. See below, pp. 234–5.
16 Bloch, *Slavery and Serfdom.*

be moderated.[17] Nevertheless, lay lords required the payment of dues of one sort or another from peasants, both regular annual payments and payments in respect of specific lordly functions like protecting the harvest; they required the performance of more or less onerous physical obligations, from castle guard duty or fetching and carrying to ploughing, mowing and threshing; and they restricted the peasant's freedom to marry and to pass on his property to his heirs.[18] Hence, according to this model, the creation of seigneurial (signorial in Italian contexts) powers, an already well-established development of the tenth to twelfth centuries,[19] is inextricably associated with the origins and establishment of serfdom. To acquire seigneurial power, they imply, was in effect to enserf.

Plenty have opposed and still oppose this approach, and there are, of course, other models;[20] it is nevertheless very dominant in the literature. An important part of the argument depends on the proposition that rural slavery continued to be significant until about AD 1000 and then very rapidly declined. Indeed, in an extreme form of the model, a period of a generation or so in the mid-eleventh century is envisaged in which neither rural slavery nor rural serfdom existed.[21] This is quite frankly incredible, given what we know of the varieties of menial dependence at that period. Moreover, the model implies that it was castle-building lay lords who were especially responsible for enserfing, although we have no trouble in finding serfs on ecclesiastical property in Western Europe. In fact, it can

17 For the Peace of God movement, see T. Head and R. Landes (eds), *The Peace of God: Social Violence and Religious Response in France around the Year 1000* (Ithaca, 1992).

18 See especially G. Bois, *The Transformation of the Year One Thousand* (Manchester, 1992); also Bonnassie, *From Slavery to Feudalism*, and R. Fossier, *La terre et les hommes en Picardie jusqu'à la fin du XIIIe siècle*, 2 vols (Paris, 1968) and so on; despite the work of the last fifteen years, G. Duby, *Rural Economy and Country Life in the Medieval West* (London, 1962), pp. 220–31, first published in 1962, remains a useful summary of the essential aspects of this model.

19 See Duby, *Rural Economy and Country Life*, pp. 224–8; and further C.J. Wickham, 'Property ownership and signorial power in twelfth-century Tuscany', in W. Davies and P. Fouracre (eds), *Property and Power in the Early Middle Ages* (Cambridge, 1995), pp. 223–6, and also the concluding piece to that volume, 'Power and property in early medieval Europe', pp. 257–60. See also comments by Robert Brenner in ch. 13, below.

20 Verriest, *Institutions médiévales*, pp. 171–248; D. Barthélemy, 'La mutation féodale a-t-elle eu lieu?', *Annales. Économies, Sociétés, Civilisations*, 47 (1992), 767–77; and, at greater length, with a review of the historiography, his 'Qu'est-ce que le servage?', *Revue Historique*, 287 (1992).

21 In south-western Europe especially; Bonnassie, *From Slavery to Feudalism*, pp. 122–5.

only be made to make sense if serfdom is defined extremely narrowly (and to define it narrowly opens up the issues of terminology discussed above).[22] It is also perfectly clear from a variety of southern and northern European texts of the ninth century (to take a well-evidenced era) that some peasants and their progeny were already hereditarily bound both to their tenures and also to certain more or less onerous obligations to their masters. These people can, of course, be discounted for the purposes of the serfdom enquiry if they be classified as slaves, but they clearly did not have the same status nor experience the same restrictions as the slaves of classical Antiquity or of continuing post-classical slavery; and, whatever we call them, their status can hardly be ignored in a consideration of the origins of serfdom. Further, while it is undoubtedly the case that seigneurial impositions could bear heavily upon the dependent peasantries of Western Europe in the eleventh, twelfth and thirteenth centuries, it is also the case that the benefits of alignment with (and of protection by) a lord sometimes openly outweighed the arduousness of the obligations. Consent to the impositions was often implicit and could be explicit.[23]

Marxist and post-Marxist historians of the Middle Ages have tended to concentrate on slavery and serfdom as economic systems rather than as social and political phenomena, and they have focused in particular on the transition from one mode of production to the next. Since it is axiomatic within this conceptual framework that the slave mode gave way to the feudal mode, Marxists have to deal with the gap between the end of classical Antiquity (and ancient slavery) and the fully fledged serfdom which characterized the feudal model of the late Middle Ages, a gap of some six or seven hundred years. Recent writing has tended to investigate varieties of proto serf and devolved slave systems, as well as the possible temporary revival of ancient modes of production.[24] Explanations for the shift from slavery have emphasized declining

---

22 If we follow Bloch's selection of *chevage, formariage* and *mainmorte* (annual poll tax, control of marriage and limitations on alienation of property) as the defining characteristics of serfdom, then of course serfdom necessarily becomes a late medieval phenomenon. These did not, in any case, apply throughout Western Europe; for example, they were absent in Lombardy: F. Menant, *Campagnes Lombardes du moyen âge* (Rome, 1993), p. 478.

23 See Wickham, 'Property ownership and signorial power', in Davies and Fouracre (eds), *Property and Power*.

24 For example, C. Parain, *Outils, ethnies et développement historique* (Paris, 1979) (which collects papers published between 1961 and 1977), esp. pp. 285–327; Perry Anderson, *Passages from Antiquity to Feudalism* (London, 1978); C.J. Wickham, 'The other transition: from the ancient world to feudalism', *Past and Present*, 103 (1984).

profitability or technological change or class struggle;[25] some analyses also draw attention to the significance of the changing power and changing mechanisms of the state and these are especially helpful in understanding the context, if not the actual process, of change.[26] What is abundantly clear, and generally agreed, is that slavery as a mode of production was very rare in the early Middle Ages; whatever we call the labourers, and whatever their legal status, the mode was much more like 'feudalism'.

The principal issues that emerge from the literature, with reference to the early Middle Ages, are therefore these: when did slavery end and serfdom begin? Why did one give way to the other? Were there continuities or a sudden break with the past? These general questions can also be posed in a specific way: were rural dependants who are described in ninth- and tenth-century texts as *censuales* or *tributarii* or *cerarii* or *coloni*, and such terms, slaves or serfs or free peasants? These questions have dominated the historiography of the last generation, and they tend to invite circular answers. The questions can be framed in other, perhaps more constructive ways: what actually changed, in the countryside, over the period 400–1100? What was the condition of menial dependants (whatever we call them)? And were there different types of menial dependant?

When did serfdom begin?

Leaving aside, for the moment, the issue of what we term them, we cannot ignore the fact that many ancient historians believe that some plantation slaves on the villa estates of the Roman Empire were given domiciles and tenures on landed property, especially on imperial property. The social and economic circumstances of these slaves therefore changed, for they acquired homes of their own and land to work at a rate they themselves determined. But legally they retained their slave status: they remained property. This is a process that seems to have begun in Italy in the second century AD.[27] Of

25 For the latter, see especially Dockès, *Medieval Slavery and Liberation*, pp. 199–246.
26 Wickham, 'The other transition', especially.
27 Whittaker, 'Circe's pigs', 91–4. Carandini's excavation of the villa at Settefinestre has been a focus of much recent discussion (see Wickham, 'Marx, Sherlock Holmes', 187–9) but the idea has long been in play: see Whittaker, *ibid*. One should not overemphasize the significance of the second-century change; the proportion of the total rural workforce constituted by villa plantation slaves was probably small, and may well have been more characteristic of Italy than other parts of the Empire, even before any changes of the second century AD. And, as Whittaker points out, there had always been tenancies on Roman estates.

course, some landlords maintained a closely directed servile labour force (slaves in the legal sense) into the tenth and eleventh centuries; there were also domestic slaves in some households throughout the early Middle Ages; the slave trade touched many parts of early medieval Europe, and was actively worked by the Vikings in the tenth and eleventh centuries; and there were slaves in industrial and urban contexts in the late Middle Ages in Mediterranean regions. All slaves did not get tenancies, but it looks as if some agricultural slaves did so, and it is in any case quite clear that the Roman law of slavery was itself changing (one might say weakening) from the second century AD.[28] Change in slave working conditions is therefore potentially a contributing factor to the development of serfdom.

It is also quite clear that some slaves in early medieval Europe could amass property to such an extent that they could buy their own freedom. In England the ninth-century laws of King Alfred allow slaves time for their own commercial dealings on four Wednesdays a year;[29] on the continent ninth-century *servi* could have property; and other texts record the purchase of their own manumission by slaves. The fact that manumission could be bought by the subject is central to the issue of declining slavery: what slaves bought was 'freedom', an escape from their slave status, an entry into humanity; but the fact that they could buy this entry means that they already had recognized rights of ownership. Although legally slaves, they were already some distance from the classic chattel slave since they could both own things and thrive economically. Society may still have classified them as slaves/unfree, but the unfree could nevertheless be owners of things and to some extent control their own labour; and the legal classification has – at least – a weaker significance.[30] The south Welsh example of Bleiddud, who in the ninth century bought perpetual freedom for himself and his family from four brothers, for 4 lb 8 oz of silver, encapsulates the point.[31]

28 W.W. Buckland, *The Roman Law of Slavery* (Cambridge, 1908). Note that even Buckland has six chapters on the slave as man, against two on the slave as *res*.
29 Laws of Alfred, 43, in Attenborough (ed.), *Laws of the Earliest English Kings*, pp. 84–6.
30 A point made by Whittaker with reference to the fifth and sixth centuries. See 'Circe's pigs', 109. Compare Bois, *Transformation of the Year One Thousand*, p. 157, following Michel Rouche: the slavery of the early Middle Ages was an 'ameliorated slavery'.
31 Lichfield *marginale*, J.G. Evans with J. Rhys (ed.), *The Text of the Book of Llan Dâv* (Oxford, 1893), p. xlvi; W. Davies, *Wales in the Early Middle Ages* (Leicester, 1982), pp. 64–7. Compare the purchase of freedom by instalments by South Carolina slaves; see comments by David Turley in ch. 10, above.

Approaching from a different angle, we should also note that – slaves apart – the condition of the free peasantry of the later Roman Empire changed over the course of the fourth and fifth centuries. There were two parallel processes: the proportion of peasant proprietors declined while that of peasant tenants increased; and the restrictions falling on peasant tenants increased while the power of landlords to constrain their tenants was reinforced by the state.[32] These processes did not of themselves make the colonate (that is, the tenant peasantry) servile at that time, but they tended to tie peasants to the land, and to tie increasing numbers of them. Moreover, the first of these processes continued during the next five or six centuries, sometimes through the initiative of peasant proprietors themselves – for a range of different reasons (sale or gift to avoid tax obligations or to get cash, donations for piety, securing a protector/patron) – resulting in an enormous increase of ecclesiastical proprietorship. Classically, free peasant proprietors made small grants or sales of their own property to religious institutions and received them back as tenures for rent, in many parts of Europe in the seventh, eighth, ninth and tenth centuries. Such gifts may have made little practical difference at the time, beyond payment of a small annual rent, but they changed the shape of proprietorship in Western Europe. A world of many small-scale owners gave way to one with far fewer proprietors, some of whom had massive accumulations of property. It was in the interests of both proprietors and tenants to make, and keep, the new arrangements hereditary.

Tying the agricultural labour force to the land is one of the keys to the establishment of the condition of the later medieval peasantry. A second key must be the enforcement of physical obligations. A workforce that is not merely committed to pay rent for its tenancies but is also subject to onerous labour service is one that is under the control of its masters in a very practical sense. While it is true that the performance of services has some small-scale precedents in the late Roman Empire, much more striking than the precedents is the fact that there are periods during the early Middle Ages when labour service demands by landlords appear to have increased. By 850 these increases are signalled both by peasant complaints and by royal and/or imperial commands to landlords to

---

32 Jones, *Later Roman Empire*, vol. 2, pp. 796–803. See also comments by William Phillips in ch. 4 above. Whittaker points out that restrictions seem to have been much heavier in the Eastern than the Western Empire ('Circe's pigs', 101–2); and makes the important observation that once *coloni* began to be exempted from military service, they became less easy to distinguish from hutted slaves (*ibid.*, 110).

limit the impositions. Peasants complained that they were subject to new impositions where there were none before and that they were subjected to heavier impositions than had been customary. So, while the eighth-century *Lex Bavariorum* from southern Germany, for example, details customary ranges of labour services that fell on free and servile tenants of great estates, and the great northern French polyptychs of the early ninth century list customary services falling on free and servile tenures and tenants, the Edict of Pîtres (864) refers to new services; *coloni* who went from Mitry to Compiègne (northern France) in 861 complained that although they were free they were quite improperly being bound to 'inferior service'.[33] The complaints are notable during the ninth century, the end of a period when it is also notable that new tenancies were created on conditions of labour service rather than (or in addition to) rent; charter evidence of 754 details harvesting and ploughing for the monastery of St Gall in Switzerland, for example. It looks as if the eighth and ninth centuries was a period of increasing physical obligations – heavier obligations, affecting more people. Labour service was increasing.

In many parts of Europe impositions continued to increase over the tenth to twelfth centuries, particularly in the context of private castle building and the establishment of seigneurial territories. In this era the range of obligations was extended and lordly monopolies created.[34] Complaints were certainly made about 'evil customs' (*mals usos, malos usaticos, mali usi, malae consuetudines*) from the late tenth century, as emphasized in the classic French model of the development of serfdom. However, different things were happening in these later centuries: firstly, while it is true to say that there were new labour impositions, the range and weight of new dues is more striking than the weight of new labour services; secondly, the creation of seigneurial territories (known as *Bannherrschaft* in Germany) was not intrinsically a landlordly act – all landlords were not *seigneurs*, for creating a *seigneurie* was to do with controlling territory, not owning it, and was at heart a political process. Of course, increased impositions added to the burdens of many rural workers, but benefits sometimes came with the burdens, for some or all of the rural population. There is an element of consent to the

---

33 See J.L. Nelson, 'Dispute settlement in Carolingian West Francia', in W. Davies and P. Fouracre (eds), *The Settlement of Disputes in Early Medieval Europe* (Cambridge, 1986), pp. 51–2, and references to other cases cited, p. 52, n. 27.

34 Duby, *Rural Economy*, pp. 220–31; Bois, *Transformation of the Year One Thousand*, pp. 162–71; see also above, p. 227–8; and comments by Brenner in ch. 13.

process;[35] and not all peasants subjected to these obligations could be described as serfs – by any definition. Since some subject peasants were clearly not serfs, I find it hard to believe that seigneurial demands could have *determined* servile status. New seigneurial impositions made life more difficult for serfs (and others); it did not create them.[36]

It would be conventional to say that a third key to the development of serfdom is jurisdictional. People classified as serfs in the later Middle Ages did not have access to a public system of justice. They could not take their cases to public courts but had to have them heard in the courts of the appropriate lords. They could not take their lords to a public court if, for example, they were ejected from their lands. And they were subject to the jurisdiction of private lords, who could punish them and take fines, as appropriate. Slaves of remote Antiquity had no place in a court of any type; if a slave killed someone, he would be subject to the jurisdiction of his master. But by the late Empire they were answerable to the public judicial system for their crimes (though they could not take part personally in judicial proceedings) and could in some circumstances give evidence.[37] The *servi* of estates of the eighth and ninth centuries seem to have been largely subject to the jurisdiction of their masters. But the tenant peasantry that complained of impositions (and of 'inferior service') in the ninth century had opportunities for redress beyond lordly jurisdictions; peasants could after all take their complaints to the king, like the peasants of Mitry did in 861; or they could successfully oppose new labour obligations in public courts, as the peasantry of Lemonta did against the church of St Ambrose in Milan in 905.[38]

When and how did the tenant peasantry become excluded from public systems, if this is indeed what happened? This issue is inseparable from the issue of the nature of public jurisdiction. It is

35 Cf. the Italian points made above, p. 231.
36 There was, of course, considerable regional differentiation; Christian conquerors in Valencia imposed new seigneurial dues: see the article by P. Guichard in Bonnassie, *From Slavery to Feudalism*, p. 268; there were new payments in England in the late twelfth century, R.H. Hilton, 'Freedom and villeinage in England', *Past and Present*, 31 (1965); in late twelfth-century Catalonia, the lord's right to mistreat his peasants (*ius maletractandi*) became generally acknowledged and in 1202 peasants were prohibited from appealing to royal courts against their lords' mistreatment. See P. Freedman, *The Origins of Peasant Servitude in Medieval Catalonia* (Cambridge, 1991), pp. 89–118.
37 Buckland, *Roman Law of Slavery*, pp. 92–3.
38 See Nelson, 'Dispute settlement'. Lemonta is cited by Duby, *Rural Economy*, p. 50; it is discussed at length by Ross Balzaretti, 'The Lands of Saint Ambrose' (University of London Ph.D. thesis, 1989), pp. 219–36.

widely maintained that in many parts of Western Europe 'public' courts fell into 'private' hands in the tenth and eleventh centuries; in other words, where formerly some 'official' would have presided in court and taken a share of the fines, now a landlord did so, sometimes notionally after delegation from the ruler. Hence, there were private courts for the tenants of a landlord (Duby's domanial jurisdiction) as well as seigneurial courts, created by particularly powerful lords for the inhabitants of the whole territory they sought to dominate, whether tenant, serf or proprietor/freeholder (Duby's *banal* jurisdiction).

It is not controversial that landlords held a wide range of courts in many parts of Western Europe by the eleventh century, but the assumption that this development made any immediate practical difference to peasant offender or peasant plaintiff is unwarranted. In the world of the tenth and eleventh centuries it made little difference whether a count or an abbot or some other aristocrat took the chair in court. And, in practice, in most of Western Europe much of the rural population became subject to a number of *different* jurisdictions, which varied with the nature of the business.[39] Very little 'public' system, in the sense that we understand it nowadays, existed. However, this did not mean that cases were necessarily settled in an unreasonable and unfair way. Indeed, one could regard the great seigneurial jurisdictions as a type of public system: not run by officials of state, nor run as a state system, but open to all within the jurisdiction, and – importantly – with their own regular procedures.[40] Lack of access to the public court did not limit the freedom of the individual.

Hence, it is reasonable to argue that the extension of private jurisdictions in the tenth and eleventh centuries provided the conditions whereby a larger proportion of the peasantry could be excluded from public systems of justice; but this only became significant if the lord of a court acted in a completely capricious way; or if public courts existed alongside private courts and different

---

39 It is broadly true to say that over the twelfth century the different jurisdictions tended to clarify; in 1180, for example, the count of Mâcon kept for himself (i.e. for his own private court) jurisdiction over cases of robbery, adultery, homicide and usury; A. Bernard and A. Bruel (eds), *Recueil des chartes de l'abbaye de Cluny* (Paris, 1876–1903), no. 4279, vol. 5, p. 646.

40 See the similar comments of Barthélemy, 'La mutation féodale', 774. Note the procedure inherited from comital courts, the oral evidence taken, the *sapientes* assisting the judgement, the use of pledges (*pignora*) to guarantee future payment, in seigneurial courts in twelfth-century Lombardy: Menant, *Campagnes Lombardes*, pp. 433–4.

things happened in them, as began to be the case in England in the late twelfth century. Lord–serf relationships did not result from the creation of private jurisdictions.[41] The establishment of private jurisdiction only becomes a key to the development of serfdom if you define serfdom as exclusion from public jurisdiction.

In similar fashion, the imposition of dues by landlords and *seigneurs* is only another key to the development of serfdom if the payment of such dues is seen as the determining criterion of servile status. New dues were created, especially in the eleventh century in continental Western Europe (though probably as late as the late twelfth century in England).[42] But seigneurial dues could fall on free as well as servile peasants. It wasn't the dues that created the serfs, rather that serfs suffered especially from them. This again is an effect, not the cause, of enserfment. (In any case tied dependants, who were liable to make annual payments to their lords, are identified in tenth- and eleventh-century texts *before* the establishment of local *seigneuries*.[43])

So when did serfdom begin? It is unconvincing to propose a single date or era. If we exclude from consideration for the moment the rural slaves of late Antiquity and their descendants, the origins of serfdom lie in continuing, though not uniformly progressive, processes stretching from the fourth to eleventh centuries AD; they lie in long continuities, not sudden rupture. There were significant beginnings in the fourth and fifth centuries with changes in the status of the colonate; there was a significant deterioration in personal condition for many in the eighth and ninth centuries with new labour impositions; and, over the whole period, the proportion of tenants to proprietors increased.[44]

If we do not exclude rural slaves from consideration, then one

---

41 Increasingly, in effect, the serf's position was protected by custom: see John Hatcher's comments on thirteenth-century England, 'English serfdom and villeinage', *Past and Present*, 90 (1981), 10.

42 Hatcher (*ibid.*, 27–33) argued against Hilton that the impositions had been laid at an earlier date, were relaxed somewhat in the mid-twelfth century, and reimposed in the 1180s.

43 See Paul Fouracre and Tim Reuter in Davies and Fouracre (eds), *Property and Power*, pp. 74–7, 176–8.

44 In southern England some dependants on estates were tied, and some were liable to provide service and some were subject to the lord's jurisdiction, at least by the late ninth century and probably by the seventh century; Laws of Ine 39, 50, 67; Attenborough (ed.), *Laws of the Earliest English Kings*, pp. 48, 52, 58. There is a recent tendency to disassociate trends of the fifth and sixth centuries from those of the ninth and tenth centuries; since there is little to suggest an *increase* in free peasant proprietorship or a dramatic rate of emancipation of hutted slaves in the seventh and eighth centuries, I remain more persuaded by the force of the long-term trends.

might very well say that there was a type of serfdom in Western Europe throughout this period. These rural slaves were also serfs: though slaves, their legal classification as such did not reflect their economic or social condition.[45] They had households and personal property and were tied.

Outside the mainstream

The preceding discussion has focused on continental Western Europe and the mainstream historiography of early serfdom in the Middle Ages. It is of some interest to look at regions which are conventionally regarded as peripheral to see if comparable processes were operating there.

In most Celtic regions very clear concepts of social stratification are evidenced throughout the early Middle Ages, that is in Ireland, Scotland, Wales and Brittany. These were highly stratified societies, in which status – which was related to honour[46] – was quantifiable. In most areas there were strong contrasts between free and unfree, noble (or privileged) and non-noble, with some finer status distinctions within these categories.[47] Although the terminology of unfreedom varies, there is some consistency about servile status across Celtic areas. There is very little to suggest gang slavery; there is plenty to suggest domestic slavery (the household slave, who may well have done agricultural work); there are also plenty of contexts that suggest agricultural slaves who had independent households. Slaves could clearly be bought and sold; they were property. However, since some purchased their freedom, those must have been able to control their own labour to some extent and amass a certain amount of personal property. This is therefore like the slavery of the late Roman period and very early Middle Ages (pre-tenth century); it is not plantation slavery.[48] To the extent that we are using slave and serf as legal categories, these people can be

---

45 Cf. Wickham, 'Marx, Sherlock Holmes', 187; Goetz, 'Serfdom and the beginnings of a "seigneurial system"', 48–50.
46 Cf. the comments of Richard Saller in ch. 6 above.
47 All Celtic areas did not, however, share the same refinements of social structure; in early Wales, in particular, it is difficult to identify a clear distinction between noble and non-noble free.
48 F. Kelly, *A Guide to Early Irish Law* (Dublin, 1988), pp. 95–7; A.A.M. Duncan, *Scotland. The Making of the Kingdom* (Edinburgh, 1975), pp. 326–48; Davies, *Wales*, pp. 64–7; W. Davies, *Small Worlds. The Village Community in Early Medieval Brittany* (London, 1988), pp. 87–9.

regarded as more slave than serf.[49] Celtic societies had servile groups, but servile overwhelmingly on the model of moderate ancient slavery rather than classic medieval serfdom.

In Ireland, in addition to the slave groups, there were highly developed, and apparently very common, clientship networks within the free population. This included clientship between free peasants and nobles, a relationship traditionally described as 'base clientship' in English. In fact, it looks as if there were relatively few independent peasant proprietors. Clientship was essentially an economic relationship: the lord provided stock (or sometimes land) and the client in return provided regular renders and performed some obligatory duties like reaping, grave-digging and road-clearing. The client, though a dependant, was free; he could terminate the relationship (by repayment of twice the value of the stock, and by other payments, depending on the initial arrangement); he was not in any sense owned by the lord; he had his business done in a public court, where his oath and his capacity to witness had value; he could amass profits and improve his own social status; he had his own honour-price[50] and could expect compensation for damage; he largely controlled his own labour; he had a household and personal property.[51] This is not remotely like servitude; nor is he an Irish version of the English or French manorial tenant. The physical obligations did not carry with them the consequence of permanent ties nor control of the body. Many things changed with the Norman Conquests of the eleventh and twelfth centuries, however, in all Celtic areas, for conquest brought foreign ideas and new relationships. My comments relate to pre-Conquest societies only.

What is interesting about the Celtic material in the overall European context is this: these are societies which had very pronounced servile elements. Note, for example, the high proportion of slaves in Cornwall (a former Celtic kingdom) in 1086, by

---

49 In Ireland, at least, there were also people who are conventionally described as 'half-free' – the *fuidir* – who could in some circumstances be released from their obligations to their lords. See N. Brady, 'Labor and agriculture in early medieval Ireland: evidence from the sources', in A.J. Frantzen and D. Moffat (eds), *The Work of Work* (Glasgow, 1994), pp. 128–9 – a very helpful paper.

50 Cf. Binchy's comment on the Irish law tract, D.A. Binchy (ed.), *Críth Gablach* (Dublin, 1941), p. 97.

51 *Críth Gablach* suggests appropriate sizes of house, outhouses, furnishings for each stratum of society; excavation at Deer Park Farms, Glenarm, has revealed evidence of buildings of early medieval date which have strikingly similar dimensions. See C. Lynn, 'Deer Park Farms, Glenarm, Co. Antrim', *Archaeology Ireland*, 1 (1987).

comparison with other parts of England.⁵² But although they did not have slave systems in the plantation sense, their servility was not the serfdom of the late Middle Ages; unfree people were owned, had negligible rights and no access to courts, and were very largely controlled by the free. The free dependants, though dependent, were not hereditarily tied, nor subject to onerous labour service, nor subject to private jurisdiction. They did not experience the progressive limitations on their freedom which affected their continental and English counterparts; or, at least, not until conquerors introduced new ideas.

In early Scandinavia and Iceland slavery was also a major social fact, though not an economic system. It came to an end, variously, in the thirteenth and fourteenth centuries and was not followed by any type of serfdom. Ruth Karras has argued strongly that the reason the end of slavery did not give rise to serfdom in Scandinavia was because new ways of viewing society developed there: in other words, because of conceptual rather than economic change.⁵³ Social differentiation developed among the free in a way that had not been characteristic of late pre-Christian and early Christian Norse societies; consequently, some became excluded from political rights which they had in theory previously held. There was therefore no need to invoke concepts of slavery or unfreedom to exclude some social groups from social and political participation, and the concepts dwindled in significance.

It is extremely interesting that in both cultures slavery did not lead into the classic serfdom of late medieval Europe, just as the decline of slavery in the Byzantine Empire did not lead into a western-style serfdom.⁵⁴ What was missing were the forces (partly political, partly religious) that led many free peasants to become tenants in continental Europe and the forces (largely economic) that led landlords to extend labour and other demands.⁵⁵ On that

---

52 D.A.E. Pelteret, 'Slavery in Anglo-Saxon England', in J.D. Woods and D.A.E. Pelteret (eds), *The Anglo-Saxons: Synthesis and Achievement* (Waterloo, Ontario, 1985), p. 122.

53 Karras, *Slavery and Society in Medieval Scandinavia*, pp. 142–63. Since she wrote, Tore Iversen, of the Historical Institute at the University of Bergen, has finished a doctoral thesis on 'Trelldommen, Norwegian slavery in the Middle Ages'; he argues that the absence of serfdom in Norway had more to do with the development of a strong public authority than with economic factors.

54 M. Kaplan, *Les hommes et la terre à Byzance du VIe au XIe siècle* (Paris, 1992), pp. 347–8, 578–9.

55 Underlying reasons (such as the increased market activity favoured by Bois) are, of course, of great importance, but it would require another paper to deal with them.

account, there remains good reason to agree with Bloch that the decline of ancient slavery did not *cause* medieval serfdom. Though some ancient slaves may have been ancestors of medieval serfs, the creation of the particular form of serfdom that characterized Western Europe in the late Middle Ages needs other explanations.[56]

What changed?

What then changed between the slavery of the second century and the serfdom of the twelfth? One change, though a change that may not be as numerically significant as once thought, is that the number of rural slave gangs declined, to be replaced by dependants working from individual households, with some element of personal control of the day. Another, major change is that the proportion of totally free peasants declined: an unmeasurable but significant proportion of the rural labour force became subject to an element of landlord control. Put simply, there seem to have been rather more medieval serfs than there were ancient slaves.[57] Thirdly, over the period to the twelfth century the range and nature of obligations which lay on this dependent peasantry tended to increase. Of course, slavery continued in some parts, even in rural contexts, and so did free peasant proprietors.

In the ninth century, there was still a clear distinction between servile and free in many parts of Western Europe.[58] The servile may or may not have descended from hutted slaves or tied *coloni* or captives or some other group; we have no way of knowing. But whatever their personal ancestry, it is perfectly clear that ninth-century servility was different from classic Roman slavery, although it may not have been too different from 'hutted slavery'.

To put flesh on this, take the example of material from the area of Redon in north-west France.[59] There is good documentation which reveals an extremely clear differentiation between 'free' and servile

---

[56] Cf. Freedman, *Origins of Peasant Servitude*, p. 207, where he points out that Catalan serfdom grew out of the freedom of early settlers; there was no continuity from ancient slavery here.

[57] Although we do not know precisely what proportion of the rural population was servile – and the issue is controversial.

[58] Cf. Barthélemy, 'La mutation féodale', 772; Bois, *Transformation of the Year One Thousand*, pp. 34–5.

[59] This is a Celtic area in the sense that the vernacular language was Celtic at this period; however, by the ninth century the region shared in the broad political and economic trends of north-west Europe.

strata in peasant communities, although the terminology is unstable (*heredes, homines, ingenui, mancipii,* and especially *coloni* and *manentes*). The free often had obligations but it is nevertheless striking that they were members of their own local communities in the fullest of senses, whether they were proprietors or tenants; they were vociferous and argumentative; they took part in dispute proceedings as parties, witnesses, judges, or sureties; they were the *plebenses,* the community of the *plebs* (village). By contrast the servile population (which was considerable in some villages) was silent and passive; we hear of them, of their dues, and of their movement with the transfer of property, but we never hear them speak; they were outside the process of community decision-making.[60] They were not members of the community in any social or political sense. By the end of the ninth century, the abbot of Redon held the local court in the *plebs* of Bains; the free peasantry thereby became subject to his so-called jurisdiction. At that period this certainly did not deny their freedom and it made no difference to the judicial processes: there were local judges, witnesses, and sureties, just as there were in cases heard by a *machtiern* (local hereditary aristocrat) or by a representative of the ruler.[61] When the peasant Justus was accused by the three peasant sons of Uesilloc over inheritance rights, the case was heard before the abbot in 892, in the presence of lay and ecclesiastical witnesses, and resolved by the sworn testimony of seven local elders.[62]

So, what did it mean to be servile in the ninth century? For the mass of the servile population, it meant being hereditarily tied and unable to relocate. It meant having no powers of negotiation. It meant being subject to the will of your master, who would in some cases have commanded the way you used your labour on a day-to-day basis; alternatively, if you controlled your own labour, you were liable to make substantial returns to your master. It meant that you could, in effect, be bought and sold, whether by dealing in your person, or by dealing in the property you worked. It meant no access to courts, whether public or private. It meant having no say in community issues and policy, and playing no part in public meetings. I am not sure that it meant being treated like an animal, though it may have done so sometimes.[63] It did not mean being

---

60 A. de Courson (ed.), *Cartulaire de Redon* (Paris, 1863); see Davies, *Small Worlds,* especially pp. 47, 87–9, 102–4, for serfs.
61 Davies, *Small Worlds,* p. 196.
62 *Cartulaire de Redon,* no. 271.
63 *Pace* Bonnassie, *From Slavery to Feudalism,* pp. 17–22, 340.

obliged to pay a wide range of different dues. In many cases it meant having your own household and nuclear family.

These were people without rights, controlled by an economically superior group. It is a type of slavery that lacks the most extreme features of developed slave systems; or a type of serfdom in which masters had a particularly high degree of power over the persons that constituted their property. But the people were permitted a degree of humanity; they may have been outside society but they were not without family. They were not citizens, but they were humans. And while *servi* and *coloni* could be bought and sold, in practice dealing in people was increasingly a consequence of dealing in the properties with which they were associated. By the ninth century, the tie between the man and the land was already much stronger than the perception of man as object.[64]

We do not know what proportion of the rural population fell into the servile category in the ninth century, but it is likely that it varied widely from region to region. Where I have looked at detail this has even varied between 10 per cent and 50 per cent per village in a small zone.

Serfdom was different by the twelfth century. The servile condition had extended to encompass more people. But some things about the state of the ninth-century rural slave/serf had changed for the better by the twelfth.[65] Although there were new obligations, payments featured more strongly than labour service. Serfs were subject to private jurisdictions and went to court: over the course of 300 years the servile had come into court; they had come into their local communities; they had acquired some rights, if only a case to maintain the status quo.[66] In effect they had acquired membership of their societies. These people were now recognized as people and were far from being objects. In terms of participation in their local communities, they had become enfranchised.

How could this have come about? Of course there were many regional differences in balance and chronology across Western Europe, but in many places acts of emancipation tailed off and the clarity of the distinction between servile and free disappeared at

---

64 *Pace* Bloch, *Slavery and Serfdom*, pp. 54–5, it is not reasonable to argue that the link between human status and the land had disappeared at this date.

65 Cf. the implications of the comments of Barthélemy, 'Qu'est-ce que le servage?', 267–71, that serfdom weakened over the eleventh and twelfth centuries.

66 This is the burden of the comments of R. Boutruche, *Seigneurie et féodalité* (Paris, 1968–70), vol. 1, pp. 145, 155–6. Cf. Bloch, *Slavery and Serfdom*, p. 63.

some point in the eleventh century.⁶⁷ In mid-eleventh-century France some serfs were still under a master's jurisdiction; others no longer were.⁶⁸ By 1050 the small proportion of unfree in Lombardy had disappeared.⁶⁹ The establishment of seigneurial powers in the eleventh and twelfth centuries (and of advocacies in Germany) must have been instrumental, for it tended to have a levelling effect on the rural population. This was for two reasons: seigneurial power was expressed in relation to a territory and fell on all within it, no matter whether their personal status was free or serf, and both freemen and serfs used the seigneurial court; secondly, it created new and overlapping jurisdictions. Paradoxically, the 'Feudal Revolution' put more control of surplus into the hands of lordly proprietors at the same time as it improved conditions for the servile population. The 'Feudal Revolution' may have given shape to a particular form of medieval serfdom, but it neither created that form nor inaugurated serfdom.

Postscript

Whether ninth-century servile people should be called slaves or serfs depends entirely on the definitions used. A perfectly good case can be made for both terms. At any point between 400 and 1100, in most parts of Western Europe, there was a spectrum of types of tied dependant, who had less or more control of their own labour, and negligible to substantial rights recognized by the community surrounding them – from the object fed by the master to the householder *censarius* who made an annual return to him. All of these

67 Cf. Ross Samson's observation that the replacement of *servi* by *bordarii* between 1066 and 1086 in England must reflect a perceived change in status; see his 'The end of early medieval slavery', in Frantzen and Moffat (eds), *The Work of Work*, p. 98. The loss of the distinction comes after a long period of unclarity in Western Europe about the force of the free/unfree divide: firstly, the unfree became able to buy freedom; secondly, although north Frankish texts used free and servile labels, the functions of the people they listed did not match the labels; thirdly, the earliest (tenth-century) Continental formulations of the 'Tripartite Society' notion, which divided society into free laity, unfree laity and clergy, were replaced. The change is reflected by Adalbero in the early eleventh century (clergy, fighters and *servi*) and by the standard tripartite formulation – with loss of any notional military capacity by west Frankish peasants. Church councils may have tried to enforce prohibition of slave/free marriages in the eleventh century, but more and more seem to have been uncertain of their status: T. Reuter, *Germany in the Early Middle Ages* (London, 1991), pp. 101–2.

68 Barthélemy, 'Qu'est-ce que le servage?', 260, 266; Duby, *Rural Economy and Country Life*, p. 188.

69 Menant, *Campagnes Lombardes*, pp. 399–401.

people were in a state of bondage. None of them would have had much power of, or capacity for, negotiation with his master; most of them were saleable. But being sold along with landed property, however the conveyancing was formulated, had nothing like the personal consequences of being sold and transported. The one kept family and humanity; the other did not.

By 1150 a lot had changed. There was still the spectrum of persons with varying rights and varying powers of control over limb, labour and goods, but sale of persons looks much less common and most of the tied could go to court. As economies and labour options diversified, being bound – however weakly – appeared more onerous. For most of the early Middle Ages serfdom existed but was not an issue; only when the options multiplied, did it become one, even as conditions improved.[70]

---

70 I am very grateful to my friend Chris Wickham for his comments on early drafts of this chapter.

XIX

Local participation and legal ritual in early medieval law courts

When I thought about the questions posed by the organisers of the *Moral World of the Law* conference, my immediate reaction was that the early middle ages did not fit into their framework at all. This was, first, because early medieval courts were places for much more than legal and judicial business: most strikingly, they were occasions as well as places, occasions when friends were entertained, visitors were received and 'policy' was discussed and determined; settlements were negotiated and business was done. Hence, to suggest that the court was in opposition to everyday life makes no sense. Secondly, law itself was often a mixture of the customary, the prescriptive and the academic; hence, to pose questions about conflict between custom and written legislation is meaningless (or, at least, it is at one level). Thirdly, early medievalists do not normally expect to find professional lawyers manipulating courtroom drama and hogging the public stage. The image seems to sit too squarely in the twentieth century, in the world of mass media, global entertainment and vast audiences.

On the other hand, it is not too difficult to think of rules and rituals in the context of early medieval law and courts; and, on deeper reflection, some of the assumptions behind the framing of the questions do become surprisingly appropriate.

This is not the place to provide a full description of the early medieval context, but the points that immediately follow provide some essential briefing for those who may be unfamiliar with early medieval western Europe. The cultures with which we are concerned in the early middle ages had levels of literacy that were exceptionally low by modern, western standards, even if we nowadays recognise that there was a higher degree of literacy than once thought.[1] Partly as a consequence of the limited place of writing in everyday life at that time, anyone investigating the period in the late twentieth century has to confront considerable problems of evidence:

---

[1] R. McKitterick, *The Carolingians and the Written Word* (Cambridge, 1989), *passim*.

there are very many things that we do not and cannot know – about life, about events and about courts; there are few accounts of court proceedings that could remotely be described as 'impartial'; we are nearly always dependent on a single record for our knowledge of what happened in a case;[2] and although some of these records have a formal status, drawn up at the conclusion of a case, they are nothing like as full as a modern recorder's transcript and are even farther from the objective. We are extremely dependent upon the eyes and ears of a single scribe, who frequently came from a church or monastery with an interest in the outcome; documents produced by beneficiaries were common.[3] However, despite the obvious problems which that circumstance creates, the repetition of elements of procedure in a multiplicity of recorded cases can be as valuable a guide to procedure, if not more, as a mass of well corroborated detail on a single incident. Useful, usable, material does exist.

Law texts themselves, that is the texts which we depend on for statements of the content of law, may in fact be records of cases rather than anything approaching legislation; and they are often found embedded within conveyancing documents and estate surveys. A body of case law may therefore be our only guide to the principles of a legal system. Where principle is stated, there is frequently a pronounced customary element, being descriptive of what was believed to be normal practice. The texts sometimes include new rules, whether deriving from a ruler's commands or a council's deliberations; they often include elements of new rules as well as custom; and both rulers and lawyers confirmed and modified custom as well as made provision for completely new situations. The fact that we have any texts at all can be for varied and different reasons: kings ordered records to be made (and distributed); lawyers collected and copied material to assist with professional practice, creating both the library reference work and the pocket book for journeys; others (usually clerics) had a scholarly habit of studying law; and others had a personal interest in 'being in the know'.[4]

The early middle ages are a long period, eight hundred years or so, and cover a multiplicity of cultures and language groups, from the Near East to

---

[2] Although, for example, some Spanish cases generated two or more documents per case; cf. a case held at Empuries in Catalonia in 843 and others in León in the tenth century; R. Collins, '"Sicut lex Gothorum continet": law and charters in ninth- and tenth-century León and Catalonia', *English Historical Review*, 396 (1985), pp. 492–4, 498–502.

[3] W. Davies and P. Fouracre, eds., *The Settlement of Disputes in Early Medieval Europe* (Cambridge, 1986), pp. 211–12; P. Chaplais, 'The origin and authenticity of the royal Anglo-Saxon diploma', *Journal of the Society of Archivists*, 3 (1965–9), pp. 55–61; cf. S. Keynes, *The Diplomas of King Æthelred 'The Unready' 978–1016* (Cambridge, 1980), p. 28.

[4] Pocket books: see D. Jenkins, *The Law of Hywel Dda* (Llandysul, 1986), pp. xxi–xxiii. Early medieval law texts: P. Wormald, '*Lex scripta* and *verbum regis*: legislation and Germanic kingship, from Euric to Cnut', in P. H. Sawyer and I. N. Wood, eds., *Early Medieval Kingship* (Leeds, 1977), pp. 105–38.

Ireland, and the Mediterranean to Iceland. It makes no sense to generalise across the lot. In order to make some sort of sense, and keep this essay graspable, it will focus on western Europe (including Ireland, but not Scandinavia) and on the period from the seventh to the tenth century, c. 650–950. It would be valid, and relevant to the issues considered in this volume, to discuss the eleventh and twelfth centuries but one would make quite different points and suggest different emphases: the issue of competing systems, for example, would become much more prominent.

I. PROCEDURE

Perhaps surprisingly, given the range of cultures, the surviving records of court cases suggest that there were considerable similarities of procedure across time, space and language group. Although, of course, there were differences, the degree of similarity is striking, as is the familiarity of some aspects of procedure (evidential aspects especially).

Legal cases were virtually always heard at public meetings, often involving a large number of people, whether they occurred in Celtic, Germanic or Latin cultures. The numbers attending could easily reach fifty or a hundred and sometimes ran into several hundreds; more than fifty might be listed by name. More than 55 individuals were mentioned as present at Valenciennes in northern France in the 690s; over 40 witnessed an inquest about mill and shipping rights at Cremona in the Po valley in 841; about 90 were present at *Clofesho* (England) in 824 – including 'the whole ecclesiastical and political "establishment"', as Patrick Wormald put it (Anglo-Saxon charters are especially notable for their long lists of witnesses who attended public meetings).[5]

Another common feature is that some person, or some group of people, presided over the meeting: there was a chairperson (sometimes literally using a special seat). In Carolingian Europe there could well be two people sharing the position, like the count and bishop who presided at Empuries (Catalonia) in 843 or the duke and bishop at Lucca (northern Italy) in 847.[6] This position of president or chair might be held by a king, or royal or other officers, or a bishop,

---

[5] P. Fouracre, ed., appendix no. 6, in Davies and Fouracre, eds., *Settlement of Disputes*, pp. 244–5; C. Manaresi, ed., *I Placiti del 'Regnum Italiae'*, 3 vols. (Rome, 1955–60), vol. I, Inquisitiones no. 7, pp. 576–81; W. de Gray Birch, ed., *Cartularium Saxonicum*, 4 vols. (London, 1885–99), vol. I, no. 379, pp. 519–22, on which by P. Wormald, 'Charters, law and the settlement of disputes in Anglo-Saxon England', in Davies and Fouracre, eds., *Settlement of Disputes*, p. 152.

[6] P. de Marca, *Marca Hispanica sive Limes Hispanicus*, ed. S. Baluze (Paris, 1688), appendix 16, pp. 779–80; Manaresi, ed., *Placiti*, vol. I, no. 51, pp. 169–73. For all aspects of procedure in Italy, see now F. Bougard, *La justice dans le royaume d'Italie de la fin du VIIIe siècle au début du XIe siècle* (Rome, 1995).

or the holder of an immunity (where the immunist had personal political power and in effect ruled his own patch of land), and it demanded especial respect.

Plaintiffs and defendants did not usually speak for themselves, for there was often an advocate to speak on behalf of the principal parties (necessarily so for women and for churches). Advocates did not have to be professional lawyers (and probably were not usually so), but they were likely to have been literate and may well have been very experienced in 'the law'; in Ireland, by contrast, a land noted for its distinctive class of high status professional lawyers, they were likely to be lawyers.

It was common for the accused to be required to make a formal denial, perhaps on oath, perhaps supported by other people. For example, at Nogent-sur-Marne in the 690s Abbot Ermenoald had to deny formally the accusation that he had failed to make good his pledge to pay oil and good wine to Chaino, abbot of the monastery of St Denis, or, failing that, to pay a fine; and at Chasseneuil in Poitou, in 828, the advocate for the monastery of Cormery denied the accusation that increased rents had been required from peasants by using the written evidence of an estate survey.[7] Records of court cases place an emphasis on the formal act of denial and its place in the procedure.

The oath was also a major recurrent element of procedure: oaths of denial, like that made at the Nogent case cited above, or others taken on the Gospels, are but one form. Oaths were also taken to underline evidence of fact: in the Loire valley in 857 (within the immunity of St Martin, Tours) nine local peasants swore to the truth of disputed facts in a case, swearing by God, their christianity, their good faith, and the relics of the saints there present.[8] Oaths might also be sworn to reinforce written evidence, as required in the case of Helmstan's claim to property in England in the early tenth century.[9] Oath-helping, essentially the procedure of making public statements of confidence in the character of one of the parties to a dispute, could also play a part: at Langon in eastern Brittany in 801, in default of evidence, the accused had to swear to the truth of his defence himself, but also had to associate twelve 'suitable' men with his oath; in Canterbury in 844 men from the three Kentish monasteries of Dover, Folkestone and Lyminge swore on behalf of the archbishop, in addition to those of his household at Christchurch, in a dispute about a grant to Christchurch.[10] In

---

[7] P. Fouracre, ed., appendix no. 5, in Davies and Fouracre, eds., *Settlement of Disputes*, pp. 243–4; L. Levillain, ed., *Recueil des actes de Pépin I et de Pépin II, rois d'Aquitaine (814–848)* (Paris, 1926), no. 12, pp. 46–7.

[8] M. Thévenin, ed., *Textes relatifs aux institutions privées et publiques aux époques mérovingienne et carolingienne* (Paris, 1887), no. 89, pp. 120–3.

[9] F. E. Harmer, ed., *Select English Historical Documents of the Ninth and Tenth Centuries* (Cambridge, 1914), no. 18, pp. 30–2.

[10] A. de Courson, ed., *Cartulaire de Redon* (Paris, 1863), no. 191, pp. 147–8; Birch, ed., *Cartularium Saxonicum*, vol. II, no. 445, pp. 22–5.

these texts the oaths sworn were Christian oaths, although early Irish material shows traces of pre-Christian oath-swearing.[11] The Christian character of the oath could well be emphasised by reference to explicitly Christian objects, such as the Gospels, the altar, or relics; one well-known thief who was denying a charge in Gwynllŵg in south-east Wales, some time in or before the eleventh century, was threatened with having to take an oath on St Cadog's holy knife: on hearing this threat, he immediately confessed.[12]

The taking of evidence was also extremely common. It was taken from written texts and also from personal witnesses to fact or to the past, and it could be provided by accuser and accused or by an independent panel. At the Chasseneuil case, it was a written estate survey that was produced as evidence against the peasants; in the Catalan case of 843 cited above the judges made a point of asking for proof, written or oral; in the Pavia case of 880 discussed below, the court asked repeatedly for a *notitia*. At one of the ruler Salomon's courts, in eastern Brittany, *c.* 857, Salomon gave the machtiern Ratfred (a petty aristocrat) ten days to produce proof and witnesses (who had to be 'law-worthy' local men) at another court; Ratfred was required to demonstrate at this second hearing that the abbot of the monastery of Redon had given him property in Bains; this he failed to do and thereby lost the case.[13]

The characteristics mentioned so far were norms. Not quite so common but still common were the use of pledges, the making of a record and the invocation of penalties for contempt. Using pledges or sureties to guarantee some part of the procedure (especially to guarantee that parties would present themselves at a deferred hearing) is particularly well evidenced in Italian material, although not exclusive to Italy, with plenty of narrative detail of comings and goings to different hearings. Pledges (both persons and things) were also used to guarantee that the judgement or settlement that terminated a case would be carried out. Making a record of the outcome of a case, listing some or all of the witnesses to the occasion, could be ordered by kings (as Pippin I of Aquitaine did for the monastery of Cormery) or requested by successful parties (as Norbert the priest did at the conclusion of the Loire valley case); the victors often generated such records in England, but public notaries did so in ninth-century Spain.[14]

[11] F. Kelly, *A Guide to Early Irish Law* (Dublin, 1988), p. 198.
[12] 'Vita Sancti Cadoci', ch. 33, in A. W. Wade-Evans, *Vitae Sanctorum Britanniae et Genealogiae* (Cardiff, 1944), pp. 94–6. See further below, pp. 56–7, on oaths and judgement.
[13] See above, nn. 7, 2; Manaresi, ed., *Placiti*, vol. I, no. 89, pp. 318–22; de Courson, ed., *Cartulaire de Redon*, no. 105, pp. 79–80. For machtierns, see W. Davies, *Small Worlds. The Village Community in Early Medieval Brittany* (London, 1988), pp. 138–42, 175–83.
[14] Cf. Levillain, ed., *Recueil des actes*, no. 12; Thévenin, ed., *Textes relatifs*, no. 89; cf. above, n. 3.

Heavy penalties could be invoked for 'contempt' of court: for producing false written 'evidence' in tenth-century Castille, for example, or for sending a substitute to answer the charge at the Valenciennes case.[15] The articulation of the idea of contempt (*contemptio ordo racionis*) in itself emphasises that these were systems with their own rules and own logic.

If one turns from consistency of procedure to its rituals, some descriptions of cases include ritualistic elements that appear decidedly quaint; on the surface what went on in these courts looks strange. Hence, in courts in Aquitaine, Francia and Italy, people grasped a *festuca* (symbolic rod) to indicate acceptance of the judges' decision; and in Spanish León, a witness to fact was submitted to the ordeal of grasping two or three stones from hot water with his right hand; in order to demonstrate the truth of his evidence, his undamaged hand had to be exposed to public scrutiny three days later. While the need for witnesses to go to the ordeal could be set aside (as it was in 940 when water rights for their mill were judged to Sancho and Nuño Gómez, after they produced twelve witnesses and three sureties), its application to innocent witnesses is very well evidenced on other occasions.[16] The value of submitting witnesses to the ordeal may be difficult for the late twentieth-century reader to grasp. However, use of the hot iron ordeal as a verification procedure for witness evidence was clearly common in late eleventh-century England too: such practices were obviously deemed appropriate in the early middle ages.[17]

Some of the procedures are described in language which will also strike the late twentieth-century reader as odd: the second formal stage of pursuing a case in eighth-century Ireland, according to the tract *Cóic Conara Fugill*, was for the plaintiff's advocate to choose the proper 'path of judgement', that of 'truth' or 'entitlement' or 'justice' or 'propriety' or 'proper enquiry', each with its own appropriate procedures; if he chose the wrong path, he was fined.[18] However, despite the unfamiliarity of the concepts here, neither odd actions nor odd language alter the similarities in what was actually done; rather, they serve to conceal the broad consistencies of practice.

Although, then, it is true that elements of the court ritual can be selected that sound alien, in fact the most essential qualities of the ritual are much more mundane (as they are also very familiar). These essentials lay in

---

[15] L. Serrano, ed., *Becerro Gótico de Cardeña* (Valladolid, 1910), no. 210, pp. 224–5; Davies and Fouracre, eds., *Settlement of Disputes*, pp. 244–5.

[16] Davies and Fouracre, eds., *Settlement of Disputes*, pp. 29, 39, 271; A. Ubieto, ed., *Cartulario de San Millán de la Cogolla (759–1076)*, vol. I (Valencia, 1976), no. 27, pp. 44–5; Collins, '"Sicut lex Gothorum continet"', pp. 503–4.

[17] R. Fleming, *Domesday Book and the Law: Society and Legal Custom in Early Medieval England* (Cambridge, 1998), Index rerum *s.v.* 'ordeal'.

[18] Kelly, *Guide to Early Irish Law*, pp. 191–2.

repetition, in doing things in the correct order, in having the correct type of person perform particular actions, and in the respect accorded (as now) to oath. Denying or ignoring the right order (both spatially and temporally) was contempt; it amounted to insult, not just to the president of the court but to the whole system: in Merovingian Francia court presidents could in theory be executed for failing to follow the proper procedure.[19] The formulaic nature of the records serves to emphasise this attitude: things had to be done in the right way and the right things had to be said, using the correct words. People consciously acted within the framework of ancient and long-established legal traditions: they used the words of formularies of the sixth and seventh centuries, even in the eighth and ninth centuries; they referred explicitly to (classical) Roman law as their standard in ninth- and tenth-century charters from Burgundy and Aquitaine; and they cited Visigothic law of the sixth and seventh centuries in Spanish charters of the ninth to thirteenth centuries, where the earlier law is often quoted verbatim.[20]

This emphasis on right order thereby proclaimed both the existence of a distinctive system and its separation from 'everyday life'. To that extent, at least, early medieval law courts are entirely within the framework of issues posed by the conference organisers, even if we cannot perceive all the rules and all aspects of the system from the present distance. As for courtroom drama: dramatic public performance is clearly indicated by some texts and is emphasised by the sometimes lengthy quotations of who said what, especially in records of Italian cases;[21] documents could be dramatically thrown on the altar, or pierced right through, or even burnt; judges could themselves walk disputed boundaries (with kings, abbots, bishops striding beside the locals), taking the court outside the courtroom. Even without particular incidents of this kind the court meeting was so insistently public that there was necessarily a performance element to the procedures.

II. THE ACTORS

The examples and elements discussed above occur overwhelmingly in rulers' courts, although they are not confined to those arenas. The courts were rulers' courts in the sense that not just a king but his officers or an

---

[19] Davies and Fouracre, eds., *Settlement of Disputes*, p. 216.
[20] W. Davies, 'The composition of the Redon Cartulary', *Francia*, 17 (1990), pp. 79–80. 'Lex Romana (e)docet...': for example, M. Deloche, ed., *Cartulaire de l'abbaye de Beaulieu (en Limousin)* (Paris, 1859), nos. 20, 104, pp. 45, 157, and A. Bernard and A. Bruel, eds., *Recueil des chartes de l'abbaye de Cluny*, vol. I (Paris, 1876), no. 81, p. 91; Collins, '"Sicut lex Gothorum continet"', p. 493.
[21] Cf. C. J. Wickham, 'Land disputes and their social framework in Lombard-Carolingian Italy, 700–900', in Davies and Fouracre, eds., *Settlement of Disputes*, p. 107.

immunist, lay or clerical, presided. The law court was often, therefore, an explicitly political instrument: it was the occasion when the ruler (or his agent) was seen to preside; since it was very public, it reinforced the place of the ruler in the world *ordo* and served to extend his practical political power. The fact that courts could meet in many locations, with no single special meeting place – royal or aristocratic palaces, within or beside churches, villages, fields – contributed to that extending power; the ruler or his agents moved about the area they ruled.

The law court could also be the place where the ruler himself gave judgement and, in extreme cases, like that against the Breton machtiern Ratfred, exercised the separate functions of presiding, judging and punishing.[22] Presiding at court could thereby be a means of controlling aristocracies. There are late ninth-, tenth- and eleventh-century cases of this overtly political combining of separate functions in south Wales, exercised through the immunity of the bishopric of Llandaff; there are tenth- and eleventh-century examples of the duke presiding and giving judgement in Aquitaine; and there are tenth-century cases of Anglo-Saxon royal intervention in disputes in clearly political contexts: both King Edwy and King Edgar intervened with reference to the disputed estate of Sunbury in the mid-tenth century, and King Edward the Elder earlier in the century forfeited Goda's properties in favour of Eadgifu.[23] Even seventh- and eighth-century Ireland sometimes fits this pattern, despite the prominence of the learned legal class: Tírechán related that people went to King Loíguire for judgement on matters of inheritance.[24]

Clearly, all rulers' courts were not political instruments in the latter sense, and these cases may be exceptional. Just how exceptional is difficult to assess, given the language of the records: in southern Europe (Italy, Spain,

---

[22] Salomon, *princeps*, asked Ratfred in court why he had threatened to burn the monastery of Redon if some property was not handed over to him; when Ratfred said that the property had been given to him freely, Salomon asked the abbot why he had made such a fuss, confiscating the property and asking Ratfred to produce proof of his claim. Ratfred could neither do that nor find witnesses. Salomon therefore restored the property to Redon; de Courson, ed., *Cartulaire de Redon*, no. 105, pp. 79–80.

[23] *The Text of the Book of Llan Dâv*, ed. J. G. Evans with J. Rhys (Oxford, 1893), nos. 212, 214, 223, 244, 245, 255; cf. W. Davies, 'Adding insult to injury: power, property and immunities in early medieval Wales', in W. Davies and P. Fouracre, eds., *Property and Power in the Early Middle Ages* (Cambridge, 1995), pp. 138–40. J. Martindale, '"His special friend"? The settlement of disputes and political power in the kingdom of the French (tenth to mid-twelfth century)', *Transactions of the Royal Historical Society*, 5 (1995), p. 47. A. J. Robertson, ed., *Anglo-Saxon Charters* (Cambridge, 1939), no. 44, pp. 90–2; Harmer, ed., *Select Documents*, no. 23, pp. 37–8.

[24] 'Tírechán', ch. 15, in L. Bieler, ed., *The Patrician Texts in the Book of Armagh* (Dublin, 1979), p. 134. See D. A. Binchy, ed., *Críth Gablach* (Dublin, 1941), ch. 41 and p. 37, and F. Kelly, ed., *Audacht Morainn* (Dublin, 1976), for judgement as exercised by kings; cf. M. Gerriets, 'The king as judge in early Ireland', *Celtica*, 20 (1988), pp. 29–52.

the Byzantine Empire) it was usual for panels of judges to make judgements, under the presidency of count, duke, bishop or whomever; the judges were local men and they clearly took some real part in the decisions. But in England and Francia, and by implication in Wales, it is very common for texts to say that 'the court' gave judgement, or king and magnates, or a council, or 'all': in 1023 in England 'all the shire granted him'; in 926 in Aquitaine judgement was by Count Ebles and his *fideles* 'with the counsel and consent of all present'.[25] Here our understanding is dependent on the language used by the recorder and the formulaic influences conditioning his writing: when he used such phrases as 'the court' or 'all', did he mean that the whole court (maybe hundreds of people) shouted out guilty or not guilty (as reported of Pontius Pilate's judgement)? Or did he mean that the president, having taken due notice of all evidence, made a judgement on behalf of the court? Or that a panel of judgement-finders made the decision, which was then announced by the chair? We usually have no way of knowing, although all three may have happened. Recourse to the notion of 'collective decision-making' does not help with the real problem since it does not tell us who in practice made the decision. There is therefore a crucially important procedural aspect of rulers' courts of which we are often unsure: who actually made the judgement?

Now for local courts. Discussion so far has focused on procedure in rulers' courts. There were other courts in Europe at this period, which did not depend on king or state apparatus (or immunist), although they are much less frequently evidenced. In eastern Brittany, for example, law courts met in most villages in the ninth century, with a local person of status presiding (sometimes sitting on a three-legged seat), in a range of possible locations (in church, in front of the church, in the president's residence, and so on). Many of the local male population would be present. Plaintiffs made accusations and the accused made denials, speaking for themselves. Evidence was provided to support the denials, by documents or by witnesses to fact giving evidence on oath; and evidence was also sometimes produced to support accusations. A panel of very local judges – as few as three and as many as fourteen members are recorded – made a judgement (failing settlement), on the basis either of the evidence produced or of their own knowledge of the parties, of the locality and of the past. Where the evidence was not decisive the judges sometimes conducted an inquest and sometimes ordered oath-helpers to swear in support of the accused. Much is made of the 'suitability' of the judges and witnesses, that is of their 'law worthiness', and sometimes formal investigation of the judges' suitability

---

[25] Robertson, ed., *Anglo-Saxon Charters*, no. 83, pp. 162–4; Martindale, '"His special friend"?', p. 28; cf. the involvement of the 'whole synod' in judging southern Welsh kings, Evans with Rhys, ed., *Book of Llan Dâv*, no. 244.

to judge was made: they had to be free, male, propertied, and of good repute.[26]

In other words, although the scale and the interests were much smaller, there is plenty here that parallels the essentials of procedure in rulers' courts: the public meeting, the chairperson or president, accusation and denial, the production of evidence, the use of oaths. What is different is the fact that people spoke for themselves; and there is rather less emphasis in the records on procedures surrounding the oath and on 'right order'. As might be expected, there was less formality, although the process was nevertheless referred to as *in lege*, going to law.

What is also different in records of these cases from procedure in rulers' courts is the fact that many local court cases ended in settlement, obviating the need for judgement.[27] And even when the judgement was that there should be an oath, this could be dispensed with (as it was in one late tenth-century English [not so parochial] shire court, in order to maintain 'friendship').[28] The drive to settle was clearly extremely strong in the villages (if for no other reason than the practical necessity of social harmony within a small community). Disputes were settled out of court too, with evidence used in a similar way to arrive at the settlement and a record sometimes being kept. Such occasions did use quasi-judicial procedures but they are differentiated from what went on in local courts: they were even less formal, had fewer procedures, are recorded in different language, and had no judges.

The Breton corpus is a particularly full and rich set of texts. There are not many other sets of material from so basic a social level, but isolated cases certainly occur in collections from all over the Carolingian world. Estey's work on the Mâcon area of Burgundy and on Languedoc in the ninth century provides a number of examples; so does the eighth- and ninth-century St Gall material from Switzerland.[29] By implication, south Wales was similar: the 'surexit' memorandum, from the region near Llandeilo Fawr, records the initiatives of *degion*, literally 'good men' (cf. *boni viri* in continental texts), in the mid-ninth century; no rulers or their representatives are mentioned in the course of this famous settlement.[30] It

---

[26] Davies, *Small Worlds*, pp. 146–60.
[27] I am not suggesting that there were never settlements in rulers' courts; cf. the 806 settlement made by the abbot of St Gall, witnessed by 42 people, P. J. Geary, 'Extra-judicial means of conflict resolution', *Settimane di Studio*, 42 (1995), pp. 579–80.
[28] Robertson, ed., *Anglo-Saxon Charters*, no. 66, pp. 136–8.
[29] F. N. Estey, 'The *scabini* and the local courts', *Speculum*, 26 (1951), pp. 119–29 (cf. G. Duby, 'Recherche sur l'évolution des institutions judiciaires pendant le Xe et XIe siècle dans le sud de la Bourgogne', *Le Moyen Age*, 52 (1946), pp. 149–94, and 53 (1947), pp. 15–38); R. Sprandel, *Das Kloster Sankt Gallen in der Verfassung des karolingischen Reiches* (Freiburg, 1958), and McKitterick, *Carolingians and the Written Word*, pp. 79–126.
[30] D. Jenkins and M. Owen, 'The Welsh Marginalia in the Lichfield Gospels, Parts I and II', *Cambridge Medieval Celtic Studies*, 5 (1983), p. 51, and 7 (1984), pp. 91–120.

therefore seems reasonable to propose that the existence of small-scale, local courts was widespread in western Europe in at least the eighth to tenth centuries, even if they understandably do not feature as prominently in the record as do rulers' courts.

While serfs sometimes went to rulers' courts to claim free status, they cannot be found as judges or witnesses there;[31] nor are they found in these roles in local courts at this period. Although serfs moved about the peasant community, had households and families, and paid dues to peasant masters, they do not appear to have participated in community business in public:[32] if they went to meetings they did not speak at them; there is therefore no sign that they participated as members of the society in meetings which were constituted as courts. These people were pre-eminently 'unsuitable' as witnesses, sureties and judges. Hence, although the material allows us to perceive the operation of the legal process at a level far below that of rulers and high politics, it certainly does not show us a society in which people had equal status and participated in the rural community on equal terms. At local level participation in legal process was limited to the free, to those of good reputation and – overwhelmingly – to males: 'citizenship' was exclusive. This was a world that was a long way from the peasant idyll of equality for all at the heart of rural society.

III. WORKING THE SYSTEM

Reflecting on the questions posed at the outset, it is evident that early medieval courts did have their own rules and their own internal logics. What went on in an early medieval court could certainly be different from what went on in everyday life (insofar as we can perceive everyday life). It was different in the sense that the world of the court was for the most part only open to a proportion of the population, adult, male and free. Courts could be used to secure personal or institutional property rights, like the suits of the bishop of Freising in the late eighth century, and were thereby an instrument for securing personal advantage.[33] Courts could certainly be manip-

---

[31] For serfs in rulers' courts see, for example, the Italian cases discussed below, p. 60, and the peasants who went from Mitry in 861 to the court of Charles the Bald at Compiègne to protest that the monastery of St Denis was trying to force them to 'inferior service' when by right they were free *coloni*; J. L. Nelson, 'Dispute settlement in Carolingian West Francia', in Davies and Fouracre, eds., *Settlement of Disputes*, pp. 50–2. In such cases the peasants were clearly protagonists, not members of the court; and they clearly were of the view that they were *not* serfs.

[32] I am using 'serf' here to refer to the unfree; they could easily be classified as a type of slave, even if they were slaves who had their own households and control of their own labour on a day-to-day basis. See further W. Davies, 'On servile status in the early middle ages', in M. L. Bush, ed., *Serfdom and Slavery. Studies in Legal Bondage* (London, 1996), pp. 245–6.

[33] P. Fouracre, 'Carolingian justice: the rhetoric of improvement and contexts of abuse', *Settimane di Studio del Centro Italiano di Studi sull' alto Medioevo*, 42 (1995), p. 785:

ulated for political ends, at least to the extent that rulers' courts could be a means of expressing, and organising, political power.

Using the court for personal interest not only happened in rulers' courts. At local level in Brittany it is noticeable that members of a judgement panel could also act for the parties in a case: in 801 at Langon the six judgement-finders judged that the accused should clear himself with his own oath and with those of twelve oath-helpers; after that, three of those judgement-finders themselves stood as oath-helpers. Forty years later, at Avessac, six local elders provided evidence about property ownership (that is, they acted as independent expert witnesses in a case) and then two of them stood as sureties for the future payment of dues by one party. At about the same time, in Guer, four judgement-finders judged that a man had no claim on property and then two of them stood as surety that the man would make no further claim. A generation later, in 867 in Peillac, four men agreed to the future payment of rent after a dispute, and then three of them stood as guarantors for two of their own number: in other words, although they were parties to the dispute it was nevertheless acceptable for them to stand as sureties for each other.[34] None of this need constitute evidence of manipulation but it certainly indicates that some people knew how to play the system. A different though comparable point might be made of the witnesses of an earlier transaction called to appear at the Loire valley case of 857, who were persuaded to assert on oath that the document they appeared to have formerly witnessed had neither been confirmed by them nor properly corroborated.[35] By the time we reach the very well documented Domesday inquests of late eleventh-century England, we can see rival gangs of witnesses 'willing to swear on oath or undertake the judicial ordeal' and lords openly using their men as jurors. As Robin Fleming says, this material 'allows us a glimpse at the real-world politics that must have operated at every court in the tenth and eleventh centuries'.[36]

The world of the court was also different in the sense that what was 'just' to the court did not always meet the deepfelt sense of injustice of plaintiffs: the court *did* have its own, different, moral framework. Although peasants could cross the boundary between local courts and rulers' courts, and enter the higher arena, they could not necessarily work the system when they got there. The twenty-three peasants from Mitry who travelled sixty km to take their complaints about status to King Charles the Bald in 861 (along with eighteen women and their children, making a group of at least sixty-one

'Freising's use of courts to defend its interests may well have amounted to an abuse of judicial privilege.'

[34] De Courson, ed., *Cartulaire de Redon*, nos. 191, 61, 180, 96, pp. 147–8, 49, 139–40, 72–3.
[35] Nelson, 'Dispute settlement', p. 56, and Davies and Fouracre, eds., *Settlement of Disputes*, p. 234.
[36] Robin Fleming has some substantial new work on the nature and use of juries in Domesday England: Fleming, *Domesday Book and the Law*, ch. 1.

people), patently felt a deep sense of injustice. But they did not succeed in their complaint because they were defeated by the landowner, who marshalled counter witnesses. When Maurinus and his son went to the count's court in Pavia in 880 to protest that the monastery of Novalesa had reduced them to servitude, it was argued that they had been given a chance earlier in the year to produce witnesses to their freedom, but had failed to do so. Though the two men maintained insistently that they had been enserfed by force, the court judged that in default of witnesses or papers they were servile; a document to that effect was then prepared for the monastery.[37]

In other cases when peasants queried a monastic landlord's powers, texts were used against them, like the written estate survey produced in 828 to demonstrate conclusively that Cormery's peasants from Antoigné in Aquitaine were paying the customary rate, as established twenty-seven years previously, when the peasants maintained that rents were much too high and had recently been increased.[38] When a couple of years earlier ten men from Fiesso in Italy, led by a man called Martin, questioned the right of the abbot of Nonantola to exclude them from fisheries and pasture on the borders of Reggio, the monastery's advocate Reginald argued that the monastery had held exclusive rights for a long time and brandished documents recording a judgement by King Desiderius in the monastery's favour (c. 758). Martin and his fellows proclaimed the document false, but others testified that it was true and enquiries were then made of local men about amounts assigned to Fiesso. It was demonstrated that, despite King Liutprand's earlier grant of limited pasture rights to Fiesso men, Desiderius had subsequently granted exclusive rights to the monastery.[39] This case is interesting because the peasants did try to argue on the basis of text (they even took their own notary with them); but they were outmanoeuvred by superior dexterity with written evidence: their own document was invalidated by the later one.

In a world in which written evidence was admissible, it could be used against people who had neither the skill nor the experience to retaliate or who had insufficient skill to use the resource conclusively; if, like the *servi* of Limonta (near Lake Como) between 882 and 957, they made some attempt to influence the record and thereby limit the growing weight of exactions, they had very little chance of success.[40] The written text thereby

---

[37] Manaresi, ed., *Placiti*, vol. I, no. 89. Cf. the cases in the Trita valley in the territory of Valva in the Apennines in the late eighth century: C. Wickham, *Studi sulla società degli Appennini nell'alto medioevo* (Bologna, 1982), pp. 20–8.
[38] Nelson, 'Dispute settlement', pp. 49–50.
[39] Manaresi, ed., *Placiti*, vol. I, no. 36, pp. 109–13.
[40] R. Balzaretti, 'The monastery of Sant'Ambrogio and dispute settlement in early medieval Milan', *Early Medieval Europe*, 3 (1994), pp. 7–12; and *passim* for using writing as a weapon.

became part of the special apparatus of the world of the law. In cultures like the Irish the written text was so special that it could not reveal its meaning without professional elucidation: lawyers were essential for the understanding of legal text, which became ever more elaborately and arcanely glossed; legal language was so distinctive it was almost secret.[41]

In all of these ways the early medieval legal experience fits the framing, and does so very clearly. But the framing does not invariably suit every situation: at aristocratic levels it does so strongly; but at peasant levels it is much less so. At local, community level the procedures look as if they were accessible to anyone qualified to participate and seem to have been freely used by them (though we should remember that the qualified did not include all people of the locality). The world of these local courts did not have so distinctive and internal a logic (just as the drive to settle took precedence over the drive to operate the rules and proceed to judgement). Everyday life was not so different; and male, free peasants clearly used the court as a means of solving their own problems. At this level the world of the law does not seem to have been so morally distinct.

---

[41] The glossing of Irish law texts, and the nature of those glosses, is a clear demonstration that the language of law was not accessible to all; Kelly, *Guide to Early Irish Law*, pp. 225–35; cf. K. Hughes, *Early Christian Ireland: Introduction to the Sources* (London, 1972), pp. 44–6.

INDEX

Agon, peasant: IX 887–8
Alain Le Grand: III 92; XVII 326, 333
Alfred, king of Wessex: XVII 331, 336
Alfrit, machtiern: XVII 323
alienation, powers of: II 270, 272; VIII 86;
　　IX 885, 890, 893; X 410–11
Anau: VIII 80
Anglo-Saxon law codes: VIII 85–6
appeal: VI 303
arable farming: VI 292–3; XI 146; XII 331;
　　XIII 347–50, 351–2
archbishops: XIV 94
aristocracy: VI 309 n15; VII 67, 72–3;
　　IX 889; X 410; XI 144, 146;
　　XIII 350; XIV 97–8, 99; XVII 333
arson: VI 296
Arthviu, elder: IX 890
assault: VI 296, 301; VIII 80
assemblies: XVI 121; XIX 50, 58
Asser: XVII 331
asylum: XV 8–9
　　see also protection
Austroberta, wife of (1) Agenhart
　　(2) Wandefred: X 411, 413

Bains, Morbihan: II 271; IV 111–12; V 185;
　　VI 297; VII 72–3; IX 890
baptism: V 194
bishoprics: XIV 92, 93
bishops: IV 100; V 195; XIV 93–4
boni viri: VI 298
Breton (language): IX 884
　　linguistic boundary: IV 98–9
brideprice: X 418–19, 423, 424
Brioverian: XII 322–3, 326, 329–31;
　　XIII 338–45
Brittany: XV 7, 18 n6
　　administration of: IV 105–6
　　geography of: VI 292–3; XVII 324
　　political system of: XVI 102–3, 107–8, 117
　　settlement of: IV 98
buildings: XII 323–5, 329, 331, 332;
　　XIII 339–45, 346, 350
burial: V 192; IX 889; XIV 98–9

cadastre, ancien: XI 144; XII 329, 331;
　　XIII 352

'Canones Wallici', *see* ELR
Carentoir, Morbihan: I 79–80; IV 107–9;
　　V 185, 188; VII 69; VIII 77, 89 n30;
　　IX 888; XI 141–6; XII 322, 331, 332
Carolingians: XVI 109; XVII 332, 333
　　see also Charles the Bald, Louis the
　　Pious
cartularies
　　see Landévennec, Redon
cemeteries: XIV 93
　　see also burial
centenarii: VII 84
Charles the Bald: IV 100, 103, 104;
　　VII 82n; XVII 332; XIX 59
charters: I *passim*; II *passim*; III 86, 87, 95;
　　VII 75
　　'Celtic': I 75; II 269; III 88, 93
　　dating of: I 70; III 85, 91, 92
　　private: I 70–71;
　　see also Liber Landavensis
châteaux: XII 323, 326; XIII 339, 340, 352
Chronicle of Nantes: I 76; III 92;
　　IV 100–101, 104
churches
　　local: V 181, 186, 190–91
　　proprietary: V 183, 190, 196
Cinaed mac Ailpín: XVII 323–4
clientship: XVI 111, 122, 124; XVIII 240
Collectio Canonum Hibernensis: VIII 85;
　　XV 8, 9, 19 n12
commemoration: V 192
communities, rural: VI *passim*; VII 84;
　　VIII 87; XVI 122; XVIII 243, 244;
　　XIX 56, 58
compensation: VII 77–8; X 420; XV 2, 4, 7
Conuuoion, abbot of Redon: VI 298;
　　VII 71, 72–3; IX 891
Cornouaille: III 87
Cornwall: XIV 96, 98; XV 5, 7;
　　XVI 108–9; XVII 331; XVIII 240
counties: VI n15
counts: IV 105, 111; VI 308 n6
courts, judicial: VI 296–303; VII 66, 68 n10;
　　XVIII 236–7, 244; XIX 56–7
cowen-ran: IX 887
credit, *see* loans, pledges
crosses: XV 6–7

cultivation: XI 145; XII 331
  see also arable, ploughsoil
cults: XIV 98–9, 100

dating practice: I 70, 78, 79; IV 103
deacons: V 190; VIII 82
debt: VIII 85
demographic decline, *see* population
di-cofrit: IX 886
diplomatic practice: I 71–80; II 268–70;
  III 87–8, 90–93
  Frankish: I 75, 76
  local: I 78–80, 82
disputes, settlement of: II 268; IV 110;
  VI *passim*; VII *passim*; VIII 79–81;
  IX 887–9; XIX 57
  informal: VI 302, 306; VII 71–2
dos: X 407, 417–18, 421, 424
dowry: X 414, 419, 421, 422, 424
Dublin: XVII 335
dues: XVIII 235, 238, 244

East Brittany Survey: XI 139–44;
  XII *passim*; XIII *passim*
elders: VI 297, 300; VII 81; VIII 81;
  XVI 120; XIX 57, 59
  see also Arthviu
ELR (sometimes known as 'Canones
  Wallici'): IV 113; V 197; VI 307,
  310 n29; VII 69 n15; VIII 85;
  X 418–19
enepuuert: IV 101
  see also morning gift
enforcement: VIII 74, 79–80
England: XV 5, 7, 10, 11; XVI 109, 113;
  XIX 55
  see also Wessex
envoys: V 184–5
  see also missi
Erispoë, Breton ruler: IV 100–101, 102
evidence: VI 300, 305; VII 75–6; VIII 78;
  XIX 52, 60

Fabrics, *see* pottery
family
  conflict: VI 295–6, 297
  interests: II 270–71, 272; III 95; IV 108;
    V 191; VIII 83; IX 887–9, 891–3
  intrusion: V 182, 183
  maternal kin: IX 892
  structure: IX 886–7
Feudal Revolution: XVIII 229–31, 245
fideiussores, *see* sureties
fideles: IV 100, 114
fieldwalking: XI 140–41

fiscal mechanisms: IV 106, 108; V 197; VII 82
Fomus, peasant: VII 71
forgery: I 77–8; II *passim*; III 85–6;
  VI 310 n27; IX 882–3
formularies: I 71–4, 79; II 268; XIX 54
formulas: VII 69; XIX 54, 56
Fracanus: IV 112
freedom: XVIII 228–9, 233, 242–3, 245 n67

geographical range: VII 79–80, 81; VIII 82
geology, solid: XII 322–3; XIII 338–9
Gesta Sanctorum Rotonensium: IV 102, 111
gifts, pious: X 415; XIV 97
girths: XV 6
godparents: IX 891–2
Govan: XIV 99–101
Gradlon, legendary king: III 85, 94; IV 105;
  XIV 99
granite: XII 322; XIII 338, 339
Grès Armoricain: XII 322, 326, 329–31;
  XIII 338–45

Haeldetwid, scribe: I 79–80; II 271–2;
  VII 68, 69
hair-cutting: IX 891–2
hermeneutic style: III 91
heroes: XVII 323, 336
Hesdren, bishop of Nantes: III 92
homicide: VI 296
honour: X 419–21, 422; XV 2
husbands: IX 889–91; X 410–11

Iarnhitin, machtiern: IV 107–8; V 184
idonei, *see* law-worthiness
immunities: VII 82; XV 10–11, 12–13;
  XVI 103
inheritance practice: III 95; X 410–14, 423–4
inquest, local: VI 297, 302
insult: XIX 54
Iona: XVII 333
Ireland: XV 5, 11; XVI 101–2, 105–7,
  110–12, 116, 123; XVII 328, 329,
  333; XIX 53, 61
Isle of Man: XVI 110
Iudicaël, *rex*: IV 105
iudices: IV 113; VI 298; VII 78–81, 83;
  VIII 81; XVI 119–21; XIX 56, 59

judgment: VI 298–300, 303; IX 888;
  XVI 119–21; XIX 56
  enforcement of: VI 301; *see also*
    sureties
  see also iudices
jurisdiction, rights of: VII 82; XVIII 236–8,
  245

kin, *see* family
kings: XVI *passim*
    Welsh: IX 890; XIV 100; *see also*
        Rhodri Mawr
    see also Alfred, overkings
kingship: IV 103–4; XVI *passim*
k-o_1: XII 322, 323, 326, 329–31;
    XIII 338–45

labour service: XVIII 234–5, 240
Lalocan, peasant: VI 297–8; IX 888
landes: XIII 346–7
Landévennec
    cartulary of: III *passim*; X 417
    monastery of: III 85, 94; XIV 94–6, 99,
        100, 101; XVII 332
    property of monastery of: III 93–4
Langon: VIII 77
language: XVI 104
    see also Breton
Latouche, R.: III 85, 91, 92, 95
law: VI 306–7; IX 885; X 408, 423; XV 2,
    4, 7, 8; XVI 101, 116–17, 119;
    XIX 49, 54
law-worthiness: VI 299, 302, 309 nn17, 18;
    VII 78
lawyers: XVI 119, 120 n42; XIX 51
Liber Landavensis, charters of: III 92
lis: IV 110–11, 112; VI 298
literacy: XIX 48
Llanbedrgoch: XVII 334
Llancarfan, monastery of: XIV 94, 101
Llandeilo Fawr: XIX 57
Llantwit Major, monastery of: XIV 100
loans: V 183–4; VIII 85
    see also pledges
lordship: XVIII 230, 231, 234, 236, 237, 245
Louis the Pious: IV 100, 111; XVII 332
Lusanger: VIII 77
lynchets: XII 326, 329, 330; XIII 342, 344,
    350

machtierns: IV 106–14; VI 298, 301,
    303–4, 310 n24; VIII 74, 81, 89 n27
    see also Alfrit, Ratfred
Máel Sechnaill mac Máel Ruanaid:
    XVII 325, 332
Maenuueten, priest: VI 296–7
mair: IV 113; VI 302, 309 n12; VII 79, 81;
    VIII 81
Malestroit Syncline: XII 322, 323; XIII 338
manumission: XVIII 233
manuring: XI 140–41; XII 326, 329, 330,
    331; XIII 342–9
markets: VI 293

marriage payments: X 414–24
married couples: IX 889–91; X 410–12, 414
meadows: XIII 350
mediators: VI 302
Merthyr Mawr: XIV 100
métairies: XII 323, 331; XIII 339
migration: IV 98; V 177–9
military expeditions: IV 100, 111
    missi: IV 102, 105–6
modes of production: XVIII 231–2
monasteries: V 195–6; IX 890–91; XIV 92,
    94, 96
    entry to: V 183
    see also Landévennec, Llancarfan,
        Llantwit, Redon
    money: V 184; VIII 78–9; IX 894n
    see also solidi
morning gift: IX 889;X 413–24
    see also enepuuert
Morvan, *rex*: IV 105

Nominoë: IV 100–101, 102, 106, 111; VI 297
notaries: VI 298; VII 68 n12
    see also scribal practice

oaths: XIX 51–2
oath-helping: VI 298, 300, 304–5, 309 n20;
    VIII 90 n42; XIX 51, 59
officials, royal: XVI 114, 118, 120, 122
ordeal: XIX 53
orthography: II 273; III 92, 93
outrage: XV 3, 4
overkings: XVI 106–7, 110–12, 113;
    XVII 325, 329

parish structures: III 95; V 177, 179, 191–4
Pascwethen, count: IV 102, 105, 106, 107
peasants: VII 82–3; VIII 83; X 414;
    XVIII 234–5; XIX 58
    see also Fomus, Lalocan, proprietors,
        Uuordoital, Wrbudic
Picts: XVI 112–13, 116; XVII 333–4
Pipriac: XII 332
pisé: XII 323, 324
Planiol, M.: IV 110, 112
plebes: III 95; IV 106–7, 108, 111–12;
    V 177–82, 188; VI 295
pledges (mortgages): V 183–4; VIII 78–9;
    IX 893, 894n; X 412, 415
    see also securities
plou: V 177–9, 181
ploughsoil: XII *passim*; XIII 342–9
political systems: XVI 110–14;
    XVII 325–31
politics: VI 303–6, 308

polities, scale of: XVI 105–10, 122–3;
  XVII 330
population, levels of: XI 143, 144
pottery: XII 330; XIII 343–5, 350
  Fabric 1: XI 141–2, 145; XIII 347–50
  Fabric 4: XI 142–3, 145; XIII 347–8
  Fabric 6: XIII 347–8
  Iron-Age: XII 330; XIII 344, 345, 347
  Roman: XIII 343, 344, 345
priests: V *passim*; VII 79, 81; VIII 82;
  XIV 96
  local: V 187–91
  mobility of: V 187–91
  see also Maenuueten
princeps: VI 308 n8; VII 78
  see also Salomon
property, rights in: VIII 84
  transmission of: IX 886, 889–92
  women's: X 409–14, 421
proprietors, peasant: VI 295; XVIII 234, 240
proprietorship: II 272–4; III 93–4; IV 107,
  112; V 182–4; VII 82; VIII 83
protection: XV 1–3; XVII 331
  breach of: XV 1–2, 3
  territorialization of: XV 4–7, 9–11
public power: IV 111–13; V 197;
  XVIII 237–8; XIX 55
punishment: VI 301; VIII 86
purchases: X 410–11

quarries: XII 323, 326; XIII 340
Quimper: III 92, 94

rangées: XII 323, 324, 328; XIII 339, 340
Ratfred, machtiern: VI 297; VII 72–3;
  XIX 52
Redon, monastery of: VI 304; XVII 332
  cartulary of: I *passim*; II *passim*;
    IV 106–12
  priests of: V 187–8
  property of: II 266; IV 111–12; VI 305
  seigneurie of: VII 79–80, 81–2; VIII 82,
    88 n12
  see also Conuuoion, Ruffiac Priory
Regino of Prüm: IV 103
Reminiac Syncline: XII 322, 323; XIII 338
rents: IX 894n
representation: XVI 115, 123
Rhodri Mawr: XVII 324–5, 333, 336
Ritcant, abbot of Redon: I 81
Riwal, *dux*: IV 104
rocks: XII 322–3, 326, 329–31; XIII 342–5
Roiantdreh: X 410, 412, 421
Roiantken, wife of Deurhoiarn: IX 888–9;
  X 415–16

Roman sites: XII 330, 331; XIII 341, 343, 345
Rome: XVII 332
roofing: XII 323, 326–7, 329–32; XIII 340,
  345–9, 350
rubble: XIII 341, 342, 343
Ruffiac, Morbihan: I 79–80; II 271–2;
  IV 107–9, 114; V 185, 188; VI 296;
  VII 69, 75; VIII 77; IX 887, 888, 890
Ruffiac Priory: XI 144
Rule of Benedict: XIV 96
rulers: IV 102–14; VI 292, 296, 297,
  300–301, 303, 310 n24; XIV 97;
  XV 3; XVII *passim*; XIX 55
  see also lordship, kings, overkings

safety: XV 2–3, 4
saints: XV 5; XVI 102–3
Saint-Maxent, monastery of: I 78
Saint-Pol-de-Léon, bishopric of: III 92
sales: I 78; II 267; III 95; V 183–4; VII 69;
  VIII 77–8; IX 886, 890
  see also purchases
Salomon, *princeps*: I 75; IV 100, 102,
  103–6; VI 297, 301; VII 72–3;
  XIV 101 n2; XVII 323; XIX 55
saltpans: VIII 77
sanctions: VII 77; VIII 78, 84
sanctuary: XV 1, 5, 7–9
sandstones: XII 322; XIII 338–9
  see also Grès
scabini: IV 100, 110; VI 298, 299
schistes: XII 322–3; XIII 338–9
scholars, Irish: XVII 332
Scotland: XV 6–7; XVI 103, 107, 112–13;
  XVII 323–4, 326–7, 334
  see also Picts, Strathclyde
scribal practice: I *passim*; III 90–92; V 185;
  VII 68–70; VIII 75; X 423; XIV 97
securities: VIII 84; XIX 52
  see also pledges
serfs: VI 295; VIII 80; XVIII *passim*;
  XIX 58
serjeants of the peace: IV 113
service: XVIII 227–8, 234–5, 240
settlement patterns: VI 294; XI 143;
  XIII 351, 352
settlements: XI 141, 144–6; XIII 347, 351;
  XVII 334
shale, *see schistes*
siltstones: XIII 338–45
slates: XII 322–3, 326, 331–2; XIII 338–9,
  340, 342–50, 351
  see also roofing
slaves: XVIII *passim*
social order: VIII 80; XVI 117–19

social organization, units of: V 180–81
  see also plebes
solidi: V 182, 183
status: XV 3, 9, 18 n12; XVIII 239
  see also honour
stones, cross-inscribed: XV 5
Strathclyde: XIV 93; XVI 107; XVII 326, 334
sureties: IV 106, 110; V 185; VI 301–2, 305; VII 75; VIII *passim*; X 415; XIX 52

taxation: XVI 113 n24
tenure: V 183; VI 305; VII 71; VIII 75; XVIII 232–3, 234–5
termonn lands: XV 4–5, 7, 12, 19 n13
theft: VI 296; XVI 118
Theodosian Code: VIII 85; XV 8
tile: XI 140; XII 330; XIII 341
tithes: V 190, 194–5
titles, rulers': IV 103, 105
tonsuring: IX 892
towns: XVII 335
transactions, performance of: II 267; IV 110, 113; V 182
Tréal: XIII 349

Uuetenoc, peasant: VII 75

Uuobrian, peasant: VII 75
Uuordoital, peasant: VI 296–7

Vannes, Morbihan: I 75
vassals: IV 100, 114
  see also fideles
Vikings: I 81; IV 104; XVII 333–6
Vilaine, river: IV 98–9; VIII 73
villages, *see* communities, rural
villes: XI *passim*
Vita Pauli: III 93
Vita Winwaloei: III 94; IV 112

Wales: X 419–21; XV 4, 7; XVI 102, 109, 116; XVII 327–9, 330
walls: XII 323, 325, 328; XIII 339–40, 341
warriors: XVI 115; XVII 332
Wessex: XVII 331–3
widows: X 412–14
witnesses: VII 70; VIII 82–3; XIX 52, 53
  expert: VI 299
  impartial: VI 300; VII 80–81; VIII 81
wives: IX 889–91; X *passim*
woods: XI 141; XII 331; XIII 350
worth, personal: VIII 80; X 419–20
  see also law-worthiness
Wrbudic, peasant: II 273; VI 305; VII 75–6